# The Great African War
## Congo and Regional Geopolitics, 1996–2006

This book examines a decade-long period of instability, violence and state decay in Central Africa from 1996, when the war started, to 2006, when elections formally ended the political transition in the Democratic Republic of Congo (DRC). A unique combination of circumstances explain the unravelling of the conflicts: the collapsed Zairian/Congolese state; the continuation of the Rwandan civil war across borders; the shifting alliances in the region; the politics of identity in Rwanda, Burundi and eastern DRC; the ineptitude of the international community; and the emergence of privatised and criminalised public spaces and economies, linked to the global economy, but largely disconnected from the state on whose territory the 'entrepreneurs of insecurity' function. As a complement to the existing literature, this book seeks to provide an in-depth analysis of concurrent developments in Zaire/DRC, Rwanda, Burundi and Uganda in African and international contexts. By adopting a non-chronological approach, it attempts to show the dynamics of the inter-relationships between these realms and offers a toolkit for understanding the past and future of Central Africa.

**Filip Reyntjens** is Professor of Law and Politics at the Institute of Development Policy and Management, University of Antwerp. He has worked in and on the Great Lakes Region of Africa for more than thirty years. Professor Reyntjens's main research interests are contemporary history, legal anthropology, political transitions and human rights, and he has published several books and numerous articles on these subjects. He co-edits a yearbook on current affairs in Central Africa, *L'Afrique des grands lacs*, which is a major reference work on the region. In addition to his academic work, Reyntjens serves as a consultant for governments, international organizations and NGOs, and as an expert witness before courts in several countries, including the International Criminal Tribunal for Rwanda and the International Criminal Court.

# The Great African War

*Congo and Regional Geopolitics, 1996–2006*

### FILIP REYNTJENS

*University of Antwerp*

CAMBRIDGE UNIVERSITY PRESS
Cambridge, New York, Melbourne, Madrid, Cape Town, Singapore,
São Paulo, Delhi, Dubai, Tokyo, Mexico City

Cambridge University Press
32 Avenue of the Americas, New York, NY 10013-2473, USA

www.cambridge.org
Information on this title: www.cambridge.org/9780521169059

First published 2009
Reprinted 2010
First paperback edition 2010

*A catalog record for this publication is available from the British Library.*

*Library of Congress Cataloging in Publication Data*
Reyntjens, Filip.
The great African war : Congo and regional geopolitics, 1996–2006 / Filip Reyntjens.
p.  cm.
Includes bibliographical references and index.
ISBN 978-0-521-11128-7 (hardback)
1. Congo (Democratic Republic) – Politics and government – 1997– 2. Congo
(Democratic Republic) – Foreign relations – 1997– 3. Civil war – Great Lakes Region
(Africa) I. Title.
DT658.26.R489 2009
967.5103'4–dc22      2009004017

ISBN 978-0-521-11128-7 Hardback
ISBN 978-0-521-16905-9 Paperback

# Contents

*Acknowledgements*                                                *page* ix

*List of Maps*                                                          xi

Introduction                                                            1

1   A Region in Turmoil                                                 10
    1.1 Kivu: Land of confrontation                                     10
        *National context*                                              10
        *Crises of identity, of land and of politics*                   13
        *The new given: Influx of Hutu refugees*                        16
        *South Kivu: The Banyamulenge*                                  21
    1.2 Rwanda: From genocide to dictatorship                           23
        *The power base*                                                24
        *The drift*                                                     25
        *'Burundisation' of Rwanda*                                     29
        *Militarisation of the political landscape*                     31
        *Continuity in managing the state*                              32
    1.3 Burundi: From putsch to civil war                               34
        *Creeping coup*                                                 34
        *Extension of the civil war*                                    39
        *Coup of 25 July 1996 and its aftermath*                        41
    1.4 Regional junctions                                              42

2   The 'War of Liberation'                                             45
    2.1 The 'Banyamulenge Rebellion' and the Rwandan
        operation                                                       45
    2.2 The other eastern neighbours: Uganda
        and Burundi                                                     58
    2.3 Angola enters the fray: Kinshasa in 100 days                    61
    2.4 Other regional allies                                           65
    2.5 U.S. involvement                                                66

|   |   |   |
|---|---|---|
| | *Logistical and political support* | 66 |
| | *Supply of material and personnel* | 70 |
| | *Incoherence* | 74 |
| | *Degree of involvement* | 77 |
| 3 | Massacre of the Rwandan Refugees | 80 |
| | 3.1 Aborted international intervention | 80 |
| | 3.2 Crimes against humanity: Genocide? | 87 |
| | *Attacks against refugee camps and concentrations* | 93 |
| | *Humanitarian assistance withheld or used as bait* | 96 |
| | *Separation of men from women and children* | 97 |
| | *Involvement of the RPA* | 98 |
| | *Massacres of other groups* | 99 |
| | 3.3 The force of manipulation | 99 |
| 4 | The Fall of the Mobutist State | 102 |
| | 4.1 The players | 102 |
| | *Laurent-Désiré Kabila and the Alliance des Forces Démocratiques pour la Libération du Congo-Zaïre (AFDL)* | 102 |
| | *The Forces Armées Zaïroises (FAZ) and their allies* | 108 |
| | 4.2 The diplomatic ballet | 118 |
| | 4.3 Meanwhile, in Kinshasa, the orchestra on the *TITANIC* | 131 |
| | 4.4 The new geopolitical situation | 140 |
| 5 | Congo: Waiting for Another War | 144 |
| | 5.1 The 'liberated territories' in the East | 144 |
| | *Two problems worse than before* | 144 |
| | *Massive human rights violations* | 152 |
| | *Practices of governance* | 153 |
| | 5.2 The end of an alliance and the prelude to a new war | 155 |
| | *The regime adrift* | 155 |
| | *The art of making enemies* | 164 |
| | *Towards a new war* | 166 |
| 6 | Impasse in Rwanda and Burundi | 170 |
| | 6.1 The civil wars | 170 |
| | 6.2 Political or military outcomes? | 179 |
| | 6.3 Justice in deadlock | 181 |
| | 6.4 Institutional developments and practice of governance | 184 |
| 7 | 'The First African World War' | 194 |
| | 7.1 From Goma to Kitona, and to military stalemate | 194 |
| | 7.2 Shifting alliances | 201 |
| | 7.3 Wars within the war | 207 |
| | *The Kivus* | 207 |
| | *Ituri* | 215 |
| | 7.4 Privatisation and criminalisation | 221 |
| | *State collapse and the privatisation of public space* | 221 |
| | *Criminalisation of states and economies* | 224 |

8   Negotiating the Transition                                         232
  8.1  The political landscape                                     232
       *The regime in Kinshasa*                                    232
       *The rebel movements*                                       238
  8.2  The false start of negotiations: From Victoria Falls to the
       death of Laurent Kabila                                     244
       *Many cooks in the same kitchen*                            244
       *The Lusaka process*                                        247
       *From Lusaka to the assassination of Laurent Kabila*        250
  8.3  Towards an imposed settlement: From the accession of
       Joseph Kabila to Sun City                                   252
       *A dynastic succession*                                     252
       *From Sun City to Pretoria, and back to Sun City*           256
  8.4  Political transition in conflict                            261
       *The bumpy road towards elections*                          261
       *The 2006 elections*                                        271

Conclusion                                                         279

*Appendix 1: Sources on the killings of Rwandan refugees
             in early 1997*                                        287

*Appendix 2: Chronology*                                           291

*Appendix 3: List of abbreviations*                                297

*References*                                                       303

*Index*                                                            319

# Acknowledgements

Writing a book like this is essentially a lonely business that can, however, be conducted only with the support and assistance of many people. After I served for seven years as Chair of the Institute of Development Policy and Management, the University of Antwerp offered me a sabbatical year. Without my employer's generosity, it would have been impossible to conduct the research that has led to this book and to another, smaller, one. During this period, my colleagues at the Institute have taken over some of my tasks, in addition to their already busy schedules. I thank them sincerely for their support.

After having worked for more than thirty years on the Great Lakes region, I have developed extensive networks of friends, colleagues and political and social actors. They have been a rich source of information, a sounding board for ideas and a platform for sharing analysis. I cannot thank them individually. However, it is my pleasure to express the debt I owe to those who have generously given their precious time to comment on draft chapters, including an earlier version in French: Alison Des Forges, Gauthier de Villers, Erik Kennes, René Lemarchand, Emmanuel Lubala and three readers who will remain anonymous, either because that is their wish or because they reviewed the manuscript for Cambridge University Press. I wish to specially mention the help of René Lemarchand, who has gone well beyond what colleagues routinely do for each other in terms of help and advice. Without his careful reading of successive drafts and his insightful and detailed suggestions, this book would probably not have been published. Of course, the usual disclaimer applies.

The maps have been drawn by the University of Antwerp media service. Craig Rollo and Stephanie Hughes, colleagues from the University of Antwerp, have revised the language and style. Frank Smith, Jeanie Lee and Cathy Felgar of Cambridge University Press and Kavitha Lawrence of Newgen Imaging Systems have turned this manuscript into a book. I sincerely thank them all.

For many years now, my companion Greet has suffered considerably due to my passion for Africa, and I am sorry to say that she will probably suffer more in the future. I thank her for her patience; unfortunately, I cannot promise that I will find more time for her.

This book is dedicated to the memory of Alison Des Forges (1942–2009), for her friendship and her unremitting struggle for the cause of human rights in Central Africa.

**Filip Reyntjens**

# List of Maps

1.  The Great Lakes region                              *page* 12

2.  Zaire/DRC and its neighbours                         46

3.  Attacks on refugee camps (autumn 1996)              52

4.  First phase of the war (autumn 1996)                56

5.  Second phase of the war (spring 1997)               64

6.  Massacre of the Rwandan refugees                    94

7.  Military situation – early 2000                     200

8.  The east–west divide                                274

# Introduction

This book examines a decade-long period of instability, violence, war and extreme human suffering in Central Africa. Whilst a great deal has been written on specific aspects and episodes of the successive Congo wars, studies attempting a global overview are almost nonexistent.[1] Interpretations have considerably diverged, with emphasis put on state failure, the resource base of the conflicts, their internal or external nature, ideological issues both regional and global, the macro or micro levels and the rationality or lack of it displayed by the actors. Three perspectives have dominated the question of why the recent wars in the region have occurred: the collapse of the Zairean/Congolese[2] state, 'warlordism' coupled with plunder and local political dynamics, and external interventions, both by neighbouring countries and by more distant international players.[3] A combination of these and other perspectives, rather than a single perspective, will emerge in this book. Indeed, in order to understand the multifaceted and complex nature of the conflicts, an eclectic approach to factors is required; some factors occurred simultaneously, whilst others were successive. Take Rwanda's motives as an example. They were a combination, changing over time, of genuine security concerns, economic

---

[1] An exception is T. Turner, *The Congo Wars: Conflict, Myth and Reality*, London/ New York, Zed Books, 2007. However, there is little overlap between this book and that of Turner, which focuses on the cultural and ideological aspects of the wars.

[2] The name of the country at the relevant time will be used, that is, Zaire until May 1997, the Democratic Republic of Congo (DRC) or Congo after that date.

[3] These perspectives are summarised in J.F. Clark, 'Introduction. Causes and Consequences of the Congo War', in: J.F. Clark (Ed.), *The African Stakes of the Congo War*, New York/ Houndmills, Palgrave MacMillan, 2002, pp. 2–4.

interests, ethnic solidarity and even (selective) humanitarian concerns, the need to 'buy' internal elite solidarity, (military) institution building and a feeling of entitlement coupled with a sense of invincibility against the background of the comfort offered by the collapse of its rich neighbour.

Considered in the past as peripheral, land-locked, and politically and economically uninteresting, in the 1990s, the African Great Lakes region found itself at the heart of a profound geopolitical recomposition with continental repercussions. Countries as varied as Namibia in the south, Libya in the north, Angola in the west and Uganda in the east became entangled in wars that ignored international borders. However, the seeds of instability were sown in the beginning of the 1960s: the massive exile of the Rwandan Tutsi, who fled to neighbouring countries during and after the revolution of 1959–1961, and the virtual exclusion of Tutsi from public life in Rwanda, the radicalisation of Burundian Tutsi who monopolised power and wealth and the insecure status of Kinyarwanda-speakers in the Kivu provinces – all these factors were to merge with others to create the conditions for war. The acute destabilisation of the region started on 1 October 1990 when the Rwanda Patriotic Front (RPF) attacked Rwanda from Uganda with Ugandan support. After the collapse of the 1993 Arusha peace accord and following the genocide and massive war crimes and crimes against humanity, the RPF won a military victory and took power in July 1994. More than 1 million people died and more than 2 million fled abroad, mainly to Zaire and Tanzania. Eight months earlier, the democratic transition had ended in disaster in Burundi: tens of thousands of people were killed, and the country embarked on a decade-long civil war. At the end of 1993, some 200,000 Burundian refugees inundated the Zairean Kivu provinces, followed in mid-1994 by 1.5 million Rwandans. This was the beginning of the dramatic extension of the neighbouring conflicts, most prominently of the Rwandan civil war.

The progressive implosion of the Zairean state, undermined by gen-eralised 'predation', was a major contributory factor to this extension. However, Zaire was also surrounded by nine neighbouring countries, seven of which were endemically or acutely unstable.[4] In a perverse cycle, the instability of its neighbours threatened Zaire, just as Zaire's instabil-ity was a menace to its neighbours. We shall see the determining impact of circumstantial alliances in a situation where borders are porous and where actors reason using the logic of 'the enemy of my enemy is my friend'. State collapse opens space for very diverse local and regional,

---

[4] I consider Tanzania and Zambia as stable.

public and private actors, each with contradictory interests. Such a context favours the privatisation of public violence and the challenging of states' territorial spaces. I therefore agree with Nzongola, when he writes that "[t]he major determinant of the present conflict and instability in the Great Lakes Region is the decay of the state and its instruments of rule in the Congo. For it is this decay that made it possible for Lilliputian states the size of Congo's smallest province, such as Uganda, or even that of a district, such as Rwanda, to take it upon themselves to impose rulers in Kinshasa and to invade, occupy and loot the territory of their giant neighbour."[5] Others are less pessimistic. Bayart argues that, as has been the case in Europe,[6] wars in Africa might be the expression, albeit a painful one, of a process of state formation. He sees conflicts as contributing to the emergence of 'trickster states', which skilfully exploit the interstices of the global economy and the interface between formal and informal, even illegal activities.[7]

Be that as it may, state collapse was not the only factor. Conversely, a unique combination of circumstances explains the unravelling of the successive wars. The main circumstance can be found in the recent history of Rwanda. Although it is the smallest country in the region, it is there that the epicentre of all the crises lay. Without it, the conflicts would not have developed to such an extent. On the one hand, the 1994 genocide is a fundamental reference: as a consequence of both the old regime's resistance to change and the deliberate strategy of tension conducted by the RPF, not only were hundreds of thousands of Tutsi killed, but the Rwandan civil war also resulted in the violent restructuring of the whole region. On the other hand, the RPF – incapable of managing its victory – chose exclusion, ethnic domination and the military management of a political space, a mode of management which it extended beyond Rwanda's

---

[5] G. Nzongola-Ntalaja, *The Congo from Leopold to Kabila. A People's History*, London/ New York, Zed Books, 2002, p. 214.
[6] He adds the important proviso that war has not been a sufficient cause of state formation in Europe.
[7] J.F. Bayart, 'La guerre en Afrique: dépérissement ou formation de l'Etat?', *Esprit*, 1998, pp. 55–73. For a similar argument, based on local-level politics, see D.M. Tull, 'A Reconfiguration of Political Order? The State of the State in North Kivu (DR Congo)', *African Affairs*, 2003, pp. 429–446, who argues that, contrary to the discourse on collapsed states, the evidence suggests that there is a resilient (if ambivalent) attachment to the idea and practice of the state in North Kivu. I disagree, because the practices Tull outlines (the mimicry of the Mobutist 'state') are precisely those that led to the demise of the Zairean state. While the continuity between Mobutu and the RCD-Goma suggested by Tull is undeniably present, it does not lead to state formation, but rather to its collapse.

borders. Encouraged by its moral high ground and by the ineptitude of
the so-called international community,[8] the new regime explored the limits
of tolerance, crossing one Rubicon after another, and realised that there
were none. (Military) success is intoxicating: the Rwanda Patriotic Army
(RPA) went from war to war, and from victory to victory (from 1981 to
1986 on the sides of Museveni in Uganda, from 1990 to 1994 in Rwanda,
from 1996 to 1997 in Zaire, though not in the Democratic Republic of
Congo [DRC] after 1998). The status of regional superpower acquired
by this very small and very poor country is truly astonishing, and it was
obtained through the force of arms, which was allowed to prevail because
of the tolerance inspired by international feelings of guilt after the genocide. Paraphrasing what was said in the late 19th century about Prussia,
Rwanda became an army with a state, rather than a state with an army,
and it emerged as a major factor of regional instability.

This book attempts to present a synthetic overview and analysis of
the complex and violent evolution of Zaire/Congo in the regional setting, between the beginning of the first war in 1996 and the elections of
2006 that marked the formal end of the transition. Given the length of
this period and the vast amount of empirical data, this book cannot go
into great detail. It does, however, provide a broad map for understanding, with references for further study. The focus is on the 'small' Great
Lakes region, with Rwanda, Burundi and Kivu at the centre. However,
successive wars have entailed a considerable geopolitical extension of
this area, so much so that the notion of the 'greater Great Lakes region'
has emerged. As many as eleven 'core countries'[9] participated in the conference on peace, security and development in the Great Lakes region,
which was held in Nairobi at the end of 2006. Although focusing on the
smaller region, this book will also take into account wider developments
where necessary.

A macro perspective has been adopted. This does not mean that the
importance of local-level dynamics should be underestimated. On the

---

[8] I use the expression 'so-called', because the 'international community' does not really
exist. Is it its institutional translation, namely the United Nations? Or does it refer to
specific countries with a particular interest in a given situation or the press or vocal non-
governmental organisations (NGOs) attempting to influence international public opinion?
As can be seen in the situation analysed here and elsewhere in the world, the international
community is all of these, and the notion lacks clarity and allows the actors to escape
their responsibilities. However, after this caveat, the expression will be used frequently
throughout this book.

[9] Angola, Burundi, the Central African Republic, the DRC, the Republic of Congo, Kenya,
Rwanda, Sudan, Tanzania, Uganda, and Zambia.

contrary, these dynamics are important in order to understand the situation fully, and they are both under-researched and highly relevant from the perspective of human agency and suffering. Moreover, there is no strict dividing line between the international, regional and national levels on the one hand, and the local level on the other: macro actors interact with local forces, while local actors interpret larger dynamics and enlist the support of macro players. Autesserre shows the joint production of violence due to the interaction of local, national and regional motivations: "[L]ocal violence was motivated not only by top-down causes (regional or national), but also by bottom-up agendas, whose main instigators were villagers, traditional chiefs, community chiefs, or ethnic leaders."[10] Although players external to the local arena feature prominently in this book, this does not suggest that the Congolese were passive objects at the receiving end of events. All the actors, including many Congolese, have exercised various degrees of agency and have engaged in violence and plunder, and, in Taylor's words, they were "not simply automatons carrying out the wishes of outside forces."[11] As an issue of *Politique Africaine* on 'the war from below'[12] clearly documents, local players were actively engaged in the violence, sometimes in a ritual fashion; marginalised groups actively seized the opportunities to renegotiate their status and/or to gain access to resources; 'civil society' and new political actors found their way into the system; and entrepreneurs of insecurity at both the micro and macro levels fully exploited the possibilities offered by instability, war, statelessness, and social, economic, and political reorganisation. In order to address the micro level, brief reference will be made to the rare studies that are available, such as those by Vlassenroot and Raeymaekers.

Chapter 1 examines the premises of the extreme violence that has cost the lives of millions of people. While Rwanda, Burundi and Kivu have been hotbeds of instability for decades, the events in Burundi and, more so, in Rwanda in 1993–1994 have been fundamental accelerators. The enormous flows of refugees, among whom there were many 'refugee-warriors', in a context of 'transborderness', the conclusion of alliances and the absence of a functioning state in Zaire, transformed domestic civil wars into a regional war in 1996, and into a continental one in 1998.

---

[10] S. Autesserre, Local Violence, International Indifference? Post-Conflict 'Settlement' in the Eastern D.R. Congo (2003–2005), Ph.D. Dissertation, New York University, September 2006, p. 298.

[11] I. Taylor, 'Conflict in Central Africa: Clandestine Networks and Regional/Global Configurations', *Review of African Political Economy*, 2003, No. 95, p. 46.

[12] RDC, la guerre vue d'en bas, *Politique Africaine*, No. 84, December 2001.

Chapter 2 analyses the first war. Without entering into the military details, the role played by national, regional and international players will be analysed. Chapter 3 studies the 'collateral damage' inflicted on hundreds of thousands of Rwandan refugees, who were massively slaughtered by the Rwandan army, whilst a divided international community turned a blind eye to their fate. Chapter 4 analyses the fall of the Mobutist state, amid the hypocrisy and ineptitude of both the international community and the Zairean political class. Chapters 5 and 6 study the inter-bellum, a period which contained all the seeds of the new war that started in August 1998. Chapter 7 addresses the dialectics of continental war. Because of shifting alliances and the rallying of regional powers behind the Kinshasa regime, contrary to the first war, the outcome was not overthrow but military stalemate, thus leading to a fragile political settlement. How this settlement came about is the subject of the final chapter (Chapter 8).

This book does not have one particular thread other than to attempt to offer an orderly presentation of a very complex episode in the region's troubled history. A number of key dimensions are analysed. They have not operated in isolation: rather, there is a logical sequence between them, and they acted against the background of a failed state in Zaire/Congo. The overarching one is the unfinished Rwandan civil war, exported in 1996, and again in 1998, to the DRC. It was at the core of the successive wars and it is going on up to the present day through the presence of the Hutu rebels of the Forces démocratiques pour la libération du Rwanda (FDLR) and Rwandan support for Congolese Tutsi renegade General Laurent Nkunda. A second recurring factor lies in the politics of identity in Rwanda, Burundi and eastern DRC. The Congolese Tutsi Banyarwanda (or Kinyarwanda-speakers) are torn between their local and national allegiance on the one hand, and their ethnic and trans-boundary loyalty on the other, with the latter offering (the illusion of) protection and being a threat at the same time. The interlocking conflicts allowed ethnic entrepreneurs to mobilise identities across boundaries, thus giving rise to instant 'ethnogenesis' under the form of a divide between 'Bantu' and 'Hamites'. Thirdly, at the regional level, the shifting alliances produce an unpredictable and constantly evolving geopolitical landscape, where players engage in cost–benefit analyses and, as previously stated, adhere to the logic of 'the enemy of my enemy is my friend'. Both these traits instill a strong element of 'realism' and of 'rationality' of sorts in the calculations, at least in the short term. International players, the United States and France in particular, functioned very much in the same vein during the first war, though much less during the second war, by which time the magnitude of Pandora's box had become clear. A fourth dimension relates to the humanitarian fallout. Wars are always costly in terms of (mainly civilian) lives lost, but the first war was marked particularly by the massive atrocities committed by the RPA against civilian Hutu refugees, while the second war caused the death of millions of Congolese, particularly in Ituri and the Kivu provinces. Although the International Criminal Court (ICC) has indicted a few Ituri warlords and former Vice President Jean-Pierre Bemba (for crimes committed in the Central African Republic), these crimes have been left largely unpunished. A fifth dimension concerns a consequence of the combination of weak Zairean/Congolese statehood and the strategies developed by local and regional entrepreneurs of insecurity. This combination has allowed profoundly privatised and criminalised public spaces and economies to emerge. These are linked to the global economy but largely disconnected from the state on whose territory they function. These networks of violence and accumulation can also be found in vulnerable peripheries elsewhere in the world. A final dimension shows the ineptitude of classical international diplomacy, despite the recent rhetoric on conflict resolution, peace-building and the duty to intervene and protect. Local and regional players, be they state or non-state, seized the initiative and largely prevailed because they had the advantage of being on site and not hindered by considerations of international (humanitarian) law. During the second war, regional powers, South Africa in particular, imposed a settlement and, together with international players, put the DRC under a *de facto* trusteeship and imposed elections on a reluctant domestic political class. The externally induced nature of the transition is also its weakness.

As a complement to the existing literature, this book seeks to provide an in-depth analysis of concurrent developments in six realms: Zaire/DRC, Rwanda, Burundi, Uganda and the African and international contexts. By adopting, as far as possible, a non-chronological approach, the dynamics of the inter-relationships between these realms become apparent. This allows the discussion of developments in different places and at different levels and times not as being peripheral to the war(s), but as a consistent and concurrent whole.

A chronology is provided at the end of the book, but, given the complexity and abundance of events, a brief timeline is proposed here to assist the reader. After the genocide and the overthrow of the Rwandan Hutu-dominated regime in July 1994, 1.5 million Hutu refugees settled just across the border in Zaire. Among them were the former government army, the Forces armées rwandaises (FAR), and militia. They launched cross-border raids and increasingly became a serious security threat to the new regime, dominated by the mainly Tutsi RPF. Under the guise of first the 'Banyamulenge rebellion' and later the 'AFDL rebellion', the RPA attacked and cleared the refugee camps during the autumn of 1996. Having security concerns similar to those of *Rwanda, Uganda and Burundi* joined from the beginning, to be followed by a formidable regional coalition intent on toppling Mobutu. In May 1997, Laurent Kabila seized power in Kinshasa. During the latter half of 1997, relations between the new Congolese regime and its erstwhile Rwandan and Ugandan allies soured rapidly. In August 1998, Rwanda and Uganda again attacked, and they did so once more under the guise of a 'rebel movement', the RCD (Rassemblement Congolais pour la Démocratie), which was created in Kigali. The invading countries expected this to be a remake of the first war, only much faster this time. The reason for this failing to occur was the result of a spectacular shift of alliances, when Angola and Zimbabwe sided with Kabila against their former allies Rwanda and Uganda. This intervention made up for the weakness of the Congolese army, thus ensuring a military stalemate along a more or less stable frontline that cut the country in two. Considerable pressure from the region led to the signing of the Lusaka Accord in July 1999. However, Laurent Kabila blocked its implementation, and only after his assassination and succession by his son Joseph in January 2001 was the peace process resumed. Again under great pressure, by South Africa in particular, and after cumbersome negotiations, the Congolese parties signed a 'Global and All-Inclusive Accord' in December 2002. It took another three-and-a-half years to implement the accord, along a bumpy road replete with incidents, obstructions, negotiations and renegotiations, and constantly threatened by the resumption of the war. An informal international trusteeship, supported by a large U.N. peacekeeping force and also by the international and Congolese civil society, imposed elections on very reluctant political players. These took place in July–October 2006, in an overall free and fair fashion, and were won by Joseph Kabila and his party PPRD. Kabila was sworn in in December 2006, both houses of parliament were installed in January 2007, and a new government was formed in early February, thus formally ending the transition.

A final introductory word must be said about sources. As this is a book on contemporary history, much of the material used is 'grey', in some cases oral, and contemporary to the events it addresses. This sort of material is often partisan, serving a political, ideological or personal cause, and untested by previous research. The advantages of such documents are obvious, as they offer immediate and sometimes very detailed information that cannot be found elsewhere. However, the drawbacks are equally clear: these sources need to be handled with suspicion, corroborated and counterchecked. In addition, their possible bias must be clearly acknowledged and, where warranted, the conditional tense must be used or conflicting versions must be put forward. Since 1996, a number of episodes and themes addressed in this book have fortunately been the subject of scholarly research, which enables the author to put the more immediate sources in context.

# I

# A Region in Turmoil

## National Context

Before addressing the region that is the focus of this chapter, the situation prevailing in the mid-1990s at the national Zairean level must be summarised briefly.[1] By the early 1990s, the Zairean state had virtually disappeared as a consequence of both internal and external factors. The external element was twofold. On the one hand, international aid policies underwent a dramatic change in the 1980s. In the context of the neo-liberal philosophy, structural adjustment programmes imposed on African states both diminished the redistributive capacity of regimes, thus threatening the survival of clientelist networks, and impoverished the populations even more than before, as well as further curtailing public spending and reducing the relevance of the state. De Villers offers a telling figure of this shrinking of public finance: between 1982 and 1985, the wage bill of the Zairean public sector decreased by one-third and in 1985, the purchasing power of civil servants had dropped to between a third and a quarter of its 1975 level.[2] On the other hand, the transformation of the

---

[1] For more details, see G. De Villers, J. Omasombo, *Zaïre. La transition manquée 1990–1997*, Brussels/Paris, Institut Africain–L'Harmattan, Cahiers Africains, No. 27–28–29, October 1997. An inside story of the last ten years of the Mobutu regime can be found in F. Vunduawe Te Pemako, *A l'ombre du Léopard. Vérités sur le regime de Mobutu Sese Seko*, Brussels, Editions Zaïre libre, 2000.
[2] G. De Villers, 'La guerre dans les évolutions du Congo-Kinshasa', *Afrique Contemporaine*, 2005, 215, 51.

international scene after the end of the cold war allowed donors to impose (or at least attempt to impose) conditionality policies aimed at democratisation, respect for human rights and good governance. Although these policies were soon weakened or even abandoned, they undermined the position of incumbent regimes and engendered a great deal of instability, in particular, in countries such as Zaire that resisted the changes wanted by the donor community. The Bretton Woods institutions and other donors 'suspended' their aid to Zaire in the early 1990s. Lemarchand notes that '[a]s the delivery of political rewards (...) became increasingly problematic, the control of the state shrank correspondingly'[3] and concludes that '[j]ust as Mobutu owed his rise to power to the penetration of East–West rivalries in the continent, in the last analysis the collapse of the Zairean state must be seen as a casualty of the cold war's end'.[4]

The fate of the Zairean state was also the outcome of a long domestic process. The increasing failure of the state preceded its collapse, and the first signs of what William Reno calls a shadow state[5] were visible in the 1970s, after the 'Zairianisation' measures allowed the transfer of large parts of the economy to political and military elites. This heralded the putting into place of a prebendary and neo-patrimonial exercise of power that progressively corrupted official institutional norms and frameworks.[6] The ensuing 'informalisation' fatally affected the state, including, as discussed later, its armed forces.

The political situation was one of total stalemate in the mid-1990s. The 'transition', which started in 1990, was leading nowhere; the political class was absorbed by never-ending disputes on a background of surreal legal discourses, and the members of the transitional parliament (Haut Conseil de la République–Parlement de transition [HCR–PT]) were not in a hurry to proceed to elections but rather preferred the relative comfort provided by their *per diem*. The promulgation of the constitutional instrument, which was to introduce the Third Republic, was constantly delayed,[7] and the National Electoral Commission (Commission nationale

---

[3] R. Lemarchand, The Democratic Republic of Congo: From Collapse to Potential Reconstruction, Copenhagen, Centre of African Studies, Occasional Paper, September 2001, p. 7.

[4] *Idem*, p. 19.

[5] W. Reno, 'Shadow states and the political economy of civil wars', in: M. Berdal, M. Malone (Eds.), *Greed and Grievance. Economic Agendas in Civil Wars*, Boulder/London, Lynne Riener, 2000, pp. 43–63.

[6] G. De Villers, 'La guerre ...', *op. cit.*, p. 54.

[7] As will be seen later, the HCR–PT approved a draft constitution only in early December 1996, when the country was fully at war.

MAP 1. The Great Lakes region.

des élections) was paralysed by internal bickering and poor relations with both the HCR–PT and civil society. The political transition was aborted, among other reasons, because of the bipolarisation between the pro-Mobutu Forces Politiques du Conclave (FPC) and the Union Sacrée de l'Opposition (USOR) and the breaking up of the opposition.[8] The impasse, the lack of perspective and the discredit, which increasingly affected the whole political class (both the *mouvance présidentielle* and the *opposition radicale*) led many national actors and international partners to lethargy and despair. The political system had retreated to Kinshasa, where it 'operated' in isolation. It did not manage 'peripheral' issues in which it had no interest, such as those affecting the Kivu region, where local and regional dynamics far exceeded the capacity of a collapsed state and an impotent political class.

## Crises of Identity, of Land and of Politics

Problems related to identity in the Kivu region are ancient; important migratory flows before, during and after the colonial period, considerable demographic pressure, the uncertain status of (neo-)traditional authorities, the political and economic dynamism of the region, its peripheral situation in the Zairean context and its partial incorporation in the East African space are the factors forming the background to recent events in eastern Zaire. The most visible and violent expression of this problem was the situation of the 'Banyarwanda', the Kinyarwanda speakers living in the Kivu. They consisted of several groups: the 'natives' established since pre-colonial days, the 'immigrants' and the 'transplanted'[9] of the colonial period, the 'infiltrators' and 'clandestines' before and after independence (1960) and the Tutsi[10] and Hutu[11] refugees. This mixture gave birth to conflict in the 1960s during the so-called Kanyarwanda rebellion, when the Banyarwanda faced the threat of expulsion from the North Kivu region.[12] After a long period of calm under the regime of Mobutu, whose influential director of the Political Bureau, Barthélémy

---

[8] An excellent survey in English of the aborted transition can be found in G. Nzongola-Ntalaja, *The Congo from Leopold to Kabila...*, *op. cit.*, pp. 189–208.
[9] The latter category of Rwandans was imported between 1937 and 1955 as workers as a result of deliberate policies by the Belgian colonial authorities, which even set up an agency (*Mission d'immigration des Banyarwanda* [MIB]) to that effect.
[10] These arrived mainly in 1959–64, 1973 and 1990–4.
[11] These arrived massively in mid-1994.
[12] See J. Gerard-libois, J. Van Lierde, *Congo 1965*, Brussels, CRISP, 1965, pp. 79–80.

Bisengimana, was himself of Tutsi origin, the problem came to the fore again during the National Conference (1991–2), when representatives of the civil society of North and South Kivu raised the question of the 'Zaireans of dual or doubtful citizenship', a coded expression referring to the Banyarwanda.

While the conflicts have older roots, this book picks up the story from early 1993 onwards.[13] The events, which started in North Kivu in March 1993, show how fluid ethnic categories are. Indeed, those who became the victims of a wave of violence waged by 'indigenous' ethnic groups, such as the Hunde, Nande and Nyanga, supported by their respective militias (the Mai-mai and the Bangilima), were the Banyarwanda, Hutu and Tutsi alike. Only two years later, the Hutu and Tutsi confronted each other in 'ethnic' strife. There are various reasons for the violence, which erupted in early 1993. First, the democratisation process underway since 1990 meant that there was a new way of competing for power. As only nationals exercise political rights, citizenship became important, particularly in regions with a high proportion of Banyarwanda (in the extreme case of the zone of Masisi, they numbered 70% of the population). Second, in this relatively overpopulated part of Zaire, conflicts over land set groups against each other in two ways. On the one hand, two types of land use, agriculture and stock breeding, entered into competition with each other; on the other, two concepts of land tenure and access to land clashed with each other: land use by members of a group, which holds corporate ownership (the customary law regime) as opposed to the concept of individual ownership of the modern law type, which allows for contractual transactions in land. A third source of conflict, not unrelated to the previous one, concerned the position of customary authorities. Groups that are immigrant or presented as such tend to try and free themselves from

---

[13] For details on earlier developments, see for example, J.-P. Pabanel, 'La question de la nationalité au Kivu', *Politique Africaine*, 41, March 1991, 32–40; A. Guichaoua, *Le problème des régugiés rwandais et des populations banyarwanda dans la région des grands lacs africains*, Geneva, UNHCR, 1992; P. Kanyamachumbi, *Les populations du Kivu et la loi sur la n ationalité. Vraie ou fausse problématique*, Kinshasa, Editions Select, s.d. (1993); 'Dossier: la 'guerre' de Masisi', *Dialogue*, 192, August 1996–September 1996; F. Reyntjens, S. Marysse, *Conflits au Kivu: antécédents et enjeux*, Antwerp, Centre for the Study of the Great Lakes Region of Africa, 1996; J.-C. Willame, *Banyarwanda et Banyamulenge. Violences ethniques et gestion de l'identitaire au Kivu*, Brussels/Paris, Institut Africain-L'Harmattan, Cahiers Africains, 25, 1997 ; P. Mathieu, J.-C. Willame (Eds.), *Conflits et guerres au Kivu et dans la région des grands lacs. Entre tensions locales et escalade régionale*, Brussels/Paris, Institut Africain–L'Harmattan, Cahiers Africains, pp. 39–40, 1999.

the authority of local chiefs, thus threatening their position and differentiating themselves from 'indigenous' populations. This attitude of distancing was more frequently adopted by pastoral communities of Tutsi extraction. Under these circumstances, the denial of citizenship became a means for the political and economic exclusion of the Banyarwanda, and the Tutsi in particular.

The conflict came to the fore again during the National Conference, and confrontations had already taken place in 1991[14] and 1992, particularly in the zones of Masisi and Rutshuru. However, conflict spread dramatically in March 1993.[15] Two days after a visit by the governor of North Kivu, violence started in Ntoto in the zone of Walikale, close to Masisi. There were large-scale killings of Hutu and Tutsi Banyarwanda; their houses were burned and their cattle were stolen. During the following days, the violence extended to the zone of Masisi, where, however, the Banyarwanda were the majority group and had organised their defence. As the casualties show, a real war broke out with many deaths: 'indigenous' and 'immigrant' communities lost about 1000 members each; tens of thousands more were displaced. Both parties accused each other: the Banyarwanda claimed that the 'indigenous' wanted to chase and even massacre them, whereas according to the 'indigenous', the Banyarwanda, and the Hutu in particular, intended to claim a territory that they allegedly considered to be part of 'Ancient Rwanda'.[16]

Two factors contributed to the pacification of North Kivu, at least for a short period. President Mobutu went to Goma, where he stayed for a month and met with most local players and units of the Special Presidential Division (Division spéciale présidentielle [DSP]); its sheer presence brought apparent calm without a shot being fired. In the long run, 'reflection days', organised in November 1993 and February 1994, consolidated the return to order. Together with the NGO ACODRI, the local Catholic church of Mweso brought together representatives of territorial units, tradespeople, teachers, local NGOs, clergymen, officers of the DSP, leaders of cooperatives, customary chiefs, civil servants and

---

[14] An important precedent took place in June 1991, when armed Hutu groups attacked state agents in charge of a census of nationals in Masisi. Offices were ransacked and registers destroyed. Already at that stage, the insecurity was linked to the Rwandan conflict: in March 1991, a retired Rwandan army officer Col. Aloys Simba was arrested in Goma while carrying weapons and funds.

[15] For details, see J.-C. Willame, *Banyarwanda et Banyamulenge...*, *op. cit.*, pp. 66–68, 124–131.

[16] As discussed later, this suggestion was reiterated in 1996–7.

simple peasants, a total of eighty-eight local actors who were joined by thirty external 'observers'.

The approach was innovative: the organisers used the method of the 'problem tree', which identified the expectations and analyses of each party, potential solution, and points of agreement and divergence. The debates showed that the two major causes of the conflicts were the problems of 'citizenship' and 'the rush for power in order to control land'. Among the solutions, many references revolved around the issue of power sharing. As to the disagreements, the cultural misunderstanding mentioned above was ever present: the perception of many Banyarwanda on the status of land and the authority of local chiefs was markedly different from that shared by the Hunde and Nyanga. However, some of these differences were bridged, partially thanks to the input of national and regional arbitrators. Although all problems were by no means solved, the two series of meetings allowed an explosive situation to be managed and the tensions in the region to diminish. This relative success, which implicated the base and which was negotiated rather than imposed, demonstrated the ability of the local communities to address their potentially violent differences.[17] However, an immense outside factor was to destroy the results of these patient efforts.

## The New Given: Influx of Hutu Refugees

Only a few months after pacification, North Kivu was flooded by over 700,000 Rwandan Hutu refugees who fled the civil war in their country and the victorious RPF, accompanied and to some extent controlled by those responsible for the Rwandan genocide. Concentrated in five huge camps (Katale, Kahindo, Kibumba, Lac Vert and Mugunga) on a limited area close to the Rwandan border, they completely upset the demographic situation and therefore the politics of the region. At the beginning of the 1990s, approximately 425,000 Banyarwanda lived in the three zones (Masisi, Rutshuru and Goma) where the refugees settled; out of a total population of about 1 million, this was about 40%.[18] Obviously, as a result of this massive injection of people, the Banyarwanda and the Rwandan refugees suddenly constituted the majority of the regional population. In addition, the Hutu (both the Rwandan refugees and the Zairean Hutu)

---

[17] On this bottom-up initiative, see J.-C. Willame, *Banyarwanda et Banyamulenge...*, op. cit., pp. 124–131.
[18] As already seen, this proportion reached 70% in the zone of Masisi.

had now become largely dominant in numbers, thus breaking the fragile balance put in place earlier in the year. The alliance of Hutu and Tutsi Banyarwanda broke up and, as in Rwanda, the two groups entered into violent conflict. The massive arrival of refugees also had other destabilis-ing effects: the environment was thoroughly disturbed by deforestation, poaching and pressure on water supplies; the economy was destabilised by the 'dollarisation' and the dramatic decrease of livestock; and basic infrastructure, already very weak before the crisis, was badly damaged.

However, large-scale violence did not start until November 1995. Probably unwillingly, the Zairean government contributed to the insta-bility in August 1995 by announcing that the Rwandan refugees were to be expelled; they were given until 31 December 1995 to leave the coun-try.[19] As a result, many refugees left the camps and attempted to settle in the zones of Masisi and Rutshuru, where they inevitably clashed with the 'natives' and Tutsi Banyarwanda whose houses and land they threatened to occupy. On a more general political level, these attempts at occupation heightened the fears of many Zaireans that a 'Hutu-land' was being put in place in North Kivu.[20] Incidents of uneven intensity in September and October 1995 were the prelude to a real war that started first in Masisi, but rapidly spread to Rutshuru and Lubero.

Massacres by Hutu militias against the Hunde and Tutsi and by Hunde militia against the Tutsi and Hutu progressively created ethnically homogenous spaces. By March–April 1996, the zone of Masisi had been 'ethnically cleansed': most local Tutsi fled to Rwanda, where about 18,000 refugees had arrived by the end of April. In March, the conflict extended to the zones of Rutshuru, Walikale and Lubero, where the Bangilima, a Hunde militia, attacked the Banyarwanda; between May and June, about 65,000 people were displaced in Rutshuru alone.

The spread of violence was enhanced by the late and ambiguous intervention of the Zairean authorities. In early April, the Zairean army launched operation 'Kimia' under the command of General Eluki, the

[19] In fact, as early as August 1995 about 15,000 Rwandan and Burundian refugees were forcibly repatriated, but the Zairean government suspended the expulsions as a result of international pressure. It should be added that the government was not solely to blame for this measure. Hunde and Nande parliamentarians from North Kivu pressured the HCR–PT into demanding radical solutions to the problem of the Banyarwanda and the Rwandan refugees. As will be seen later, the government was also forced into intransigent positions by the interim parliament on other related issues.
[20] Azado, *Nord-Kivu: Etat d'urgence*, Kinshasa, April 1996, p. 4; On 3 August 1996, the NGO SIMA–Kivu organised a conference in Brussels around the theme 'Zaire–Rwanda–Burundi: Who would profit from the creation of a Hutu-land and a Tutsi-land?'.

chief of staff of the Forces Armées Zaïroises (FAZ). Elite elements of the DSP rapidly brought something resembling calm to areas where they operated. However, troops from other units, poorly equipped, badly trained and barely paid, were not only inefficient, but even participated in looting and abuse. Although these elements of the FAZ appear to have often fought on the side of the Hutu against the Tutsi and Hunde, this was more the result of economic calculations than of political or ethnic bias: they essentially fought for those who paid for their services. The ambiguity was also very clear in the attitude of the local authorities, used to manipulating ethnicity for plutocratic purposes. Thus, in May 1995, the governor of North Kivu, Christophe Moto Mupenda, stated during a public meeting before a Hunde audience in the town of Masisi that 'hospitality has its limits' and that it was necessary 'to strike and strike now against the immigrants'. During the following year, two Goma-based radio stations fuelled anti-Tutsi feelings, and megaphones were used to call on residents to chase the Tutsi out of town; Tutsi businessmen were arrested by local authorities without specific charges.[21] In November 1995, General Eluki declared publicly that 'the Hunde, Nyanga and Batembo are right to fight for the land of their ancestors and to chase the foreigners away from it'.[22]

The situation was further compounded by the presence, among the refugees, of the former Rwandan army, FAR, and militiamen. After they arrived in July 1994, they were only partly disarmed; and some of the weapons and ammunition seized were later resold to them by the FAZ. In addition, until the middle of 1996, military equipment continued to reach them in the Goma region, despite an embargo decreed by the UN Security Council. Several UN commission of inquiry reports established that former FAR and militia were armed and trained in preparation for an invasion of Rwanda and that some Zairean authorities played a central role in these activities; also, a considerable mobilisation effort had been conducted among the refugee populations, including in the form of the levying of 'war tax', and Rwandan and Burundian insurgents had joined forces to destabilise their respective countries of origin from Zaire.[23] As early as May 1995, research conducted by Human Rights Watch arrived

---

[21] U.S. Committee for Refugees, *Masisi, Down the Road from Goma: Ethnic Cleansing and Displacement in Eastern Zaire*, Washington D.C., June 1996, p. 16.
[22] *ANB–BIA*, 1 April 1996.
[23] International Commission of Inquiry (Rwanda), Reports of 17 January 1996, 14 March 1996, 28 October 1996, 26 January 1998 and 19 August 1998. Final report 18 November 1998 (Security Council document S/1998/1096).

at similar conclusions.[24] These illegal activities had the support both of the Zairean regime, and also of France, as many indications show.[25] Kinshasa and Paris thus combated the Kampala–Kigali axis. There were a considerable number of 'refugee-warriors'[26] among the refugees. These 'refugee-warriors' were not just the passive beneficiaries of international assistance, but actors in their own right with a clear goal in mind: they intended to recapture power in their country of origin. For a number of these Rwandans in 'humanitarian sanctuaries',[27] the reaching of this objective probably included finishing an unfinished job: the genocide. The fact that humanitarian assistance also reached armed elements and objectively supported their project of violent return forced Médecins sans frontières (MSF) to end their work in the Kivu camps in mid-1995. The instability caused by the presence of Rwandan refugees was not limited to eastern Zaire. From the beginning of 1995, the western *préfectures* of Rwanda (Cyangugu, Kibuye and Gisenyi) increasingly became the theatre for raids and infiltration. Although these insurrectionist activities were initially of low intensity, the RPA had a great deal of trouble containing them and the number of civilian victims grew constantly as detailed later in the text.

Nevertheless, the question arises as to whether the new Rwandan regime really wanted the refugees to return home. Contrary to what has often been claimed, the Zairean government did not feel that the prolonged presence of over a million Rwandans was in its best interest. Between the end of 1994 and mid-1996, the government made many representations to the UNHCR and Rwanda to ensure their repatriation or the resettlement elsewhere of those unwilling or unable to return. According to Honoré N'Gbanda, 'Kagame did not want the Hutu back in Rwanda',[28] and he refers to an incident, which appears to confirm this

---

[24] Human Rights Watch Arms Project, *Rearming with Impunity: International Support for the Perpetrators of the Rwandan Genocide*, New York, May 1995.

[25] A summary can be found in F.-X. Verschave, *La Françafrique. Le plus long scandale de la République*, Paris, Stock, 1998, pp. 239–252.

[26] See A.R. Zolberg, A. Suhrke, S. Aguayo, *Escape from Violence: Conflict and Refugee Crisis in the Developing World*, New York, Oxford University Press, 1989, p. 278.

[27] The expression comes from J.-C. Rufin, 'Les économies de guerre dans les conflits internes', in: F. Jean, J.-C. Rufin (Eds.), *Economie des guerres civiles*, Paris, Hachette, 1996, p. 27.

[28] H. N'Gbanda Nzambo Ko Atumba, *Ainsi sonne le glas! Les derniers jours du Maréchal Mobutu*, Paris, Editions Gideppe, 1998, p. 95. This book is referred to on several occasions, but a caveat is in order. N'Gbanda is a former intelligence chief, minister and, above all, was special security advisor to Mobutu from 1992 to 1997. He is therefore an important player, who relates his version of events. The risk of bias and apology is ever-present; in addition, many facts are based on the author's sole testimony. However,

thesis. During a visit to President Mobutu in Gbadolite at the end of 1994, Rwandan president Bizimungu reportedly accepted a proposal to solve the issue of refugees. When N'Gbanda went to Kigali some weeks later to finalise the details, one of Bizimungu's advisors refused the solution, apparently without consulting with the president or offering an explanation. N'Gbanda concludes that 'the centre of decision was elsewhere' (that is to say with Vice-President Kagame, the real holder of power).[29]

As the UNHCR erroneously believed in a rapid return of the Rwandan refugees,[30] camps that were both too large and too close to the Rwandan border were maintained. When the Zairean government asked the UN to move the refugees away from the border by resettling them in the former military training centres of Irebu, Lukandu and Kongolo, the UN refused because of the 'high cost' of the operation. In addition, no effort was made to separate the civilian refugees from the armed elements among them. Moreover, the strong control of populations, very typical of Rwanda, was exported to the camps, where the refugees were organised into cells, sectors, municipalities and *préfectures* (districts) and tightly 'administered'. Some have concluded that these people were 'hostages', even 'living shields' behind which former military and militia were hiding. However, whilst there was undoubtedly some violence and intimidation in order to discourage the refugees from returning to Rwanda, this population was also in a sense 'voluntarily hostage': used to a pyramid structure of administrative presence, socially conformist and worried about the practices (arrests, massacres and 'disappearances') carried out by the new regime, which they did not trust, most refugees did not really consider repatriation to be a viable option.[31] Finally, contrary to what some sources, bent on intoxication rather than on information, have

---

N'Gbanda is a privileged witness and his book sheds such unique light on a number of events that, read with the necessary caution, it is a useful source of information.

[29] On this episode, see H. N'Gbanda, *Ainsi sonne le glas...*, *op. cit.*, pp. 89–92.

[30] This belief was shared by the Zairean authorities who signed several agreements (e.g., on 24 October 1994, 27 January 1995, 25 September 1995 and 20 December 1995) with the UNHCR and/or Rwanda on measures supposed to incite the refugees to return home. Applying the December 1995 accord, Zaire undertook the 'administrative closure' of the camps of Kibumba and Nyangezi in February 1996.

[31] These sentiments are echoed in J.-P. Godding, *Réfugiés rwandais au Zaïre. Sommes-nous encore des hommes?* Paris, L'Harmattan, 1997. Besides intimidation, the refugees also quoted the insecurity inside Rwanda and disputes about property as the main reasons for their refusal to return (see Joint Evaluation of Emergency Assistance to Rwanda, *The International Response to Conflict and Genocide: Lessons from the Rwanda Experience*, Vol. 4 (*Rebuilding Post-War Rwanda*), March 1996, p. 92).

claimed, the number among the refugees implicated in the 1994 genocide did not exceed 15%.[32]

In early 1996, a plan called the 'Tindemans Plan',[33] though the author was in fact Christian Tavernier (see below), might possibly have been able to deal with this explosive issue. Although the plan essentially concerned the FAZ, which were to be partly demobilised and transformed into an 'army at the service of development', it also contained a part discussing the former FAR. These were to be transferred to the Kamina army base in Shaba, about 1000 km from Rwanda; those among them suspected of genocide were to be judged by the International Criminal Tribunal for Rwanda (ICTR), where they would be defended by Belgian lawyers; in the case of a conviction, they were to serve their prison term outside of Rwanda. On 5 January 1996, Tavernier signed a document in Mugunga camp with General Bizimungu, the chief of staff of the FAR; this provided for a meeting to finalise the project. Because the international community was unwilling to commit the necessary funds, and also because of internal problems related to Belgian politics too complex to explain here, Tindemans did not obtain the required support at the Belgian and European levels, and the plan was abandoned.[34] Had it been applied, the Great Lakes region might have avoided two successive wars and immense human suffering.

### South Kivu: The Banyamulenge

Contrary to North Kivu, South Kivu remained relatively quiet until 1996, even if the arrival of 200,000 Burundian refugees at the end of 1993 and half a million Rwandan refugees in mid-1994 had an undeniable destabilising effect. As early as November 1995, the secretary general of the Milima Group, one of the 'tribal solidarity organisations' very common in the region, drew the attention of the international community to the discrimination the Banyamulenge were suffering. In a letter of 15 November 1995 to the Carter Center in Atlanta, Ruhimbika warned that 'the present situation could soon lead to armed conflict which will spread beyond the Kinyarwanda speakers concerned, all the more so since the

---

[32] Joint Evaluation of Emergency Assistance to Rwanda, *The International Response...*, *op. cit.*, Synthesis Report, p. 39.

[33] Named after Leo Tindemans, Belgian MEP and former prime minister.

[34] Details of the plan and the obstacles encountered can be found in *Afriq'Events*, 29, November–December 1996 and *Le Soir Illustré*, 23–29 November 1996.

circulation of weapons in the region is intense. The recent inter-ethnic war in North Kivu which has claimed thousands of victims and displaced persons, is a precedent which must be taken into account'.

Before addressing the debate, which was triggered by Ruhimbika's claims, the meaning of the term 'Banyamulenge'[35] must be discussed. In a document sent on 11 July 1996[36] to the UN Human Rights Commission, Ruhimbika claimed that there were between 350,000 and 500,000 Banyamulenge, adding that before 1959,[37] the Banyamulenge were called Banyarwanda; according to him, the new term was used to 'distinguish them from the other Tutsi of the region'. Indeed, the Banyamulenge are Banyarwanda who arrived from Southwest Rwanda in South Kivu before 1885, the formal beginning of the colonisation of Zaire; in other words, these are 'native' Banyarwanda, as opposed to 'immigrant', 'transplanted', 'infiltrated', 'clandestine' or refugee populations (see earlier text concerning North Kivu). However, if this is the case, the number of Banyamulenge quoted by Ruhimbika was a huge overestimation. Based on the small amount of information available on the Banyamulenge before the 1990s,[38] they did not exceed 50,000; the real number is probably even lower.

As they immigrated before 1885, the Banyamulenge possessed Zairean citizenship, even if the most restrictive legislation, that of the 1981 Act on Nationality is applied (' (...) Every person of whom one of the ascendants is, or has been, a member of one of the tribes established on the territory of the Republic of Zaire in its limits of 1 August 1885 is Zairean'). The warnings of Ruhimbika can be explained by new attempts aimed at calling into question the political rights of 'populations of doubtful citizenship' in South Kivu. Thus, an April 1995 resolution of the HCR–PT was relayed in the region by local authorities, including the district commissioner of Uvira and the vice-governor of South Kivu. In his report of 29 January 1996, the UN Special Rapporteur Roberto Garretón drew attention to the threats

---

[35] For more details, see F. Reyntjens, S. Marysse, *Conflits au Kivu...*, *op. cit.*, pp. 5–8.

[36] As will be seen subsequently, by this time the war was being actively prepared and Ruhimbika was fully involved. Therefore, his letter could well be part of a campaign to prepare the international opinion for the Rwandan operation in the region under the cover of the 'rebellion of the Banyamulenge' (see later text).

[37] The year of the Rwandan revolution as a result of which the first Tutsi refugees left the country.

[38] G. Kajiga, 'Cette immigration séculaire des Rwandais au Congo', *Bulletin du CEPSI*, 1956, 32, 5–64; G. Weiss, *Le pays d'Uvira*, Brussels, ARSC, 1959; J. Depelchin, From Pre-Capitalism to Imperialism. A History of Social and Economic Formations in Eastern Zaire (Uvira zone, c. 1800–1965), Stanford University, Ph.D. Dissertation, 1974.

against the Banyamulenge;[39] this immediately caused an angry reaction by a group of people from the Kivu living in Canada who claimed that Garretón had been manipulated by the Banyamulenge.[40] The 11 July 1996 document of the Milima, quoted earlier, sees proof in this reaction that 'South Kivu is now embarked on the same course as its Northern neighbour', a clear reference to the violence of which the Tutsi Banyarwanda were the victims in North Kivu at the end of 1995 and the beginning of 1996.

Clearly, tensions grew dramatically in June–July 1996. The Banyamulenge were the victims of discrimination, violence and expulsion from their land. In July, the governor of South Kivu called for an economic boycott of the Banyamulenge. In August, the Milima Group was banned and Ruhimbika fled to Rwanda. At the same time, the Banyamulenge armed themselves and, above all, Rwanda was fully preparing the ground for the operation, which was to become the 'rebellion of the Banyamulenge' (see later text).

## 1.2  RWANDA: FROM GENOCIDE
## TO DICTATORSHIP

Between 1990 and 1994, Rwanda went through a twofold evolution: on the one hand, a 'classical' political transition as seen elsewhere in Africa in the context of post-Cold War developments (see earlier text); on the other, a civil war, which started when the RPF invaded from Uganda. This combination and the radicalisation that ensued led to political stalemate, the collapse of the Arusha peace accord, the resumption of the civil war and massive violence, under the form both of genocide committed by radical Hutu against the Tutsi and crimes against humanity and war crimes committed by the RPF.[41]

---

[39] United Nations, Economic and Social Council, Commission on Human Rights, Report on the situation of human rights in Zaire, prepared by the Special Rapporteur, Mr. Roberto Garretón, in accordance with Commission resolution 1995/69, E/CN.4/1996/66, 29 January 1996, paragraphs 33–37.

[40] Forum Baraza La Kivu, *'Banyamulenge', Roberto Garretón's report and Human Rights in Fizi, Uvira and Mwenga, Zaire: The anatomy of fraud and genesis of a conflict*, Montreal, 10 May 1996.

[41] For the period preceding the genocide, see F. Reyntjens, *L'Afrique des grands lacs en crise. Rwanda, Burundi 1988–1994*, Paris, Karthala, 1994; G. Prunier, *The Rwanda Crisis. History of a Genocide*, New York, Columbia University Press, 1995. The account offered here is limited to the period between the genocide and mid-1996. For an analysis of Rwanda up to late 2003, see F. Reyntjens, 'Rwanda, Ten Years On: From Genocide to Dictatorship', *African Affairs*, 2004, 177–210.

## The Power Base

When, after the genocide and the military defeat of the old regime, a new government took office on 19 July 1994, the victorious RPF reaffirmed its adhesion to the spirit and, to the largest possible extent, the letter of the 1993 Arusha peace accord and the logic of power-sharing it contained. However, a number of amendments made to the fundamental law by a declaration made on 17 July by the RPF profoundly modified the nature of the political regime agreed in Arusha: it introduced a strong executive presidency, engineered the dominance of the RPF in the government and redrew the composition of the parliament. The new fundamental law was in effect a piece of subtle constitutional engineering, which attempted to hide the monolithic nature of political power.

Of course, it is the context in which power is exercised that determines the way a state is run, rather than the constitutional order. This context was one of domination by the RPF, which created and maintained a closely controlled political environment. From early on under the new regime, the power base proved to be very narrow: the army and the security services, the party officials (*abakada*) and a fraction of the urban population, in particular the old Tutsi diaspora, in particular from Uganda, which returned to the country in the wake of the RPF's victory. While initially a number of politicians, civil servants, judges and military in place before mid-1994 either stayed or returned and were willing to cooperate with the RPF, very soon the increasing number of defections was to destroy the illusion.

Apart from a large number of anonymous Rwandans who wished to leave the country,[42] the list of well-known figures, throwing in the towel, rapidly increased throughout 1995–6. Among the most prominent exiles were a prime minister and several ministers, superior judges and high civil servants, diplomats, army officers, leaders of civil society and even players of the national soccer team. As soon as they arrived abroad, they made similar allegations of concentration and abuse of power, outrage by the army and intelligence services, massive violations of human rights, insecurity and intimidation, discrimination against the Hutu and even the Tutsi genocide survivors.[43]

---

[42] Many were unable to do so, because they lacked a passport or a visa or because they feared their flight would threaten their families.

[43] For a few examples, see V. Ndikumana, J. Afrika, *Lettre ouverte au Conseil de sécurité de l'ONU sur la situation qui prévaut au Rwanda*, Nairobi, 14 November 1994; E. Ruberangeyo, *Mes inquiétudes sur la gestion actuelle rwandaise des fonds publics*,

The Hutu elites who remained in the country often became the victims of imprisonment and even death. District administrators (*préfets*), local mayors, headteachers, judges and other judicial staff were killed. In most cases, the responsibility of the RPA was well documented. Many judges were arrested under unclear charges: the former justice minister Alphonse Nkubito quoted thirty cases of judges and prosecutors in jail.[44]

The political landscape did not just oppose Hutu and Tutsi. Indeed, many Tutsi felt ill-at-ease, particularly those who lived in Rwanda at the time of the genocide. The latter increasingly became second-rate citizens suspected of having 'done business with the devil' in order to ensure their physical survival. They resented the feeling that one dictatorship had replaced another and tried to challenge what they saw as an authoritarian regime disrespectful of human rights. Some reputedly 'Tutsi' newspapers in Kigali, such as *L'Ere de Liberté*, *Intego* and *Le Tribun du Peuple*, quite openly voiced these concerns. Differences existed even within the RPF, which was less monolithic than it looked from the outside.

## The Drift

When the RPF took power, it inherited a country that had been profoundly destroyed both in human and material terms – over 1 million people had been killed,[45] 2 million refugees were abroad, over 1 million were internally displaced, survivors were profoundly traumatised, hundreds of thousands of 'old caseload' refugees returned in a chaotic fashion, the infrastructure had been destroyed, banks had been plundered, administration, courts, health care and education had disappeared. Clearly, some credit and the benefit of the doubt had to be given to a regime facing the

---

31 May 1995; S. Musangamfura, *J'accuse le FPR de crimes de génocide des populations d'ethnie hutu, de purification ethnique et appelle à une enquête internationale urgente*, Nairobi, 8 December 1995; F. Twagiramungu, S. Sendashonga, F.R.D. *Plate-forme politique*, Brussels, March 1996; T. Lizinde, *Rwanda: la tragédie*, Brussels (in fact: Kinshasa), 1 May 1996.

[44] A. Nkubito, *Le harcèlement, les tracasseries, les menaces, bref la persécution du personnel judiciaire*, Kigali, 10 May 1996. Quite tellingly, the author did not sign this text for fear of persecution; after his death in February 1997, his name can be revealed.

[45] The figure commonly quoted is 'between 500,000 and one million', which of course leaves an unacceptable gap; at any rate, this figure is not based on any research. On the basis of three sets of demographic data (June 1995, September 1996 and January 1997), the author arrives at a total number of between 1,050,000 and 1,150,000 victims. See F. Reyntjens, 'Estimation du nombre de personnes tuées au Rwanda en 1994', in: S. Marysse, F. Reyntjens (Eds.), *L'Afrique des grands lacs. Annuaire 1996–1997*, Paris, L'Harmattan, 1997, pp. 179–186.

colossal task of reconstructing the country under such adverse circumstances. When the first indications of worrying developments emerged soon after the RPF seized power, it seemed premature to challenge the good faith and the political will of the new regime.[46]

However, less than a year later, increasing doubt emerged and it became clear that a number of practices were a consequence of a lack of political will rather than of a lack of resources. While initially the regime seemed to hesitate between political openness (witness the appointment of a government of national union and the return to Rwanda of some non-RPF civilian and military office-holders) and violent repression, to which large numbers of civilian victims bore testimony (see later text), signs of a worrying drift soon appeared. Killings by the RPF abated for a while at the beginning of October 1994 as a result of the threat that the Gersony report (see later text) was to be released if the situation did not improve. They then started to increase in number again during the early part of 1995. It appears that this was due, at least in part, to the outcome of a donors' roundtable organised in Geneva in January 1995, during which a total amount of almost US$600 million was pledged by bilateral and multilateral partners.[47] As there were virtually no strings attached, the Rwandan government interpreted this as a signal that blank cheques were being issued and that it could act unfettered. The highly publicised killing of thousands of internally displaced persons at Kibeho camp in April by the RPA was merely the visible side of the resumption of government-sponsored violence.[48]

The victim[49] turned bully;[50] like elsewhere, this phenomenon happened in Rwanda, although it was not considered politically correct to

---

[46] The author was among the first observers to express concern: F. Reyntjens, 'Sujets d'inquiétude au Rwanda en octobre 1994', *Dialogue*, 179, November–December 1994, pp. 3–14; translated and summarised in English: F. Reyntjens, 'Subjects of concern: Rwanda, October 1994', *Issue. A Journal of Opinion*, 1995, 2, 39–43.

[47] However, it should be pointed out that, as often happens with pledges, only 60% of the amount was effectively committed and only about one-third eventually disbursed.

[48] On Kibeho, see Médecins sans Frontières, *Report on Events in Kibeho camp, April 1995*, 25 May 1995. The report published on 18 May 1995 by an 'International Commission of Inquiry' was very understanding and had more to do with diplomacy than with fact-finding, a reality later admitted by at least one member of the commission.

[49] As a matter of fact, the Tutsi living inside the country, not the RPF, were the victim of genocide. As discussed again later, the RPF, however, astutely played the role of victim, a status which engendered a considerable political dividend.

[50] The idea is reflected in the title of Mahmood Mamdani's book *When Victims Become Killers: Colonialism, Nativism, and the Genocide in Rwanda*, Princeton, Princeton University Press, 2001.

acknowledge the reality of widespread 'disappearances', assassinations and massacres. An increasing number of Rwandan and expatriate sources from inside and outside the country indicated that before, during and after the genocide, the RPF killed tens of thousands of innocent civilians. Some of these incidents are well documented and a few even received international condemnation. However, most of them were unknown or, at times deliberately, underestimated.[51] From the first days after the RPF's victory, abuse was veiled in a conspiracy of silence, induced in part by an international feeling of guilt over the genocide and a comfortable 'good guys–bad guys' dichotomy.[52] An early report by UNHCR consultant Robert Gersony, who reportedly estimated that between 25,000 and 45,000 civilians had been killed by the RPF between April and August 1994, was suppressed and never released.[53]

Apart from considerations of guilt and political correctness, other factors explain the conspiracy of silence. On the one hand, most massacres occurred in a discreet fashion and investigations were made difficult. Thus, the areas where they were committed were declared 'military zones', which could not be entered by outsiders, the remains of victims were removed, and entire regions, such as the Akagera Parc[54] were closed to access and even air traffic.[55] On the other hand, observers had an interest in keeping silent. NGOs and international organisations feared expulsion, while Rwandans ran the risk of reprisals against themselves or their

[51] However, see S. Desouter, F. Reyntjens, *Rwanda. Les violations des droits de l'homme par le FPR/APR. Plaidoyer pour une enquête approfondie*, Antwerp, Centre for the Study of the Great Lakes Region of Africa, June 1995; S. Smith, 'Rwanda: enquête sur la terreur tutsie', *Libération*, 27 February 1996; N. Gordon, 'Return to Hell', *Sunday Express*, 21 April 1996. A seminal book written by Alison Des Forges for Human Rights Watch and the Fédération internationale des droits de l'homme, *Leave None to Tell the Story. Genocide in Rwanda*, published in March 1999, contains a section (pp. 692–735) on the crimes committed by the RPF.

[52] A good example is P. Gourevitch, *We Wish to Inform You That Tomorrow We Will Be Killed with Our Families. Stories from Rwanda*, New York, Farrar Straus and Giroux, 1998. Although this book was extremely well received and became something of a Bible, particularly in the United States, it adds nothing to our knowledge of the genocide. In addition, the book is a thinly veiled apology for the RPF whose crimes are systematically minimised or explained away.

[53] On the saga of the Gersony mission, see A. Des Forges, *Leave None...*, *op. cit.*, pp. 726–731.

[54] Where several sources indicated the existence of cremation sites, for example, close to Gabiro military camp. Later, we shall find the same phenomenon of 'cremation ovens' in Zaire, where the RPA killed tens of thousands of Rwandan refugees in 1996–7.

[55] The dossier published by *Libération* on 27 February 1996 is very revealing with regard to this aspect of the cover-up.

families. Bradol and Guibert of *Médecins sans Frontières* denounced a
real 'law of silence' on the part of the aid organisations: '[C]losed eyes
and mouths are a condition for the perpetuation of these crimes. Apart
from the political and legal impunity automatically offered by the states,
the authorities thus benefit from the moral and media impunity resulting
from the resignation of the witnesses'.[56] The issue of information management in situations of war and gross human rights abuse will be discussed again later.

The final reason for this complicity of silence was the 'genocide credit'
that the new regime in Kigali enjoyed. It was a source of legitimacy
astutely exploited to escape criticism, not unlike the invoking of the
holocaust by certain extremists in Israel to justify violating the human
rights of Palestinians. The use of the genocide as a political trump card
was made easier by the fact that the massacres by the former Rwandan
army and the Hutu militia were committed almost 'live', which encouraged the international community to reason in terms of good and bad
guys. As the 'bad guys' were known, the others (i.e., the RPF) had to be
the 'good guys'. This presentation even allowed the RPF and its sympathisers to accuse those who denounced its crimes of being 'negationist'
or 'revisionist',[57] even if these same persons vigorously condemned the
genocide of the Tutsi.

The drift was accompanied by two other worrying developments. On
the one hand, tens of thousands of Hutu were jailed for their alleged
participation in the genocide. While many were undoubtedly guilty, many
others had empty files with no charges brought against them; they were
victims either of political or personal settling of scores or involved in property litigation after their houses or land were seized by RPF sympathisers.
On the other hand, a strong and very effective[58] 'security machine' was
soon put in place. In an emerging police state, the press and civil society
were put under increasing control, party political activities were prohibited, mail was opened, telephones and other communications were
monitored and movements inside the country and abroad were carefully
watched.

---

[56] J.-H. Bradol, A. Guibert, 'Le temps des assassins et l'espace humanitaire, Rwanda, Kivu,
1994–1997', *Hérodote*, 86–87, 1997, 131.
[57] A good example can be found in J.-F. Dupaquier, 'Rwanda: le révisionnisme ou la poursuite du génocide par d'autres moyens', in: R. Verdier, E. Decaux, J.-P. Chretien (Eds.),
*Rwanda. Un génocide du XXe. siècle*, Paris, L'Harmattan, 1995, pp. 127–136.
[58] In the past, General Kagame was a chief of Ugandan military intelligence. According to
Ugandan sources, his nickname was 'Pol Pot'.

## 'Burundisation' of Rwanda

The narrowing of the power base was only one element of an evolution, which neighbouring Burundi experienced in the past with disastrous consequences. This 'Burundisation' expressed itself in two ways: on the one hand, the Tutsification of the state, the economy and the urban population; on the other, the birth of Hutu irredentism, which contained the seeds of continuing civil war.

Let us discuss Tutsification first. While the RPF officially rejected ethnic discrimination and even the notion of ethnicity, it rapidly reserved access to power, wealth and knowledge to Tutsi, except in the cabinet, which remained the symbolic expression of 'national unity'. This policy was founded on the formal denial of the ethnic factor, a denial which was an essential element of the hegemonic strategies of a small Tutsi élite, and which can be compared to the situation in the 1950s in Rwanda and after 1965 in Burundi. Bradol and Guibert rightly feel that 'to stress the absence of ethnic identities has become a means of masking the monopoly by Tutsi military of political power. In this case, political discourse opposed to ethnism attempts to hide the domination of society by the self-proclaimed representatives of the Tutsi community'.[59] This state of affairs was explained away in a paradoxical fashion: when in the past, the Hutu were a majority in one or the other institution, this was called 'ethnic discrimination'; however, now that the Tutsi were a majority, this became 'meritocracy'. As representatives of the new regime made their baffled audience understand during a scientific meeting in Arusha in September 1995, 'quality now prevails over quantity'. This is of course an implicit return to the 'Hamitic hypothesis',[60] rightly challenged by the Tutsi when they were not in power.

The former priest Privat Rutazibwa, one of the ideologues of the RPF, has proposed a revealing, though implicit, explanation. 'The Hutu élites as a whole entirely subscribe to the fundamental thesis of the ethnist ideology, namely that power belongs to the Hutu because they

[59] J.-H. Bradol, A. Guibert, 'Le temps des assassins ...', *op. cit.*, p. 119.

[60] This hypothesis, which was prominent in the Africanist literature of the late 19th and early 20th centuries, stated that 'everything of value found in Africa was brought there by the Hamites, alledgedly a branch of the Caucasian race' (E.R. Sanders, 'The Hamitic Hypothesis: its Origin and Functions in Time Perspective', *Journal of African History*, 1969, 521). For the Europeans, the attraction of this hypothesis was that physical characteristics could be linked to intellectual capacities: the 'Hamites' were born leaders and were entitled to a past and a future almost as noble as their European 'cousins'. In Rwanda, the Tutsi were considered Hamites.

are a majority'. To make things absolutely clear, Rutazibwa explained that 'fundamentally, the Hutu élites adhere to the fundamental heresy that as a result of their being an ethnic majority, power naturally belongs to them, a bizarre conception of democracy indeed'. Such an observation obviously allows for the exclusion of 'the Hutu élites' in their entirety, in order to base the exercise of power on 'the qualification of competence and personal merit'.[61] The government-owned weekly *La Nouvelle Relève* meant exactly the same thing when it expressed the hope that the road followed would be 'the result of a popular consensus between the leaders and the *enlightened part* of the people'.[62] This 'enlightened part' clearly does not include the Hutu, or at least their élites; therefore, the combination of 'meritocracy' and the exclusion of the élite of one ethnic group allows the élite of the other ethnic group the right to govern.

This Tutsification, which was also a means of consolidating the RPF's hold on the system, was quite spectacular at most levels of the state: by 1996, the majority of MPs, four of the six presiding judges of the Supreme Court, over 80% of mayors, most permanent secretaries and university teachers and students, almost the entire army command structure and the intelligence services were Tutsi. This phenomenon was further amplified and supported by a socio-political reality, namely the Tutsification of urban Rwanda, which had become the sociological and economic foundation of the RPF. Many of the returned old diaspora ('old caseload refugees') indeed settled in towns and cities, where they became the majority, 'squatting' in homes, shops and businesses.

Next, irredentism and the threat of civil war emerged increasingly. Even though, until the autumn of 1996, Rwanda was the victim of armed incursions, which emanated mainly from Zairean territory, there was no real rebellion or insurrection, much less a civil war. Assailants operated commando raids, committed attacks and briefly engaged the RPA, and then retreated to their sanctuaries on the other side of the border. While the intensity and frequency of these incidents were limited, they were an undeniable security problem for the Rwandan government. As the threat grew, Rwanda eventually decided to neutralise the danger under the cover of the 'Banyamulenge rebellion' (see later text).

---

[61] P. Rutazibwa, 'Cet ethnisme sans fin', *Informations Rwandaises et Internationales*, 5, November–December 1996, 19–20.
[62] *La Nouvelle Relève*, 323, 31 May 1996 (Emphasis added, FR).

## Militarisation of the Political Landscape

While, during the period of political transition (1991–1993), opposition parties and civil society had entered the public scene,[63] the resumption of the civil war, the genocide and the seizure of power by the RPF eliminated these actors from a 'normal' political life. Upon assuming power, the RPF decreed a transitional period, which was to last five years and suspended the activities of political parties, which, however, were not dissolved. Parties effectively ceased functioning: a last-ditch attempt was made by the main opposition party Mouvement démocratique républicain (MDR), which on 6 November 1994 published a document, *Position du parti M.D.R. sur les grands problèmes actuels du Rwanda*. This document was quite critical of the new regime and heralded the silencing of the MDR.

For its part, civil society withered away as a result of two complementary phenomena: militarisation of the political system and ethnic polarisation. Just like the population, and the élites in particular, it was physically divided. Most association leaders lived in exile, scattered over a large number of countries in Africa, Europe and North America. Remnants of Rwandan civil society, however, remained active abroad in two ways. On the one hand, intense activity rapidly developed in the refugee camps, particularly in Zaire. Besides organisations with a humanitarian, health or educational vocation, 'reflection groups' of all sorts emerged, such as 'La Chandelle' in Goma and 'Ihuriro' in Bukavu.[64] On the other hand, leaders of organisations, which existed in Rwanda prior to the genocide continued to meet and produce analyses; however, these activities were generally quite unstructured, even though some new associations (such as 'Rwanda pour tous') were created in exile. Inside Rwanda, some existing groups resumed their activities, while others were created to cater for new needs. Among the old ones, the NGO umbrella organisation Comité de concertation des organisations d'appui aux initiatives de base (CCOAIB) soon became active again, but its initiatives and those of its constituent organisations were heavily controlled by the regime. Most of the new associations grew out of the sequels of the genocide: assistance for orphans and widows, as well as catering for the needs of memory and reparation; among these, *Ibuka* ('Remember') became the most influential one.

---

[63] On this, see F. Reyntjens, 'Rwanda et Burundi: les acteurs politiques', in: Y. Verhasselt (Ed.), *Rwanda-Burundi*, Brussels, Royal Academy of Overseas Sciences, 1997, pp. 111–126.

[64] See J.-P. Godding (Ed.), *Réfugiés rwandais au Zaïre...*, *op. cit.*

The importance of armed actors increased in a way that was proportional to the decline of political parties and civil society. Roles were reversed; the former rebellion was in power and the RPA, the armed wing of the RPF, was now the national army; the former government army FAR, as well as the extremist Hutu militia, fled abroad, to Zaire in particular, where they remained a potential invasion force. The most relevant actors had, thus, become military. Domestically, these were the RPA, the powerful Department of Military Intelligence (DMI) and the *abakada*, the local cadres of the RPF; Dorsey has shown to what extent they became the cornerstone of the system and how the physical control of the populations was an obsession of the RPF as early as at the beginning of the Rwandan civil war in 1990.[65] The former FAR and militia, some of which had received paramilitary training were abroad.

This militarisation of the political space, which civilian actors increasingly abandoned willy-nilly, progressively became a prime political factor.[66] Violent action waged by elements of the old regime and the military operations of the new army mostly hit civilians, whilst at the same time, the violent stalemate increasingly discredited a political approach and forced the actors towards the logic of military confrontation. Thus, for instance, some opponents to the new regime, who initially believed that it would be possible to negotiate a political solution, increasingly feared that they would achieve nothing if they were unable to mount a credible military threat. For its part, the regime reacted by becoming even more intransigent, thus contributing to deepening the impasse.

### Continuity in Managing the State

The continuity from one regime to the next was striking. Indeed, the practices in the way the RPF exercised power echoed those of the days of single party rule. A small inner circle of RPF leaders took the important decisions, while the cabinet was left with the daily routine of managing the state apparatus. Impunity was another element of continuity. Under the former regime, attacks, murders and massacres of civilians during the early 1990s were never judicially investigated, let alone prosecuted, and

---

[65] M. Dorsey, 'Violence and Power-Building in Post-Genocide Rwanda', in: R. Doom, J. Gorus (Eds.), *Politics of Identity and Economies of Conflict in the Great Lakes Region*, Brussels, VUB Press, 2000, pp. 311–348.

[66] Incidentally, this shift also showed in the national budget. In 1996, just over 50% of the then current expenditure (wages, goods and services) was military (civilian: 19.4 billion Rwanda francs; military: 20.6 billion).

this practice was maintained under the RPF. Elements of the RPA who murdered individuals and committed massacres, sometimes on a large scale,[67] were not worried. True, some military were prosecuted, but their trials generally concerned common law offences, such as a hold-up at the Tanzanian embassy in Kigali or a murder committed during the theft of a motorcycle; others were sentenced for breaches of the military criminal code (desertion, insubordination). In the rare cases where military were tried for the killing of civilians, sentences were lenient and the facts were attributed to individual officers, found guilty of negligence (case of Col. Ibingira) or revenge (Maj. Bigabiro). Organised massacres of civilians were never recognised as such and the commanding officers responsible were not brought to trial.

Continuity was not just visible in the exercise of power, but also in the nature of the state. An ancient state tradition again reemerged: a mere two years after the extreme human and material destruction of 1994, the state was rebuilt. Rwanda was again 'administered' from top to bottom, territorial, military and security structures were in place, the court system was reestablished and tax revenues were collected and spent. In short, life carried on. In a brief span of time, the regime was able to put into place a policy of near-total control of state and society. This project expressed itself in the maintaining of an efficient army, which was able to operate inside and, as will be seen later, far beyond the national borders; the setting up of 're-education', 'solidarity' and 're-groupment' camps; the 'villagisation' policy ('*imidugudu*'); tense relations filled with distrust with the UN and NGOs; and the establishment of an important intelligence capacity, with the DMI operating inside the country and the External Security Organisation (ESO) in charge of operations abroad. While many other African countries that had not nearly experienced the catastrophe Rwanda underwent, tended towards state collapse, the Rwandan state reaffirmed itself vigorously. The strength of the state tradition also showed in the refugee communities in Zaire and Tanzania, where quasi-state organisations and practices were immediately put into place in the camps: extra-territorial creation of cells, sectors, municipalities and *préfectures*; keeping of registers of all sorts; emergence of political–administrative authorities; 'war tax' collection; maintenance of

---

[67] For a few early examples, see Human Rights Watch, Rwanda. A New Catastrophe?, December 1994; Rwanda. The Crisis Continues, April 1995; Local Rwandan Leaders Assassinated, August 1995; HRW and FIDH Condemn New Killings in Rwanda, July 1996.

the structures of the former FAR, which, as discussed later, was much more effective in combat than the Zairean army.

## 1.3  BURUNDI: FROM PUTSCH TO CIVIL WAR

After having been excluded from power since 1965, the Hutu were reintegrated progressively in the context of the policy of 'national reconciliation' launched by the regime after violent confrontations in 1988.[68] As a result of the post–Cold War requirements discussed earlier, this process was coupled with a 'democratic transition' from 1992 onwards. Although democratisation probably followed reconciliation too soon, elections were held in 1993, when the opposition party Frodebu convincingly won the presidential and the parliamentary polls. The Tutsi political and military elites, which had been privileged in the past, reacted a mere three months later: the army staged a coup on 21 October 1993; Hutu President Ndadaye and other Frodebu leaders were assassinated, and massive violence all over the country claimed the lives of tens of thousands of civilians, both Hutu and Tutsi.[69]

### Creeping Coup

As the coup collapsed, at least officially, in the face of both domestic and international condemnation, the conspirators were forced to devise other, more discreet and subtle, means to control the political situation. From early 1994 onwards, the army and opposition forces successfully practised a creeping *coup d'état*. The strategy deployed included (i) the destruction of the legitimacy of Frodebu, obtained through the June 1993 elections, by accusing it of being responsible for a planned genocide against the Tutsi; (ii) the use of the Constitutional Court to paralyse both government and parliament; (iii) the organisation of urban and rural violence with the complicity of the armed forces, and the physical intimidation of Frodebu officials, in order to progressively make it impossible to manage

---

[68] An interesting and empathic insider's account of this period is offered by the then U.S. Ambassador to Bujumbura and his wife: R. Krueger, K.T. Krueger, *From Bloodshed to Hope in Burundi. Our Embassy Years during Genocide*, Austin, TX, University of Texas Press, 2007.

[69] For more on the period preceding the one analysed here, see F. Reyntjens, *L'Afrique des grands lacs en crise...*, op. cit.; F. Reyntjens, *Burundi. Breaking the Cycle of Violence*, London, Minority Rights Group, 1995.

the state; and (iv) the imposition of a *de facto* constitutional order, which allowed the consolidation of the putsch.

From the first days of the crisis initiated by the putsch, Tutsi opposition groups started to formulate positions and issue statements attempting to minimise the importance of the action by the army, to put both the 1992 constitution and the June 1993 elections between brackets and to discredit the government and Frodebu. A document published on 27 October, less than a week after the coup, neatly illustrated these attempts.[70] Although the memorandum stated that the problems, which had existed before the coup could not justify the action of the military, in fact, the long litany of reproaches heaped upon the government and Frodebu could only be read as an implicit legitimisation of the army's action. The attitude of the government, towards the putsch, 'perpetrated by a small group of soldiers', was qualified as 'irresponsible'. While the document condemned the violence against Tutsi civilians, no mention was made of the killing of Frodebu officials and Hutu civilians by elements of the army and by Tutsi civilians. The argument attempted to weaken and even destroy the legitimacy conferred on Frodebu by the elections: the 'acquis de juin 1993' (Frodebu's electoral victory) was counterbalanced by the 'acquis d'octobre' (the genocide plan allegedly concocted by Frodebu).

The Constitutional Court proved to be a major trump card. As a consequence of the putsch, the country faced a major constitutional impasse. It is as if the plotters proceeded with the constitution in mind: they not only assassinated President Ndadaye, but also Pontien Karibwami, the Speaker of the National Assembly, who, according to Article 85 of the Constitution, was to be entrusted with governing in the interim in the event of the president's death, as well as the Deputy Speaker Gilles Bimazubute. Fresh general elections were obviously impossible with about 20% of the population displaced or in exile abroad as a result of the violence; moreover, the tensions inherent in a new electoral exercise would have further destabilised the country and, at any rate, the administrative apparatus had become non-existent in many places. In order to break the deadlock, the National Assembly approved a constitutional amendment allowing Parliament to elect a successor to President Ndadaye. On 13 January, the Assembly elected the 'consensus candidate' Cyprien Ntaryamira of Frodebu by a joint Frodebu–Uprona majority of 78 out of 79 members, participating in the vote. However, the Constitutional Court used its

---

[70] *Mémorandum sur l'état de la situation engendrée par le coup de force de quelques militaires contre le pouvoir en date du 20 au 21 octobre 1993*, Bujumbura, 27 October 1993.

power to block this solution. Indeed, on the one hand the government had asked the court to validate Ntaryamira's election; on the other, several plaintiffs had seized the court in order to have the amendment of Article 85 declared unconstitutional. As a result of the political–ethnic divide (five Tutsi members close to Uprona against two Hutu members close to Frodebu), the court failed to agree. Leaks indicated that the Tutsi majority was inclined to declare the amendment unconstitutional and would, therefore, invalidate the election of Ntaryamira. After two weeks of fierce wrangling, the two Hutu members resigned, and on 29 January, the five remaining judges were dismissed for 'seriously failing to discharge their function'. Only after the violent episode of the 'dead city days', which will be dealt with later, was it possible to proceed with the inauguration of President Ntaryamira on 5 February 1994 and the formation of a new government a few days later.

However, this was by no means the end of the constitutional warfare. On 12 and 18 April, the court, reinstated as a result of the political deal of Kajaga, rendered two judgments. The decision of 12 April ascertained the vacancy of the presidential office following the death of President Ntaryamira, killed together with his Rwandan colleague Habyarimana on 6 April in the plane, which was shot down in Kigali. However, the judgment of 18 April, rendered by the five Tutsi judges only, held the January constitutional amendment to be invalid. This decision caused renewed deadlock and further increased tension. Following another political agreement on 10 September 1994 (see later text), a new constitutional amendment was approved on 23 September in order to fill the post left vacant by the death of Ntaryamira.

Street violence in Bujumbura, rural disorder, the physical intimidation of Frodebu officials and the campaign of terror conducted by the security services and the Tutsi militia were even more important for the success of the creeping coup than the actions of the Constitutional Court. The intimidation by extremist opposition groups became increasingly violent, but it started from the first days of the putsch and made it impossible for Frodebu to function as a political party and the main actor in the institutions. It is impossible here to even begin to enumerate the long list of provocations, violence and murders used to weaken Frodebu, intimidate moderate political leaders, including those in the main opposition party Uprona and paralyse public life.[71] This strategy of tension gained in

---

[71] Some examples can be found in F. Reyntjens, *Burundi. Breaking the Cycle...*, *op. cit.*, pp. 17–19.

intensity during 1994 and 1995 and eventually made any kind of normal political life impossible.

The effectiveness of this strategy is shown by the evolution of the political system, which was amended from one concession by Frodebu to the next, from one compromise to another, under the pressure of violence. Although Frodebu had emerged from the 1993 elections as a clear winner, it effectively became a political minority, merely exercising the symbolic signs of power. This evolution became clear when a new agreement was signed on 10 September 1994. This was extremely far-reaching, not because the opposition increased its share in government to 45% but rather because the 1992 constitution was effectively suspended and replaced by mechanisms that annihilated Frodebu's electoral victory. The 'Government Convention' had supra-constitutional status, as 'the Constitution remains valid (only) insofar as it is not contrary to this Convention' (Article 6) during a transitional period, which was to last until 9 June 1998 (Article 7). There were numerous important amendments to the constitutional structure.

The 'Negotiation Framework' of the political parties, which signed the Government Convention, was institutionalised and given considerable powers: it was to appoint the president of the republic, whose designation was merely 'confirmed' by the National Assembly; its agreement was also needed on the appointment of the prime minister. More important still was the extension of powers given to the National Security Council, which became in reality the single most important body of the state. It was to be consulted on a number of major presidential decisions, and even had veto power regarding the request for foreign military assistance. The majority of its ten members came from the opposition, which was thus in a position to block any move by the president. Furthermore, Article 33 stated that during the transitional period 'the National Assembly accepts to suspend (...) its constitutional prerogatives regarding the mechanisms of dismissing the government'. Clearly, the 'Government Convention' was the institutional translation of the October 1993 *coup d'état*: the constitution was shelved and the outcome of both the presidential and parliamentary elections was swept aside as the president and parliament were placed under the trusteeship of an unconstitutional body.

Apparently these considerable concessions by Frodebu did not satisfy the opposition, which continued to press for even more. This was borne out by a new conflict, which erupted over the succession of President Ntibantunganya as Speaker of the National Assembly. The election on 1 December 1994 of Jean Minani (Frodebu) was immediately

challenged by the chairman of Uprona, Charles Mukasi. He claimed
that Minani had appealed for the killing of Tutsi in the wake of the
October 1993 putsch and ordered Prime Minister Kanyenkiko and the
Uprona Ministers to leave the government if Minani was to stay in
power. Although the accusations levelled against him were factually
false, Frodebu was again forced to cede: Minani was given the chair
of Frodebu on 8 January 1995, and the party's former general secretary, Léonce Ngendakumana, became the new Speaker of the National
Assembly on 12 January. This was achieved after another round of
violence (dozens of people were killed in Bujumbura during December
1994, a curfew was imposed on 21 December) and after bitter wrangling inside Uprona, where the party chairman was in open conflict
with Prime Minister Kanyenkiko.

'Dead city days' organised in Bujumbura by Uprona and other 'opposition' parties forced Kanyenkiko out of the cabinet. Abandoned by his own
party Uprona, which felt that he was too 'moderate', Kanyenkiko eventually resigned on 15 February 1995. The Uprona leadership was in turn
taken hostage[72] by Tutsi extremists, belonging to Solidarité jeunesse pour
la défense des droits des minorités (SOJEDEM) among others. They succeeded in imposing Antoine Nduwayo, said to be close to former President
Bagaza, as the new prime minister, although he was not Uprona's first
choice. Nduwayo was appointed on 22 February. In the cabinet, which
took office on 1 March, Uprona lost four portfolios in favour of Tutsi
micro-parties, which did not have an electoral base, but which possessed
a considerable capacity to harness urban violence. Again, political hooliganism was thus rewarded. The radical opposition gained another victory
when the cabinet was again reshuffled on 12 December 1995: Frodebu
and its allies hung on to only eleven of twenty-six portfolios; for a party
holding 80% of seats in parliament, this was a new proof of the success of
the creeping coup.

In the meantime, the militarisation of the territorial administration
continued. In February 1996, four provinces were led by a military
governor. The persecution of Frodebu officials intensified: in mid-1996,
some twenty Frodebu MPs were dead or in exile; dozens of party leaders at local, provincial and national level were in jail, and Frodebu was
unable to exercise any activity, which would be expected of a political
party.

---

[72] In the physical sense of the word: the party headquarters were occupied and the leaders
prevented from leaving the premises.

## Extension of the Civil War

Apart from the political and constitutional evolution hitherto discussed, the strategy of tension developed by some of the Tutsi élites had two major consequences. The first was the radicalisation of the political landscape. In response to the coup of October 1993, the ensuing violence in the provinces and the spreading of urban political hooliganism, Frodebu started arming some of its members. While initially this was a measure of self-defence, the threats, which increasingly affected the party leadership, transformed this into an offensive armament effort. The first elements of a 'popular army' (*Intagoheka*), constituted in April 1994, vowed to replace the 'Tutsi army'; during the following months, units of the Burundian army were attacked by skeleton rebel forces. In June, some leaders of Frodebu created the Conseil national pour la défense de la démocratie (National Council for the Defence of Democracy [CNDD]) and its armed wing the Forces pour la défense de la démocratie (Forces for the Defence of Democracy [FDD]). Both were led by the former home minister Léonard Nyangoma, who fled the country during the violence of the spring of 1994. On the Tutsi side, extremist urban militia ('*Sans Echec*', '*Sans Peur*', SOJEDEM and others) had been active since early 1994.

Moreover, the two main parties grew further apart and their structuring capacity was undermined by radical tendencies within them, as well as by the pressure exercised by smaller parties and other groups. We have already seen how division in Uprona forced Kanyenkiko to resign in favour of Nduwayo, imposed on the party by radicals and extremist micro-parties. Within Uprona, the moderates were increasingly marginalised, victims as they were of intimidation and even assassination attempts.

For its part, Frodebu split into at least three factions. The smallest continued to support President Ntibantunganya, although many in the party felt that the increasing concessions made to the opposition and the army were an almost total surrender and an attempt to cling to what was rapidly becoming a symbolic shred of power. A second faction supported the party chairman Jean Minani, who, while supporting the Government Convention, became increasingly vocal in condemning violence, whether from the army or the militia. By 1996, the third faction, the CNDD, appeared to have become the most representative of the feelings of the party militants. It rejected the Government Convention as anti-constitutional, demanded the return to barracks and the reform of the army, which it vowed to fight as long as this objective was not reached, and insisted on political negotiations under international auspices.

The gradual but steady extension of the civil war was the second consequence. During 1995, between 15,000 and 25,000 civilians were killed at least. Most of them were Hutu killed by the army and by Tutsi militia, but the number of Tutsi and military killed started to rise in the second half of the year. Starting in the first months of 1995, the FDD attacked army positions in a sustained way, particularly in the provinces of Cibitoke and Bubanza. As they attempted to consolidate their positions there, and, later, in other parts of the country, they put in place parallel local administrations and even collected taxes.

The spreading violence and the increased radicalisation contributed to the further extension of the civil war. At the end of March 1995, a new round of anti-Hutu ethnic cleansing in Bujumbura left hundreds dead; the Frodebu headquarters were set ablaze and there was a new massive exodus of Hutu and Zaireans[73] from the city. The situation deteriorated rapidly. On 6 June, the army killed scores of civilians in the Bujumbura suburb of Kamenge in the course of a so-called disarmament operation. On 12 June, dozens of Hutu students were killed on the university campus; most other Hutu students fled and the university became almost mono-ethnic. On 25 June, Foreign Minister Jean-Marie Ngendahayo, a Tutsi from the Frodebu party, resigned and went into exile in South Africa, after having escaped (together with U.S. Ambassador Krueger and OAU representative Bassole) an attempt on their lives[74]; he said his departure was due to the incapacity of the government to ensure the security of its citizens, and he later joined the CNDD–FDD. In August, the minister of transport, post and telecommunications Innocent Nimpagaritse (a Hutu from the Parti du Peuple [PP]) followed suit and left for Nairobi.[75]

During the period from July to September, the armed wing of Palipehutu (Parti pour la libération du people hutu) launched numerous attacks in the region of Mabayi in the Cibitoke province and massacred Tutsi civilians; the army retaliated by killing Hutu civilians unrelated to the rebellion. During the first months of 1996, a similar scenario developed in the South and Southwest, where rebels (probably elements of Frolina) attacked both military installations and civilian targets. By mid-1996,

---

[73] Being 'Bantu', the Zaireans were often seen as allied with the Hutu. The 'Bantu' vs. 'Nilotic' ethnogenesis in the region will be discussed again later.

[74] On this event, see R. Krueger, K.T. Krueger, *From Bloodshed to Hope...*, op. cit., pp. 228–245.

[75] The fear of these two Ministers was understandable: on 11 March, the chairman of the *Rassemblement du Peuple Burundais* (RPB) and Minister of Energy and Mines Ernest Kabushemeye was assassinated in broad daylight in the centre of Bujumbura.

the civil war was raging in eleven of the fifteen provinces, and the army was under increasingly severe pressure. The government was divided and impotent, and Parliament did not function. Clearly, what was left of the system faced imminent implosion. On 18 January 1996, the UN Special Rapporteur for Burundi, Professor Sergio Pinheiro, stated that a 'genocide by attrition' was taking place. During the first months of 1996, other observers, including UN Secretary General Boutros Boutros-Ghali, the UN High Commissioner for Refugees Sadaka Ogata and President Ntibantunganya himself issued similar warnings.

## Coup of 25 July 1996 and its Aftermath

It is in this context that regional talks on Burundi took place on 25 June in Mwanza (Tanzania).[76] As a result of the meeting, Ntibantunganya and Nduwayo both agreed to request 'international military assistance', the nature of which was not specified. For the Burundian army and some Tutsi circles, such an initiative implied the risk of the neutralisation of the army, an unacceptable perspective. Uprona and Parena[77] immediately opposed the proposal forcefully. As a result, Prime Minister Nduwayo accused President Ntibantunganya of undermining the army; he even personally participated in a demonstration of thousands of people in Bujumbura in opposition to any military intervention. A grave incident then occurred: on 20 July, over three hundred Tutsi were massacred in a displaced persons' camp at Bugendana (Gitega province); although the perpetrators were not formally identified, it was generally assumed that they were Hutu rebels. When President Ntibantunganya attended the funeral on 23 July, he was threatened by a hostile crowd and evacuated to Bujumbura. On 25 July, he sought refuge in the residence of the U.S. Ambassador. The prime minister announced the resignation of the government. After having been symbolic for a while, power was now formally vacant.

The creeping coup was made official when the former president Major Pierre Buyoya took over power again. The coup and the return of Buyoya only confirmed the existing situation. The president and the parliament

---

[76] These followed three meetings organised by former Tanzanian president Julius Nyerere. For information on international and regional attempts at mediation, see P. Dupont, 'La crise politique au Burundi et les efforts de médiation de la communauté internationale', in: F. Reyntjens, S. Marysse (Eds.), *L'Afrique des grands lacs. Annuaire 1997–1998*, Paris, L'Harmattan, 1998, pp. 39–61.

[77] *Parti pour le redressement national*, a small Tutsi-dominated parti, headed by former President Bagaza.

had become mere figureheads, the cabinet was divided and unable to carry out anything resembling coherent policies and the army already possessed the substance of power. In that sense, the coup created some degree of clarity: the reality of the power relations was made explicit and the political–military players became more visible.

Following pressure from Nyerere and Tanzania, the regional heads of state decreed sanctions at the end of July. At least theoretically, landlocked Burundi was vulnerable to a wide-ranging embargo. Three conditions were set out for the lifting of the regional measures: the unbanning of the political parties prohibited by the putsch, the reinstatement of the suspended parliament and the start of immediate and unconditional negotiations between all groups concerned. Whilst a decree of 13 September 1996 reinstated parliament and allowed 'political parties and associations with a political vocation' to function again, the third condition was not met. For the regional leaders, this was the most important one, and they announced on 25 September that the sanctions would not be lifted. The embargo was to remain in force until early 1999.

From a regional geopolitical point of view, Buyoya seized power at a crucial juncture. Without suggesting that this was part of a larger master plan, his accession took place merely one month before the beginning of the first Great Lakes war. The taking of control by a Tutsi officer allowed Burundi to be integrated into a coalition, which was taking shape at that very moment. Even though relations between Burundi and Uganda were far from cordial,[78] from a military point of view it was thus made easier to put the Kampala–Kigali–Bujumbura axis in place.

## 1.4 REGIONAL JUNCTIONS

While the sources of instability in the Great Lakes region were, in essence, domestic, reflecting as they did the political conflicts in Rwanda, Burundi, the Kivu and Zaire more generally, their repercussions were increasingly felt throughout the larger region. This regionalisation of violence was reinforced by the geographic proximity of conflicts, by the game of alliances and by population flows.

First, let us discuss geographic proximity. At the beginning of the 1990s, Rwanda, Burundi and the two Kivu provinces had a combined

---

[78] Uganda very actively supported the regional embargo against Burundi and President Museveni was suspected by Bujumbura of supporting former President Bagaza, Buyoya's arch-rival.

population of almost 20 million for an area of some 180,000 sq. km., that is, about 110 per sq. km., by far the highest regional density of the continent. Demographic pressure was particularly high in Rwanda and Burundi, but, as has been seen, North and South Kivu also experienced considerable pressure on land, especially in the areas bordering Rwanda and Burundi. Second, the alliances have already been briefly mentioned. At the macro level, these were, for instance, the Mobutu–Habyarimana and Museveni–Kagame axes, while at the local level, for instance in the Kivu, 'natives' coalesced against the Banyarwanda first, the Hutu against the Tutsi later. Third, the population flows were ancient, and they rendered the international borders porous. The debate on citizenship was the most visible recent expression in Zaire, and the sudden arrival of almost 200,000 refugees from Burundi at the end of 1993 and of over one-and-a-half million Rwandans in the middle of 1994 was a culminating point. The combination of these three phenomena engendered a very unstable political–military landscape in the Great Lakes region.

In addition, this conflict zone could not be isolated from the larger setting. On the contrary, the Great Lakes conflict tended to merge with two others, the Sudanese and Angolan civil wars. Zaire constituted the junction between these zones for two reasons. First, the Zairean state had virtually disappeared,[79] thus leaving a 'black hole' with porous borders, almost no effective national army or administration, very poor communications between the centre and the periphery and between peripheries and an essentially informalised economy. Just like nature, geopolitics abhors the void, which is filled under these circumstances by other actors, both internal and external. Second, the Mobutu regime was implicated in the neighbouring wars: it supported the Khartoum government in its war against the southern Sudanese rebellion, which was in turn supported by the United States, Uganda, Ethiopia and Eritrea; Zairean territory served as a rear base for attacks by armed movements against Uganda, Rwanda and Burundi; and the support offered by Mobutu to the Angolan rebel movement UNITA had not ceased with the 1994 Lusaka peace accord.

---

[79] While subscribing to most of what he writes, I do not agree with Vlassenroot's claim that '[t]he end of Mobutism (...) was not the result of state collapse, but was caused by local and regional dynamics that fell completely outside the zone of control of the central government' (K. Vlassenroot, The Making of a New Order. Dynamics of Conflict and Dialectics of War in South Kivu (DR Congo), University of Ghent, Ph.D. Thesis, 2002, p. 1). The local and regional dynamics he mentions have, of course, played a major role, but they could not have had the profound consequences they had in the presence of an (even moderately) functioning state in Zaire.

Likewise, international actors were present in the wings, France on the side of Khartoum and the Rwandan Hutu, the United States on that of the Sudanese SPLA, Uganda, Rwanda and Luanda. As all reasoned using the logic 'the enemy of my enemy is my friend', circumstantial alliances were very visible along two axes: on one side, France, Khartoum, Mobutu's Zaire, the Hutu rebels and UNITA; on the other, the United States, Eritrea, Ethiopia, the SPLA, Uganda, Rwanda, Burundi and the MPLA. While the three conflicts were not intrinsically linked, the game of alliances and the geographic proximity, with Zaire as the glue, thus opened the perspective of a war zone stretching from Luanda to Asmara. The role and motives of these actors will be discussed in detail later.[80]

[80] Note that the presentation above refers to the situation in 1996; as will be seen later, alliances have dramatically shifted since.

# 2

# The 'War of Liberation'

## 2.1 THE 'BANYAMULENGE REBELLION' AND THE RWANDAN OPERATION

Within the regional setting just described, Rwanda occupied a particular position. Although its civil war formally ended with the RPF's victory in July 1994, the flight of the defeated army, the militia and 1.5 million civilians to Zaire exported the conflict. As these insurgent forces were intent on resuming the war, the situation that developed just a few kilometres across its borders was Rwanda's affair, and a vital one at that.

Notice of a Rwandan intervention in the Kivu was given by the Kigali press close to the RPF. Under the title 'A war which Zaire will wage against Rwanda will destroy the Mobutu regime', *Ukuri*, No. 4 of May 1996, concluded that 'Kigali hopes war will break out so that the refugees can be taken care of'. *Amani*, No. 8 of June, wrote that 'if the present process of decay, characterised by incidents, raids, murders and massacres, continues, a war between Rwanda and Zaire is inevitable'. *Rwanda Libération* No. 17 of July announced 'the response of the RPA and thus, the Great Lakes Region will witness the end of Mobutu'. The official weekly *La Nouvelle Relève* No. 325 of 15 August carried three articles on the same theme and mentioned the problem of the Banyamulenge under the title 'A genocide under incubation in Mulenge (Zaire)'. Conversely, on the Zairean side, *Le Potentiel* of 6 May wrote that 'the Parliament of transition is close to authorising war against Rwanda' and *Le Palmarès* of 13 July carried the title 'Kagame at the heart of a plot against Mobutu'; the article

MAP 2. Zaire/DRC and its neighbours.

was accompanied by a photograph showing the Ugandan, Rwandan and Burundian chiefs of army staff sitting together on a podium.[1]

As previously stated, Rwanda had been facing a security threat since 1995,[2] particularly in the three western *préfectures*, affected by commando

---

[1] These bellicose echoes followed the return to Kinshasa of Mobutu aide Vangu Mambweni from Paris, where he had met with Jacques Foccart, '*Monsieur Afrique*' at the Elysée. Vangu declared that 'Parliament is ready to allow a declaration of war against Rwanda', a country, which aimed to 'establish the Anglo-American hegemony in the Great Lakes region at the expense of *la Francophonie*' (quoted by F.-X. Verschave, *La Françafrique...*, *op. cit.*, p. 250). This clearly reflects the so-called Fashoda syndrome (this expression refers to the 'secular resistance of France to Anglo-Saxon imperialism'; Fashoda is the place in present-day Sudan where the Marchand expedition was forced to retreat in 1898 in the face of Lord Kitchener's troops. This heralded the end of French ambitions in East Africa).

[2] Turner (*The Congo Wars...*, *op. cit.*, pp. 15–16) rightly points out that this threat applied to the regime, but not *per se* to Rwanda as a whole. Indeed, the majority of the population may well have considered those posing this threat to be its allies and potential liberators. Likewise, when Kigali argued that it needed to protect the Congolese Tutsi, this may

operations emanating, at least in part, from Zairean territory. During a speech in Tambwe on 19 February 1995, General Kagame set the tone: 'I wholeheartedly hope that these attacks take place! Let them try! I do not hide it. Let them try' (translated from Kinyarwanda). During the same period, he confirmed candidly to the journalist François Misser that 'if another war must be waged, we shall fight in a different fashion, elsewhere. We are prepared. We are ready to fight any war and we shall contain it along the border with Zaire'.[3] Officials from the United States and The Netherlands, two countries close to the Rwandan regime, confirmed that they had had to dissuade Kagame on several occasions from 'breaking the abscess' of the Rwandan refugees in Zaire the hard way.[4] During a visit to the United States in August 1996, one month before the start of the 'rebellion', Kagame told the Americans that he was about to intervene,[5] the more so since, according to some sources,[6] the ex-FAR were preparing a large-scale offensive against Rwanda from Goma and Bukavu. Faced with the unwillingness or inability of the international community to tackle this problem, Kigali's patience obviously reached its limits. It was revealing that Rwanda was the only country that refused to sign a non-aggression pact among the Central African states at a summit held in Yaounde from 8 to 10 July 1996. Despite all the warning signals, the arms embargo imposed on Rwanda during the 1994 genocide was lifted on 1 September 1996.

The most important Rwandan refugee organisation, the Rassemblement pour la Démocratie et le Retour des Réfugiés (RDR), clearly realised what

well have reflected the feelings of many Rwandan Tutsi, but probably not those of many Hutu.

[3] F. Misser, *Vers un nouveau Rwanda? Entretiens avec Paul Kagame*, Brussels, Luc Pire, 1995, p. 121.

[4] The EU Special Representative for the Great Lakes region Aldo Ajello has confirmed this information.

[5] According to the then U.S. Ambassador to Kigali, Robert Gribbin, Kagame had already told him in March 1996 that 'if Zaire continues to support the ex-FAR/*Interahamwe* against Rwanda, Rwanda in turn could find anti-Mobutu elements to support', adding that 'if the international community could not help improve security in the region, the RPA might be compelled to act alone' (R.E. Gribbin, *In the Aftermath of Genocide. The U.S. Role in Rwanda*, New York, iUniverse, 2005, pp. 144–145).

[6] The existence of this project was later confirmed by documents discovered in Mugunga camp in November 1996. Although these documents have never been published, some echoes can be found in extracts published in newspapers, for example, *Le Monde*, 19 November 1996 and *Le Figaro*, 20 November 1996. It is surprising that neither the AFDL (see later text) nor the RPA have kept these archives; on the contrary, they reportedly burned them (S. Boyle, 'Rebels repel Zaire counteroffensive', *Jane's Intelligence Review*, 1 April 1997). However, I have copies of a number of these papers.

was in the offing. In a communiqué of 17 June 1996, it warned that an attack against the refugee camps was being prepared 'by allied Ugandan, Rwandan and Burundian troops'; it mentioned troop concentrations in the Kisoro region (Uganda) and in the volcano region of northwest Rwanda. According to the RDR, a recent attack against the commercial centre of Bunagana close to the Ugandan border had served to test the Zairean reaction.[7] A communiqué of 1 July mentioned a raid conducted against the refugee camp at Kibumba on 26 June, said to be a new attempt to test Zairean defences. A few months later, when the war was raging, the RDR was left only with the painful consolation of being able to state 'we told you so'.[8]

Whilst the first signs of aggression were thus visible in North Kivu, in South Kivu, the 'Banyamulenge affair' was to offer the context needed to start the war. Moreover, Rwanda had clearly exacerbated a latent problem in order to create a pretext for launching its operation. Although the Banyamulenge had genuine grievances (see earlier text), the decision to engage in military action was not taken by them, but in Kigali.[9] President Museveni later recalled that, probably as early as 1995, Kagame had recruited 2000 Zairean Tutsi (including a number of Banyamulenge) into the RPA with a view to carrying out military action against the refugee camps. These men, reinforced by another 2000 additional recruits, launched the 'Banyamulenge rebellion'.[10] In June 1996, the RPA was training Banyamulenge rebels in northwest Burundi; according to diplomatic sources in Kigali, 700–800 Rwandan soldiers 'deserted' the RPA in July and infiltrated into South Kivu.[11] According to Vlassenroot,[12] based on interviews with Banyamulenge leaders, a delegation was sent from Kigali to the Hauts Plateaux in July, in order to inform the Banyamulenge population about the impending military operations. In early July, the town and refugee camp of Kamanyola were hit by shelling that came from Rwanda. From early September onwards, several witnesses mentioned the RPA moving men and equipment into South Kivu via Burundi.[13] During the night of 31 August to 1 September, about sixty 'Banyamulenge infiltrators'

[7] As early as 8 June, Zaire asked for an urgent meeting of the UN Security Council with regard to the 4–5 June incursions into Bunagana by a force from Uganda.

[8] Communiqué 97 of 22 October 1996.

[9] K. Vlassenroot, *The Making of a New Order...*, op. cit., p. 235.

[10] *The Monitor*, Kampala, 1 June 1999.

[11] This recalls the 'desertion' of Rwandan elements of the Ugandan army, when the RPF launched its attack on Rwanda in October 1990 from Ugandan territory.

[12] K. Vlassenroot, *The Making of a New Order...*, op. cit., p. 235.

[13] These infiltrations are confirmed by Müller Ruhimbika (*Les Banyamulenge (Congo-Zaïre) entre deux guerres*, Paris, L'Harmattan, 2001, p. 45).

from Rwanda were intercepted in the vicinity of Luberizi; the exchange of fire with the Zairean army caused casualties. A local spokesperson from Uvira, later interviewed by *Le Figaro*, confirmed that the first skirmishes took place on 31 August, when Zairean 'green berets' (commando troops) exchanged fire with 'over 600 Tutsi of Rwandan origin'.[14] On 21 September, some twenty trucks accompanied by three Landrovers and two armoured vehicles transported Rwandan soldiers to the Uvira region through the Burundian province of Cibitoke. A similar operation, this time with seven trucks, took place on 10 October.[15] On two occasions during the second half of September, the RPA opened mortar and machine-gun fire on targets north of Bukavu (Birava) and more to the south across the Ruzizi River.[16] According to the Zairean Minister of the Interior, exchange of fire, including rockets and mortar, between Cyangugu and Bukavu between 22 and 23 September was 'a diversion to cover the bellicose activities of the Banyamulenge'.[17] The RDR claimed that these bombardments were designed to force humanitarian organisations out.[18]

On 13 September, the Zairean government claimed that Rwanda and Burundi 'were stirring up trouble' in South Kivu. On 22 October, Zaire formally accused the Rwandan and Burundian armies of having launched an attack involving about 1700 men in the Kamanyola area. At the same time, it claimed that the FAZ had 'repulsed attacks by the Rwandan army at Kibumba, Rugari and Bunagana' in North Kivu.[19] Likewise, the local NGOs sounded the alarm. In a note published on 24 September, the South Kivu Civil Society and the Regional Council of NGOs (Conseil régional des organisations non-gouvernementales de développement [CRONGD]) warned of infiltrations, during the previous couple of months, by armed elements coming from Rwanda via Burundi; they were said to be proceeding to the highlands of Fizi, Uvira and Mwenga. Later, both the archbishop of Bukavu Mgr. Munzihirwa[20] (who was killed by the RPA at the end of October) and the 'Groupe Jérémie'[21] condemned the 'aggression coming from Rwanda and Burundi'.

---

[14] *Le Figaro*, 19 November 1996.
[15] Several witnesses in South Kivu.
[16] Reuters, Kigali, 30 September 1996.
[17] AFP, Kinshasa, 24 September 1996.
[18] AFP, Nairobi, 24 September 1996; the last 'humanitarians' indeed left Bukavu on 28 October.
[19] AFP, Kinshasa, 22 October 1996.
[20] For example, in letters of 27 September and 11 October 1996.
[21] Letter of 28 October 1996.

This being said, it must be recalled that the Banyamulenge were the victims of abuse and that they had good cause to fear undergoing the same fate as the Banyarwanda of North Kivu at the beginning of the year. On 9 September, 'native' populations organised a 'dead city' day in Uvira, demanding the departure of the 'foreigners' and pillaging some of their houses. According to Amnesty International, dozens of people, most of them Tutsi, were arrested; the document referred to allegations that dozens of Banyamulenge were illegally executed or 'disappeared'.[22] As in Uvira, demonstrators in Bukavu denounced the 'aggression by Tutsi invaders' on 18 September and a 'march of anger' resulted in pogroms during which dozens of Tutsi were killed. Over 1000 refugees arrived in Burundi and Rwanda. On 8 October, the vice-governor of South Kivu, Lwabandji Lwasi, announced the creation of a 'humanitarian corridor' to evacuate those Tutsi not involved in the rebellion. Those who did not leave the area were to be considered rebels; he stated that within a week, 'the cleaning up of the highlands will begin.'[23] On 10 October, Rwandan president Bizimungu announced in Cyangugu that his country was ready to offer hospitality to women and children, but that the Banyamulenge men 'must fight (…) in order to defend their rights as Zaireans'.

Clearly, two phenomena were at play. On the one hand, the Tutsi of South Kivu organised their self-defence; on the other, the Rwandan regime stoked the fires, trained and equipped the Banyamulenge, whilst at the same time introducing troops on the ground and bombarding the border area. In this precise and contingent setting,[24] the Rwandans and the Banyamulenge were objective allies. A Banyamulenge leader was later to be very lucid about the fact that the Banyamulenge 'had their interests and the Rwandans had theirs, i.e. dismantling the refugee camps (…) Our children had gone to Rwanda where they had become soldiers, and for this reason we asked for Rwanda's support'.[25] Pourtier rightly

---

[22] Amnesty International, Zaire: Amnesty International Condemns Human Rights Violations against Tutsi, 20 September 1996.

[23] Excerpts from this speech can be found in *Le Soft International*, 729, 20–23 February 1998. The day after his speech Lwabandji was suspended by Prime Minister Kengo wa Dondo. Lwabandji later explained that his intentions were strictly humanitarian ('*Réaction de Monsieur Lwabandji Lwasi Ngabo, vice-gouverneur honoraire du Sud-Kivu, à la déclaration du porte parole des Banyamulenge à la conférence de Goma*', Brussels, 15 January 2008).

[24] Indeed, we shall see later that this alliance broke up when the setting and the perception of interests changed.

[25] Enoch Ruberangabo in *Comment rétablir la paix à l'Est du Congo (ex-Zaïre)?*, Geneva, GRAZ–Congo, November 1997, p. 10.

stressed that 'the Banyamulenge were the spearhead and a fifth column at the same time (...) The strategic choice (of Kigali) to attack the camps clearly shows the fundamental objectives of a 'rebellion' that was no longer (a rebellion), because what really happened was the extension of the Rwandan civil war into Zairean territory'.[26]

Facing a disorganised and unmotivated Zairean army, the 'Banyamulenge rebels' supported by the RPA, rapidly conquered South Kivu: Uvira fell on 28 October, followed by Bukavu on 30 October. The rebel advance was accompanied by the flight of hundreds of thousands of civilians, Zaireans and Burundian refugees at first, followed by Rwandan refugees. From the early beginning, very grave human rights abuses were committed by both sides, but mainly by the 'rebels': a particularly grave incident took place on 4–5 October at Lemera hospital, where many patients and staff were killed in cold blood by 'armed groups' of Banyamulenge. This was to be the start of a long series of crimes against humanity, which will be addressed later.

As the 'rebellion' spread over the two Kivu provinces, the objectives and the implication of the neighbours became clearer. As has been discussed, the main concern of the Rwandan regime was to eliminate the threat emanating from refugee concentrations, and in particular from the armed elements among them. This goal was achieved by the combination of their physical elimination, forced repatriation and the move further westwards, far from the Rwandan border. The mechanism was the same everywhere: the camps were heavily shelled, which caused many casualties and forced the refugees out.

These operations were conducted almost simultaneously in South and North Kivu. As the 'Banyamulenge rebellion' was initially limited to South Kivu, this shows the extraneous character of the war. UNHCR spokesperson Ron Redmont referred to fighting between Zairean soldiers and 'armed men coming from Burundi' in the Uvira region.[27] Attacked by 'infiltrators coming from Burundi',[28] some 250,000 Burundian and Rwandan Hutu refugees fled their camps around Uvira on 21 October.[29] RPA units with armoured vehicles and mortars crossed the Ruzizi River at Kamanyola and killed refugees in four camps along the border.[30]

[26] R. Pourtier, 'Congo–Zaïre–Congo: un itinéraire géopolitique au coeur de l'Afrique', *Hérodote*, 86–87, third–fourth term 1997, p. 27.
[27] AFP, Geneva, 18 October 1996.
[28] AFP, Bujumbura, 23 October 1996.
[29] AFP, Bujumbura, 21 October 1996.
[30] AFP, Bukavu, 24 October 1996.

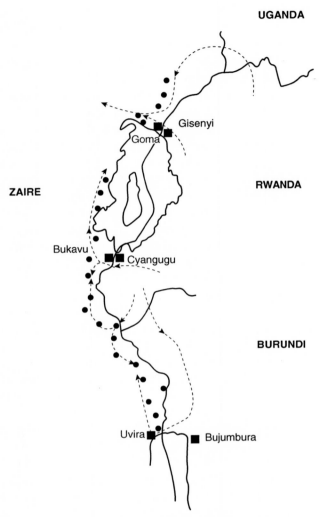

MAP 3. Attacks on refugee camps (autumn 1996).

Likewise, camps in the Bukavu area were attacked from Rwanda on 25 and 26 October.

While these incidents in South Kivu could be presented as part of the 'rebel' advance, similar attacks took place in North Kivu, where there was no rebellion at all. According to the UNHCR, on 21 October 'non-identified armed men' attacked villages and a position of the Zairean contingent charged with security in the North Kivu refugee camps. The

Zairean press agency AZAP claimed that sixty 'Tutsi combatants' and thirty porters entered the country on 20 October, from Rwanda en route to Masisi. Other sources claimed that 'armed Tutsi' attacked and occupied the village of Camunganga, 70 km north of Goma.[31] Starting on 21 October, the camps to the north of Goma were systematically shelled, one after the other, by 'non-identified elements' from Rwanda, who on a number of occasions transited through Uganda. Kibumba refugee camp was attacked on 21 October,[32] Kahindo on 23 October, Katale on 26 October. On 30 October, the FAZ camp at Rumangabo was shelled by mortars. The refugees fled towards Goma; by the end of October, Mugunga camp, about 20 km west of Goma, had become the largest refugee concentration in history, with a population of over 600,000.

On 22 October, a communiqué from the Rwandan Foreign Ministry invited the Rwandan refugees, 'adrift between Uvira and Bukavu (to) return to the Motherland, Rwanda', thus escaping 'the miseries of fratricidal war'. On 25 October, the UN High Commissioner for Refugees, Sadako Ogata, relayed this appeal through local radio stations; at the very same moment, however, the refugees were being attacked by the Rwandan army. Two weeks earlier, the United States had gone even further. During a meeting organised in Geneva by the UNHCR, the Assistant Secretary of State for Refugees and Migrations Phyllis Oakley advocated the ending of all assistance to the Rwandan refugees, in order to promote their return to Rwanda, a country where, in her words, 'we have seen a great improvement'. This astonishing position in fact echoed the one defended by USAID's Richard McCall at the round-table on Rwanda held in Geneva in June 1996.[33]

On 28 October, Rwandan president Bizimungu declared that 'if Zaire wants to expel the Banyamulenge to Rwanda, it should also return their land'. During a press conference, he attempted to show, with the help of maps, that the region inhabited by the Banyamulenge historically belonged to Rwanda.[34] Two days later, during a press conference by

---

[31] AFP, Kinshasa, 21 October 1996.

[32] An anonymous humanitarian source accused the RPA of being responsible for this attack, 'launched with assault weapons and heavy artillery' by men of the RPA's 7th battalion based in Kigali. Most assailants wore military attire, but some were dressed in civilian clothing (AFP, Goma, 27 October 1996).

[33] On this subject, see D. De Schrijver, 'Les réfugiés rwandais dans la région des grands lacs en 1996', in: S. Marysse and F. Reyntjens (Eds.), *L'Afrique des grands lacs. Annuaire 1996–1997*, Paris, L'Harmattan, 1997, pp. 249–250.

[34] AFP, Kigali, 28 October 1996. We have shown elsewhere that the idea of the pre-colonial 'Greater Rwanda' does not correspond to reality; see 'Rwanda: territoires et frontières', in: F. Reyntjens and S. Marysse (Eds.), *Conflits au Kivu...*, *op. cit.*, pp. 17–18.

General Kagame, a document from the president's office, calling for the organisation of a 'Berlin Conference II', was distributed. The suggestion that Rwanda was challenging existing borders was, of course, reinforced. In addition, Kagame announced that Rwanda would have to react in the event of 'Zairean agression'.[35] In Brussels, the Rwandan foreign minister spoke in the same vein: at the very moment the RPA occupied Goma, he stated, without batting an eyelid, that 'if the Zairean army continues to provoke us, we have the right to defend ourselves'.[36] Clearly, the aggressor claimed to be aggressed in order to justify his aggression.

Indeed, the Rwandan army was clearly present in Zaire well before these statements were made. Its involvement in the capture of Bukavu was even implicitly acknowledged: Lt. Col. Firmin Kagame, the RPA Cyangugu commander, stated that he sent a 'good sized force' to Bukavu 'in retaliation for Zaireans firing into Rwanda'.[37] According to Voice of America's (VOA) correspondent Chris Tomlinson, Rwandan authorities, speaking on the condition of anonymity, admitted that the Rwandan government was sympathetic to the Banyamulenge, and that some officers from the Rwandan army had helped organise the rebel group.[38] The Ugandan newspaper *The Crusader* wrote in its edition of 4 December 1997 that one of the main commanders of the rebellion was Lt. Col. James Kabarebe (alias Kabari or Kabere), formerly of the National Resistance Army (NRA) in Uganda, commander of the RPA's Republican Guard and very close to General Kagame, whose close protection he had assumed during 1990–94. Kabarebe will prominently reappear later in this book.

Refugees interviewed by Agence France-Presse (AFP) said they saw six Rwandan soldiers taken prisoner by the FAZ, as well as armoured vehicles of the RPA.[39] The direct implication of the RPA was particularly clear in the Goma area, which was attacked from Rwanda by land and across Lake Kivu. On 2 November, Reuters correspondent Christian Jennings 'entered Goma on Saturday morning behind troops of the Tutsi-led Rwandan army

---

[35] The previous day, Kagame put forward another argument during an interview with Reuters. He claimed that the FAR were in charge of Goma and Bukavu: 'If they are allowed to continue to reign over that region, the implications will be profound'. However, based on independent sources, including foreign journalists in Bukavu, Reuters felt that Kagame was exaggerating. According to the press agency, there was coordination between officers of the FAZ and the FAR and the presence of a few FAR soldiers at one checkpoint in Bukavu, while no FAR were present in Goma (Reuters, Kigali, 29 October 1996).

[36] *La Libre Belgique*, 2–3 November 1996.

[37] Reuters, Cyangugu, 30 October 1996.

[38] VOA, 28 October 1996.

[39] AFP, Bukavu, 23 October 1996; AFP, Bukavu, 24 October 1996.

from Gisenyi'.[40] Before that, on 28 October, USAID's Brian Atwood stated that the RPA supported 'Tutsi rebels' in their offensive in the Goma region.[41] A diplomatic source confirmed the presence of the RPA in Goma: 'They came in by land and across Lake Kivu on boats landing on the city beach. We are 110 percent certain the RPA is in Goma. It is confirmed'.[42] Staff at the U.S. Embassy in Kigali was later to admit to a Dutch correspondent that they knew all along 'that the Rwandan army was the brain behind the attack against the Hutu. It was in their interest'.[43] The sequence of events actually shows the crucial role played by the RPA: Goma indeed fell well before the 'rebels' from South Kivu moved from Bukavu to Goma.

By early November, the Rwandan and Burundian borders were secured by a buffer zone stretching from Uvira to Goma, which was about 250 km long. On 20 November, Masisi fell, Butembo was taken on 27 November, while, on 30 November, the Ugandan army (Uganda People's Defence Force [UPDF]) took Kasindi and opened the way to Beni. The Bukavu–Goma junction was not made until early December. As Bunia was captured with the help of the UPDF on 25 December, the area under 'rebel' control at the end of 1996 stretched from Lulimba (about 150 km south of Uvira) in the South, to Kamituga (about 90 km west of Bukavu) and Walikale (about 120 km west of Goma) in the West and to Bunia (about 400 km north of Goma) in the North. Thus a buffer zone of about 800 km long and some 100 km deep ran along the Ugandan, Rwandan and Burundian borders. This ended the first phase of the war.

The role of Rwanda during this phase has obviously been central. Indeed, the 'rebellion' in the Kivu was to a large degree an extension of the Rwandan civil war; first, the Banyamulenge, and all Congolese Tutsi were instrumentalised by the Rwandan regime. When, much later, on 29 January 1997, Belgium stated publicly what everyone knew, namely, that thousands of Rwandan soldiers had fought alongside the rebellion; this nevertheless met with an ascerbic rebuttal. Claude Dusaidi, advisor at the Rwandan presidency, immediately stated: 'I believe that Belgium has gone senile (…). It looks like they don't know where the borders are, nor do they distinguish between Zaireans and Rwandans'.[44] The next day, the Rwandan foreign minister called the Belgian accusations 'erroneous

[40] Reuters, Gisenyi, 2 November 1996.
[41] Reuters, Kigali, 29 October 1996.
[42] Reuters, Bukavu, 2 November 1996.
[43] *NRC–Handelsblad*, 25 November 1996.
[44] AFP, Nairobi, 29 January 1997.

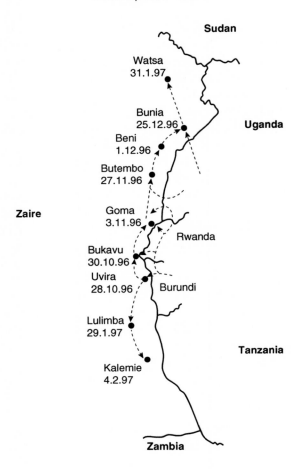

------➤ Itinerary of the AFDL and its allies.
The dates indicate the capture by the "rebellion"
of the locations on the map.

MAP 4. First phase of the war (autumn 1996).

and partisan'.[45] The executive committee of the rebel Alliance des forces
pour la libération du Congo-Zaïre (AFDL) denounced the 'interference' and stated that 'Belgium is not impartial and even less qualified to
deal with our problems'.[46] These denials, of course, sound very hollow
since Kagame himself unveiled the public secret in a famous interview

[45] AFP, Nairobi, 30 January 1997.
[46] AFP, Goma, 2 February 1997.

in *The Washington Post* on 9 July 1997.[47] He said that 'the Rwandan Government planned and directed the rebellion', that 'Rwandan forces participated in the capture of at least four cities' and that 'Rwanda provided training and arms for (the rebel) forces even before the campaign to overthrow Marshal Mobutu began last October'. Kagame added that it would have been 'more suitable if Congolese rebels had done most of the fighting', but they were not 'fully prepared to carry it out alone'.

Why did the international community, which knew very well that Rwanda was destabilising its neighbour, do nothing? Why were Zairean protests never listened to, when the Rwandan operation was such a clear violation of international law? As early as October 1996, a diplomat in New York told *Le Monde* under the cover of anonymity that 'the role played during the Zairean crisis by the Kigali government and its motives have nothing democratic about them, but the international community still suffers a guilt complex towards the regime, which underwent the genocide of 1994'. He added that 'any action undertaken against the regime in Kigali is always perceived as offering moral support to those guilty of genocide; it is true that the Rwandan regime is benefiting from this ambivalence, and we know it'.[48] The Rwandan authorities themselves clearly realised this: Minister Mazimhaka later stated that 'we were (diplomatically) stronger because nobody could argue against us'. An American diplomat acknowledged that 'the Americans were terribly manipulated by this (Rwandan) government and now are almost held hostage by it'.[49] The extent that this was the case at the U.S. embassy in Kigali will be seen later.

Without false modesty, General Kagame stated that '[w]e used communication and information warfare better than anyone. We have found a new way of doing things'.[50] Throughout the war, the management of (access to) information was very efficient. The press was excluded from the centre of events, and, frustrated and impotent, it was forced to follow events from a distance on the sidelines. It was barred from access to every battle, every massacre: thus, at the beginning of the war, when the refugee camps were 'emptied', reporters were blocked first in Gisenyi, later in

---

[47] J. Pompret, 'Defence Minister Says Arms, Troops Supplied for Anti-Mobutu Drive', *The Washington Post*, 9 July 1997.

[48] *Le Monde*, 26 October 1996.

[49] *The Washington Post*, 14 July 1998.

[50] N. Gowing, New Challenges and Problems for Information Management in Complex Emergencies. Ominous Lessons from the Great Lakes and Eastern Zaire in late 1996 and early 1997, London, 27 May 1998, p. 4.

Goma, and the only event they were allowed to witness was the massive return of refugees to Rwanda. In Baghdad and Belgrade, CNN reported live; in Central Africa, it was confined to the periphery of the conflict. This theme of information management is taken up again when discussing the plight of the Rwandan refugees.

While the Rwandan involvement during the first phase of the war was prominent, Uganda and Burundi shared similar security concerns. The role played by these two other eastern neighbours will now be analysed briefly.

## 2.2  THE OTHER EASTERN NEIGHBOURS: UGANDA AND BURUNDI

In the communiqués of 17 June and 1 July 1996 quoted earlier, the RDR mentioned Ugandan and Rwandan 'allied forces' and expressed concern about a concentration of Ugandan troops in Kisoro, close to the Zairean border. As already stated, Zaire seized the Security Council after the attack on Bunagana. A non-identified 'French expert', quoted by *Le Figaro*, claimed that 'there is a Rwandan–Ugandan plan for the destabilisation of Zaire, (a plan) which has the support of Washington'.[51] According to Jacques Isnard,[52] French and Belgian intelligence discovered that a 'Tutsi legion', trained by Uganda, supported Kabila's rebellion. This 'legion' allegedly mobilised some 15,000 men recruited in Uganda, Eritrea and Burundi, under the command of officers of the Ugandan army. According to the same source, the operation was funded by private means totalling US$ 280 million, from Colombian, Lebanese and Israeli 'mafias' engaged in the diamond and gold business.

In fact, the prolonged implication of the Ugandan army is less well documented than that of Rwanda. When the 'rebellion' started in North Kivu on 24 October 1996, some elements of the Rwandan army moved from Rwanda, crossing the border with Uganda at Cyanika and transiting through the Kisoro region in Uganda, to attack Kibumba camp; this transit would obviously have been impossible without Ugandan approval. At the beginning of December, in pursuit of elements of the rebel Allied Democratic Forces (ADF) in the Ruwenzori region,[53] the UPDF took the

[51] *Le Figaro*, 7 November 1996.
[52] *Le Monde*, 13 May 1997.
[53] At the end of October 1996, General Salim Saleh, Museveni's half-brother, asked the Ugandan parliament to authorise UPDF deployment against rebel bases in Zaire and the Sudan (DHA–IRIN, *Update on South Kivu*, 26 October 1996).

Zairean town of Kasindi, thus opening the way for the rebel seizure of Beni, again with Ugandan support.[54] According to several sources, UPDF units also participated in the capture of Bunia at the end of December,[55] thus ensuring the control of a strategic city for the establishment of the buffer zone intended by Kampala.

As will be seen later, now that Uganda's borders were secure, Museveni became reticent and initially opposed the extension westwards of the Zairean rebellion.[56] A communiqué published on 29 January 1997 by the General Staff of the FAZ nevertheless mentioned several thousand Ugandan soldiers progressing to the west on the Walikale–Kisangani and Bunia–Mambasa axes. These accusations were hotly denied by Uganda: according to presidential advisor John Nagenda, 'this is rubbish. That's my answer to it. Total and absolute rubbish, as usual'.[57] On 31 January, Zairean television showed 'prisoners of war', said to be a Ugandan corporal and a Rwandan lieutenant.[58] The next day, the Ugandan foreign minister rejected this 'totally false and idiotic' accusation.[59] On 11 February, the Zairean army claimed that a Ugandan military aircraft transporting men and equipment had crashed in the Ruwenzori area. The communiqué specified that a number of survivors had been taken prisoner, a claim which considerably weakened the story, as the FAZ had abandoned this region close to the Ugandan border two months earlier.[60] Uganda again immediately denied this.[61] The Zairean authorities later accused Uganda of having participated in the Watsa and Kisangani campaigns, but this involvement has never been confirmed by independent sources. However,

---

[54] Ugandan officers actually claimed that Beni was taken by the UPDF (AFP, Kinshasa, 2 December 1996).

[55] The mercenary commander Christian Tavernier (cf. *infra*) claimed that 'soldiers of Museveni's regular army massively supported the rebels. I assess their number at some 6,000 in the battle for Bunia. 15,000 of them captured Kisangani' (*La Libre Belgique*, 4 April 1997). Interviewed by a Belgian reporter, the population of Bunia spoke without reservation about the presence of Ugandan and Rwandan forces (F. Francois, 'A la rencontre du Kivu libéré: carnet de route (janvier–février 1997)', in: *Kabila prend le pouvoir*, Brussels, GRIP-Editions Complexe, 1998, p. 60).

[56] However, this was to change when the war entered its second phase with the Angolan intervention (see later text).

[57] AFP, Kinshasa, 29 January 1997.

[58] AFP, Kinshasa, 31 January 1997.

[59] AFP, Kampala, 2 February 1997.

[60] Later, it will be seen that another source stated that a US C-130 carrying troops of the Special Forces crashed in the Ruwenzori area in January 1997. There might thus be confusion over this incident which, at any rate, has never been proven.

[61] AP, Kinshasa, 11 February 1997.

an article published in *The Washington Post* of 4 March 1997 provided
a number of elements suggesting a profound Ugandan implication; in
addition, as late as the end of January 1997, several witnesses confirmed
that truckloads of Ugandan soldiers entered Zaire through Rutshuru on
their way further north.[62] It was at that time, on 30 January, that Zaire
reactivated its complaint to the Security Council. Indeed, no one was
really fooled: asked about the reasons for the speedy advance of Kabila's
men, a diplomat in Kinshasa replied: 'Rwanda and Uganda'.[63]

This being said, the role of Uganda was not unidirectional. During
the first phase of the war, President Museveni attempted to mediate
and promote a negotiated settlement. At a meeting, which he organised
in Kampala on 16 November 1996 with Zairean and Rwandan[64]
representatives, Museveni submitted a list of twelve 'suggestions'
aimed at ending the conflict.[65] According to the Ugandan newspaper
*New Vision* of 20 November 1996, Museveni also asked for Mobutu's
'advice' after an attack by the rebel ADF against the Ugandan army. It
may well be that the refusal of the Kinshasa regime to engage in mean-
ingful dialogue with the neighbouring countries and the rebel movement
convinced Museveni to support the rebellion beyond the initial objective, which was to establish a security zone at the border, and to opt
for a final solution. This did not prevent him, when in Paris in February
1997, from advocating a ceasefire, to be followed by a conference on
security in the Great Lakes region.[66] Moreover, Museveni later stated
that he disapproved of the direct involvement of the Rwandan army in
military operations in Zaire, as such actions 'artificially falsify the outcome of conflicts (...). In a scenario which combines "artificial winners"
and political exclusion, the stage is set for future political problems'.[67]
Formulated with hindsight, this analysis is convincing, but it does not, of
course, explain why the Ugandan army has also been so deeply involved
in the war on Zairean soil.[68]

---

[62] AFP, Goma, 29 January 1997.
[63] *The New York Times*, 8 February 1997.
[64] It is interesting to note that Kabila's rebel alliance was not invited; this of course confirms
the impression that the Ugandan and Rwandan regimes felt that they represented the
interests of the AFDL.
[65] These 'suggestions' are reproduced later in this book.
[66] AFP, Paris, 11 February 1997.
[67] *The Monitor*, 2 June 1999.
[68] However, Museveni's concern was to return during the second war, which started in
1998. As will be seen later, this is one of the causes of the conflict that then broke out
between Uganda and Rwanda.

Burundi, for its part, probably benefited most from the 'Banyamulenge rebellion', as the rear bases of the Burundian rebel groups, in particular the CNDD–FDD, in South Kivu were destroyed. From October 1996 onwards, rebel activity in the northwestern provinces (Cibitoke and Bubanza), separated from South Kivu only by the Ruzizi River, decreased considerably. However, contrary to the Rwandan anti-government forces at the time, the Burundian guerrilla movements maintained elements inside Burundi; in addition, large groups of CNDD–FDD fighters managed to escape to Tanzania and even to the interior of Burundi. The involvement of the Burundian army in Zaire seems to have been rather limited and confined to complicity rather than to active operations.[69] Thus, the infiltration of troops and equipment by the RPA into South Kivu in mid-1996 was carried out through Burundian territory, in obvious connivance with the freshly installed military regime in Bujumbura. The lesser involvement of Burundi is not surprising. Its army had enough problems at home: harassed by three rebel movements, this rather inefficient force of about 20,000 men could hardly afford a foreign adventure, all the more so since Burundi was facing an embargo decided by the region's countries as a response to Buyoya's *coup d'état*. However, William Barnes argues that the embargo was also one of the reasons for Burundi's involvement in Zaire. The main concern was to avoid abandoning exclusive control of the area west of its border, essential to bypass the embargo, to Rwanda and Uganda.[70]

## 2.3 ANGOLA ENTERS THE FRAY: KINSHASA IN 100 DAYS

Up to early 1997, the advance of the 'rebellion' was rather limited. During the first four months of the war, about 80,000 sq. km. were occupied, that is, less than 5% of the total surface area of Zaire. The advance halted for a short time after the fall of Bunia. According to several sources, among whom John Pomfret figures prominently,[71] once the buffer zone was put in place to secure the eastern neighbours, there was some hesitation and

---

[69] There is one major exception. In mid-September 1996, when the 'Banyamulenge rebels' fought in the highlands, the Burundian army crossed the border and 'cleansed' the Ruzizi plains; in addition to fighting the CNDD–FDD rebels, it killed large numbers of unarmed Burundian refugees.

[70] W. Barnes, 'Kivu: l'enlisement dans la violence', *Politique Africaine*, 73, March 1999, p. 127.

[71] J. Pomfret, 'In Congo, Revenge Became Rebellion', *The Washington Post*, 6 July 1997.

even controversy within the AFDL and its regional sponsors. As seen earlier, Uganda, in particular, was very reluctant to engage in the conflict beyond its immediate security interests.[72] Likewise, Kagame mentioned the overthrow of the Mobutu regime as only the third objective of the Rwandan intervention.[73] In addition, the fact that Eritrean and Ethiopian mercenaries were said to have been hired by the rebellion on three-month contracts and solely for operations in the Goma–Bukavu area seems to confirm the initial limitation of territorial ambitions.

At the end of 1996, the involvement of Angola on the side of the Zairean rebellion was unclear. Inter-governmental relations appeared normal: the Zairean foreign minister visited Luanda at the end of November, while a high Angolan security official met with President Mobutu at Cap Martin in France. According to Misser and Vallée, President Dos Santos and Prime Minister Kengo Wa Dondo met in Brazzaville on 3 December and agreed to meet both countries' security concerns. Angola was to prevent the 'Tigres' (Katangese Gendarmes) from crossing into Zaire, while Zaire was to suppress the right of passage, which UNITA used to sell diamonds and buy weapons, and it was to dismantle UNITA bases in Zaire.[74]

However, even if one were to admit that the Zairean government honestly subscribed to these commitments, at the same time, other more obscure forces were engaged in activities that could only worry Luanda. According to several sources, people close to President Mobutu[75] fraudulently sold hundreds of tons of weapons and ammunition to UNITA. [76] This embezzlement of Zairean army resources not only sabotaged the efforts of General Mahele to fight the rebellion (see later text), but may also have contributed to the decision of Angola to enter the war by supporting the AFDL.

At any rate, by the end of 1996, Angola realised that its security concerns had not been met by the situation created in eastern Zaire and decided to make a difference.[77] Luanda's position, which was to expand

---

[72] Kagame confirmed that '[t]he most serious objection to direct involvement in the anti-Mobutu rebellion came from Uganda' (*Weekly Mail and Guardian*, 8 August 1997).

[73] Interview quoted earlier in *The Washington Post*, 9 July 1997.

[74] F. Misser, O. Vallee, *Les gemmocraties. L'économie politique du diamant africain*, Paris, Desclée de Brouwer, 1997, pp. 123–124.

[75] Those mentioned included Generals Likulia, Nzimbi and Baramoto, as well as civilians such as N'Gbanda and Seti Yale.

[76] For an interesting inquiry into these practices, see J. Rupert, 'Zaire Reportedly Selling Arms to Angolan Ex-Rebels', *The Washington Post*, 21 March 1997.

[77] The more historical causes for the Angolan intervention in the war are addressed by T. Turner, 'Angola's Role in the Congo War', in: J.F. Clark (Ed.), *The African Stakes...*, *op. cit.*, pp. 77–81.

the ambitions of the rebellion to the whole of Zaire, eventually prevailed.[78] Angola provided the crucial impetus through the Katangese Gendarmes, known as the 'Tigres'.[79] At the end of December 1996, the Angolan General Kopelipa (whose real name was Vieira Dias), President Dos Santos' security advisor, together with Katangese Gendarmes Generals Mulanda and Kafunda, paid a visit to Kigali to prepare for the operation. During two weeks in mid-February 1997, several battalions (2000–3000 'Tigres') were airlifted to Kigali, and taken from there by road to Goma and Bukavu. This operation was logistically supported by the Angolan army, obviously in close cooperation with Rwanda.

The Gendarmes played a major role in the capture of Kisangani, which they approached via two axes: Bunia–Bafwasende and Shabunda–Tingi–Tingi. Kisangani fell on 15 March. Another group progressed southwards, from Bukavu to Kalemie and further on to Kamina. Only in mid-March, a month after the beginning of the 'Tigres' operation, did the Zairean General Staff formally accuse 'Angolan military of fighting on the side of Kabila's men'. Although the direct participation of the Angolan army started only later, the confusion is understandable as the Gendarmes were incorporated into the Angolan army (Forças Armadas Angolanas [FAA]), they spoke Portuguese and the logistics were provided by the FAA. Mbuji–Mayi and Lubumbashi fell in early April. Only towards the end, in late April, did the FAA intervene directly, when they crossed the border and captured Tshikapa on 23 April. This expeditionary corps went on to take Kikwit and participated in the battle for Kenge (about 100 km east of Kinshasa), where the Angolan army came face to face with elements of UNITA brought there in support of the FAZ (also see later text).

The massive direct and indirect entry of Angola on the side of the rebellion and its eastern sponsors occurred at a moment when, according to the official broadcasting station *La Voix du Zaïre*, the Zairean foreign minister received the Angolan ambassador who transmitted a 'message of friendship' from his country. On 7 February, when preparations for military intervention were underway, the Angolan government expressed its solidarity with the Zairean people 'in the face of external interference in the internal affairs of Zaire'.[80] The increased involvement of Angola gradually expressed itself

---

[78] Thus, the Angolan weekly *Espresso* of 3 May 1997 affirmed that President Dos Santos insisted that Kabila should pursue his offensive to the end.

[79] Having fled to Angola after the collapse of the Katangese secession in early 1963, a number of them were eventually integrated into the Angolan army, of which they (or rather their sons) became the 24th Regiment in 1994.

[80] UN DHA IRIN, *Update 97*, 7 February 1997.

CAR                                          Sudan

Lisala
2.5.97                          Isiro
Congo                                        11.2.97              Uganda
(Brazzaville)
                                    Kisangani
Mbandaka                            15.3.97                       Rwanda
13.5.97
                                                                  Burundi
Kinshasa                            Kindu
17.5.97                             28.2.97
                                                                  Tanzania
Kikwit
29.4.97
                        Mbuji-Mayi    Kalemie
                        6.4.97        4.2.97

Angola

                        Lubumbashi
                        9.4.97

                                    Zambia

- - - - - →   Itinerary of the AFDL and its allies.
              The dates indicate the capture by the "rebellion"
              of the locations on the map.

MAP 5. Second phase of the war (spring 1997).

in the transfer of the centre of political gravity. Although Laurent Kabila initially paid many visits to Kigali and Kampala, Luanda progressively became
the place for meetings between the rebellion and its regional supporters.
Luanda was later to become the focal point of the unsuccessful efforts by
South Africa, the United States and the UN to achieve a negotiated settlement
(see later text). Vice-President Thabo Mbeki and ambassadors Richardson
and Sahnoun were frequent guests, at the same time remaining in contact
with the other key players, Kagame and Museveni.

The entry of the Gendarmes and the Angolan army caused the rebellion
to pick up speed. While it took four months (October 1996 to January
1997) to occupy less than one-twentieth of the country, the remainder of

Zaire was captured in the three months that followed the arrival of the 'Tigres' (mid-February to mid-May 1997).

## 2.4 OTHER REGIONAL ALLIES

The coalition aimed at toppling Mobutu included not just the eastern neighbours and Angola, but went further. However, while countries such as Eritrea, Ethiopia, Zambia and Zimbabwe offered varying degrees of support to Kabila's rebellion, a brief mention of their role will suffice here. Beyond political and diplomatic support, there is no proof that Eritrean or Ethiopian government forces engaged in the conflict. However, several sources mentioned the presence of 'mercenaries' from these two countries. The story in *Le Monde* on the 'Tutsi Legion' quoted above also refers to recruitment in Eritrea. Of course, the possibility that the regimes of Asmara and Addis Ababa tolerated or even facilitated the hiring of mercenaries cannot be excluded.

Zambia, at very least, allowed rebel forces to transit through its territory during the advance towards Lubumbashi. In early April 1997, Lusaka allowed Katangese Gendarmes to land in Ndola. These Gendarmes took Lubumbashi from the west, after entering Zaire through Kipushi on the border with Zambia. According to the South African weekly *The Sunday Independent*, Zambia also contributed 1000 troops.[81] Zimbabwe, for its part, contributed much more substantially than was initially thought. During the war, *The East African* had already claimed that Zimbabwe was supplying arms and uniforms and that the state-owned Zimbabwe Defence Industries (ZDI) had been shipping material for several months.[82] A week after this revelation, the dominant Zimbabwe African National Union–Patriotic Front (ZANU–PF) party congratulated Kabila on his efficient campaign, whilst at the same time denying that Zimbabwe was supplying the rebels with weapons or other material.[83] Nevertheless, the extent of Zimbabwe's involvement later became clear. It played a crucial role by supplying weapons, aircraft, pilots, paratroopers and special forces. The value of ZDI's supplies totalled US$39 million.[84] Two

---

[81] *The Sunday Independent*, 13 July 1997.
[82] *The East African*, 14 April 1997.
[83] UN DHA IRIN, *Update 154*, 19–21 April 1997.
[84] This is a huge amount, which at first sight seems implausible. Where would the rebel movement have found such funds? However, Kabila incurred a debt towards Zimbabwe, which is one of the factors explaining Mugabe's position during the second Congo war (see below).

Zimbabwean airforce Casa transport planes were used to ship arms and food to the rebel forces and to airlift troops to advanced positions.[85]

The composition of the regional alliance was visible the day Kabila swore the oath of office in Kinshasa on 29 May 1997. The foreign heads of state present were the presidents of Burundi, Rwanda, Angola, Uganda and Zambia, the 'frontline' neighbours that had made him king.

### 2.5  U.S. INVOLVEMENT

### Logistical and Political Support

The remarkably well-coordinated and efficient nature of a 'rebellion' that was new, virtually without proper military capacity and functioning in a circumstantial alliance raises the issue of the support provided by forces external to the region. Even facing a very poorly performing government army, the rapid progression of the rebel alliance on several large fronts extending over considerable distances was possible only with excellent logistics in terms of reconnaissance, communication, transport and supply logistics. This is all the more obvious since the rebellion was the work of a very heterogeneous alliance of several Zairean and foreign forces.

The United States had always maintained very cordial relations with the new Rwandan regime and shown a great deal of understanding for its security concerns. According to Human Rights Watch, the Americans, just like the Rwandans, felt that the refugee camps in Zaïre were a threat to the stability of Rwanda and the region. Although they were unwilling to tackle this problem themselves,[86] as early as August 1995, the Pentagon decided not to oppose a Rwandan operation, provided that it was 'clean', that is, causing the lowest possible number of civilian casualties. In August 1996, Kagame was in Washington and announced to the State Department that he was going to 'empty' the camps, if no one else took care of this problem. The United States reportedly did not object.[87] As previously discussed, the RPA

---

[85] *The Sunday Independent*, 13 July 1997; *The Zimbabwe Independent*, 22 August 1997.

[86] As will be seen later, the United States felt that an operation of separation and disarmament was not to be part of the mandate of an international force that never materialised.

[87] Human Rights Watch, *Democratic Republic of The Congo. What Kabila is Hiding. Civilian Killings and Impunity in Congo*, October 1997, p. 33. However, in a letter Assistant Secretary for Legislative Affairs Barbara Larkin addressed on 15 December 1997 to Christopher Smith, chairman of the House Subcommittee on International Operations and Human Rights, she was more cautious: 'During his August 1996 visit to Washington, Vice President Kagame expressed frustration with the international community's apparent inability to resolve the refugee crisis in eastern Zaire. (...) Kagame expressed scepticism

effectively conducted the operation, which however proved to be anything but 'clean' (see later text). As a matter of fact, there are many indications that the United States went far beyond giving Kagame the green light.

On 15 July 1997, a news network, NCN, published a report suggesting, albeit cautiously, that the United States had installed a C3I centre (command, control, communications and intelligence) in Kigali, from whence the rebel operations were coordinated.[88] Based mainly on an unidentified Finnish source, NCN used the conditional tense and warned against grand conspiracy theories. However, the document offered a number of elements worthy of careful examination, which need to be linked to other available information. To quote but a few examples: the direct contacts between Kabila and the Pentagon during the war; the presence of American demining units in Rwanda allegedly used to transfer troops across the Zairean border; the presence in Kigali of 'old hands' of the CIA; and the sighting of American armoured vehicles in the Kisangani area. NCN also referred to information provided by the Chinese press agency Xinhua that the United States installed communications stations in Fort Portal (Uganda),[89] Brazzaville and Kigali.[90] This is corroborated by one of the author's own sources who, in November 1996, saw a high mast and two large parabolic antennas between Gisenyi (Rwanda) and Goma (Zaire). The French DC8 Saringue communications monitoring aeroplane, based in the Central African Republic, reportedly established that the United States was

---

with [regard to our] approach, but at no time stated that he would soon take action on his own (...)'. Ambassador Gribbin believes that Kagame's visit to Washington ended in a misunderstanding: 'Kagame judged that he was honest about Rwanda's intent to dismantle the camps in the absence of an international undertaking to do so. In turn Secretary of Defense William Perry thought he laid down a clear marker that unilateral action was not advisable. Kagame thought he got an okay. Perry thought he had quashed the idea. Each went away happy' (R.E. Gribbin, *In the Aftermath of Genocide...*, *op. cit.*, pp. 175–176).

[88] NCN Intelligence Reports, A U.S. inspired covert coalition command and control center in Kigali?, Washington D.C., AfIS News Service, 15 July 1997.

[89] The installation in Fort Portal was confirmed by a Ugandan source. This information was considered very embarrassing by the Americans, so much so that the U.S. embassy in Kampala had the story blocked from publication in *The New Vision* (W. Madsen, *Genocide and Covert Operations in Africa 1993–1999*, Lewiston, The Edwin Mellen Press, 1999, p. 197). The station was shut down after Kabila had made it to Kinshasa (*Idem*, p. 198). As this is the first quote from Madsen's book, it should be stressed that it is unreliable on many points. Much information is based on a single source, often of doubtful quality, and the author often accumulates unchecked data, out of which he then extracts a story. In addition, he insufficiently sees the context, thus making him unable to put information into perspective, and to assess the relevance of some of the facts presented. That said, Madsen's research has also unearthed data that can be useful if cross-checked.

[90] Xinhua, Nairobi, 31 March 1997.

assuring communications between Rwanda and combat units in Zaire.[91]
A plane operated by Mountain Air, flown by an American named Tim,
shipped weapons to the front and evacuated rebel wounded to Entebbe.
Mountain Air was said to be a CIA operation.[92]

There are more puzzling facts. The International Rescue Committee
(IRC), an American NGO active in the Kivu region, is said, by several
witnesses, to have installed anti-aircraft artillery in Bukavu and Goma;
in addition, in Bukavu, it paid the first wages to the civil servants of the
rebel administration in the form of food. The IRC is suspected of being
an executing agency for certain U.S. government services; its links with
the CIA appear to be close.[93] It is possible that the U.S. Committee for
Refugees (USCR), whose director Roger Winter was very close to the
Rwandan and Ugandan regimes, as well as to the Southern Sudanese
rebellion, played a similar role.[94]

A number of actions and positions of the U.S. embassy in Kigali were
ambiguous, to say the least. Ambassador Gribbin's revealing and, in a
way, candid memoirs allow for a better understanding of that attitude.
Indeed, Gribbin 'went native' and showed extraordinary sympathy for
the RPF's positions.[95] He 'judged that Rwanda had a solid foundation
for institutional growth, expansion of participation, widening input, and
democratic growth',[96] and he toed the regime's line on nearly every single

---

[91] P. De Barba, 'L'engagement américain pendant la guerre au Zaïre', *Raids-Magazine*, 138,
November 1997.

[92] The use of this aeroplane was confirmed by a reporter who used it on 7 March 1997 for
a visit to Goma: *An evening with Kabila*, Goma, 9 March 1997, posted on Rwandanet
via Ugandanet, 10 April 1997.

[93] On the clandestine activities of the IRC, see E. T. Chester, *Covert Network. Progressives,
the International Rescue Committee, and the CIA*, Armonk/London, M.E. Sharpe, 1995.

[94] The USCR actively participated in the campaign to bury the plans for the deployment of
an international force (see later text). Returning from a visit to the region at the end of
November 1996, Winter stated that he met Kabila on several occasions in order to get
a better insight into the military and political objectives of the rebel movement. He concluded that a military operation would be counterproductive and suggested instead helping
Rwanda to settle the repatriated refugees (USCR, 'Military Deployment in Eastern Zaire
Would Be Misguided; Talk of Deployment Threatens to Impede Humanitarian Relief',
28 November 1996). In an op-ed piece, Winter later criticised the human rights organisations for denouncing the abuse perpetrated against the Rwandan refugees (R. Winter,
'How Human Rights Groups Miss the Opportunity to Do Good', *The Washington Post*,
22 February 1998).

[95] The difference between Gribbin and the U.S. Ambassador in Bujumbura could not be
greater. Robert Krueger was very concerned about human rights abuse and openly confronted those in power, thus even putting his own life at risk. See R. Krueger, K.T. Krueger,
*From Bloodshed to Hope...*, *op. cit.*

[96] R.E. Gribbin, *In the Aftermath of Genocide...*, *op. cit.*, p. 150.

issue (a few examples are offered below).[97] He even went as far as echoing the regime's position that, when criticising the human rights situation, organisations like Amnesty International 'regurgitated Hutu power propaganda as truth'.[98] From the start of the rebellion, the deputy chief of mission Peter Whaley paid frequent visits to Bukavu and Goma, where he had several meetings with Kabila.[99] On 16 November 1996, the day after the attack against Mugunga refugee camp, Roger Winter organised a meeting at the embassy with Kabila, U.S. special envoy Ambassador Richard Bogosian, Ambassador Robert Gribbin, Peter Whaley and a colonel of General Smith's staff.[100] The false statements made by Ambassador Gribbin and General Smith concerning the Rwandan refugees remaining in Zaire, at a moment when a macabre and cynical game of numbers was played in the context of plans to deploy an international force, will be discussed again later. In a cable on 21 January 1997, the embassy was even more cynical: it urged humanitarian agencies to pull out of the refugee camp at Tingi–Tingi and 'stop feeding the killers (...). If we do not, we will be trading the children in Tingi–Tingi against the children who will be killed and orphaned in Rwanda'.[101]

The role played by the defence attaché, Major Richard Orth, at the embassy in Kigali must also be mentioned. An old hand of the Defence Intelligence Agency (DIA), he expressed his sympathies for the RPF in such an open manner that it became a source of embarrassment for the State Department.[102] In a letter sent to President Clinton

---

[97] This is all the more surprising since Gribbin realised that 'RPF luminaries proved to be masters of spin (...) The RPF played the genocide card shamelessly (correctly so, in my view, because genocide had defined the Rwandan tragedy) and staked out the moral high ground. The claim to righteousness was then misused to shield or justify political decisions' (*Idem*, p. 199).

[98] *Idem*, p. 160. Interestingly, Gribbin does not mention U.S.-based Human Rights Watch, which overall made the same observations as Amnesty International.

[99] Whaley also played a doubtful role in the saga of the UN inquiry into the massacres of Hutu refugees (see later text). In her testimony before the U.S. Congress in July 1997, Kathi Austin said that Whaley told her that he urged Kabila not to cooperate with the inquiry.

[100] Testimony of Roger Winter before the House Subcommittee on International Operations and Human Rights, 4 December 1996.

[101] UN DHA IRIN, *Update 88*, 28 January 1997. In his memoirs, Ambassador Gribbin conveniently glosses over Tingi–Tingi and the statements made by the Kigali Embassy on this tragedy.

[102] Strong RPF bias appears to have been a common characteristic of U.S. Defence attachés in Kigali. Orth's predecessor, Lieutenant Colonel Thomas Odom showed unwavering sympathy for the Kigali regime, as can be seen throughout a book he published on his experience in Zaire and Rwanda (T.P. Odom, *Journey into Darkness. Genocide in Rwanda*, College Station, Texas A&M University Press, 2005).

on 28 August 1997, the chairman of the House Subcommittee on
International Operations and Human Rights, Christopher Smith wrote
that 'a few U.S. diplomats in Rwanda have been (...) strong and obvious enthusiasts of the Rwandan government and their Congolese allies'.
In his view, this would explain the fact that U.S. policy was dictated
by 'reports from people who tended to discount negative reports about
their friends in the RPA and the Kabila forces'. Officially at least, this did
not seem to worry the State Department. In her letter of 15 December
1997, quoted earlier, Barbara Larkin assured Smith 'of the confidence
we place in Ambassador Gribbin and his staff in Kigali. Throughout the
conflict in Zaire, Embassy Kigali reported consistently and profession-
ally on the events as they unfolded'.

## Supply of Material and Personnel

Several sources mention the supply of arms, ammunition and equipment,
and even the presence of U.S. military. A South African pilot stated that, in
September 1996, he shipped a cargo of rifles from Pretoria to Bujumbura,
where the shipment was received by a Burundian army officer and a man
the pilot recognised as a member of the U.S. embassy; according to the
same source, the destination for the cargo was Uvira.[103] This occurred at
the time the 'Banyamulenge rebellion' started in that region.[104] According
to another source, as early as July–August 1996, American military and
'civilian'[105] planes transported tons of supplies out of Uganda and, to
a lesser extent, out of Rwanda. Later, Hercules and Galaxy planes of
the U.S. Air Force (USAF) are reported to have offloaded arms, ammunition and other equipment in Goma.[106] American armoured personnel
carriers (APCs), stationed in Uganda, supposedly for use in the aborted
humanitarian operation (see later text), were 'stolen' and used in the campaign against Kisangani and even further west.[107] In the same vein, a
high-ranking Zairean army officer claimed on 5 February 1997 that the
Ugandan army were using equipment delivered at the end of 1996 in

---

[103] R. Block, 'Lost In Africa: How U.S. Landed On Sidelines In Zaire', *The Wall Street
    Journal*, 21 April 1997.
[104] We have seen that witnesses saw about thirty Rwandan trucks crossing the Burundian–
    Zairean border at the same place and time.
[105] Inverted commas are used as some of these aircraft operated for the CIA. Mountain Air
    (see earlier text) was again mentioned.
[106] P. De Barba, 'L'engagement américain ...', *op. cit.*
[107] *Zaire News Watch*, 16 May 1997.

Kampala for the international force; this included transmission material, listening posts and support weapons.[108]

The 5 December 1996 issue of *Le Monde* said that, according to French intelligence, between 60 and 100 'American advisors' supported the RPA and even made incursions into Zaire. In its issue of 30 August 1997, the French journal *Valeurs Actuelles* published extracts of a note drafted by a 'French service', which, however, was not identified. The text mentioned the airlifting of arms and ammunition to Goma from Uganda in October and November 1996. This has already been referred to, but the note goes on to claim that about twenty officers of the U.S. special forces based in Fort Bragg were operating in Zaire; one of them was said to have been killed during fighting near the Oso bridge.[109] The note also confirmed the presence of a sophisticated system of communications and transmission. The most serious accusation claimed that American military was involved in machine-gunning refugee camps, notably by using a C-130 gunship belonging to the special forces.[110]

In addition, humanitarian sources suspected the United States of transmitting information on the movements and concentration of refugees to the Rwandan military. This information was obtained through air reconnaissance missions in the context of the decision-making process on the deployment of the international force (see later text). However, it appeared that this intelligence was used to localise the refugees, not in order to assist them, but to exterminate them. Referring to refugee concentrations, a U.S. general spoke of 'targets of (military) opportunity'.[111] Kagame himself recognised that 'at a certain stage we shared information (with the Americans) on refugee movements'.[112]

In an enigmatic fashion, Burundian President Buyoya said on 20 April 1997[113] that 'the influence of powers [external to Africa] is obvious' and

[108] AFP, Goma, 5 February 1997.
[109] Also see *Le Figaro*, 28 March 1997; *Le Monde* of 29 March 1997 carried more or less the same information. In addition, Belgian reporter Colette Braeckman wrote that 'credible witnesses say they have seen black American soldiers with the RPA' (*Le Soir*, 13 November 1996). Madsen (*Genocide and Covert Operations...*, *op. cit.*, p. 205) quotes sources as saying that white men wearing 'green berets' murdered thousands of Hutu refugees, but also that black U.S. Special Forces participated in the attacks.
[110] This type of information must, of course, be read with a great deal of caution. The source of the document, which the article's author Hubert Coudurier refused to share with this author, is unknown. Moreover, the story in *Valeurs Actuelles* contains a number of elements that are false or factually impossible.
[111] N. Gowing, 'New Challenges and Problems...,' *op. cit.*, p. 58–59.
[112] *Idem*, p. 60.
[113] AFP, New York, 20 April 1997.

that 'no African power helps Kabila as much as certain exterior powers', which, however, he refused to name. Nevertheless, the fact that he
mentioned 'a struggle between Western powers in Africa' suggests that he
was referring to France and the United States; he would logically place
the latter in the camp of the rebellion and its eastern supporters. Later,
during testimony before the House International Relations Committee,
Physicians for Human Rights accused the U.S. army of having trained
Rwandan troops who were guilty of atrocities against unarmed civilians in
Zaire and inside Rwanda. A few days earlier, the European Commissioner
for Humanitarian Affairs Emma Bonino, referring to the famous Kagame
interview in the 9 July 1997 issue of *The Washington Post*, expressed her
surprise at Kagame commending the United States for 'taking the right
decision to let it (the rebellion) proceed'. She wondered whether 'someone in Washington could perhaps provide some explanations' on the role
played by the United States.[114] In her habitual direct style, Bonino later
said that 'the US have lied throughout' with regard to their knowledge of
Rwandan plans to attack the refugee camps.[115]

The explanations sought by Bonino have never been given, even after
many sources brought increasingly precise indications with regard to
American involvement. A memo[116] submitted to the House Committee on
International Relations by Under Secretary of Defense Walter Slocombe
mentioned, for the period from 15 July to 30 August 1996, the training
by nine U.S. instructors of thirty elements of the RPA in 'small unit leader
training, tactical skills, land navigation, first aid, and basic rifle mark-
manship'. These activities took place just prior to the beginning of the
'Banyamulenge rebellion' and the entry into the Kivu of elements of the
RPA. During the period from 2 to 27 November 1996, that is, just prior
to and during the episode of the 'voluntary-forced' return of the refugees
(see later text), five instructors trained about forty elements of the RPA
and the National Police (*Gendarmerie*) in 'civilian' skills, such as multi-
media information campaigns with emphasis on refugee repatriation. As
this training started ten days before the RPA operation against Mugunga
camp, it is likely that the Americans knew about Kagame's intentions and
that they expected a large influx of repatriated refugees.[117]

---

[114] Reuters, Brussels, 13 July 1997.
[115] Interview with the weekly *La Vie*, as reported by AFP, Paris, 29 October 1997.
[116] U.S. Military Activities in Rwanda Since 1994. Summary, 19 August 1997.
[117] In addition, a few weeks before the massive return, the Rwandan authorities organised
meetings with the local administrators to explain how to handle sudden and large
influxes of returnees. Similarly, a memorandum dated 6 November 1996 from the UN

Reports by Amnesty International and Human Rights Watch were more precise. In September 1997, Amnesty observed that U.S. military assistance to Rwanda had intensified during the months preceding the RPA's operation in Zaire. The report said that a U.S.-supported public information campaign 'played a significant role in convincing foreign governments and humanitarian organizations that it was safe for Rwandese refugees to return home, where many of them have subsequently been subjected to human rights violations, including extrajudicial execution and "disappearances"'.[118] The organisation concluded that 'the apparently uncritical political support of the USA for the Rwandese government can only be encouraging the Rwandese authorities to believe that they can carry on violating human rights with little fear of criticism from their most important allies'.[119] Human Rights Watch quoted several testimonies on the presence of American military in Zaire between November 1996 and August 1997. A witness saw elements of the special forces from Fort Bragg in uniform in North Kivu on 23–24 July 1997. Other witnesses reported U.S. military in Goma in November 1996 and in the Ruwenzori region in August 1997 together with elements of the UPDF.[120] The story of a Rwandan priest contains the following passage, which seems genuine in the context:

On 19 December 1996, we met a group which had captured a white soldier, who had been lost in the forest. He spoke poor French with an English accent. During his interrogation he said he was a Frenchman who had come to save the refugees and that he had been separated from the others by accident. Despite his explanations, his language betrayed him. He was found to be an American who had become separated from the Tutsi soldiers during the attack of 15 December 1996 at Musenge. The wrath of the traumatised came over him and he disappeared [i.e. he was killed].[121]

A great deal of uncertainty as to the extent of the U.S. involvement remained, and Christopher Smith, in his letter to President Clinton (mentioned earlier), expressed discontent with the explanations, which

---

human rights field operation outlined a number of measures to be taken in the case of a massive return (HRFOR *Preparation for a Massive Influx of Rwandan Refugees from Zaire*, 6 November 1996).

[118] Amnesty International, *Rwanda. Ending the Silence*, 25 September 1997, p. 45.

[119] *Idem*, p. 46.

[120] Human Rights Watch, *Democratic Republic of the Congo. What Kabila is Hiding...*, op. cit., pp. 34–35.

[121] Abbé Jean, *Neuf mois de tragédie à l'Est du Zaïre. Mon journal*, Nairobi, 14 November 1997, p. 8 (author's translation).

had been offered by Slocombe a week earlier. After reminding the U.S. president of the massacres committed in Zaire and Rwanda by the RPA ('a deliberate and systematic policy of targeted ethnic killing') and of the absence of any U.S. reaction to this abuse, he demanded clear answers to a number of questions concerning the sort of training given to the RPA,[122] the military operations of the RPA in Zaire, the violations of the refugees' human rights and the tolerant attitude of the United States toward the regime in Kigali. Smith did not receive a satisfactory answer and told President Clinton in a new letter on 24 April 1998 that 'I have not received much information that is responsive to the obvious point of my request'.

## Incoherence

There appeared to be a disparity between the publicly formulated policy of the United States, and of the State Department in particular, and the evidence of its profound involvement on the side of the rebels and their sponsors. Indeed, quite soon after the war began, the State Department acknowledged that Zaire was the victim of external aggression; it insisted on respect for the country's territorial integrity and asked the neighbours to stay out of the conflict. In a letter of 22 November 1996 to the Zairean foreign minister, Secretary Warren Christopher confirmed that 'Rwandan troops entered Goma and Bukavu in October and that Ugandan troops entered North Kivu in November'. The United States 'have strongly recommended their withdrawal, in order to avoid an escalation of the conflict'.[123] On 9 January 1997, the U.S. Ambassador in Kinshasa Daniel Simpson said on Zairean television that 'we know perfectly well that Zaire has been attacked by Rwanda and Uganda. This poses a political

---

[122] Returning to the testimonies before his Subcommittee on 4 December 1996, Smith wrote: 'I was also assured that our military training of Rwandan forces "deals almost exclusively with the human rights end of the spectrum as distinct from purely military operations" (testimony of Ambassador Bogosian) and that "we are talking about the softer, kinder, gentler side of the military training... We have not provided Rwanda with any sort of basic military training that – what you would get at Ft. Bragg officer training, those sorts of things" (testimony of [Deputy Assistant Secretary of Defense] Vincent Kern). It now appears, however, that we were providing Rwandan forces with training in a broad array of military skills (...) whose connection to "the human rights end of the spectrum" is attenuated at best (Ironically, some of the U.S. trainers apparently came from Fort Bragg)'.

[123] This letter (in French) is reproduced in H. N'Gbanda, *Ainsi sonne le glas..., op. cit.*, pp. 387–388.

and humanitarian problem'.[124] At a conference organised on 16 January in Washington by the U.S. Institute of Peace and the State Department, all participants, including the American officials, agreed that 'Rwanda, Uganda, Burundi, and more recently Angola have been deeply involved in the civil war'.[125] On 24 January, the State Department called for 'the withdrawal of all foreign forces, including the mercenaries' and underlined that the United States 'have asked since the beginning for neighbouring governments to stay out of the conflict'.[126] On 7 February, Madeleine Albright urged neighbouring countries, Rwanda, Uganda and Burundi, to stay out of the escalating conflict;[127] thus, the United States pointed their finger at close allies in the region. A week later, at a meeting of the UN Security Council, U.S. Ambassador Bill Richardson warned another ally, Angola, against any involvement in the conflict.[128] On 25 April, Assistant Secretary of State for African Affairs George Moose expressed 'deep concern' over Angola's military involvement in the Zaire conflict; he said this could represent a 'complicating factor' for both Angola and Zaire.[129]

It would be tedious to continue this enumeration of declarations and positions, which all show that the State Department was worried about the direct support given to the rebellion by the countries of the region. The genuine nature of this concern was underscored by the irritation it caused in the rebel camp. On 6 February, Kabila criticised the 'interference' of the United States in the conflict. The AFDL's spokesperson Raphaël Ghenda stated that the warnings by countries such as the United States, France and Belgium 'are just crocodile tears (...). The situation is what it is because they have supported Mobutu for over thirty years'.[130]

Clearly, the American policy was incoherent, to say the least. It is possible that other actors such as the Pentagon, the CIA and even the National Security Council developed a discreet and autonomous course, contrary to the one publicly formulated by the State Department. It is well known, for instance, that certain military circles in the United States had excellent relations with the Ugandan and Rwandan military; a number of Ugandan and

---

[124] According to *The Monitor* (Kampala) of 13 January 1997, Uganda and Rwanda qualified Simpson's remarks as 'an unfortunate personal opinion'.
[125] U.S. Institute of Peace, *Special Report. Zaire's Crises of War and Governance*, Washington D.C., April 1997.
[126] AFP, Kinshasa, 24 January 1997.
[127] UN DHA IRIN, Update 96, 7 February 1997.
[128] UN DHA IRIN, Update 111, 28 February 1997.
[129] UN DHA IRIN, Update. 158, 25 April 1997.
[130] AFP, Goma, 6 February 1997.

Rwandan officers had received training in the United States. When the war started in Rwanda in October 1990, Paul Kagame himself was actually following a course at the Staff Command College in Fort Leavenworth, and American officers did not hide their admiration for this 'brilliant strategist'.[131] There might well be some form of comradeship between the U.S. military on the one hand and the Rwandan and Ugandan militaries on the other.

Other players on the ground were linked to (former) military and old hands of the CIA and the DIA. The IRC has already been mentioned. Ronco Consulting, a private company run by former U.S. military, worked in Rwanda for the National Demining Office. Its operation was, of course, perfectly legitimate, but meant that it had people on site. According to Kathi Austin (Human Rights Watch Arms Project), Ronco imported military equipment such as explosives and armoured vehicles. This material was then allegedly transferred to the Rwandan army, with the Pentagon's blessing.[132] Military Professional Resources Inc. (MPRI) was another company active in the region. Founded by retired U.S. high-ranking officers and based in Virginia, one of its advisors was Herman Cohen, Assistant Secretary of State for African Affairs under George Bush; its Vice-President, Harry Soyster, was the former number two at the DIA, also during the Bush Sr. presidency.[133] The privatisation of military operations and the training of foreign armies offer deniability: even though, according to a former DIA official, '[t]he programmes are designed to further our foreign policy objectives. If the [U.S.] government doesn't sanction it, the companies can't do it',[134] this allows the U.S. administration to deny any implication in operations that evade the usual forms of public control. This policy became official to the extent that, on 24 June 1997, the DIA organised a symposium on 'The Privatization of National Security Functions in Sub-Saharan Africa'. Among those present in Washington were Ed Soyster (MPRI), Eben Barlow (Executive Outcomes) and Tim Spicer (Sandline), and also representatives of private companies such as Exxon and Texaco, diplomats from Uganda and Angola, and even humanitarian organisations such as World Vision, UNICEF and the UNHCR.

---

[131] Officials at the State Department claimed in private that 'the Pentagon has fallen in love with Kagame'.

[132] K. Silverstein, 'Privatizing War. How Affairs of State are outsourced to corporations beyond public control', *The Nation*, 2 July–4 August 1997.

[133] On MPRI, see 'Generals for Hire', *Time Magazine*, 15 January 1996; 'For US firms, war becomes a business', *The Boston Globe*, 1 February 1997; 'Private US companies train armies around the world', *U.S. News and World Report*, 8 February 1997.

[134] K. Silverstein, 'Privatizing War ...', *op. cit.*

## Degree of Involvement

In her 5 May 1998 testimony before the U.S. House Subcommittee on International Operations and Human Rights, Kathi Austin was very severe. She claimed that the killing of tens of thousands of refugees, considered as 'collateral damage', had been facilitated by U.S. assistance to Rwanda and other governments in the region. U.S. officials continually provided political, consultative and logistical support to the Kagame regime: 'U.S. policy was mistaken in becoming partisan'. Nevertheless, with the available information, it is difficult to conclude on the nature and the extent of the role played by the United States as such or by certain individual civilians or military. Rather than a large conspiracy, this could well be considerable confusion in the absence of a real policy for a region, which the Americans did not know well.[135] At the same time as stating 'categorically' that '[n]o U.S. military personnel were deployed to Kivu at this time or later, in any capacity'[136] and that 'the U.S. did not provide Laurent Kabila or his AFDL rebels with any equipment, material, training, intelligence, or any other tangible support of any kind',[137] Ambassador Gribbin attempts an explanation: 'What the U.S. did was to refrain from all-out opposition to the Rwanda/rebel struggle (...) We did not use all the leverage at our disposal to limit Rwandan involvement. The Rwandan leadership interpreted our restraint as acquiescence in their Congo adventure'.[138] Just like during the phase leading up to the war (see earlier text), this seems to boil down to a 'misunderstanding'. The incoherence of Washington was also noted by certain American specialists. Herman Cohen stated: 'I wish I could give credit to the US government for the broad vision and policy of doing something like this, but I can't.

---

[135] In his letter of 28 August 1997 to President Clinton (cf. *supra*), Christopher Smith expressed concern over 'the apparent unfamiliarity of United States policy makers with the basic facts on the ground throughout the Zaire operation'. I was myself struck by the relative incompetence of two staff of the National Security Council in charge of the dossier. These young White House staff were very conscious of their influence (and, therefore, rather arrogant), but failed to grasp the complexity of the region they were dealing with. Michael Barnett, who was encharged with the Rwanda dossier in the US Mission at the UN, candidly expressed the problem: 'That I might be presented as a Rwanda expert still strikes me as rather incongruous (...) I was a seasoned veteran of Rwanda for nearly four months when President Habyarimana (...) was killed and all hell erupted' (see M.N. Barnett, 'The UN Security Council, Indifference, and Genocide in Rwanda', *Cultural Anthropology*, 1997, pp. 551–578).

[136] R.E. Gribbin, *In the Aftermath of Genocide...*, *op. cit.*, p. 189.

[137] *Idem*, p. 194.

[138] *Idem*, pp. 194–195.

It's day-to-day policy. One problem at a time builds up, and the French, with their paranoia[139], see a grand design'.[140] Another former Assistant Secretary of State, Chester Crocker, said he 'could not see a coherent policy by the US government' and that 'the Americans are not competent enough to engineer anything in the region'.[141] An inquiry by *Le Monde* among American officials showed a similar picture. Fearful of Kabila's drift, a 'very high U.S. source' stated that 'whatever our European allies seem to think, Kabila is not our creature or our puppet. We do not give him anything, so there is nothing we can take back. If he refuses to listen to us, he becomes largely uncontrollable'.[142]

Despite the many ambiguities, a number of facts emerge:

(i) The policy articulated by the State Department seems to have been sidelined by the Pentagon and intelligence agencies, and possibly by the National Security Council. This involvement was partly privatised. The U.S. mission in Kigali, both its diplomatic and military branch, actively supported and coordinated these clandestine operations.

(ii) The United States was aware of the intentions of Kagame to attack the refugee camps and probably assisted him in doing so. In addition, they deliberately lied about the number and fate of the refugees remaining in Zaire, in order to avoid the deployment of an international humanitarian force, which could have saved tens of thousands of human lives, but which was resented by Kigali and the AFDL (see later text).

(iii) The United States supplied the forces of the AFDL and the RPA operating in Zaire with logistical and material support, and probably some command structure on the ground; this means that they had knowledge of the massacres of Rwandan refugees by their allies.

(iv) Through its diplomatic and military support, the United States gave the signal or at least the impression, to the Rwandan government and the AFDL that anything was permitted and that they were ensured impunity. By action and omission, they therefore bear part of the responsibility for the crimes committed by their

---

[139] A reference to the 'Fashoda syndrome' (see earlier text).

[140] H.W. French, 'In Zaire, France Sees the Hand of Washington', *The International Herald Tribune*, 5 April 1997.

[141] Interview in *Le Vif/L'Express*, 16 May 1997.

[142] *Le Monde*, 29 April 1997.

allies. In that sense, their position toward the new Rwandan regime was comparable to that of France towards the old one.

(v) More generally, the incoherent involvement of the only remaining superpower has generated dynamics of which it insufficiently measured the consequences. In Central Africa like elsewhere, the United States has been an apprentice sorcerer incapable of accompanying a process, which span out of control, with the disastrous consequences later described.

# 3

# Massacre of the Rwandan Refugees

## 3.1  ABORTED INTERNATIONAL INTERVENTION

It has been seen that, under the guise of the 'Banyamulenge rebellion', the Rwandan refugee camps in South and North Kivu were systematically attacked with heavy arms. This was just the beginning of a humanitarian disaster. On 29 October 1996, European Humanitarian Affairs Commissioner Emma Bonino accused the international community of remaining idle in the face of a situation she called 'explosive': 'Five hundred thousand people today, probably one million in the coming days are in mortal danger (…). If the Security Council does not act now, I wonder when it will ever act'.[1] The idea of intervention gained momentum on 4 November, when the UNHCR explored the views of the governments in the region with regard to the creation of 'humanitarian corridors' for the refugees blocked in Zaire. On the same day, the French section of Médecins sans frontières (MSF) insisted on immediate military intervention to create security zones and to disarm the armed elements among the refugees. Bernard Kouchner launched a vibrant appeal for intervention in *Le Monde*.[2] MSF evaluated the number of dead among the refugees at over 13,000, a figure that did not include the war casualties. On 8 November, a consortium of some twenty American humanitarian NGOs

---

[1] AFP, Brussels, 29 October 1996. On 1 November, the chairman of the UN Security Council Razali Ismail recognised his impotence: 'Both collectively and individually, we are incapable of acting sufficiently to prevent the enormous humanitarian tragedy which is happening before our eyes'.

[2] B. Kouchner, 'Monsieur Mandela, peut-on les laisser mourir?', *Le Monde*, 5 November 1996.

and a platform of European NGOs in turn demanded the rapid deployment of an international force, while insisting on the need to separate armed and non-armed refugees. France and Spain considered contributing to such a force, while other countries such as the United Kingdom immediately expressed their reticence.

In fact, two diametrically opposed views collided, one insisting on the need for the protection of the refugees, the other on their repatriation. The latter implicitly felt that the conflict was the consequence of the lack of solution to the situation created in mid-1994 and that a considerable loss of life was the price to be paid to solve the problem. Needless to say, this was also the position of the Rwandan government and of those supporting it.

A regional summit held in Nairobi on 5 and 6 November apparently attempted to reconcile these two positions: it asked the Security Council to deploy an international force and to establish corridors, whilst at the same time requesting 'the separation of intimidators and *bona fide* refugees'. This position was initially supported by the Rwandan government, but not without ambiguity. Indeed, on the one hand, President Bizimungu insisted on 6 November that refugees were to be repatriated and separated from 'intimidators', while on the other, Foreign Minister Gasana stated in Brussels a day earlier that Rwanda would oppose a military–humanitarian intervention 'by all means and not just politically (…). If such a force were to be deployed without the consent of the sub-region, we shall fight it'. Nevertheless, the plan seemed to be gaining momentum: the United States, the United Kingdom and Germany appeared to be in favour of the idea, and South African president Nelson Mandela announced that his country would contribute troops if the UN asked for them. In an interview to the daily *Libération*, President Mobutu, clearly without consulting his government, agreed to the plan: 'The UN Secretary General and President Chirac told me about it, and I have said yes. I accept a *de facto* truce'.[3] Despite this apparent consensus, vetoes were immediately expressed: on 7 November, Kabila excluded French participation; the next day, Bizimungu opposed any French, Belgian or Rwandan involvement.

In Resolution 1078, adopted on 9 November, the Security Council recommended that a multinational force be set up 'for humanitarian purposes in eastern Zaire'. However, the idea was only adopted in principle and member states were asked to 'draw up a concept of operations and

---

[3] *Libération*, 9–10 November 1996.

framework for a humanitarian task force, with military assistance if necessary'. At the same time, the UN mediator appointed on 30 October,
Canadian Raymond Chrétien, started his diplomatic mission. As he shuttled between Kinshasa and Kigali, it was clear that he understood who
was fighting whom: he was in Kigali on 8 November, in Kinshasa on 9
November, and back in Kigali on 11 November. Likewise, on 11 November,
European commissioner Bonino travelled from Kinshasa to Kigali, where
she chided the Americans for sabotaging the military–humanitarian intervention, rightly so as it turned out. The State Department declined to
commit itself 'in the absence of a coherent plan', which was indeed lacking. At the same time, several African countries (Chad, Congo, Ethiopia,
Mali, Senegal and South Africa) indicated that they were ready to commit troops. For its part, the OAU demanded 'with insistence the rapid
deployment of a neutral force' and insisted on the need for a clear mandate. It also underlined 'the need (...) to create a mechanism ensuring the
effective participation of Africa'.

On 12 November, Canada offered to assume the command of the multinational force. For those opposed to deployment, in particular Rwanda
and the AFDL, the threat became real. They feared that the intervention would have two consequences contrary to their interests: on the
one hand, it could stabilise the military situation and thus prevent the
further progression of the rebellion, even allowing the Zairean army to
reorganise; on the other, the problem of the Rwandan refugees could
remain unsolved, and the Rwandan security objectives would not be
achieved.[4] The latter risk became even more real when Canada stated on
14 November that it would accept the command only if disarmament
and separation was not to be part of the mandate, a position shared by
the United States when announcing that they were willing to contribute
1000 troops. However, this position was contrary to that of the UNHCR,
the European Union and several NGOs who all felt that separation was
to be one of the main objectives of any kind of intervention, a point of
view also expressed by the Nairobi Summit (5–6 November), the Security
Council (10 November) and the OAU (11 November). It was soon to

---

[4] This concern was openly shared by those close to the Rwandan regime. Thus, Belgian
Senator Alain Destexhe published an op-ed piece in *Le Monde* of 14 November 1996
under the title 'Contre une intervention au Kivu' ('Against intervention in Kivu'). He
claimed that the refugees would return to Rwanda only 'if they are forced to by power or
by hunger'. Coming from a former general secretary of Médecins sans frontiers, this position was particularly cynical, especially knowing what the fate of these refugees 'forced
(to return) by power or by hunger' eventually became.

become clear that the United States and Canada did not really intend to support an international force.

Despite all the ambiguities, the preparations seemed to genuinely continue. On 13 November, a team of forty American army personnel, accompanied by some British, Canadian and French, arrived in the region to assess the humanitarian situation and the military opportunities. In his famous interview in *The Washington Post* of 9 July 1997 (see above), Kagame revealed that, while Canadian, American and British diplomats and officers were in Kigali preparing for deployment (or acting as if they were), he was busy 'burying that plan'. An essential element of his strategy was the management of information, something Kigali did very skilfully (see below). In order to avoid the 'CNN Effect' ('there is no humanitarian disaster and, therefore, no reason to intervene, if there are no images'),[5] the area surrounding Goma was closed off to both humanitarian organisations and impatient but powerless journalists.[6] The manipulation of opinion was constant and frustrations accumulated. A doctor on the spot said he feared that 'the Tutsi military authorities will again stage a "show" and then block everything, just as they did before'.[7] On 15 November, ten days after Kabila announced a 'unilateral cease-fire' to please the international community, the RPA attacked the huge camp at Mugunga and forced many of the refugees into Rwanda. In a matter of days, hundreds of thousands crossed the Zairean–Rwandan border.

This massive return seemed at first glance to confirm the thesis of the 'refugee-hostages', because it appeared that the refugees, freed from their intimidators, 'voted with their feet'. However, the situation was less obvious, even though, as said before, intimidation and violence were mechanisms used to control these populations. First, the refugees did not have much of a choice, as they were fired upon and the only safe passage opened to them led into Rwanda. Second, the fact that the refugees interviewed by the international press upon their arrival in Gisenyi claimed they were 'happy to come home' and expressed relief at being 'freed from their intimidators' was not convincing for those who know how Rwandans communicate.[8] For many returnees, declarations of that kind

---

[5] The editorial in the Belgian daily *Le Soir* of 12 November 1996 was entitled 'Attend-on CNN?' ('Do we wait for CNN?').

[6] This is well described in L. Bijard, 'Zaïre. La faim fera le travail ...', *Le Nouvel Observateur*, 14–20 November 1996.

[7] *Le Soir*, 13 November 1996.

[8] On this, see the interesting article by C.M. Overdulve, 'Fonction de la langue et de la communication au Rwanda', *Nouvelle Revue de science missionnaire*, 1997, pp. 271–283.

were part of a survival strategy: they said what they felt they had to say in view of the expectations of those who held the power over life and death in their hands; saying the opposite would entail all the unpleasant consequences of being considered *interahamwe*. Third, observers were struck by the fact that the refugees walked back like sheep, without showing the slightest enthusiasm for being 'freed' and returning to their home country at last. Bradol and Guibert noted that 'we are far removed from the naive image showing a population, taken hostage by the authors of the 1994 genocide, who decided to return spontaneously and in security, after being 'freed' by Laurent-Désiré Kabila's troops'.[9] In addition, as will be seen later, this massive return, while initially looking like a great victory for the RPF, did not solve its problem. On the contrary, in November 1996 Rwanda re-imported its civil war.

This repatriation was not the end of the discussion on the deployment of an international force, and a cynical game of figures started with regard to the number of refugees remaining in Zaire and their humanitarian condition. Indeed, hundreds of thousands of refugees did not return and moved westwards after abandoning their camps in North and South Kivu. Colette Braeckman even argued that the AFDL/RPA deliberately forced the refugees from Bukavu deeper into Zaire, because they were considered politically more difficult to deal with than those from Goma. Thus a column of refugees who moved from Bukavu to Goma with the intent of crossing into Rwanda was stopped and diverted to Walikale, from whence they continued towards Kisangani.[10] This was to be the beginning of a dramatic trek, which will be described later.

On the very same day of the attack against the Mugunga camp, the Security Council voted in Resolution 1080, allowing for deployment under Chapter VII of the UN Charter. The Rwandan Ambassador at the UN immediately claimed that the force was no longer needed for the protection of the refugees; the next day, Kabila expressed the same point of view. Some 30 Canadian military were prevented from leaving Kigali airport and a further 100 were blocked in Nairobi pending authorisation to land in Kigali. On 19 November, the Rwandan foreign minister confirmed that the international force was no longer needed and that, at any rate, Rwandan territory could not be used for such an intervention.[11] The

---

[9] J.-H. Bradol and A. Guibert, 'Le temps des assassins ...', *op. cit.*, p. 139.
[10] C. Braeckman, 'La campagne victorieuse de l'AFDL', in: *Kabila prend le pouvoir*, *op. cit.*, pp. 72–73.
[11] AFP, Kigali, 19 November 1996.

next day, Kagame declared that most refugees had returned; 'just a few scattered refugees' remained in Zaire and he accused the humanitarian agencies of exaggerating the figures. At the same time, the WFP estimated that 700,000 refugees were unaccounted for.

The new situation created by the massive repatriation and the uncertainty surrounding the number of those remaining in Zaire reopened the opposition between two positions, one defended by France, the other by the United States. Whilst President Chirac insisted that 'the situation is far from being stabilised' and that international intervention remained necessary, the United States suggested reviewing the mission and made it clear that their support would be only logistical. Canadian Defence Minister Doug Young indicated that 'it is possible that the evolution of the situation renders this mission unnecessary, at least at the military level'. The day before a meeting scheduled in Stuttgart on 21 November to discuss deployment, U.S. Ambassador in Kigali Robert Gribbin stated in a BBC interview that the number of remaining refugees in Zaire amounted to 'some tens or twenties of thousands, rather than a large mass'.[12] On the same day, U.S. General Edwin Smith, during an inspection visit to Kigali, announced that the international force was no longer necessary. He claimed that '202,000' refugees remained in Zaire and that many of them would probably not return to Rwanda. Smith made these statements at the very moment the UNHCR stated that the number of those stranded in Zaire could be as high as 600,000.[13] The momentum decreased rapidly. The Stuttgart meeting ended without a real decision: the governments involved stating that they would 'study a number of options'. On 25 November, UK Defence Minister Malcolm Rifkind stated that 'the day of a decision has not yet come'.[14] The protests of his Belgian colleague Jean-Pol Poncelet and European Commissioner Emma Bonino did not help.[15]

---

[12] As a reaction, the organisation Refugees International asked for Gribbin to be recalled for having deliberately lied about the plight of the refugees.

[13] The Rwandan authorities of course supported the American thesis. Presidential advisor Claude Dusaidi claimed that 'the UNHCR always exaggerates the figures. We believe the American estimates to be correct'.

[14] The British position has consistently been favourable to the rebellion and its sponsors. Thus, during closed door consultations which preceded a declaration by the Security Council asking for 'an end to hostilities and the withdrawal of all external forces, mercenaries included', the UK expressed reservations, particularly with regard to a reference to the inviolability of borders (AFP, New York (UN), 8 February 1997).

[15] Early February 1997, when visiting the camp of Tingi-Tingi, Bonino denounced what she described as an 'international scandal'. She just met 'these people 'who do not exist'. All

By the end of November, it was clear that the intervention was not going to take place, although it was largely admitted that hundreds of thousands of refugees remained in Zaire without assistance or protection while an increasing number of sources reported that these refugees were the victims of large-scale massacres. The cynical numbers game continued up to the last moment. On 6 December, the Commander Designate of the force, Canadian General Maurice Baril, stated that air reconnaissance missions could not find more than 165,000 refugees, while the UN Department of Humanitarian Affairs claimed that 'the most basic arithmetic shows that a minimum of 439,500 remain in Zaire'.[16]

The formal abandonment of the international force was decided in New York on 13 December, following the presentation by Raymond Chrétien of a report he made after a five-week mission in the region.[17] After having stated a week earlier that 'the humanitarian force is indispensable',[18] he now felt that 'the usefulness of the intervention of a multinational force will decrease'. What he saw on the ground had been 'very encouraging', all the more so since the rebels had let him know that they would not oppose humanitarian actions, an assurance which, as will be seen, was to be cruelly contradicted by subsequent events.[19] Cynically or naively, Canadian prime minister Jean Chrétien declared that the international force had served as 'a catalyst' for the return of hundreds of thousands of refugees; his foreign minister Lloyd Axworthy added that 'the fact that this return has taken place at the time the international force was announced, is no coincidence'. That is true, but obviously not in the sense suggested by Chrétien and Axworthy, as it has become apparent that it was the prospect of deployment that prompted General Kagame to 'clean out the camps'. Lionel Rosenblatt, chairman of Refugees International, stated on 4 December 1996 before the House Subcommittee on International

the Generals and international powers, with their planes and radar and 'hardware', have never been able to locate them' (AFP, Kinshasa, 2 February 1997).
[16] Reuters, Butembo, 7 December 1996.
[17] AFP, New York (UN), 13 December 1996.
[18] *Le Monde*, 5 December 1996.
[19] A resolution carried by the European Parliament on 12 December did not have much influence. The Parliament expressed 'surprise over the reduction to a small staff in Uganda of a force of 10,000 initially foreseen' and stated that it was 'unacceptable that the deployment of an international force to get humanitarian aid to the refugees is being obstructed' (AFP, Strasbourg, 12 December 1996). The final statement voted in on 6 December by the Franco-African summit in Ouagadougou asked for the deployment of an international force. Rwanda was the only participant expressing reservations over the adopted text.

Operations and Human Rights that 'a reversed form of the "CNN factor" is at play here. As the humanitarian disaster in eastern Zaire is not shown on television, many people do not believe it is taking place (or feel they can afford to ignore it politically)'.

As a matter of fact, despite appearances, the international force was never seriously considered. An officer involved in the operation testified: 'It was clear from Day One in mission planning that began in Germany that when the One Stars [Brigadier-Generals] came in there was an acceptance that the mission would never happen. Still, planning went ahead up and down through the national structures'.[20] Disinformation, dubbed 'Operation Restore Silence' by Oxfam emergencies director Nick Stockton, in which 'the U.S., U.K. and other governments (...) managed the magical disappearance',[21] was crucial: the cynical numbers game and the manipulation of information have been decisive in a process that proved extremely costly in terms of human lives.

### 3.2 CRIMES AGAINST HUMANITY: GENOCIDE?

As has been seen hitherto, sources on the ground mentioned massacres against Rwandan and Burundian refugees and certain Zairean groups from the early days of the rebellion onwards.[22] However, international opinion initially reasoned in terms of a 'humanitarian drama' rather than in terms of crimes against humanity.[23] At the end of 1996 and in early 1997, when the size of the massacres became increasingly known, more precise accusations were levelled and new attempts were made to resuscitate the aborted international intervention. The AFDL felt the danger when, after Belgium accused Rwanda of engaging thousands of troops in the rebellion (see above), the Belgian foreign minister went to Washington and New York. According to the AFDL, his mission was to 'try and renew the possibility of a military intervention in the crisis of our country'.[24] This was probably true, as Minister Derycke and his Canadian colleague

---

[20] N. Gowing, *New challenges and problems...*, *op. cit.*, p. 56.
[21] *Idem, ibid.*
[22] For an attempt at a legal explanation of these crimes, see V. Parqué, F. Reyntjens, 'Crimes contre l'humanité dans l'ex-Zaïre: une réalité?', in: F. Reyntjens, S. Marysse (Eds.), *L'Afrique des grands lacs. Annuaire 1997–1998*, Paris, L'Harmattan, 1998, pp. 273–306.
[23] It is interesting to note that similar confusion, involuntary for some, deliberate for others, had surrounded the genocide in Rwanda two and a half years earlier.
[24] AFP, Goma, 2 February 1997.

Lloyd Axworthy discussed the prospects of a multinational force with
Kofi Annan, the then UN Secretary General. In an interview with *Le Vif/
L'Express* of 14 February, Derycke virulently denounced the 'lack of EU
and US interest' toward the crisis in the Great Lakes region.

This feeling was shared by the French Secretary of State for Humanitarian Action, Xavier Emmanuelli. During a meeting with Kofi Annan,
he indicated he was 'among those who regret that Resolution 1080 [of
November 1996 concerning the international force] was never implemented'. While admitting that there were political problems, he asked
'not to write off these people on the loss side of the balance sheet'.[25]
The idea was picked up by the UN Secretary General after a meeting in
Paris on 1 March with French foreign minister Hervé de Charette: 'The
humanitarian situation is very serious. I hope that it will be possible to
convince the member states to reconsider the decision to send a multinational force to Zaire'.[26] When returning to the theme in Kinshasa on
10 March, Emmanuelli issued a real distress signal: 'Without organised
help, all those men, women and children adrift are condemned to death
through starvation, exhaustion, illness or assassination by those who
have been chasing them for months'.[27] President Chirac launched a sol-
emn appeal for 'the implementation of humanitarian intervention that is
urgently needed in Zaire'.[28] However, because London and The Hague,
close to the regime in Kigali and, by extension, to the AFDL, were firmly
opposed to the 'international mechanism of humanitarian protection'
proposed by the French, the EU failed to come to an understanding, and
the project was finally buried in mid-March. Dutch cooperation minister
Jan Pronk, who never hid his sympathies in the region, went as far as to
claim that 'France is attempting to start a discussion on a situation that
does not exist'.[29]

In the meantime, the 'G-word' entered public discourse.[30] On 24
February 1997, the *Osservatore Romano* denounced the indifference
of the international community towards a 'creeping genocide'. The next

[25] AFP, New York (UN), 20 February 1997.
[26] AFP, Paris, 1 March 1997.
[27] *Le Monde*, 12 March 1997.
[28] *Idem.*
[29] *Le Monde*, 13 March 1997.
[30] In fact, the term had been used months earlier, but in a less clear fashion and in the context of the 'humanitarian disaster'. Thus, on 25 October 1996 Emma Bonino affirmed
that the international community 'must clearly say that new genocide, which seems to be
under preparation, will not be tolerated'. The *Osservatore Romano* of 28 October mentioned 'the threat of genocide'. On 9 November, UN Secretary General Boutros-Ghali

day, the spokesperson for the Belgian Secretary of State for Development Cooperation Réginald Moreels stated that 'we have received information from different sources in the region that genocide is indeed taking place'.[31] This statement led to angry exchanges in the Belgian Parliament. Accused of 'revisionism' by members with close links to the Rwandan regime, Moreels reacted: 'It is not because one condemns the massacres and the threat of genocide in the opposite sense that one can be treated as a revisionist of the (Rwandan) genocide of 1994'. Senator Destexhe, whose cynical attitude toward the plight of the refugees has been noted above, was not to be moved: 'It is your conscience against mine. Each time you use the term genocide (with regard to the situation of the refugees) you will find me in your way'.[32]

Likewise, some scholars engaged in denial and rejected the accusations levelled against the AFDL/RPA without even examining them. Thus Christian Scherrer[33] claimed that the accusations were 'out of context and unfair if not baseless': 'the genuine refugees (...) have taken the chance to return to Rwanda (...). Those who continued running away from their homes must have had good reason to do so. (...) The vast majority of women and children have returned to Rwanda (...). It seems highly unlikely that the AFDL has a policy of massacres and genocidal atrocities'.[34] He was to be terribly contradicted. No less suspect sources attempted to put up a smoke screen. Ambassador Gribbin systematically played down the gravity of the refugees' fate: between Kisangani and Ubundu, 'hundreds, if not thousands of people perished'; in Mbandaka, 'several hundred or more died'.[35] As will be seen later, these were gross underestimates, and the 'hundreds' turned out to be tens of thousands. The Hema[36] bishop of Goma, Mgr. Faustin Ngabu, claimed that 'he not even once heard about large-scale massacres' and did not exclude

warned against the threat of the Rwandan refugees becoming the victims of 'genocide by starvation'.

[31] AFP, Brussels, 25 February 1997.

[32] Belgian Senate, *Compte-rendu analytique*, session of 18 March 1997.

[33] A former member of the UN Human Rights Field Operation in Rwanda (UNHRFOR), Scherrer defended positions very close to the RPF. See C.P. Scherrer, *Ethnisierung und Völkermord in Zentralafrika: Genozid in Rwanda, Bürgerkrieg in Burundi und die Rolle der Weltgemeinschaft*, Frankfurt, Campus, 1997.

[34] C.P. Scherrer, Central Africa: Conflict Impact Assessment and Policy Options, Copenhagen Peace Research Institute, Working Paper 25/1997, pp. 61–62.

[35] R.E. Gribbin, *In the Aftermath of Genocide...*, *op. cit.*, p. 219.

[36] As will be seen later, in the Ituri region (northeastern Zaire) the Hema are a minority traditionally engaged in cattle-breeding. In their relations with the Lendu majority, they are in a situation comparable to the Hima in Ankole and the Tutsi in Rwanda and Burundi.

the possibility of 'manipulation'. Revealingly, he added that the rebels 'bring to Zaire the hope of new leaders for the salvation of the nation'. Paradoxically, using an argument developed by the Hutu extremists to deny the 1994 genocide, Mgr. Ngabu asked the question 'why always present the facts as massacres of the innocent when two armies are engaged in a war?'[37] A similar interpretation was proposed by Belgian journalist Colette Braeckman who wrote that 'these groups of fleeing people were more the shreds of a defeated army (armed men surrounded by civilians) than genuine refugees in the strict sense of the word'.[38] However, it has been seen that not more than 10–15% of the refugees were suspected of being involved in the genocide. Bradol and Guibert have noted that 'this type of presentation results more from a political will to deny the responsibility of the AFDL in the massacre of refugees than from a serious study of the (refugee) population structure'. They concluded that 'to assimilate women and children of under fifteen, i.e. the large majority of this (refugee) population, with the "shreds of a defeated army" is an attempt to justify the unjustifiable: their physical extermination'.[39]

While the reality of massive slaughter was undeniable, the international community did not budge. On 24 February, the Council of the EU decided to do nothing, except 'examine' the possibility of sending a 'fact-finding mission' that was never to materialise. Only when it was too late for the victims were efforts deployed to at least establish who was responsible for the disaster. This was the beginning of the saga of the UN inquiry, which was to last for over a year.

This protracted process will not be discussed in detail here,[40] and will be limited to a summary presentation. On 6 March 1997, faced with increasingly numerous and precise accusations, the High Commissioner for Human Rights proposed sending a human rights observer mission to Eastern Zaire and asked the special rapporteur for Zaire to look into the allegations. The next day, the Chair of the Security Council agreed to send a mission to the region. As a result of a first summary report, which mentioned widespread massacres, the UN Human Rights Commission

---

In the context of a 'coalition of minorities' in the region, the Tutsi sympathies of Mgr. Ngabu were well known.

[37] *Le Monde*, 12 March 1997; *La Libre Belgique*, 13 March 1997.

[38] C. Braeckman, 'Zaire: récit d'une prise de pouvoir annoncée', *Politique internationale*, 1997, 76, 68.

[39] J.-H. Bradol, A. Guibert, 'Le temps des assassins ...', *op. cit.*, p. 137.

[40] A detailed survey and analysis can be found in V. Parque, F. Reyntjens, 'Crimes contre l'humanité ...', *op. cit.*

decided to despatch a three-member commission, which included the special rapporteur Roberto Garretón. Difficulties immediately arose and the AFDL refused to allow the commission to move freely in the territory it occupied. The team was forced to leave, but assured that it was ready to return once assurances were given of 'total and unconditional cooperation, including guarantees of security'. After Kabila came to power, he appeared to accept the principle of an inquiry and promised that a commission to that effect would be given access to all areas it wished to visit.

However, when a preparatory team went to Congo, as Zaire had been renamed by then, the mission proved particularly difficult because of the obstacles put in its way by the new regime. As early as 19 June 1997, *The Washington Post* learned that Kabila had warned local authorities not to help the mission in locating mass graves and contacting direct witnesses of the massacres. According to the same article, Kabila and his government were under intense pressure by Rwanda and Uganda to sabotage the inquiry. A new mission sent in August 1997 encountered problems similar to the previous ones. It remained blocked in Kinshasa for weeks and, on 1 October, Kofi Annan decided to recall the team 'for consultations'. When the team was eventually redeployed on 11 December, new difficulties immediately emerged in the form of travel restrictions, 'spontaneous' demonstrations organised by the government, intimidation of witnesses and physical threats against members of the team. On 13 February 1998, the team's number two, Zimbabwean Andrew Chigovera resigned, stating that he had 'great difficulty in believing that an environment favourable to an independent and impartial inquiry on human rights existed in the RDC or could present itself'.[41] In a *note verbale* presented to the Congolese government on 26 February 1998, the team said it was 'extremely preoccupied' by the way in which it had been treated. The government replied by accusing it of 'interfering in the internal affairs of our state'. When the team moved to Goma, one of the staff was arrested and his documents were seized or copied. This was the proverbial last straw.

Although the team left Congo, this time not to return, it did produce a report which Secretary General Kofi Annan submitted to the Security Council on 29 June 1998, after having communicated it to Congo and Rwanda, the two countries challenged in the report. The report concluded that the RPA had committed large-scale war crimes and crimes

[41] AFP, Kinshasa, 13 February 1997.

against humanity. It went further by suggesting that genocide might have occurred. However, this needed additional investigation: 'The systematic massacre of those (Hutu refugees) remaining in Zaire was an abhorrent crime against humanity, but the underlying rationale for the decision is material to whether these killings constituted genocide, that is, a decision to eliminate, in part, the Hutu ethnic group'.[42] In letters of 25 June, the Congolese and Rwandan missions to the UN transmitted their government's response; they predictably rejected all the allegations.[43] On 13 July, the Security Council condemned the massacres, other atrocities and violations of international humanitarian law, including crimes against humanity. It requested that the Congolese and Rwandan governments carry out inquiries and punish the guilty. By demanding a report on the steps taken by 15 October at the latest, the Council kept its options option, as it envisaged, if need be, taking the 'additional measures' necessary to judge the culprits. Without saying so explicitly, it thus left the possibility of taking them before an international tribunal, an option suggested by the inquiry report.

International human rights organisations expressed their disappointment. Amnesty International labelled the declaration 'weak': 'It is surprising that the Security Council has escaped its responsibilities by asking the authorities identified as guilty of these horrible atrocities to take the guilty to justice'. The organisation could only 'hope that on 15 October, the Security Council will place human rights, peace and the security of ordinary people above political expediency'.[44] The fear implicit in this statement was to prove justified, as 15 October was to pass without the issue returning to the agenda, and it has not done so since. Of course, the situation was very different by then, as the second war had started in the meantime (see below). For all concerned parties, the message was clear: impunity was to prevail. As will be seen, a year later, they were to

---

[42] UN Security Council, Report of the Investigative Team Charged with Investigating Serious Violations of Human Rights and International Humanitarian Law in the Democratic Republic of Congo, S/1998/581, 29 June 1998, para. 96.

[43] After a new war broke out between Rwanda and the DRC (see below), the Congolese government was to recognise the facts, but blamed them on Rwanda. Minister Victor Mpoyo claimed that the AFDL was unaware of the massacres: 'The Rwandan army controlled the area and, therefore, the information. (...) We could not imagine that those men who survived a genocide could behave in such a bloodthirsty fashion'. Even after coming to power in Kinshasa, 'we were gagged by the Rwandans on this subject' (*Libération*, 17 September 1998).

[44] Amnesty International, UN Security Council shamefully abandons victims in Democratic Republic of Congo, 15 July 1998.

remember that message, and a new round of massive human rights violations was to start.

As a matter of fact, the UN Investigative Team did not add much to what was already known. Numerous other sources provided data that was precise, emanating from different quarters and collected independently of each other. The accumulation and cross-checking of this documentary mass gives a convincing idea of events which the UN inquiry has only confirmed and detailed on some points. In order to draft the summary analysis that follows, a large number of sources have been used, references to which are listed in a separate Appendix 1, in order to show how abundant the documentation is on this grave matter and how soon it was available. This extensive documentation outlines a number of coherent practices, which are briefly summarised in the following pages.[45]

## Attacks against Refugee Camps and Concentrations

Earlier the attacks on the refugee camps at the beginning of the war were discussed. Elements of the AFDL and, more so, of the RPA systematically shelled numerous camps in South and North Kivu, where massacres were also committed with light weapons. Since the first days of the 'rebellion', attacks had taken place against the camps of Kagunga, Runingo, Luberizi, Chimanga, Kashusha and Inera in South Kivu and Katale, Kahindo, Kibumba, Sake and Mugunga in North Kivu. Thousands of refugees, most of them unarmed civilians, were killed. These attacks continued and intensified as the refugees moved westwards. The largest massacres occurred between Shabunda and Kingulube, at Shanji, Walikale, Tingi-Tingi, Kasese and Biaro, and finally between Boende and Mbandaka. The report of the UN joint mission referred to information received concerning 134 sites where atrocities had been committed. At the end of May 1997, when the AFDL had taken control of the whole country, the UNHCR found that 246,000 refugees were unaccounted for. On 8 July 1997, the acting UN High Commissioner for Human Rights stated that 'about 200,000 Hutu refugees could well have been massacred'. After detailed calculations, Emizet arrives at a death toll of about 233,000.[46]

---

[45] Facts described here are not individually referenced, as they appear in several sources and because this would create a confusing accumulation of footnotes. All these data can be found in the sources listed in appendix 1. Also see K. Emizet, 'The Massacre of Refugees in Congo: a Case of UN Peacekeeping Failure and International Law', *The Journal of Modern African Studies*, 2000, 163–202.

[46] K. Emizet, 'The Massacre of Refugees ...', *op. cit.*, pp. 173–179.

MAP 6. Massacre of the Rwandan refugees.

It would be fastidious to describe or even simply enumerate the many massive and focused killings, most of which are quite well-documented by several independent sources. However, the nature and the extent of this tragedy can be illustrated with two examples. As the rebels were moving in, the refugees left Tingi-Tingi camp at the end of February 1997. They initially headed for Kisangani, but at Pene-Tungu they were diverted towards Ubundu by the FAZ, which wanted to prevent this wave of people from reaching Kisangani. In mid-March, the Tingi-Tingi survivors, who numbered approximately 135,000, set up camp near the villages of Biaro and Kasese on the railway line between Ubundu and Kisangani. Around mid-April, journalists and humanitarian agencies were denied access beyond km 42 of the railway line from Kisangani. The refugees were then out of reach of assistance or protection. On 17

April, between 200 and 400 'search and destroy' elements of the RPA landed in Kisangani and were despatched to the south and then, across the river, deployed to the camps.[47] Between 21 and 25 April, the camps were attacked by RPA and AFDL military. As in Kasese camp alone, 9000 refugees were, in UN terms, 'extremely vulnerable' and incapable of moving, the number of victims there probably exceeded 10,000; 2500 of them were children in a severe state of malnutrition. When assistance finally arrived in Biaro on 29 April, soldiers escorted the starving, sick and exhausted survivors to Ubundu, 80 km to the south, an area in turn declared a no-go zone. Several reporters who visited Kasese and Biaro after 28 April made analogous and incriminating observations. In Biaro they heard the sound of a digging machine requisitioned a week earlier by the rebels, but they were prevented from proceeding any further 'for reasons of security'. Congolese soldiers and civilians said there was an 'open air incinerator' at km 52, next to a quarry. A Belgian entrepreneur running a logging operation in the area confirmed this information to the author. A soldier told a photographer working for Associated Press that 'there is much work to do, digging up the bodies and burning them. When the UN eventually comes to investigate, there will be no evidence'.

The second example is the sequel to the first. About 45,000 survivors of the Kasese-Biaro carnage managed to escape through the forest to Opala via Yaleko. They continued their trek westwards towards Mbandaka, following the Ikela–Boende–Ingende–Wendji route. RPA/AFDL elements who chased them made a detour via Isangi–Yakuma–Djolu in an attempt to cut off the refugees at Boende. A phased massacre then began between Boende and Mbandaka. Thousands were killed in Boende and on the road from Boende to Nsamba, in Mpenzele, between Djoa and Ingende, in Wendji and, finally, in Mbandaka itself. The Mbandaka massacres are particularly incriminating for the RPA/AFDL, because all arriving refugees were disarmed on the orders of the

---

[47] It is interesting to note that this RPA 'cleansing team' arrived just two days after a visit to Kasese and Biaro by Dr. Ephraïm Kabyija, advisor in the Rwandan president's office and chairman of a commission for the repatriation and reintegration of refugees. Invited by the UNHCR, which wished to convince the Rwandan government to accept refugee repatriation by air rather than overland, Kabayija was thus able to exactly identify the refugees' location and transmit their whereabouts to the RPA. If this can be proven to be the case, he played the same role as 'facilitators' did elsewhere in eastern Zaire (see below). Kabayija subsequently became a Minister in the Rwandan government.

military governor of the Equateur region. In addition, the killings took place in front of numerous Mbankada residents who were profoundly shocked by the cruelties committed against inoffensive civilians.[48] The cross-checking of sources suggests an estimate of the number of victims in southern Equateur, *grosso modo* between Boende and Mbandaka, at about 15,000. This estimate includes those killed, those who died from illness and exhaustion and those who drowned in the Ruki and Zaire-Congo rivers.

### Humanitarian Assistance Withheld or Used as Bait

On a number of occasions, rebel forces and their Rwandan allies made it impossible to get humanitarian aid to starving, exhausted and sick refugees, either by blocking access to them or by relocating them out of the reach of assistance. As early as November 1996, humanitarian agencies were denied access to the area around Goma, declared a military zone. A similar decision was taken in Bukavu, where access was made impossible beyond a 30 km radius around the town; even within that radius, freedom of movement was severely restricted. It should be noted incidentally that this technique is similar to the one used by the RPF in Rwanda in 1994: on many occasions the areas where the RPA committed massacres were declared 'military zones' with prohibited access.[49] As has been hitherto discussed, similar strategies were used in April 1997 to the south of Kisangani: first Biaro and later Kasese were made no-go areas; next, when the humanitarian agencies were allowed in, the surviving refugees were herded to Ubundu, in turn declared inaccessible. In November 1996, Secretary General Boutros-Ghali claimed that 'two years ago, the international community was confronted with the genocide of the Tutsi by weapons. Today we are faced with the genocide of the Hutu by starvation'. Six months later, his successor Kofi Annan said that 'it is possible to kill by weapons or by hunger. The killing is done by hunger today'.

Humanitarian aid was also used as bait. Several sources mentioned a similar scheme used on a number of occasions. Humanitarian

---

[48] The combination of these two elements probably explains why the Congolese authorities were so opposed to the deployment to Mbandaka of the UN investigative team (see above).

[49] Examples can be found in S. Desouter, F. Reyntjens, *Rwanda. Les violations des droits de l'homme par le FPR/APR...*, *op. cit.*

organisations would typically locate the whereabouts of refugee concentrations and make them leave the bush. The area would then be declared a military zone with prohibited access. When the humanitarian agencies were allowed back in, the refugees had disappeared. This strategy used so-called 'facilitators', designated by the AFDL, who were supposedly in charge of liaison with the aid organisations, but who, in reality, directed the 'rebel' forces to the refugee concentrations. Thus a certain Marc Kazindu, described as 'Tutsi' without further specification, was mentioned as having 'facilitated' the massacres along the axes Bukavu–Walikale, Bukavu–Kalonge and Bukavu–Shabunda. In April, Rwandan refugees and village chiefs in South Kivu had asked the UNHCR and the ICRC to end the search for refugees, because they feared that these operations exposed both the refugees and certain Zairean groups to attacks by AFDL and RPA troops. In mid-May 1997, the ICRC decided to stop accepting the use of facilitators.

### Separation of Men from Women and Children

As early as 26 November 1996, in a communiqué concerning the Chimanga massacre, Amnesty International mentioned the separation of men and women/children by AFDL forces, after which the men were killed. In his report of 28 January 1997 special rapporteur Garretón found that 'many witnesses (...) underline the habit of the AFDL to separate men from women and children. The fate of the latter is generally known, but no news is heard from the former'. According to UN sources reported in *The Washington Post* of 19 June 1997, RPA 'Commander Jackson' admitted that it was his job to kill Hutu refugees, adding that all the male refugees were members of the *Interahamwe* militia responsible for the 1994 genocide of the Tutsi. Médecins sans frontières found that by March–April 1997 these gender distinctions were no longer made: women and children were exterminated too. A commander confirmed to MSF that 'all those who are in the bush are the enemy'. Indeed it is striking that the massacres became more widespread and systematic at the same time as the Biaro–Kasese episode. The supposition cannot be excluded that this was the moment the Rwandan authorities decided that repatriation was no longer a viable option, as the insurrection inside the country started to expand. Kigali realised that the civil war had been re-imported with the returnees in the autumn of 1996. The only avenue remaining then became pure and simple extermination.

## Involvement of the RPA

In most cases, the massacres were committed by the RPA, and maybe by their Congolese Tutsi allies, but much less so by the AFDL *per se*.[50] Kabila's aim was the overthrow of Mobutu and he had no particular interest in the extermination of the Rwandan refugees, that is to say, of the unarmed elements among them. An RPA colonel, interviewed in Goma by John Pomfret of *The Washington Post*, candidly admitted that the military campaign in Zaire had a dual objective: to take revenge against the Hutu and ensure the security of Rwanda. A Tutsi official at the Congolese Ministry of the Interior told the same reporter that the Rwandan troops and their Congolese allies had been given authorisation to attack the Hutu refugees, provided that they (the troops) contributed to the overthrow of Mobutu, another illustration that this was an extra-territorial extension of the Rwandan conflict into Zaire.[51]

While the initial massacres, for instance those at Lemera and Chimanga, were blamed on 'Banyamulenge rebels' or 'AFDL troops', it later became apparent that most killings were committed by elements of the RPA. As seen earlier, this was already the case when the camps were attacked in the Goma region, but the presence of Rwandan military could then still be seen in the context of the campaign aimed at putting a buffer zone into place (see above).

On the other hand, the operations of the RPA in the Kisangani and Boende–Mbandaka regions clearly focused on the refugees who became the object of a real extermination project. Many sources mentioned military who spoke Kinyarwanda and/or who wore uniforms donated to the RPA by Germany. As previously stated, several witnesses saw Rwandan 'search and destroy' units land at Kisangani, to be deployed on the Kisangani–Ubundu axis. Names of Rwandan officers were cited, but the fact that they used their (real or fake) first names renders their identification difficult. However, it is possible to establish the implication of James Kabarebe, who was later to become Chief of Staff of the Congolese army, Godfrey Kabanda and Jackson Nkurunziza (alias Jack

---

[50] At any rate, apart from Kisase's men (see below) and the Banyamulenge, the 'AFDL *per se*' did not amount to much in the early stages of the war.

[51] General Kagame implicitly admitted this reality when he expressed surprise at the emotion surrounding the fate of the refugees: 'People see this in terms of human rights (...), which is a poor analysis. One must understand that every conflict is not bad. There are conflicts that are a sort of purification. In certain cases, conflicts erupt in order to make a real transformation possible' (AP, Kigali, 7 June 1997).

Nziza), nicknamed 'The Exterminator', who is also suspected of the murder of Kisase Ngandu in January 1997 (see below). The Mbandaka massacres were organised by Colonels Richard and Wilson, nicknamed 'Khadafi', while the officer commanding the Katangese gendarmes, Gaston Munyangu, formally in charge of the military region, was unable to oppose them. Congolese elements of the AFDL showed their powerless reprobation of these practices. Under the cover of anonymity, some of them expressed their regret to the press, for example, during a moving testimony broadcast by French television on 4 June 1997.

## Massacres of Other Groups

Much has been said about the fate of the Rwandan refugees, but Zairean groups were also the victims of very grave abuse in the area controlled by the rebellion, particularly in the Kivu region. Many civilian Fulero, Bembe, Vira and, in particular, Zairean Hutu were killed, followed later by Hunde and Nyanga when the Mai-mai turned their weapons against the AFDL. The most significant massacres took place in North Kivu, specifically in the zones of Masisi and Rutshuru. Adding up the figures provided by several documents emanating from Congolese sources in the region, some of which are very detailed, the toll of Congolese victims could well exceed 15,000.

Finally it must be noted that many Burundian refugees living in South Kivu shared the fate of their Rwandan companions. Many were killed when their camps were attacked or while fleeing to the west with the Rwandans. Others drowned, together with many Congolese, when they attempted to cross Lake Tanganyika in search of safety. Others still were massacred by the Burundian army when they were forcibly repatriated to Burundi, especially at Gatumba border post, but also elsewhere along the Ruzizi river, which they attempted to cross in order to reach the Burundian provinces of Bubanza and Cibitoke.[52]

### 3.3  THE FORCE OF MANIPULATION

As already mentioned, a detailed study by Nik Gowing provides some useful insights as to how this tragedy was possible, despite everyone

---

[52] In a joint communiqué released on 7 November 1996, the UN special rapporteurs for Rwanda, Burundi and Zaire expressed concern over the large number of 'disappearances' of men, separated from women and children, at the Gatumba transit centre: 'Only women and children are allowed to pass, while the fate of the men is uncertain (...) Allegations of massacres of many refugees or returnees in the Gatumba perimeter add to the consternation'.

concerned being aware of it. The central pillar of the strategy of Rwanda and the AFDL was the management of information. The technique of the 'closure of the conflict scene' was successfully used by the RPF in Rwanda: Kagame confirmed that, since early 1994, 'the aim was to let them [the NGOs and the press] continue their work, but deny them what would be dangerous to us'.[53] Intimidation was the next tool: 'Kagame does not like NGOs, so he paralysed them completely and terrorised them. If he did not like what they did with information, he kicked them out'.[54] Likewise, reporters 'knew the Rwandan government could make life unpleasant'.[55] The fear of expulsion was constant and, in certain cases, justified.[56] An ICRC delegate went further: 'I was scared that we would have a full stop, then a dead delegate at the end of sentences in reports'.[57] This fear was reinforced by monitoring and leaks: thus 'one particular NGO partial to the Rwandan government' (USCR, IRC?) would fax sit-reps directly to Kagame's office.[58] Another source explained how 'I was present in the (Rwandan) Ministry of Defence as (...) information would come across the fax lines from NGOs in Britain. One NGO was particularly notorious on this'.[59] Along the same lines, a humanitarian agent indicated that 'if the Save the Children person in Bukavu radioed that he had refugees (...), then those refugees would be under threat because networks were bugged'.[60] Humanitarian staff themselves were uneasy, a feeling exacerbated by the assassination in January 1997 of three Spanish Médecins du Monde workers by the RPA.

The international media became 'a tool for Rwandan manipulation': the Kigali government 'blocked information from inside the conflict zone', 'prevented the deployment of the multinational force' and 'wrong-footed the international perceptions of what was taking place'.[61] The 'natural sympathy', which benefited the RPF in the press played a considerable role. The logic being used was that of the 'good guys versus the bad guys', a logic dear to many Americans: fully banking on the pretence that 'its people were a victim of genocide', the RPF were the good guys. A number

---

[53] N. Gowing, *New challenges and problems...*, *op. cit.*, p. 15.
[54] *Idem*, p. 22.
[55] *Idem*, p. 36.
[56] *Idem*, p. 43, 52.
[57] *Idem*, p. 45.
[58] *Idem*, p. 47.
[59] *Idem*, p. 50.
[60] *Idem*, *ibid.*
[61] *Idem*, p. 38.

of reporters were 'RPF groupies'; one of them recognised that 'journalists and NGOs were in bed with the RPF'.[62] At any rate, the choice was simple: 'The RPA's line was that you are either with the RPA or against them'.[63] However, even though the skills of the RPF, which realised as early as in 1990 that a modern war is as media-oriented as it is military, were undeniable, these manipulation and disinformation techniques were only able to succeed with the complicity of governments, organisations, journalists and scholars who threw their weight behind the regime in Kigali and chose to ignore the 'collateral damage' caused by those they supported. In a detailed and convincing demonstration, Johan Pottier explains why and how the RPF succeeded in 'converting international feelings of guilt and ineptitude into admissions that the Front deserves to have the monopoly of knowledge construction'.[64] He shows that the RPF's 'rewriting project' benefited from the empathy and services not only of (mainly Anglophone) journalists unfamiliar with the region, but also of newcomer academics, diplomats and aid workers.

[62] *Idem*, p. 41.
[63] *Idem*, p. 62.
[64] J. Pottier, *Re-Imagining Rwanda: Conflict, Survival and Disinformation in the Late Twentieth Century*, Cambridge, Cambridge University Press, 2002, p. 202.

# 4

# The Fall of the Mobutist State

Having analysed the role played by external actors in Chapter 2, it is important to now return to the unravelling of the war, by looking at the domestic players, the futile and ambiguous attempts at diplomatic management of the crisis, the ineptitude and indeed self-destruction of the Zairean political system, and the impact of the rebels' victory on the regional political situation.

## 4.1 THE PLAYERS

### Laurent-Désiré Kabila and the Alliance des Forces Démocratiques pour la Libération du Congo-Zaïre (AFDL)

The AFDL was officially[1] founded in Lemera (South Kivu) on 18 October 1996, more than a month after the beginning of the 'Banyamulenge rebellion'. The document detailing the founding of the AFDL was signed by representatives of four political movements: the Parti de la Révolution Populaire (PRP; represented by L.D. Kabila), the Conseil National de Résistance pour la Démocratie (CNRD; represented by Kisase Ngandu), the Mouvement Révolutionnaire pour la Libération du Zaïre (MRLZ; represented by Masasu Nindaga) and the Alliance Démocratique des Peuples (represented by Déo Bugera). The document did not say much, other than that the decision-making body was the Alliance's Council composed of representatives of the four organisations, that a Liaison Bureau was to be created and that Laurent Kabila was to act as the

---

[1] As will be seen later, the AFDL was, in fact, created in Kigali.

AFDL's spokesman.[2] The statutes adopted in Goma on 4 January 1997[3] provided for the merger of the founding parties 'into a large political movement aimed at assembling all the live forces of the Congolese nation'. The bodies were the Congress, the Council and the Executive Committee, which had fifteen members, among whom was the chairman, also in charge of the Department of Defence. From 'spokesman', Kabila formally[4] became the chairman of the AFDL, although no decision to that effect by a competent body of the movement is known, a preview of how he was to function later as president.

Among the component parts of the Alliance, the PRP and Kabila were not unknown.[5] Kabila was among the leading figures of the Congolese rebellions of 1964–65: vice-chairman in charge of external relations and trade in the provisional government of the National Liberation Council (Conseil national de libération [CNL]), Eastern Section, in Albertville (Kalemie) in July 1964, Kabila became the second vice-chairman of the Supreme Council of the Revolution (Conseil suprême de la révolution [CSR]) in April 1965. He then left the Congo and lived in several East African countries. In 1967, he returned and created the PRP on 24 December 1967 in the area of Fizi-Baraka south of Uvira. His Marxist–Leninist-inspired political action was based on the analysis of what he saw as the errors of the previous rebellions:[6]

• Lack of political education;
• Dependency on the outside, which ignores the 'qualitative contradictions' of Congolese society;
• Neglect of the countryside;
• 'Tribalist and sectarian' nature of the war;

[2] The text of the 'Lemera Accord' can be found in G. De Villers, J.-C. Willame, *République démocratique du Congo. Chronique politique d'un entre-deux-guerres, octobre 1996–juillet 1998*, Brussels-Paris, Institut Africain/L'Harmattan, Cahiers Africains, No. 35–36, 1998, p. 20.
[3] Text in *Idem*, pp. 27–31.
[4] The word 'formally' is used because Kabila already referred to himself as the chairman before 4 January 1997. In an interview with *Le Monde* of 13 November 1996, he said he was 'in a way' the AFDL's chairman.
[5] A biography of Kabila can be found in E. Kennes, *Essai biographique sur Laurent-Désiré Kabila*, Brussels/Paris, Institut Africain/L'Harmattan, Cahiers Africains, 57–58–59, 2003, 436 pp. A hagiography of limited interest also exists: G. Mukendi, B. Kasonga, *Kabila. Le retour du Congo*, Ottignies, Quorum, 1997.
[6] PRP, *Makosa saba katika mapinduzi ya kwanza* ('The seven errors of the last revolution'); see C.K. Lumuna Sando, *Zaïre: quel changement pour quelles structures?*, Brussels, Editions A.F.R.I.C.A., n.d., pp. 141–142.

- Struggle for power, individual reputation and nepotism;
- Lack of coordination between the fighters and the people;
- Lack of a revolutionary party, in the absence of which a revolution is impossible.

Despite the fact that this analysis was by and large adequate, in reality, the PRP was unable to get anywhere beyond a low-intensity guerrilla war waged by a small and peripheral *maquis*. A few actions, such as the kidnapping of foreigners and attacks on Moba and Kalemie, were of little operational value and did not really bother the central government. During this period, Kabila survived economically thanks to commercial activities, for example, gold smuggling.[7] The *maquis* rapidly lost ground at the end of the 1970s and completely disappeared in 1986–7. By then, Kabila had left Zaire and set up business in Tanzania, though this did not mean the total end of his political activities. Some sources claim that he spent some time with the Southern Sudanese rebellion at the end of the 1980s, and that he went to Gbadolite to meet with Mobutu on behalf of John Garang on several occasions. This occurred at a time when Garang and Mobutu were still allies, and, if true, would, of course, contradict Kabila's claim that he never had any dealings with Mobutu. In addition, the PRP published documents during the 'transition' of the early 1990s, including a long and bizarre open letter to Mobutu and the chairman of the HCR–PT.[8]

The three other movements in the Alliance were much less well-known. The CNRD, which presented itself as the armed wing of the Mouvement national congolais (MNC) – Lumumba, was supposedly founded in the early 1990s. Its leader André Kisase Ngandu was a Tetela of the Kasaï who, with about 300 of his men, received some military training in Libya under the auspices of the Mathaba (Libyan secret service) in 1990 and 1991. When Libya closed these 'terrorist' training camps under international pressure, Kisase went to Uganda in early 1992. He is said to have seized the opportunity of the RPF victory in 1994 to send his men to Rwanda to continue their military training. Together with the Banyamulenge who served in the RPA, these troops were probably the

---

[7] Details on this period can be found in a book that paints a rather depressing picture of Kabila: Wilungula B. Cosma, *Fizi 1967–1986. Le maquis Kabila*, Brussels/Paris, Institut Africain/L'Harmattan, Cahiers Africains, No. 26, 1997. The image of Kabila 'the rebel' painted in J.-C. Willame, *L'odyssée Kabila. Trajectoire pour un Congo nouveau?*, Paris, Karthala, 1999, pp. 16–29 did not offer more cause for optimism.

[8] L.D. Kabila, *Naufrage du processus de re-démocratisation*, Hewa-Bora III, 6 December 1993, p. 29.

only 'autochthonous' elements to participate in the initial phase of the 'rebellion'. The two other movements appear to have been created for the occasion. The leader of the MRLZ Masasu Nindaga, formerly of the RPA, was a Mushi of the Bukavu region. The Alliance démocratique des peuples (ADP) supposedly represented the Zairean Tutsi, and both the Banyamulenge of South Kivu and the Banyarwanda from North Kivu; its leader Déo Bugera was a Tutsi from Masisi. Kigali obviously was the link between these people: as will be seen later, Museveni introduced Kabila and Kisase to Kagame; Masasu was a veteran of the RPA; many Tutsi from Masisi joined the RPF's struggle from 1990 onwards. Müller Ruhimbika (see earlier text), acting as the spokesman for the ADP,[9] announced the creation of the AFDL in Kigali.[10]

Although Kabila embarked on this adventure without troops of his own, he recruited fighters as he progressed. On 6 February 1997, the AFDL paraded several thousand recruits in Goma; according to Kabila, they had been trained in Rumangabo military camp. Clad in brand new fatigues and black rubber boots, they marched without weapons.[11] A week later, Kabila presided over a similar parade in Bukavu.[12] In both cases, the recruits were mainly youngsters in their teens: this was the beginning of the phenomenon of the *kadogo* (literally 'the little ones' in Swahili), the canon fodder that was to cross most of Zaire on foot. According to UNICEF, they reached 18,000 in number by early 1998. These recruitments allowed Kabila to build his own military base, and also to dilute the strong Tutsi presence in the rebel ranks. This aim is well rendered by a statement made in confidence to Belgian reporter Colette Braeckman. It was necessary to seek a counterweight to the Tutsi, who dominated the rebel army and whose supremacy irritated most Zaireans: 'They now behave like victors; tomorrow they will have to behave like compatriots'.[13] With the benefit of hindsight after what started in August 1998 (see later text), this sounds almost prophetic. At the political and administrative level, many intellectuals of the Zairean diaspora joined the

---

[9] Ruhimbika (*Les Banyamulenge...*, *op. cit.*, p. 54) confirms that the ADP was created in Kigali under the auspices of RPA's Colonel James Kabarebe.

[10] Reuters, Kigali, 24 October 1996. According to Ruhimbika (*Les Banyamulenge...*, *op. cit.*, p. 55), 'in mid-October 1996, still following the instructions of Rwanda, Laurent Kabila and other Congolese, Ngandu Kisase, Nindaga Masasu, Déogratias Bugera and Joseph Rubibi met in Kigali in the office of Colonel James Kabarebe to launch the AFDL'.

[11] AFP, Goma, 6 February 1997.

[12] AFP, Goma, 12 February 1997.

[13] 'Les jeunes soldats de Kabila, profondément zaïrois', *Le Soir*, 26 February 1997.

AFDL as soon as the rebellion took shape, and the perspective of victory became real. The All-North America Conference on Zaire (ANACOZA) in particular was a breeding ground for qualified staff whose expertise was precious to the Alliance.[14]

As seen earlier, the 'Banyamulenge rebellion' was part of a Rwandan–Burundian–Ugandan strategy aimed at securing borders. Kabila only appeared in the picture later. While his activities had become essentially commercial by the mid-1980s, Kabila did maintain contact with insurrectionist groups that never disappeared completely, in North Kivu in particular.[15] In 1994, a report commissioned by the Zairean interim parliament (the so-called Vangu report) referred to Zairean refugees in Uganda 'where, with the blessing of the Ugandan political authorities, a certain Kabila, chairman of the Parti pour la lutte pour la démocratie au Congo (sic), is involved in guiding these rebels, who often organise incursions by attacking places in the zone of Beni'.[16] While Kabila did not lead these insurrections, some of his people joined Kisase after leaving the Fizi *maquis*; this probably explains the reference to 'a certain Kabila' in the Vangu report.[17] In addition, because of his past military activities and his long residence in East Africa (Tanzania and Uganda), Kabila was known to certain leaders in the region. His commercial networks provided another resource base; thus, several sources claim that Banyamulenge middlemen were involved in smuggling gold and ivory from Kabila's *maquis*. Finally, although he was not involved at the start

---

[14] Other exiled groups were more reticent. Thus, a 'co-ordination of the Zairean diaspora', created during a congress held in Belgium from 31 October to 3 November 1996 and chaired by Professor Elikia Mbokolo 'formally rejects the presence of a foreign army [a reference to the RPA] on the national territory' and invited 'the Rwandan government to voluntarily withdraw as soon as possible'. A communiqué of 27 October 1996 by SIMA-KIVU denounced 'the hegemonic dream of the Tutsi powers of Rwanda, Burundi and Uganda to impose their supremacy on the Great Lakes Region' and 'whatever exploitation by Zairean movements such as that of Laurent Kabila who, for opportunistic reasons, are tempted to seek alliances with the enemies of the Zairean people'.

[15] Thus the Parti de la libération congolais (PLC) of Antoine Marandura was active in the second half of the 1980s, particularly in the Ruwenzori region, which straddles the DRC and Uganda. Marandura enjoyed Libyan support, which he embezzled to a sizeable extent to fund his transport and construction businesses in Tanzania. Kisase's CNRD was active in the same area in the early 1990s, again, as said before, with Libyan help; Kisase enjoyed at very least the passive support of the Ugandan regime.

[16] Haut Conseil de la République-Parlement de Transition, *Rapport de la commission d'information du HCR–PT sur la situation des personnes déplacées dans les régions du Nord et du Sud-Kivu*, Kinshasa, 30 November 1994, p. 16.

[17] E. Kennes, 'La guerre au Congo', in: F. Reyntjens, S. Marysse (Eds.), *L'Afrique des grands lacs. Annuaire 1997–1998*, Paris, L'Harmattan, 1998, p. 255.

of the rebellion, Kabila tried to get his foot in the door, as soon as things started to move. In mid-September 1996, the PRP sent out a communiqué, claiming that 'an assault platoon of the Forces armées populaires (FAP) of the PRP under the command of Laurent Kabila' had launched attacks in the area of Jomba (where the borders of Zaire, Uganda and Rwanda meet) from 12 September onwards.[18] However, it is very unlikely that the PRP was active in that area; the actions claimed by Kabila were probably those of the Rwandan army (cf., the attack on Bunagana mentioned earlier). At any rate, during the following weeks, Kabila appeared as a leader of the rebellion in South Kivu, but he could not have moved his 'troops' between the two Kivus without anyone noticing.

Clearly, Kabila drew attention to his existence at a time when the foreign sponsors of the 'Banyamulenge rebellion' were facing a public relations problem. In order to avoid the blame, as formulated by the Zairean government from 13 September onwards, terming this as external aggression, it was necessary to exhibit leadership, the 'Zaireness' of which could not be challenged. Kabila was not a Tutsi and, while his erstwhile *maquis* was in South Kivu, he was a Katangan. This made it possible to present himself as a 'national' leader. As both Nyerere and Museveni knew Kabila, it was not that surprising that they called upon him.[19] President Museveni later shed some light on the way in which Kabila entered the scene. According to the Ugandan president, Kabila came to see him in Kampala after the National Resistance Movement (NRM) in Uganda seized power in 1986. Introduced by a Tanzanian intelligence agent, Kabila asked for Museveni's support in his struggle against Mobutu. He returned to Kampala after the victory of the RPF. Around the same time, Kisase Ngandu also met with Museveni, who, then, introduced Kabila and Kisase to General Kagame. After the start of the 'Banyamulenge rebellion', the Rwandans brought together the four leaders of what became the AFDL.[20]

Just like the regional coalition that supported it, the Alliance was, therefore, artificial and circumstantial. As will be seen later, the AFDL was to completely evaporate. On 6 January 1997, during the rebellion, Kisase Ngandu was assassinated. According to someone close to the victim, his execution was ordered by Kabila and carried out by RPA Major Jack Nziza, whose role in the massacres of Hutu refugees has been mentioned earlier.

---

[18] Undated press release published by Gaëtan Kakudji, General Secretary of the PRP; the press did not pick up the story at the time.
[19] Because of his past commercial dealings, Kabila was also known to the Banyamulenge.
[20] *The Monitor*, 1 June 1999.

At the origin of Kisase's elimination were disagreements, in the leadership within the AFDL,[21] on the attitude towards the local populations and their property and on the predominance of the Rwandans in the rebellion.[22]

## The Forces Armées Zaïroises (FAZ) and Their Allies

In 1996, the FAZ were the mirror of the Zairean state: most of them existed on paper only. About 75,000 in size,[23] the army was funded by a modest budgetary outlay of between 2% and 3% of the GDP in the 1990s. Certain 'elite units' were supposedly better off than the average FAZ. The Division spéciale présidentielle (DSP) officially had 15,000 men, but, in reality, it numbered about 7000, with the majority coming from Mobutu's Equateur region, mostly Ngbaka troops and Ngbandi (Mobutu's ethnic group) officers. Commanded by General Nzimbi, a relative of Mobutu, the DSP did not, in practice, follow the ordinary military hierarchy. The *Garde civile* was about 10,000 strong, most of them Ngbandi. Commanded by General Baramoto, another relative of Mobutu, just like the DSP, it obeyed the president and not, in practice, the general army staff. Generals Nzimbi and Baramoto were not professional soldiers, but politicians-cum-businessmen, a fact that obviously did not contribute to the quality of command in these units. More generally, the FAZ were undermined by politicisation, nepotism, corruption and embezzlement. As a consequence, the unpaid, untrained and unequipped officers and soldiers were forced to 'make ends meet' by preying on the population; '*clochardisé*' (turned into tramps) as it was, this army was unsurprisingly neither committed nor professional, and it is understandable that it lost the war, or, more accurately, that it did not fight the war. In certain well documented cases, officers even sold weapons and ammunition to the rebel forces before fleeing their advance.[24]

---

[21] It may well not be a coincidence that Kisase was killed just two days after Kabila 'captured' the chairmanship of the AFDL.

[22] Masumbuko Musemakweli, *Toute la vérité sur l'assassinat du général-major André Kisase Ngandu, commandant en chef de l'Alliance (AFDL)*, Goma, 7 March 1997. The author behind the pseudonym is Daniel Mayele, General Secretary of the MNC-L.

[23] An annex to a document, Zaïre. L'armée au service du développement, published in March 1996 by the Belgian NGO Coopération et Progrès gives a total of 77,000. This figure includes 12,000 civil guards and 25,000 gendarmes. The text said about certain 'elite units' that they were 'left in decay' or that 'they virtually ceased to exist'. The Air Force (FAZ) 'has no C-130s in flying condition'.

[24] For more information on the dire state of the FAZ, see E. Kennes, 'La guerre au Congo', *op. cit.*, pp. 243–250 and E. Kennes, 'Du Zaïre à la République Démocratique du

Fighting took place only at the beginning of the conflict, when the rebellion, which at the time was still that of the Banyamulenge supported by the Rwandan army, was attempting to carve out some territory between Uvira and Bukavu. The rebellion used the tactics that the RPA had applied successfully in Rwanda in 1994: a combination of infiltration and encircling, but at the same time leaving an escape route for the FAZ, thus limiting unnecessary losses. A source local to the fighting nicely illustrated this process: 'In Nagero (...), two men unknown to local people and travelling on a bike were arrested. On the luggage rack was a bundle in cloth. Inside it were two disassembled AK-47s... This is the infiltration technique of the rebels. They arrive as civilians with disassembled weapons and mingle with the local population. When they have infiltrated sufficiently, they appear in arms and it is then generally too late'.[25]

Later, another scenario was to be repeated throughout the campaign. The AFDL announced it was about to attack a particular place and in some cases even announced before it happened that a target had been taken. Even before the first contact, the FAZ would typically loot the place,[26] requisition vehicles and flee. This not only allowed the rebellion to advance easily, but also to get hold of sizeable stocks of arms and ammunition on their push westwards. Thus, for instance, an aeroplane loaded with military equipment was simply abandoned by the FAZ at Kalemie airport. Rebel victories were easy under these circumstances: 'The fall of Wamba (100 km south of Isiro) was the work of three rebels arriving on a motor bike, one carrying a lance, another a knife and the third a pistol which might or might not have been loaded'.[27] Even in Lubumbashi, taken in a pincer movement through Zambia (see earlier text), the FAZ hardly put up a fight. Kolwezi is said to have been captured by vehicles previously seized in the town by a small group of 'infiltrated' rebels.[28] During the war, the FAZ only put up brief spells of resistance in Goma, Beni, Bunia, Lubumbashi and Kenge. As will be seen, forces other than the FAZ fought the rebellion elsewhere.

Congo: une analyse de la guerre de l'Est', *L'Afrique politique 1998*, Paris, Karthala, 1998, pp. 184–190.

[25] T. Charlier, 'Les mercenaires français au Zaïre', *Raids-Magazine*, 132, May 1997, pp. 24–25.

[26] It should be added in fairness that the FAZ were not the only looting forces. Bukavu and Goma were largely 'emptied' by the RPA, which took a considerable bounty of hi-fi equipment, domestic appliances, vehicles and PCs back to Rwanda.

[27] AFP, Kisangani, 18 February 1997.

[28] E. Kennes, 'La guerre au Congo', *op. cit.*, p. 242.

At the start of the war, the political–military class in Kinshasa did not take the issue seriously. They were not concerned by what was happening in faraway Kivu. On 2 November 1996, following the fall of Goma, the army Chief of Staff General Eluki belatedly blamed the government for 'not having done anything to provide the army with the means necessary to wage the war'. Only after defeat followed defeat did the regime attempt, in moves that were too little too late, to organise some resistance against the advancing rebellion.

Three ways of organising resistance were explored. The first was diplomatic: from early November 1996, President Mobutu's special advisor on security matters Honoré N'Gbanda started travelling in order to secure support in the face of what Zaire, not altogether wrongly, claimed was an outside aggression. The diplomatic ballet that involved Zairean and many other players will be discussed later.

A second approach attempted to improve the performances of the FAZ. On 20 November 1996, Eluki was sacked and replaced by Baramoto, who, however, was no better than his predecessor. Only with the appointment of General Mahele on 18 December did a professional officer of undeniable quality (though not a graduate of a military academy) assume the command of the FAZ.[29] The day after he took charge, reinforcements were sent to Bunia in a vain attempt to halt the rebel progression to the northeast. At the same time, commando and DSP units restored a certain degree of order in Kisangani, which was the scene of looting by deserting soldiers.

On 2 January 1997, the government announced a 'total and lightning counter-offensive' and asked the army to be 'a force deserving the confidence of the Nation' and 'to become, as of now, a truly Republican army'. A statement of the army high command was firm: the high command 'puts at the disposal of the Chief of Staff all the strategic and logistical means necessary to conduct without delay the counter-offensive of the Zairean Armed Forces. It will have to be total and lightning and will not spare any Zairean or foreign actor collaborating with the enemy'.[30]

---

[29] According to Ambassador Fernand Wibaux (see later text), he and George Moose insisted with Mobutu that Mahele be appointed. However, Wibaux admitted that Mahele 'was unable to do anything due to lack of resources, because of the European weapons embargo' (interview in *Le Figaro*, 18 April 1997). According to the then Prime Minister Kengo, it was President Chirac himself who, after a meeting with Kengo in Ouagadougou, obtained the appointment of Mahele from Mobutu (personal communication).

[30] AFP, Kinshasa, 3 January 1997.

Mahele tried to reconstruct the army by improving equipment, discipline and morale. As far as equipment was concerned, with the aid of funds from outside bodies (see later text), the Zairean government acquired material that was, however, in part unsuitable and unusable, and in part diverted. Thus, in the middle of the war, Generals Nzimbi and Baramoto, in an attempt to sabotage Mahele's efforts and at the same time to earn an income, reportedly sold considerable stocks of newly bought Zairean army equipment to UNITA.[31] On 29 January, Prime Minister Kengo promised Parliament that 'whatever his grade, every member of the armed forces involved in the sale of arms to the enemy will be severely sanctioned'; he added that inquiries were underway and that, in addition to the fourteen soldiers condemned to death by a court martial in Kisangani, others would soon be put on trial.[32] The statement of the army high command mentioned earlier had already announced 'the army will have to get rid of criminals, cowards, looters and vagrants'; court martials were to punish all offenders 'in a severe and spectacular fashion'. Death sentences were supposed to bring discipline, while the disbursement of soldiers' pay was to stimulate morale: in mid-February soldiers received twenty dollars each,[33] a luxury not seen for years. In addition, a recruitment drive in early February brought in 26,000 youngsters aged between 15 and 18 years that were to provide the canon fodder necessary for the counteroffensive.[34] However, obviously an army left in decay for many years could not be reconstructed, either materially or morally, in a couple of weeks.

That is why a third strategy was used. This strategy aimed to mobilise external support. The implication of 'friendly states' failed, if only because the Zairean authorities were clumsy enough to publicly state that support had been offered, which caused the countries in question to renege on their commitments. Countries such as Togo, Chad, Israel, Egypt, China, Libya and Morocco, quoted as allies by the Zairean and international press, were one after the other embarrassed and forced to deny their involvement. Certain high-level contacts, however, suggest that support was indeed negotiated. The visit of the Sudanese foreign minister to Kinshasa on 31 December 1996 was no coincidence. As stated earlier,

---

[31] J. Rupert, 'Zaire Reportedly Selling Arms ...', *op. cit.*; on the 'Generals' war', see H. N'Gbanda, *Ainsi sonne le glas...*, *op. cit.*, pp. 46–52.

[32] AFP, Kinshasa, 29 January 1997.

[33] AFP, Kisangani, 18 February 1997.

[34] Reuters, Kisangani, 4 February 1997.

the Mobutu regime supported the Khartoum government in the context of the alliances around the southern Sudanese conflict. The 'humanitarian' NGO Dawa al Islamaya, a fundamentalist organisation established in Khartoum, opened an office in Kinshasa in 1995 and was active in the Hutu refugee camps in the Kivu region.[35] Louis Farrakhan, the leader of the radical 'Nation of Islam' in the United States, visited Mobutu in February 1996, in order to demonstrate his support for Hassan el Turabi and the Sudanese cause. Ten days after the visit of the Sudanese delegation, the Chief of Staff of the Chinese army General Fu Quanyu was received by Mobutu. According to Zairean television, the Chinese delegation agreed to resume military cooperation.[36] On 4 February 1997, *The Jerusalem Post* wrote that both Israel and China had decided to provide the Zairean army with technical assistance. In addition, when, at the same time, the presence of Israeli mercenaries in Zaire was mentioned, the Ministry of Defence in Jerusalem refused any comment.[37] Some forty instructors of the Israeli army reportedly trained the DSP under a contract signed in 1994 between Kinshasa and an Israeli arms production company.[38] Other sources claimed that Kuwait, in recognition of the political support of Zaire (which at the time chaired the Security Council) during the first Gulf war, transferred US$ 64 million for the purchase of weapons. However, as a reaction to a declaration by the mercenary commander Christian Tavernier[39] that 'it may be Kuwait that is funding our operation', Kuwait immediately denied all involvement in Zaire.[40]

Support was also found elsewhere. While most of the 'Tigres' or 'Katangese gendarmes' fought on the side of the rebellion (see earlier text), some of them had returned to Zaire in the early 1990s. These troops in part joined the cause of the autonomist Katangese party Union des fédéralistes et des républicains indépendants (UFERI), and in part were incorporated in the *Garde civile*.[41] In a declaration made on 4 November 1996, Colonel Songolo, who presented himself as one of the leaders of the Front pour la libération nationale du Congo (FNLC) but was an

---

[35] A number of ex-FAR officers, initially settled in Nairobi, moved on to the Sudan during 1997 'to resume the struggle'.

[36] Reuters, Kinshasa, 10 January 1997.

[37] *La Libre Belgique*, 5 February 1997.

[38] G. Berghezan, 'Une guerre cosmopolite', in: *Kabila prend le pouvoir, op. cit.*, pp. 95–96. However, it must be added that other sources put Israel on the side of the Ugandan–Rwandan alliance.

[39] *Le Soir*, 27 January 1997.

[40] AFP, Kuwait, 29 January 1997.

[41] E. Kennes, 'La guerre au Congo', *op. cit.*, p. 249.

adventurer without much of a following, offered the support of his men to the FAZ. He demanded the logistics needed 'for us to go to the front in order to defend our territory invaded by foreign Rwandan troops'.[42] When Laurent Kabila announced the seizure of Bunia on 25 December 1996, he claimed that Katangese gendarmes had fought on the side of the FAZ.[43] Several other references to the presence of 'Tigres' fighting the rebellion are found elsewhere.[44]

Support also came from UNITA, an old Mobutu ally. In order to secure both its assault and retreat bases and the transit of its diamonds through the Bandundu region, for UNITA the support for a friendly regime in Zaire was essential. Several thousand UNITA men reportedly fought alongside the Zairean army in Bunia, where UNITA's commander of the northern zone General Abilio Kamalata 'Numa' was severely wounded.[45] On 6 January 1997, Kabila claimed that 2000 UNITA troops were engaged with the FAZ.[46] UNITA was also directly involved in Isiro and Kenge. In the latter case, elements of UNITA and the Angolan armed forces entered into direct confrontation. After sustaining heavy losses, UNITA abandoned the theatre and retreated into Angola.[47]

A third source of military support came from an old alliance that, by the autumn of 1996, had become a question of survival. Even if old ties had not existed between the FAZ and the former FAR, for the latter, fighting the rebellion was vitally necessary for several reasons. First, the RPA was a major spearhead of the rebellion, and it attacked refugee concentrations, including of course the armed elements among them. Second, the FAR, while attempting to control the Rwandan refugees, also had to protect them. Third, the loss of territory close to the Rwandan border was to deprive the FAR of the assault and retreat bases used for their incursions into Rwanda. Until the fall of Kisangani, the resistance

---

[42] Reuters, Nairobi, 4 November 1996. During the second war, Songolo was to choose the side of the anti-Kabila rebellion, although this too was supported by Rwanda. Since then, nothing has been heard from Songolo.

[43] *Le Soir*, 26 December 1996 (following Reuters and AFP). The deputy chairman of the Red Cross for the Bunia region repeated this accusation in an interview with the *Voice of America* on 2 January 1997.

[44] For example, T. Charlier, 'Les mercenaires français au Zaïre', *Raids-Magazine*, 132, May 1997, pp. 18, 22, and 24; H. Van Dyck, *Rapport sur les violations des droits de l'homme dans le Sud-Equateur, République démocratique du Congo, du 15 mars 1997 au 15 septembre 1997*, Antwerp, mimeo, 29 September 1997, p. 3.

[45] According to *Le Soir*, 3 March 1997.

[46] AFP, Goma, 6 January 1997.

[47] According to N'Gbanda, UNITA troops were attacked from behind by their FAZ 'allies' at Maindombe bridge near Kenge (*Ainsi sonne le glas...*, op. cit., p. 324).

against the rebels' progress was to a large extent waged by the FAR, first around Bukavu and Goma, then, at Walikale, and finally, around Kindu and between Walikale and Lubutu, where the advance of the AFDL/RPA was contained for over a month. According to humanitarian sources, out of 126 wounded military taken to Lubutu hospital at the end of February 1997, more than 100 were Rwandans.[48] The capture of Buta followed intensive fighting between Rwandans on both sides, Tutsi with the AFDL, and Hutu with the FAZ.[49]

By mid-February, Secretary General Kofi Annan and the European Union expressed concern over the introduction of weapons, ammunition and uniforms into Tingi-Tingi refugee camp, and they demanded its demilitarisation.[50] Kofi Annan asked 'all the concerned parties to cease transforming the camp into a military base and to ensure the security of the refugees and the staff working for the humanitarian agencies'. Clearly, Tingi-Tingi had become a FAR base for the combat it was waging a few dozen kilometres to the east, particularly at the Oso river. This militarisation, of course, increased the danger to the refugees by exposing them to military action taken against the armed elements among them.[51] After the loss of Kindu, Punia and Lubutu, which all fell in late February and early March 1997, the FAR appear to have stopped participating in the war. They then attempted to exit, either by fleeing to the west and later to neighbouring countries or by maintaining pockets of refuge in the vast territory only nominally controlled by the AFDL.[52] It will be seen that the FAR resurfaced later and remained an important military factor.

The fourth type of military support sought by Kinshasa was mercenary. Two distinct operations were launched. The first, led by Christian Tavernier,[53] involved some thirty men, most of them French. This small force, which was to operate in support of the few FAZ units that remained

[48] IRIN, Update 108, 25 February 1997.
[49] C. Braeckman, 'La campagne victorieuse ...', *op. cit.*, p. 74.
[50] AFP, The Hague, 14 February 1997; AFP, New York (United Nations), 15 February 1997.
[51] In this sense, see H.W. French, 'Zaire, in Arming the Hutu, is Making Human Shields of the Refugees', *The International Herald Tribune*, 20 February 1997.
[52] The latter strategy is attested to by the fact that attacks by ex-FAR were reported in zones occupied by the rebellion, for example, at less than 50 km west of Goma in mid-December 1996 and near Katale, north of Goma, in January 1997.
[53] This Belgian officer was trained on the job during the Katangese secession in the early 1960s. He then became battalion commander under Mike Hoare during the mercenary campaign against the rebellions in 1964–5. At the end of the 1960s, he became an advisor to President Mobutu.

operational, arrived in Zaire at the end of 1996 with the intent of moving from Bunia to Goma via Beni. The fall of Bunia and the Ugandan support for the rebellion frustrated this project, and the mercenaries pulled out in mid-February 1997, after a vain attempt to hold on to Watsa first, and their rear base Nagero next. They were repatriated after spending some time at the SARM headquarters in Kinshasa. This old-fashioned mercenary presence lasted for one-and-a-half months only.[54] The second operation depended directly on General Mahele and involved about 100 Serb mercenaries based in Kisangani, where they arrived in mid-January 1997. Besides relatively light weapons, they had three MI-24 helicopters and three Aermacchi light aeroplanes. Apart from the useless and, from a public relations point of view, counter-productive bombardments of Bukavu, Shabunda and Walikale, the role of this force was limited. The MI-24s were briefly used with some success in raids in the Walikale region, but the logistics of these aircraft posed enormous problems in a country where infrastructure was virtually non-existent. Poorly adapted to the military and physical conditions prevailing on the ground, discredited by the atrocities they allegedly committed and in the face of the rebel threat against Kisangani, the Serbs left the city on 14 March, after an operation that had lasted only two months. Contrary to the situation prevailing thirty years earlier, the mercenary presence did not make the slightest difference to the eventual outcome of the war. Perhaps this failure is the symbol of the end of a bygone type of 'mercenariat', which, however, is being replaced by a more modern, more professional, more international and more worrying one.

A (semi-)official French implication, either in support of mercenary operations or unrelated to them, has been suggested by several sources. François-Xavier Verschave has accumulated an impressive set of data on this subject. A few elements of his dossier, still largely undisclosed, will now be presented. In a broadcast on 5 November 1996, the Swiss television channel TSR revealed that former French minister Charles Pasqua met with Mobutu on 31 October 1996 at the request of President Chirac. TSR claimed that Mobutu asked for logistical support and the recruitment of mercenaries. According to *Le Figaro* of 5–6 April 1997, Ambassador Fernand Wibaux, a close collaborator of Jacques Foccart in the 'Africa cell' (Cellule africaine) of the Elysée, gave the green light (some claim it was an 'orange light') for the recruitment of 100 Serb mercenaries by

---

[54] On this operation, see T. Charlier, 'Les mercenaires français ...', *op. cit.*; C. Braeckman, 'Christian Tavernier, du Zaïre au Congo', *Le Soir*, 3 October 1997.

a company called Geolink; the contract was reportedly made through 'Commander Dominic',[55] a 'correspondent' of the French internal security service Direction de la surveillance du territoire (DST).[56] Based on information provided by unidentified American intelligence and diplomatic sources, *The New York Times* of 2 May 1997 confirmed the *Le Figaro* story, adding that it was possible that French 'services' conducted the operation without the knowledge of the French government. The bill was said to have amounted to FRF25 million. Interviewed in Gbadolite by *Le Monde* (issue of 10 May 1997), 'Colonel Dominic', who said he was 'Serb, but also French', suggested asking 'Place Beauvau,[57] they know I am here'.[58]

Tavernier, for his part, claimed that his operation enjoyed the support of Ambassador Wibaux.[59] He argued that the aim was to recapture the territory lost by the FAZ starting from Bunia, where elements of the French Commandos de recherche et d'action en profondeur (CRAP) were to be based. Between late 1996 and early 1997, other sources also mentioned the presence of elements of the CRAP and the 13th Régiment de dragons parachutistes (RDP).[60] In addition, CRAP elements are said to have discretely recovered the bodies of American military killed near the Oso river (see earlier text) and returned them to the United States; this story has never been confirmed, but if it were true, this would mean that (French) soldiers 'that were not there' recovered the bodies of (American) soldiers 'that were not there either'. On 8 January 1997, *Le Monde* wrote that military previously working at the Elysée assisted in the recruitment of mercenaries: the newspaper quoted the names of Allain Le Carro, a former Lieutenant-Colonel of the Groupe

---

[55] The name of 'Colonel Dominic Yugo' does indeed come up in Kisangani, where he was alledgedly involved in atrocities (cf. J. McKinley, 'Serb Who Went to Defend Zaire Spread Death and Horror Instead', *The New York Times*, 19 March 1997).

[56] He is said to have been involved in the restitution of two French pilots shot down over Bosnia and captured by the Serbs in December 1995.

[57] The square in Paris which houses the interior ministry, of which the DST depends.

[58] The information of *Le Figaro* and *The New York Times* is confirmed in S. Boyle, 'The White Legion: Mercenaries in Zaire', *Jane's Intelligence Review*, 1 June 1997.

[59] However, Wibaux denied any implication in an interview with *Le Figaro* (18 April 1997). While recognising that he had been contacted by Geolink and that he had met with Christian Tavernier, he said he thought that the mercenaries were recruited by mafia-like networks run by Seti Yale, a former Mobutu advisor. This may well be true, but it is also known that Seti Yale maintained links with certain French '*services*' and '*réseaux*'.

[60] However, it cannot be excluded that the 13th RDP was deployed in preparation for the aborted international intervention. In 1988, these paratroopers preceded the Foreign Legion into Kolwezi (*Libération*, 14 November 1996).

de sécurité de la présidence de la République (GSPR), who formerly had been in charge of the close protection of President Mitterrand, and Robert Montoya, a former *gendarme* in the anti-terrorist cell at the Elysée who maintained close links with the private security firm Executive Outcomes. The Elysée spokesperson denied this: 'The French authorities categorically deny any implication whatsoever in the actions of the people *Le Monde* refers to', without, however, stating that the officers mentioned were not involved. On several occasions, Kabila accused France of intervening on the side of Kinshasa, but every time the denial of Paris was 'categorical'.[61]

Even more than American involvement, the involvement of France is shrouded in mystery, linked to the way in which France traditionally manages its relations with Africa: a number of '*officines*' acting in a relatively autonomous fashion, the opaqueness of political decision-making and of actions on the ground, the Fashoda syndrome, intoxication and manipulation of information. Dumoulin adds that 'this murkiness of centres of decision and operation on the ground often shows struggles of influence that only partly follow the traditional left–right political rivalries'.[62] This being said, a sufficient number of diversified sources suggest that (semi-) official France has been engaged, in a clandestine and temporary fashion, on the Zairean government's side. Whilst the information on the physical presence of the French army is limited and certainly insufficient to draw conclusions, some support of the 'cellule africaine' and probably of one or other '*service*' and the '*réseau Pasqua*' to the mercenary operations is likely. It must be recalled in this context that the alliances of France in the region (hostility towards the Kampala–Kigali axis and support for the Khartoum regime) were very clear before and during the 1996–7 rebellion. In order to maintain a minimal presence in the face of an 'Anglo-Saxon ploy', France needed at least to give the 'orange light' to players able to support its allies.

---

[61] Thus, on 23 December 1996, 'the French authorities scrupulously respect the arms embargo decided on by the European Union in 1993. As a consequence, they have not offered any military assistance to this country (Zaire), nor have they authorised any supply of military material' (AFP, Paris, 23 December 1996). On 6 January 1997, after Kabila, obviously falsely, accused France of sending 1000 soldiers to Kisangani, the French defence ministry stated 'that there is not one single French soldier in Zaire, except five *gendarmes* and a military attaché at the French embassy in Kinshasa' (AFP, Paris, 6 January 1997).

[62] A. Dumoulin, *La France militaire et l'Afrique*, Brussels, GRIP-Editions Complexe, 1997, p. 51.

## 4.2 THE DIPLOMATIC BALLET

A number of regional and international actors, who pursued divergent and often hidden agendas that changed throughout the crisis, attempted (or pretended to attempt) a negotiated settlement.[63] Initiatives followed one after the other, straddling and often even short-circuiting each other. In mid-October 1996, EU special envoy Aldo Ajello toured the region's capitals in order to promote dialogue between Kinshasa and Kigali, showing that he knew full well who was fighting whom. He was immediately rebuffed by the Rwandans: Foreign Minister Gasana said that it was impossible to envisage mediation or a ceasefire with Zaire and he restated the position that his country was not involved in the war.[64] On 25 October, Secretary General Boutros-Ghali advocated holding an international conference, an idea supported by France and the United States. The Security Council called for a ceasefire and accepted the Secretary General's proposal to appoint a special representative.[65] On 30 October, the Belgian foreign minister announced in the Senate that 'if all parties agree to sit around a table, Belgium is willing to host a conference on the Great Lakes region'; this proposal was made after the Rwandan ambassador in Brussels asked Belgium to play a constructive role in the settlement of the crisis. On 1 November, the conflict prevention body of the OAU in turn demanded a ceasefire and negotiations, and insisted on the respect for the territorial integrity of member states.[66]

The first (Nairobi-I) summit was chronologically the first attempt to internationalise the conflict. Worried by the fact that the Zairean rebellion was actively supported by Rwanda and Uganda, the two countries in the region with which his relations were less than cordial, Kenyan president Daniel Arap Moi invited Presidents Bizimungu (Rwanda), Afewerki (Eritrea), Museveni (Uganda), Chiluba (Zambia) and Mkapa (Tanzania), Ethiopian prime minister Meles Zenawi, as well as the OAU chairman (Cameroon's President Biya was represented by his foreign minister), OAU general secretary Salim Salim and former President Julius Nyerere. Zaire refused to talk in a situation of aggression and remained absent; the AFDL was not invited. In a communiqué released on 5 November 1996,

---

[63] Although I have already indicated that it must be read with caution, the book written by Honoré N'Gbanda (*Ainsi sonne le glas...*, *op. cit.*,), who was closely involved in most initiatives and steps throughout this process, is a rich source 'from within'.

[64] AFP, Kigali, 29 October 1996.

[65] AFP, New York (United Nations), 25 October 1996.

[66] PANA, Addis Ababa, 1 November 1996.

the summit asked the Security Council to urgently take the measures needed to establish humanitarian corridors in Eastern Zaire and to create secure zones protected by a neutral international force (it will be recalled that this occurred during the saga surrounding the aborted military intervention: see earlier text). It also insisted on the urgent need to conclude a ceasefire, to respect the territorial integrity of Zaire, to put an end to cross-border incursions and to respect the inalienable rights of all the populations inside the country (the latter was of course a reference to the citizens' rights of the Banyamulenge and other Banyarwanda). Finally, it demanded the voluntary repatriation of the refugees and the separation of 'intimidators from the bona fide refugees'. These resolutions seemed to translate a consensus among the regional states, including on the issue of military intervention. However, the next day, Zaire reiterated its resolve not to participate in any negotiation as long as 'the Rwandan, Burundian and Ugandan aggressors' had not left its territory.

Other summits were to take place in Nairobi, but in the meantime, intense diplomatic activity developed elsewhere. In November 1996, the U.S. special envoys Ambassadors Richard Bogosian and Howard Wolpe visited most of the region's capitals. From 8 to 13 November, the UN special representative Raymond Chrétien shuttled between Kigali and Kinshasa, followed on 11 and 12 November by European Commissioner Emma Bonino. On 15 November, an OAU delegation met with President Mobutu in France. At the end of a meeting with Mobutu in Cap Martin on 4 December, Ambassador Chrétien said that the Zairean president 'is central to the resolution of the crisis. He is in permanent contact with his Prime Minister and government. I found him in good physical shape and perfectly informed about the situation'.[67] Likewise, in the region Mobutu remained an acceptable interlocutor. The diplomatic tour undertaken by his special advisor Honoré N'Gbanda has already been mentioned. This tour brought him to Kampala on 16 November, when, in the presence of a Rwandan representative, President Museveni submitted a list of twelve 'suggestions' that deserve to be reproduced entirely:

1. Declare a ceasefire and maintain it.
2. Rebels to acknowledge publicly that HE President Marshall Mobutu is the President of the Republic of Zaire.
3. Rebels to acknowledge and recognise the Government of the Republic of Zaire.

---

[67] *Le Monde*, 5 December 1996.

4. To urge the Government of Zaire and the neighbouring states to observe the UN Charter.

5. The Government of Zaire to restore citizenship to those entitled to it in accordance with international law.
   Citizenship is acquired by:
   (a) birth
   (b) registration
   (c) naturalisation.

6. To observe all international treaties on human rights.

7. To grant indemnity to all those engaged in the present conflict in Eastern Zaire and thus contribute to the ending of the rebellion.

8. To integrate some of the rebels into the Zairean army.

9. To introduce political reforms in the country within two years from 1 January 1997, leading to an internationally supervised general elections (sic).

10. To expel all Interahamwe, former Rwanda Government leaders and soldiers from Zaire territory and relocate the refugees who may not wish to go back to Rwanda, far away from the border as provided for by international conventions.

11. To convene a regional conference of Heads of State as a prelude to an international conference to discuss issues of general concern to the countries in the Great Lakes Region, so as to find a lasting solution to current and future problems.

12. With the cessation of hostilities, regional leaders to lobby the international community for the removal of the economic embargo on Zaire.

I have reproduced this document in full because it is surprising, not so much because the AFDL was not even involved in this initiative, which shows that Museveni knew the reality very well (obviously, to him the Rwandan envoy also represented the 'rebellion'), but more so since the Zairean regime refused a proposal that required virtually no concessions and that would nevertheless have ensured its survival. N'Gbanda offers an explanation for this astonishing refusal. Having heard indirectly about the Kampala meeting and opposed to any form of dialogue before the withdrawal of foreign troops, the Kengo government sabotaged any prospect of a deal. Even though, according to N'Gbanda, Mobutu 'felt that (the proposal made by Museveni) contained many positive points that could have served as a base for useful negotiations',[68] he could not afford to be

---

[68] H. N'Gbanda, *Ainsi sonne le glas…, op. cit.*, p. 171.

seen to submit himself to a 'diktat', thus risking 'undermining his authority and creditworthiness in his own country'.[69] However, N'Gbanda omits to add that the government's intransigence was to a large extent imposed by the HCR–PT which, under the pressure of the Kivu MPs and Anzaluni Bembe in particular, insisted on a radical position. While Kengo was initially favourable to talks with Rwanda, the threat of destitution (together with accusations that he was 'in league with the Rwandans') forced him to align himself with the hard line drawn by the Assembly. As stated earlier, the radical position of Zaire may well have convinced Uganda to commit itself more resolutely to the side of the rebellion.

A second summit (Nairobi-II) took place in Nairobi on 16 and 17 December, again in the absence of Zaire, but with the South African and Zimbabwean presidents joining the meeting. Nothing much new happened compared to the meeting of early November, beside the fact that the presidents of Kenya, South Africa, Zimbabwe and Cameroon (the latter in his capacity as chair of the OAU) agreed to manage the dossier on behalf of the other countries present. This marked South Africa's entry into the fray, a country which until then had remained very reluctant to get involved,[70] but which was strongly encouraged by the United States, committed to the search for a negotiated settlement,[71] but wishing to avoid too much public exposure in this delicate matter. The centre of diplomatic activity was to gradually shift towards Pretoria. On 23 December, a South African delegation led by the deputy foreign minister visited Kigali. On 27 and 28 January 1997, delegations from Kenya, Zimbabwe, Cameroon, Tanzania, Congo (Brazzaville) and the OAU met in Pretoria. The 'peace quartet', composed of the foreign ministers of Kenya, South Africa, Cameroon and Zimbabwe, was charged with continuing the efforts. The 'quartet' went to Kinshasa on 18 February in order to prepare a third regional summit.

---

[69] *Idem*, p. 168.

[70] See F. Chambon, 'La grande prudence de la diplomatie sud-africaine', *Le Monde*, 6 November 1996. It should be added that the South African diplomacy, which was not particularly efficient in itself, was also short-circuited by the South African arms industry, which delivered weapons and ammunition to almost all parties involved in the conflicts of the Great Lakes region. In addition, what Landsberg writes with regard to the second war also applies to the first: 'South Africa's commercial interests, and especially perceptions of South Africa's presumed imperialist tendencies, (unintentionally) frustrated some of its diplomatic ambitions' (C. Landsberg, 'The Impossible Neutrality? South Africa's Policy in the Congo War', in: J. F. Clark, *The African Stakes...*, *op. cit.*, p. 181).

[71] At least, the State Department was; as we have seen, some other parts of the executive branch were at the same time stoking the fires.

However, just as before, Zaire refused to accept the invitation as long as foreign troops had not withdrawn.[72]

Nevertheless, at the end of February, N'Gbanda and the AFDL's Foreign Affairs Commissioner Bizima Karaha, who was later joined by Kabila, went to South Africa for talks surrounded by a great deal of discretion and actively encouraged by the United States (Assistant Secretary of State for African Affairs George Moose, National Security Council advisor Susan Rice and Ambassador Howard Wolpe were present in the wings).[73] The parties claimed that there were no direct contacts and that they exchanged views using Mandela as a go-between.[74] N'Gbanda felt that the Americans were the real interlocutors: during a meeting on 22 February, they told him they spoke on Kabila's behalf and presented the text of an 'accord', which in fact was an ultimatum addressed to Mobutu.[75] During the Cape Town meeting, South Africa increased its weight by announcing it was willing to contribute two battalions to the international force being discussed at the time (see earlier text).

Somewhat sidelined since the failure of the Chrétien mission, the UN attempted to regain the initiative. At the end of January, Algerian diplomat Mohamed Sahnoun was appointed UN special representative for the Great Lakes region. After brief but very intense consultations, he proposed a five-point peace plan that was adopted by the Security Council on 18 February (Resolution 1079). The plan included:

- the immediate cessation of hostilities;
- the withdrawal of all foreign forces, including the mercenaries;

---

[72] AFP, Nairobi, 20 February 1997.

[73] AFP, Pretoria, 21 February 1997.

[74] At the time, N'Gbanda denied any contact with the rebel leadership: 'There has never been any question of meeting someone from the rebellion' (AFP, Cape Town, 21 February 1997). However, he later acknowledged that a meeting between him and Kabila was scheduled on 20 February in Cape Town, but that it had been cancelled as a result of an indiscretion by Mandela who told Radio France Internationale (RFI) about the meeting, while it was supposed to remain secret. When the news broke in Kinshasa, it caused uproar. Kengo accused N'Gbanda of 'high treason' (H. N'Gbanda, *Ainsi sonne le glas...*, *op. cit.*, p. 230). Kengo told this writer that upon hearing the news on RFI, he called Mobutu to learn from him whether he mandated N'Gbanda. Mobutu replied he was to 'challenge' N'Gbanda and get back to Kengo. He later called Kengo to tell him that he had spoken to Mandela, who promised him he would make a statement to the press to deny the information, which he did not do.

[75] H. N'Gbanda, *Ainsi sonne le glas...*, *op. cit.*, p. 233; the text of the document ('agreement') is reproduced on pp. 383–384 of N'Gbanda's book.

- the reaffirmation of the national sovereignty and territorial integrity of Zaire and the other states in the Great Lakes region;
- the protection and security for all refugees and displaced persons, as well as the facilitation of access for humanitarian assistance;
- the speedy and peaceful settlement of the crisis through dialogue, the electoral process and the holding of an international conference on peace, security and development in the Great Lakes region.

During an informal meeting convened in Paris by the Director of African and Malagasy Affairs at the *Quai d'Orsay* on the same day that Resolution 1079 was adopted, at a meeting, which brought together senior officials from Germany, the United States, Belgium, the UK, Spain and The Netherlands, as well as Aldo Ajello, a consensus emerged to back Sahnoun's efforts (possibly through a support group), promote a cease-fire (all participants were asked to put pressure on their 'friends' in the region), encourage the electoral process and organise an international conference. In substance, this was the same line as the one taken by the Security Council.

The reactions to Resolution 1079 were initially not encouraging in the region. Rwandan presidential advisor Claude Dusaidi expressed the view that the peace plan did not take into account the rebels' position. Zairean foreign minister Gérard Kamanda wa Kamanda felt it was 'timid', because it failed to condemn the aggressors. Despite these reservations, Zaire accepted the plan on 5 March, while adding the demand of 'the immediate deployment of an international control mechanism in order to make Mr Sahnoun's and the Security Council's plan operational and to verify the withdrawal of all foreign troops, mercenaries and militias included'. Following a pressing demand made by the Security Council on 7 March, Kabila announced on 8 March that he was ready to negotiate a ceasefire according to the framework of the plan. After a long discussion with Sahnoun on 15 March (the day the rebellion captured Kisangani, which considerably strengthened his position) Kabila, on the one hand, reaffirmed his adherence to the peace plan, but, on the other, rejected the ceasefire and demanded direct negotiations with Kinshasa. His lukewarm support for the UN plan showed clearly when, after the meeting with Sahnoun, Kabila told reporters that he intended 'to march on Kinshasa' and that Mobutu had to resign. The Zairean president was, of course, further weakened by the fall of Kisangani. Thus, the day after this turning point in the war, the Belgian government expressed the view that there could be no solution without taking Kabila into account. For

Foreign Minister Erik Derycke, 'the Mobutu era has been gone for some time now' and 'Kabila cannot be ignored'. The rebellion immediately welcomed Belgium's 'salutary turnaround'.

In the meantime, the OAU had taken a more active interest in the Zairean affair, which eclipsed the other crises on the continent during the inter-ministerial meeting in Tripoli on 26–27 February. The only resolution taken was the organisation of a summit, scheduled in Lomé in mid-March; among other subjects, it was to discuss the usefulness of the deployment of a 'buffer' military force.[76] In an attempt to regain the diplomatic initiative, lost to South Africa, the Kenyan government called a new summit in Nairobi on 19 March, which was the date originally set for the Lomé meeting. 'Not being a head of state or of government', Kabila was not invited, though Kisangani had just fallen in his hands. Like the previous Nairobi meetings, the third summit (Nairobi-III) did not achieve anything new: another appeal for an immediate ceasefire, the implementation of the UN plan and a recommendation that the OAU central organ for conflict resolution, scheduled to meet in Lomé on 26 March, address the Zairean problem. It is not surprising under these conditions that Kabila called the summit 'irrelevant', adding that President Moi 'is another Mobutu'.[77]

Ambassador Sahnoun nevertheless met with Kabila again in Kisangani on 22 March and invited him to attend the Lomé meeting; Kabila agreed to despatch an AFDL delegation. This was the first time since the war had started that the rebellion was invited to an international meeting on the situation in Zaire. South African vice-president Thabo Mbeki arrived in Kinshasa on the same day. He brought Mobutu a message from Mandela and expected a reply before the beginning of the Lomé summit. The aim was obvious: Lomé was to be used to initiate the first direct contact between Kinshasa and the rebellion. To achieve this, Paris and Washington even launched a joint initiative that showed a certain *rapprochement* after a long period of disagreement caused by the proximity of both powers to

---

[76] AFP, Tripoli, 27 February 1997.
[77] Kabila's position was understandable. On 6 January, Moi visited Mobutu in Gbadolite; the communiqué issued after the meeting reaffirmed the commitment of both presidents to the principles of the integrity and inviolability of internationally recognised borders (which implied that Moi agreed that Zaire was the victim of external aggression) and criticised the 'lack of resolve' of the international community for its failure to implement Security Council resolutions 1078 and 1080 (on the deployment of the international force) (AFP, Nairobi, 6 January 1997). Both these positions were of course hostile to the rebellion and to those who supported it.

one or other party to the conflicts in the region. *Le Figaro* of 28 March 1997 claimed that this joint effort was also facilitated by the discreet recovery and restitution by the French of an American 'advisor' killed in the Kivu region (see earlier text). Both governments pleaded with the OAU central organ of conflict resolution for a ceasefire and the start of direct negotiations between Kinshasa and Laurent Kabila. The French–American convergence was probably also inspired by the fact that the United States was becoming increasingly concerned about Kabila's style and intentions and were worried about his capacity to run Zaire, if he were to take power as the result of a military victory.[78]

All these initiatives appeared to be bearing fruit. On 27 March, the final communiqué of the Lomé meeting announced the start of negotiations and the conclusion of a ceasefire, after the government and the AFDL delegations consulted with their respective authorities; the communiqué added that the negotiations and the ceasefire were to lead to the application of the UN peace plan.[79] This time, the roles were reversed, as it was now the Zairean government that insisted on negotiations after having refused them for so long, while the AFDL was in a position of strength after the capture of Kisangani. Declarations made in the margins of the Lomé summit bore this out very well. On the one hand, Zairean deputy prime minister Banza Mukalay announced that a power-sharing offer, which was to be valid during the transition towards elections, would be made to the AFDL. On the other hand, Bizima Karaha told the BBC that the AFDL would never enter into a power-sharing arrangement with the government. As far as the ceasefire was concerned, this was only 'a principle'. Another AFDL leader, Mwenze Kongolo, insisted that 'we consider ourselves to be in a state of war and our troops are advancing normally. We do not negotiate because we are weak, we are in good shape'.[80]

These differences of opinion did not prevent a meeting between the government and the AFDL from taking place in Mataba (South Africa) on 6 April. The delegations were headed by Foreign Minister Kamanda wa Kamanda and Bizima Karaha respectively, with Vice-President Thabo

---

[78] The American hesitation towards the end of the rebellion were expressed adequately in the title of an article in *The International Herald Tribune* of 28 March 1997: 'Washington Hopes Mobutu Loses and Kabila Doesn't Win'. In early April, the State Department's spokesperson Nicholas Burns said that 'Laurent Kabila has stayed in the jungle for thirty years and we have no idea about the ideology he would apply once he takes power' (quoted in *Le Figaro*, 11 April 1997).

[79] Reuters, Lomé, 27 March 1997.

[80] AFP, Goma, 31 March 1997.

Mbeki and Ambassador Sahnoun being present. Of course, the fall of Mbuji-Mayi on 6 April and the threat against Lubumbashi (which was to fall on 9 April) further weakened the position of the government delegation, which, despite Mobutu's overtures,[81] did not obtain the much hoped for ceasefire. The 8 April final communiqué did not contain anything concrete, although five 'points of convergence'[82] were enumerated, but these were only vague declarations of intent and did not commit anyone. Obviously, the rebels gave signs of goodwill to please the international community, but their objective remained the total military victory that was within reach.[83] The day after the Pretoria communiqué, Kabila gave Mobutu three days 'to negotiate his departure', failing which the AFDL was to march to Kinshasa. Even Mobutu's final ally, France, now saw the situation turning and, well after the Americans and the Belgians, publicly expressed its distance. After the Lomé summit, Paris, for the first time, did not refer to the 'rebels' any longer, but used the name of the rebel organisation (AFDL). On 9 April, the *Quai d'Orsay* stated that it was up to the Zairean population to determine its own fate: France did not support anyone, 'what we support is Zaire and the future of its people' and it added that, at any rate, France recognised states and not governments.[84] From that moment, Paris was to try and secure Mobutu's 'soft' exit and promote the setting up of a transitional government that would be the outcome of a negotiated settlement.

Even after the fall of Lubumbashi, the international community continued to (pretend to) promote a negotiated solution. However, it was progressively to limit its ambitions to ensuring a 'soft landing' of the rebellion

---

[81] In an interview published in the South African *Sunday Times* of 6 April 1997, Mobutu called Kabila 'a nationalist patriot. I urgently invite him to sit around the table with his Zairean brothers and sisters in order to restore peace and participate in the current democratic process'.

[82] Urgent need to address the problems of political structures and of governance;
Negotiations leading to a political and peaceful solution to the conflict;
Recognition of the territorial integrity and sovereignty of the country;
Need for fundamental democratic change and a transition process leading to transparent, fair and inclusive elections;
Search for ways and means of promoting good relations between states in favour of regional stability.

[83] Echoing Museveni's tactics during the Ugandan civil war, Bizima Karaha told the Australian Broadcasting Corporation that the rebels' strategy was to 'talk and fight and fight and talk' (*Zaire Watch News Briefs*, 12 May 1997, quoted by W. Madsen, *Genocide and Covert Operations...*, op. cit., p. 286).

[84] As late as 1 March, Foreign Minister Hervé de Charette said that 'Mobutu is undoubtedly the only person capable of contributing to the solution of the problem'.

in Kinshasa. During a visit to Lubumbashi on 5 May, U.S. Ambassador Bill Richardson stated that 'the aim of my urgent mission is to prepare a soft landing for Mr. Kabila's rebels when they reach Kinshasa, a landing that avoids bloodshed and chaos'.[85] In the meantime, U.S., Belgian, British and French army units were positioned in the Republic of Congo (Brazzaville and Pointe-Noire) as a dissuasion and evacuation force. As a reaction, Kabila raised the stakes on an issue that is, and has always been, very delicate in the west, that is, the security of expatriates. A communiqué of 18 April claimed that 'Mobutu has ordered the military intelligence services and the Division spéciale présidentielle to kill expatriates in Kinshasa, in order to invite the American, French and Belgian forces to invade our country with the aim of preventing our victory'. Mobutu's son Nganza Mobutu immediately denied the allegation, which, indeed, was just a transparent attempt to sow panic in the expatriate community, which, however, was not duped. After new contacts between the two sides in Pretoria and a visit by Kabila to South Africa in mid-April, Mandela sent official invitations for a face-to-face meeting between Mobutu and Kabila. As Mobutu replied that he was in no condition to travel to South Africa due to health reasons, this was to be the start of the bizarre episode of the South African military vessel Outeniqua.

It was bizarre indeed, as it was obvious to all observers that the chances of reaching a negotiated settlement were nil. After Mobutu made it known on 12 April that he was not willing to receive an ultimatum from a 'gang leader' but that, 'if Mr. Kabila asks politely, I cannot refuse to meet with a Zairean compatriot', Bizima Karaha stated on behalf of the AFDL that 'a cease-fire would only prolong the suffering of our people'. In his first public speech in Lubumbashi on 19 April, Kabila confirmed that 'the war must continue until the liberation of Kinshasa', that he would never accept a government of national union and that 'Mobutu must negotiate the conditions of his departure from power with me'. This episode also increased the concerns of the internal opposition, which feared marginalisation. An advisor to Etienne Tshisekedi stated his opinion that 'organising negotiations with which the unarmed opposition is not associated would be a way of prolonging the crisis. If the summit is to discuss future elections, a three-way dialogue is indispensable'.[86] Nevertheless, the machine was running, or at least wanted to convey

---

[85] Reuters, Lubumbashi, 5 May 1997.
[86] *Le Monde*, 20–21 April 1997.

that impression. While Ambassador Richardson[87] embarked on a new whistlestop tour (during which he met Museveni, Kagame, Kabila, Dos Santos and Mobutu),[88] the South African Foreign Minister announced on 29 April that a Mobutu–Kabila summit was to take place aboard a military vessel in international waters. On 2 May, Mbeki, Richardson and Sahnoun met in Luanda to prepare for the meeting and, above all, to ensure the presence of the two parties; Kabila's participation, in particular, remained uncertain.[89] Kagame was also present and, according to a press article, Kabila 'was given a final briefing by the two men, Kagame and Dos Santos, who made him king'.[90]

On 4 May, Mobutu and Kabila met aboard the SAS Outeniqua, docked in the port of Pointe-Noire rather than sailing in international waters.[91] The meeting, chaired by Mandela, achieved nothing and confirmed that the differences between Mobutu and Kabila were insurmountable: Kabila intended to put in place a transitional power structure under his own terms,[92] while Mobutu was adamant that he would relinquish power only as a result of elections organised by a broad-based transitional authority.

[87] Even at this advanced stage of the rebellion, Richardson thought (or proclaimed to think) that a negotiated issue was still possible: 'There can be no military solution to this crisis. President Mobutu and rebel leader Kabila must meet face-to-face' (Mike Hanna, CNN, 29 April 1997).

[88] Richardson gave Mobutu a letter dated 25 April from President Clinton, who expressed the hope 'that your withdrawal from active political life (...) would serve the best interests of your country' (reproduced in F. Vunduawe Te Pemako, *A l'ombre du Léopard...*, *op. cit.*, annex II). During the meeting, Richardson formulated a real ultimatum. He stated that 'it is time for you to withdraw from the political scene in honour and dignity, now that it is still time'. The United States were to ensure Mobutu's security and possessions 'with the respect due to a Head of State' (H. N'Gbanda, *Ainsi sonne le glas...*, *op. cit.*, p. 300; F. Vunduawe Te Pemako, *A l'ombre du Léopard...*, *op. cit.*, p. 405). According to N'Gbanda, Mobutu accepted the offer and had a letter drafted in which he asked President Clinton to confirm these guarantees in writing. However, the letter was never sent, but one with a similar message was addressed to President Chirac (on this confused episode, see H. N'Gbanda, *Ainsi sonne le glas...*, *op. cit.*, pp. 303–306; the two letters are reprinted on pp. 433, 437). According to Vunduawe, the letter was effectively given to Richardson, but Mobutu refused to sign it (F. Vunduawe Te Pemako, *A l'ombre du Léopard...*, *op. cit.*, annex III).

[89] Reuters, Luanda, 2 May 1997.

[90] *Le Soir*, 5 May 1997.

[91] According to Vunduawe (*A l'ombre du Léopard...*, *op. cit.*, pp. 428–435), Kabila's seers advised him not to meet Mobutu on firm land and never to look in his eyes. Footage of the meeting indeed shows that Kabila watched the ceiling and never looked at Mobutu, whose spell he clearly feared.

[92] The AFDL plan, which provided for the rendition of Mobutu and the accession of Kabila to the presidency, is reproduced in F. Vunduawe Te Pemako, *A l'ombre du Léopard...*, *op. cit.*, annex IV.

However, it was agreed that a new meeting was to take place within ten days, an unrealistic perspective as the battle for Kenge, the last stage before Kinshasa, was to start only two days later. Nevertheless, Bill Richardson remained 'optimistic'. During a visit to Paris on 8 May, he claimed that 'the ingredients of a peaceful transition are there', a feeling shared by the *Quai d'Orsay*: the objective remained 'a political exit to the crisis, with a transition mechanism', which was to lead to 'free elections with international supervisors'. In fact, by then the Americans had for some time lost control over Kabila, who had become a loose cannon they now openly and belatedly distrusted.

Knowing that he could not hope for an agreement, Mobutu then attempted *in extremis* to relaunch another option he had in reserve; he tried to muster the support of a number of Francophone countries to face the eastern and southern axis that sided with the AFDL. On 8 May, he met in Libreville with the leaders of Gabon, Togo, Equatorial Guinea, Congo (Brazzaville), the Central African Republic, Chad and Cameroon.[93] At the end of the summit, Mobutu announced that he would not be a candidate for his own succession. In addition, he asked the HCR–PT to elect a new speaker, who in virtue of the transitional constitutional act was to assume the interim post of President of the Republic.[94] The next day, the Libreville plan[95] was rejected by the AFDL; Bizima Karaha announced that 'the transition will be led by the Alliance, and by the Alliance alone'. On the same day, Thabo Mbeki, again engaged in a diplomatic whistlestop tour that took him to Luanda, Dar Es Salam, Kigali and Lubumbashi, announced that a second meeting aboard the Outeniqua was to be held on 14 May. On 13 May, the day before the scheduled meeting, Kabila, however, clearly indicated that he was not interested in a negotiated settlement. In the 'Democracy Now' programme on American Pacific Radio, he reiterated his opposition to a transitional government and insisted that power be directly transferred to the AFDL. He also accused the United States and European countries of 'manipulation' and 'intrigue', aimed at replacing Mobutu while leaving Mobutism intact: '(the foreign powers) cannot come in like that, imposing upon us a lot of conditions and deciding for our people who should be its leader (...) The time has come for

---

[93] As we shall see later, Kabila was to play the same card some three years later.

[94] The position of Speaker of the HCR–PT had been vacant since early 1995, when Mgr. Monsengwo was forced to resign after a vote of no-confidence. On 10 May 1997, Monsengwo was indeed re-elected as Speaker after a vote contested by the radical opposition, which called Monsengwo a 'Mobutist' (see later text).

[95] Reproduced in F. Vunduawe Te Pemako, *A l'ombre du Léopard...*, *op. cit.*, annex V.

these great powers to leave the people of this country in peace'.[96] On the scheduled day, Mandela, Mobutu and Sahnoun were in Pointe-Noire, but Kabila, who was in Luanda, failed to appear. Invoking security concerns,[97] he announced on 15 May that he was not coming to the meeting: a real insult to President Mandela[98] and the Americans who had done their utmost to organise the meeting. Kinshasa fell two days later.

From the start, diplomatic efforts were characterised by ambiguity and a good deal of hypocrisy. After the initial refusal of the Zairean regime to negotiate with the rebellion, the AFDL pretended to pursue a negotiated settlement and the international community pretended to believe it. However, after the fall of Kisangani, the AFDL used a recipe applied with success by Museveni in Uganda: 'Talk and Fight', where 'talking' is part of a military strategy rather than a genuine willingness to achieve a political agreement. Moreover, as is the case elsewhere in the world, the 'international community' does not really exist. Until March 1997, the American and French agendas were so divergent and their mutual distrust so deep that coordinated action proved impossible. The responsibility of the United States is particularly heavy: combating the Khartoum regime and intent on toppling Mobutu, the Americans actively supported their Ugandan and Rwandan allies and thus took the risk, a risk which eventually materialised, of durably destabilising the entire region. The French also engaged in *Realpolitik*: gravely discredited in the region, they lacked the moral authority to influence the course of events, even supposing that their intentions were honest and their actions better informed than those of the United States. When a certain *rapprochement* occurred between Washington and Paris, it was too late for concerted action, as Kabila felt that victory was in sight. By then, he had become uncontrollable, an 'unguided missile' in the words of a U.S. official.

In addition, coordination was consistently lacking: first Kenya, later South Africa and a host of special envoys of the UN, the EU, the OAU, the United States and other bilateral players were all, at one time or another, trying to get their foot in the door. In early April 1997, Kofi Annan expressed concern over this proliferation of mediators. He feared

---

[96] IPS, New York, 13 May 1977.

[97] The AFDL radio was more specific and claimed that Gabon and Togo were preparing for Kabila's assassination in Pointe-Noire. It will be seen later that Kabila became obsessed by real or imaginary attempts on his life.

[98] According to N'Gbanda, Mandela lambasted Kabila for his 'lack of political culture and respect for heads of state and elders' (H. N'Gbanda, *Ainsi sonne le glas...*, *op. cit.*, p. 320).

that 'there (were) too many cooks in this kitchen' and hoped that all
would pull together to support Ambassador Sahnoun.[99] However, without U.S. support and therefore, without much leverage, there was nothing
Sahnoun could do and Kabila understood this perfectly well. Finally, the
1996–7 war showed that the capacity of international players to influence
a given situation considerably decreased in favour of local and regional
actors, who pursued their own agendas and had the major advantage of
being militarily and politically present on the theatre. In this sense, as
Prunier has rightly stressed,[100] the importance given (e.g., by the press)
to a French–American confrontation was probably exaggerated. The
impotence of the so-called international community was to become even
more glaring during the second war (see later text).

### 4.3 MEANWHILE, IN KINSHASA, THE ORCHESTRA ON THE *TITANIC*

As previously stated, 'the Kivu was not its affair' for the political class
in Kinshasa.[101] This feeling, together with a political practice that had
become increasingly surreal and where excessive legalism and the constant negotiation of personal and factional interests pretended to further
the 'transition', explains why in Kinshasa it was 'business as usual', even
well after the beginning of the war in the east. Lye Yoka described the
illusion of a capital city where 'the workers do not work, the students
do not study, the ministers do not administer, the presidents do not pre-
side, the educators do not educate'[102]; one is tempted to add 'and where
fighters do not fight'... The broken vessel was sinking, but the orchestra
continued to play.

The events in the east initially generated a rise in nationalist sentiment,
coupled with anti-Tutsi hysteria. At the end of October 1996, the Tutsi
in Goma were the victims of abuse by certain 'autochthones' with the
approval, if not upon the incitement of, local authorities. Many Tutsi fled
to Gisenyi, just across the border in Rwanda. In Kinshasa, the HCR–PT

---

[99] *Le Monde*, 2 April 1997.

[100] G. Prunier, 'La crise du Kivu et ses conséquences dans la région des Grands Lacs', *Hérodote*, 86–87, third–fourth term 1997, p. 55.

[101] The politics of Kinshasa towards the rebellion are only briefly addressed here. For more details, see G. De Villers, J. Omasombo, *Zaïre. La transition manquée...*, op. cit., in particular pp. 259–280.

[102] Yoka Liye, *Lettres d'un Kinois à l'oncle du village*, Brussels/Paris, Institut Africain/ L'Harmattan, Cahiers Africains, 15, 1995, p. 16.

demanded that diplomatic relations with Rwanda and Burundi be broken off, all Rwandans and Burundians working in the civil service be sacked, the Munyarwanda-run Telecel company be seized and all refugees be repatriated. Pogroms against Tutsi started. On 1 November, thousands of students took to the streets and looted homes and businesses belonging to Tutsi; they also demanded the resignation of Prime Minister Kengo wa Dondo, whose grandmother was a Tutsi.[103] Many Banyarwanda went into hiding or crossed the river to seek shelter in Brazzaville, while the more affluent fled to Europe or Rwanda. On 7 November, 1000 students occupied Parliament and again asked for the sacking of Kengo and his replacement by Etienne Tshisekedi. They also demanded the appointment of General Mahele as chief of staff replacing General Eluki: '(Mahele) is a leopard, a fighter. He will bring us Kagame's head. Eluki can go and watch the catch on television'.[104]

Kengo attempted to regain the initiative. Playing the nationalist card, he referred to 'serious signs of intelligence of certain Zaireans with the enemy'. Moreover, he, of course, announced that the recapture of lost territory in Kivu was 'ineluctable', that Marshall Mobutu was to return soon, that the suspension of diplomatic relations with Rwanda, Burundi and Uganda was 'under examination' and (business as usual) that the elections were to take place in May 1997.[105] As in the past, the crisis and the accompanying nationalist feelings were immediately seized upon by President Mobutu. Accustomed to 'governing from a distance',[106] whether in Gbadolite or in Roquebrune-Cap Martin, despite his debilitating illness, he claimed to be in charge. In an interview with Stephen Smith, he stated that 'up to now, no one, I repeat: no one, has questioned my authority over the armed forces'. He also announced that he was to be a candidate for his own succession and that he was to return to Kinshasa soon: 'today, Zaire needs me'.[107] Moreover, he succeeded in breaking through his international isolation[108]: after his arrival in his French residence, the

[103] Kengo's mother had a Ngbandi father and a Tutsi mother; his father was a Belgian Jew of Polish origin.
[104] *Le Monde*, 9 November 1996.
[105] *Le Monde*, 23 November 1996.
[106] The expression is from Stephen Smith, *Libération*, 9–10 November 1996.
[107] *Libération*, 9–10 November 1996.
[108] It must however be added that Mobutu's isolation had already considerably decreased since 1993–4, due to the way in which the internal opposition increasingly discredited itself and also, even more, to the crises in the Great Lakes region. On the way the Phoenix rose from the ashes, see G. De Villers, 'Dernier acte au Zaïre de Mobutu: le Phénix et le Sphinx', in: *Kabila prend le pouvoir...*, *op. cit.*, pp. 15–30.

villa 'Del Mare' on the *Côte d'Azur*, on 4 November he received UN envoy Raymond Chrétien, President Lissouba, Vice-President Thabo Mbeki, President Omar Bongo, and several foreign ministers, and also was in frequent telephone contact with Jacques Chirac and Boutros-Ghali, among others.

While the rebellion was not interested in a negotiated settlement (see earlier text), the internal opposition continued to reason following the logic of the 'achievements (*acquis*) of the Sovereign National Conference (CNS)' and the 'transition'. Thus, the main opposition leader Etienne Tshisekedi, elected prime minister by the CNS, attempted to seize the opportunity offered by the crisis to recover that position. On 21 November 1996, he visited Mobutu in Cap Martin. After a meeting that lasted only half an hour, Mobutu made no declaration, but Tshisekedi announced that the two men agreed on 'national reconciliation': 'Now the two chiefs will come together as a matter of responsibility'. From then on, the two political families involved in the transition[109] were to work together. Upon leaving Mobutu's residence, Tshisekedi announced on RFI that he was now 'the Prime Minister of a government of national union, with the approval of President Mobutu'. This was immediately denied by Mobutu's special advisor N'Gbanda, who stated that this issue was not raised during the conversation. Still according to Tshisekedi, Kabila, 'an authentic Zairean' subscribing to the CNS project,[110] would realise that the rebellion had lost its rationale.

When returning to Kinshasa on 27 November, 'Tshitshi' was welcomed at the airport by close to 1 million *Kinois* shouting '*Mobali ya Mobutu ayé*' (the husband of Mobutu arrives)... On 17 December, Mobutu returned to the country he had not seen since August. He too was greeted by huge crowds ('Welcome Papa Mobutu, our saviour').[111] The next day, he appointed General Mahele as chief of staff (see earlier text), thus replacing 'politician-businessman' Baramoto with a professional officer.

---

[109] The FPC on the president's side and the USORAL for the opposition. In fact, these 'families' had ceased to be homogenous blocs for quite a while (see earlier text).

[110] This was clearly wishful thinking on behalf of Tshisekedi: in an open letter quoted earlier ('Naufrage du processus de la démocratisation', 6 December 1993), Kabila called the CNS 'futile' (p. 7). In an interview with Colette Braeckman, Kabila confirmed his claim: 'this conference (...) was infiltrated from day one and manipulated by Mobutu's agents. Its results were flawed and its resolutions have never been applied' (*Le Soir*, 23–24 November 1996).

[111] 'We are very happy. With him being back, we will all win the war together', said a young newspaper vendor to *Le Monde* (18 December 1996), 'he alone can give orders to his generals'. In addition, the mere news of Mobutu's arrival in Kinshasa caused people to flee Goma, where a FAZ offensive was feared now that the 'chief' was back.

Mahele was also to control, at least in principle, the DSP, the *Garde civile* and the Service d'action et de renseignement militaire (SARM) (military intelligence), which in practice did not follow the regular military structures. Generals Baramoto and Bolozi, who commanded the *Garde civile* and the SARM respectively, were replaced, while General Nzimbi remained the DSP commander, which was now theoretically placed under the authority of the Chief of Staff.

Contrary to popular hopes and expectations, Mobutu did not, however, appoint Tshisekedi as prime minister. On 20 December, after 'consultations' with the two political families on the previous day and positioning himself as the 'guarantor of the nation', thanks to the profound divisions in the opposition,[112] Mobutu confirmed Kengo as the head of a reshuffled government; the only minister from the Union pour la démocratie et le progrès social (UDPS) came from the wing opposed to Tshisekedi.[113] After signing the decree of appointment, Mobutu left Kinshasa to 'take part in the Christmas celebrations' in his Gbadolite fiefdom. Another sign of surreal 'normality' was that after the HCR–PT had approved a draft constitutional amendment at the beginning of the war (5–6 October 1996), on 28 December, Mobutu signed the law providing for the organisation of a constitutional referendum. Likewise, the radical opposition continued to function as if nothing had happened. During a meeting on 4 January 1997, the chairman of the Union sacrée de l'opposition radicale et alliés (USORAL) declared that he did 'not recognise Mr. Mobutu as head of state and guarantor of the Nation'. He announced the launching of a campaign of civil disobedience and called upon members to be ready 'to shed blood for the overthrow of Mobutu's dictatorship'. Observers noted that 'the war, the ongoing process of the country's dismemberment did not discourage the political elites from continuing their game of musical chairs ...'.[114] After 'having put the house in order', on 8 January 1997, Mobutu returned to France for medical checks.

---

[112] The UDPS–Tshisekedi continued to prevail itself of the 'legitimacy' of the CNS. According to his spokesman, 'Etienne Tshisekedi has been elected Prime Minister by the National Conference; he alone can today assume this office, and there can be no discussion about this' (*Le Soir*, 21 December 1996).

[113] Apart from the ministers of the Mouvement populaire de la révolution (MPR), the Union pour la République et la démocratie (URD) and Tabiana of the Parti démocrate et social-chrétien (PDSC), the members of the government did not hold office with the consent of their respective parties, from which they were immediately excluded; so they sat in their individual capacity.

[114] G. De Villers, J. Omasombo, *Zaïre. La transition manquée...*, *op. cit.*, p. 240. Another example of the practices of an irredeemable political class: just a few days before the

Surprisingly, it was not just the Zairean political class that continued to reason following the logic of the 'transition'. The 'international community' too seemed to believe that elections were to be the way forward. On 17 October 1996, Aldo Ajello welcomed the adoption of the draft constitutional amendment: 'I believe that we are now on the right track', he said, referring to the process that was supposed to lead to elections in May 1997.[115] At the end of November, the Belgian Minister for Development Cooperation visited Kinshasa and announced the payment of a first instalment of US$ 1 million to the National Electoral Commission. On 24 February 1997, three weeks before the fall of Kisangani, the Council of Ministers of the EU reaffirmed the importance of the holding of elections for which it earmarked ECU 30 million. On 21 January, the Belgian foreign minister '(remained) convinced that the continuation of the transition process and the holding of free and fair elections (...) are the only framework for a durable solution'.[116] Even after the fall of Kisangani, Minister Derycke stated on 20 March in the Belgian Senate that he remained convinced that 'the holding of free and serious elections in Zaire is the only way to relaunch the country'. Belgian journalist Colette Braeckman expressed understandable surprise at 'this precipitated project, at a time when vast regions occupied by the rebels would remain excluded from the (electoral) consultation', adding that this perspective 'risks provoking the falling apart (of Zaire), which everyone says must be avoided'.[117]

At one single moment, which coincided with a pause in the rebellion's progression (see earlier text), an internal negotiated settlement seemed a possibility. On 17 January 1997, Kabila invited the Zairean government to the negotiating table. He proposed holding a 'national conference' in Goma aimed at putting into place a 'transitional government'[118] However, such an appeal fell on deaf ears in Kinshasa, where

fall of Kisangani, the distribution of state allowances continued. Some sixty members of the HCR–PT were appointed CEO or member of the board of public corporations in a vast operation aimed, according to the government, at ensuring 'an equitable division of power', but which mainly served to open access to comfortable salaries.

[115] AFP, Kinshasa, 17 October 1996.

[116] AFP, Brussels, 21 January 1997. In line with the logic of the 'transition', the UDPS representative in France called the Belgian Minister's position 'unacceptable': 'The UDPS reaffirms its position to start negotiations between President Mobutu, the democratic opposition of Etienne Tshisekedi and the armed opposition of Laurent-Désiré Kabila, before the organisation of general elections' (AFP, Paris, 7 February 1997).

[117] *Le Soir*, 15–16 February 1997.

[118] AFP, Goma, 18 January 1997.

at the time there was a large consensus in support of the war effort, following the announcement in early January of the 'total and lightning
counter-offensive' (see earlier text). At any rate, the venue proposed for
the meeting was unacceptable for the political class of Kinshasa, both
for reasons of security and because Goma was in a zone 'under foreign
occupation'. In early February, the AFDL launched a final ultimatum: if
negotiations did not start on 21 February, the rebellion was to launch
a 'general offensive'.[119] At the time this ultimatum was announced, the
offensive was, however, being fully prepared, particularly by the airlifting of Katangese *gendarmes*, who spearheaded the second phase of the
war (see earlier text).

In the meantime, the position of Prime Minister Kengo had become
increasingly uncomfortable. As has been stated earlier, students asked
for his resignation in November 1996. On 10 February 1997, the radical opposition movement Forces novatrices pour l'union et la solidarité
(FONUS) organised a 'dead city' day widely followed in Kinshasa and
Kisangani.[120] FONUS leader Joseph Olenga Nkoy again demanded
Kengo's departure for his 'incapacity to tackle the challenge posed by
the war in the east', but also because of his 'delaying manoeuvre' on
the electoral timetable and the introduction of bills of 100,000, 500,000
and 1 million New Zaires,[121] which the population feared would fuel
inflation.[122]

The fall of Kisangani sealed Kengo's fate. On 18 March, the HCR–PT
sacked the government in a vote that was illegal as the quorum was not
reached.[123] According to some sources in the parliament, Kengo's demo-
tion was part of a deal between the opposition and a moderate wing of
the army. Under the leadership of Mahele, reportedly the deal was to prevent a *coup* by the 'falcons' (among whom were Nzimbi and Baramoto)
and to provide the army with the means necessary to fight the war more
efficiently, while the opposition was to attempt to enter into contact with
the rebellion, in order to seek a negotiated political transition.

---

[119] AFP, Goma, 3 February 1997.
[120] AFP, Kinshasa, 10 February 1997.
[121] The latter banknotes were immediately nicknamed 'prostates', a reference to President
Mobutu's disease.
[122] At the end of February, Olenga Nkoy fled Zaire. During a press conference in Brussels,
he suggested a *rapprochement* with Kabila (*La Libre Belgique*, 1–2 March 1997).
[123] Instead of a vote of 445 members out of a total of 464 present, a three-quarter majority
of all members was needed, that is, 552 out of a total of 736. However, a great deal of
confusion surrounded these numbers, very different from one source to another.

Mobutu returned to Kinshasa on 21 March. His welcome was markedly less enthusiastic than that of December.[124] Before leaving France, he appealed for a ceasefire and the creation of a 'National Council representing all tendencies and sensitivities', in order to 'find with all our brothers (...) the appropriate means to find a way out of the situation that affects our country so badly'.[125] Happy to rid himself of an increasingly unpopular government, Mobutu 'took notice' of the decision of the HCR–PT and, after some unconvincing resistance, Kengo resigned on 24 March.[126] On 1 April, the 'political family' of the opposition proposed Tshisekedi, among five candidates,[127] for the post of prime minister. Mobutu immediately accepted, a move that allowed him to pit two of his adversaries, Tshisekedi and Kabila, against each other, as well as dividing the opposition,[128] all the more so since declarations made by Kabila in Kisangani on 25 March worried the internal opposition: indeed Kabila, doubting the opposition's integrity, announced the prohibition of political parties in the areas under rebel control and made it clear that, after taking power, he intended to run the country through a transitional government composed exclusively of the AFDL. Although the AFDL warned that whoever would become prime minister would be considered a 'traitor', Tshisekedi accepted the appointment. He announced his cabinet on 3 April: without consulting anyone, and by invoking the 'legitimacy' of the CNS, he reconstituted his team of March 1993, but he did not fill six portfolios which he reserved for the AFDL. Again following the logic of the legitimacy derived from the CNS, he revived the CNS constitution and, as a consequence, announced that the HCR–PT had disappeared in favour of the HCR instituted by the CNS.

[124] Probably for reasons of ill health, he remained for hours in the aeroplane on the tarmac at Ndjili airport, and he was driven almost incognito to Tshatshi military camp in town.

[125] AFP, Roquebrune–Cap–Martin, 20 March 1997.

[126] He left the country a few weeks later. On 15 April, the new Information and Press Minister Kin-Kiey Mulumba accused him of having emptied the treasury and announced that an international arrest warrant was to be issued against him. According to a document released by Kengo in reply to these accusations, the 'treasury' contained a mere US$ 80,000 at the time he left office. The arrest warrant never materialised.

[127] Apart from Etienne Tshisekedi, the candidates were Frédéric Kibassa Maliba (the leader of a dissident wing of UDPS), Thomas Kanza (a Lumumbist veteran), Pierre Pay Pay (former Governor of the Central Bank and Finance Minister) and Arthur Z'Ahidi Ngoma (an international civil servant with UNESCO). The latter became a leader of the rebellion against Kabila in August 1998 and an interim vice-president in 2003.

[128] One of Mobutu's tried and tested tricks, and it worked again.

As was to be expected, both the FPC and the other members of his own political family rejected Tshisekedi's moves. In a joint declaration issued on 5 April, the FPC and USORAL 'decide to withdraw their confidence in Mr. Etienne Tshisekedi wa Mulumba as Prime Minister'. The AFDL reacted with disdain. It refused even to talk to Tshisekedi and pursued its contacts with Mobutu's representative in South Africa, whereas Tshisekedi called the Pretoria meetings 'useless'.[129] According to Raphaël Ghenda, the AFDL wanted 'the departure of Mobutu and his administration. Etienne Tshisekedi is his Prime Minister. We do not see why we would enter his government'. The rebellion also confirmed that it expected 'Mobutu to retire and hand over power to us. We will then appoint a government composed exclusively of members of the Alliance, before organising elections in one, two or three years'. As will be seen later, Tshisekedi finally ended his own political destruction and that of the UDPS during the transition in 2003–6.

The day after the fall of Mbuji-Mayi and a few days before that of Lubumbashi, the country was thus left without a government. Sacked due to lack of a majority in parliament, Tshisekedi accused Mobutu of high treason for having violated the constitution and called upon the army to cease fighting the AFDL.[130] Mobutu declared a state of emergency on 8 April and, the next day, asked General Likulia, who was vice prime minister and defence minister in the last Kengo administration, to form a 'government of national salvation', which was presented on 11 April, two days after the fall of Lubumbashi. This was the first time since the start of the 'transition' in 1990 that a government had been led by an officer. In addition, the portfolios of defence and the interior were given to generals. While other factions of the radical opposition were included, the Tshisekedi faction was not represented in the cabinet. It was as if the Tshisekedi interlude had not even existed, as the handover of affairs occurred between Kengo and Likulia. Echoing the declarations made at the start of the year, Likulia announced the restructuring of the FAZ, in order to put into place 'a republican army respectful of human rights and liberties'. As seen earlier, the war was by then, of course, completely lost, and these words must have sounded very hollow in the ears of both the FAZ and the AFDL.

---

[129] 'Those who want to go to South Africa are free to do so, but I fail to see the usefulness of the Pretoria meeting (...) Kabila is my brother, I do not need an intermediary to meet with him'.

[130] Reuters, Kinshasa, 10 April 1997.

The circle of institutional 'normality' was closed on 10 May, when Monsignor Monsengwo was reelected as speaker of the HCR–PT. According to the interim constitution, he was to take interim power if a presidential office vacancy were to occur.[131] While remaining very vague about whether or not he accepted the post ('The decision has not yet been notified officially'), Monsengwo, who was in Brussels at the time, suggested he would fill the position 'if national and international guarantees are given that the constitutional scheme of the CNS will be respected' and subject, of course, to the authorisation of the ecclesiastic authorities. It came as no surprise that both the AFDL and the radical opposition immediately denounced Monsengwo's election as a manoeuvre of the Mobutists to save the regime. On the other hand, in a statement that was quite astonishing in the light of the actual situation, the Belgian foreign minister welcomed the move; he felt that Monsengwo could play a rallying role within the opposition and act as a mediator in the negotiations with Kabila,[132] adding that 'the aim is not to replace Joseph-Désiré Mobutu by Laurent-Désiré Kabila'.[133]

On 14 May, Mobutu left Kinshasa for Gbadolite. After a meeting of the council of ministers, the government issued a surreal communiqué stating that President Mobutu 'decided to stay aloof' of political affairs and that he was not to present himself for re-election, 'in order not to appear as an obstacle to a negotiated settlement and to the constitutional order'. However, there was no question of resignation and, according to the government spokesman, henceforth, Mobutu 'reigns but does not govern'. The communiqué invited the AFDL to enter into the search for 'a satisfactory compromise between the theses defended by the belligerents' and finally indicated that it was now 'incumbent upon Mgr. Monsengwo to ensure the mediation of the crisis'.[134] The next day, the AFDL entered Kinshasa. The regime was so inept that it was not even able to organise the 'bloodbath' feared by the international community.[135] De Villers and

---

[131] It will be recalled that this election followed the Libreville summit of 8 May, when Mobutu made a last desperate bid to save the situation (see earlier text).

[132] *La Libre Belgique*, 12 May 1997.

[133] *Le Soir*, 12 May 1997.

[134] Large extracts of the communiqué can be found in *La Libre Belgique*, 17 May to 19 May 1997.

[135] General Mahele, who according to some sources was killed by Mobutu's son Kongolo, became the means of atonement. Intent on avoiding a bloodbath in Kinshasa, he maintained contacts with the AFDL for several weeks. According to one of N'Gbanda's sources (*Ainsi sonne le glas...*, *op. cit.*, p. 253), the U.S. Ambassador established the link between Mahele and Kabila. N'Gbanda also claims that he heard Mahele ask General

Omasombo conclude that 'while the audience has long left the theatre, the players of the 'transition' play their role up to the very end. However a competing company enters the scene and lowers the curtain'.[136]

## 4.4 THE NEW GEOPOLITICAL SITUATION

The seizure of power by the AFDL through the support of a formidable regional coalition created a complex situation. This was due not only to the fact that the AFDL itself was a circumstantial and therefore fragile alliance, but also to its foreign sponsors not adhering to the same agenda *per se*. The crimes committed against the Rwandan, Burundian and Zairean Hutu and the claim by Kagame (e.g., in *The Washington Post*, see earlier text) on the predominant role played by Rwanda during the war only compounded a volatile situation.

Kagame's claims first embarrassed Kabila. Wanting to be seen as a Congolese nationalist, he always denied the implication of foreign forces beyond providing political support. Although he was already being confronted with dissatisfaction about the perceived domination of the AFDL by Zairean and Rwandan Tutsi, Kagame's statement reinforced those who accused Kabila of being a mere puppet with very limited autonomy.[137] It will be seen later that Kabila's attempts to be seen to 'liberate' himself from the Rwandan influence was to be one of the causes of the next war. Kagame's admission was also, paradoxically, a potential embarrassment for Rwanda and its regional allies. It indeed acknowledged that elements of the Rwandan army were present at times and places where crimes against humanity were committed, and thus reinforced the many accounts of the RPA's involvement in the massacres. For Rwanda's allies, the Ugandans in particular, the 'revelation' to *The Washington Post*

---

Ilunga to instruct his soldiers not to fight in Kinshasa (*idem*, p. 328). In a similar vein, members of a small leftist opposition party, the Front patriotique (FP), guided the rebel forces through Kinshasa. The FP was to be the only party to obtain portfolios (Sondji and Kinkela) in the first AFDL government put into place by Kabila.

[136] G. De Villers, J. Omasombo, *Zaïre. La transition manquée...*, *op. cit.*, p. 280.

[137] The embarrassment of the new Congolese authorities was considerable. Kabila immediately denied the claims and said that he had 'summoned' Kagame to explain his statement (*The Washington Post*, 12 July 1997; Reuters, Nairobi, 16 July 1997); Minister Etienne Mbaya refused to comment on the Kagame interview and accused the press of having Kagame say things he did not say (AFP, Kinshasa, 15 July 1997); Minister Mwenze Kongolo would not confirm that the RPA had participated in the war and added: 'This country is ours (...) It is not Kagame's territory' (AFP, Johannesburg, 13 July 1997).

rendered more difficult and less plausible the denial of their own involvement in the war.

The two problems that were the immediate roots of the war had not been solved. These were, on the one hand, the status of the 'populations of doubtful citizenship', a coded expression for Kinyarwanda-speakers in eastern Zaire/Congo; indeed the resentment against the Banyarwanda by the 'autochthonous' populations had become worse than before. On the other hand, the Rwandan security concerns did not disappear: the massive return of Hutu refugees during the fall of 1996 simply displaced, at least in part, the problem from outside to inside the country; in addition, pockets of former FAR and Interahamwe remained active in South and North Kivu. As will be seen later, the main political problem of Rwanda, the exclusion of growing numbers of Hutu and even of Tutsi, even increased.

The persistence of these problems contributed to the regional extension of the ethnic bipolarisation that showed its destructive potential in Rwanda and Burundi. Rapid ethnogenesis was underway: increasing numbers of voices in Zaire/Congo and in the Kivu region in particular developed the theme of a conflict between 'Bantu' and 'Hamites', 'Hima' or 'Nilotics'. The issue was presented in these terms as early as December 1996, when a Council for the Resistance and Liberation of Kivu (Conseil de résistance et de libération du Kivu [CRLK]), identifying itself as a 'Bantu' organisation, stated one of its objectives to be to 'chase the Hima from the territories of East Zaire'. Similar suggestions are found in Professor Kabuya-Lumuna Sando's introduction to a publication by the Zairean Ministry of Information and Press. 'Faced with the hegemonic doctrine of the Tutsi', he identified 'sort of an objective alliance between the peoples of Zaire and the Hutu'.[138] The obvious influence of Congolese and Rwandan Tutsi in the AFDL leadership and the frustrations this caused reinforced the temptation of an ethnic drift, which even infected Uganda: at the end of July 1997, the rebel ADF declared it wanted to save Uganda from 'Tutsism'.[139]

While already facing a dangerous stalemate inside its borders, Rwanda seemed to claim some regional leadership. On 15 June 1997, the RPF general secretary Denis Polisi stressed in Brussels that Rwanda had become the 'master player' of the Great Lakes region and that 'henceforth, nothing can happen (in the region) without Rwandan consent'. He added that

---

[138] *Conflits de l'Est du Zaïre. Repères et Enjeux*, Kinshasa, Editions Secco, p. 18.
[139] UN DHA, Nairobi, 31 July–1 August 1997.

'Rwanda has just solved the Zairean problem and is ready to settle other problems in the region'.[140] This ambition of the military management of a regional space posed an obvious problem: the position of Rwanda as a 'master player' had been gained through the barrel of a gun by a small and intrinsically very poor country. As both the second war and the political drift inside Rwanda was to demonstrate later, this ambition contained the seeds of profound regional instability.

The European Commissioner for Humanitarian Affairs Emma Bonino called the intervention of Zaire's neighbours 'the ugly face of African assertiveness'.[141] Indeed, the question arises as to whether a new practice of interference in the internal affairs of other states constituted real progress compared to the past experience with French, Belgian or U.S. interventions on the African continent. Just like their predecessors from the North, the countries of the region were driven by considerations of *Realpolitik* and the pursuit of personal, factional or national interests, while concerns related to democratic governance and human rights were clearly absent. African leaders, in fact, admitted to this explicitly: when almost a dozen heads of state and government met in Kinshasa on 20 July 1997 to express their support for President Kabila, they criticised 'the attitude of donor countries that link their aid to the DRC to the respect for human rights and democratic reform'. They denounced the 'disinformation campaign' against the DRC and other countries in the region about the massacres of refugees and the violation of human rights, and they went so far as to claim that 'the refugees dispersed in several parts of the DRC have been completely repatriated to their country of origin',[142] a statement which was obviously false.

By intervening in the way they did, the states of the region not only operated in a fashion that was clearly contrary to international law and to conflict prevention mechanisms provided by both the UN[143] and the OAU,[144] they also opened a Pandora's box that was to fully show its contents from mid-1998 onwards. In addition, besides the unilateral

---

[140] These quotes are based on notes taken by two people who were present at the meeting, which took place at the Rwandan embassy in Brussels.

[141] Reuters, Brussels, 13 July 1997.

[142] AFP, Kinshasa, 20 July 1997.

[143] An Agenda for Peace: Preventive diplomacy, peace-making and peace-keeping. Report of the Secretary-General pursuant to the statement adopted by the Summit Meeting of the Security Council on 31 January 1992, UN Doc. A/47/277, S/24111, 17 June 1992.

[144] Mechanism on Conflict Prevention, Management and Resolution, adopted by the 29th Assembly of the OAU in Cairo, 30 June 1993.

intervention of regional states, the phenomenon of the privatisation of public space and, therefore, of crisis management increased dramatically. Mafia-like and highly speculative networks entered the fray, accompanied by private instruments for the maintenance of 'order' such as Executive Outcomes, MPRI and Ronco. The withdrawal of the state offered expanding manoeuvring space for all sorts of particular interests, including under the form of warlords, rebel movements and 'entrepreneurs of insecurity', functioning in a context of increasingly hazy territorial boundaries. In the pursuit of their perceived interests, these state and non-state, legal and illegal, visible and less visible actors concluded short-term and rapidly shifting alliances, thus creating a complex, moving and unpredictable politico-military environment. These phenomena, which became more explicit during the second war, will be addressed in Chapter 7.

The new Congolese regime, in addition to being confronted with many internal contradictions, was expected to reconstruct the state and to integrate its many regional, ethnic, political and social forces under these adverse and turbulent circumstances. Rwanda and Burundi continued to face severe political and security problems. In the next two chapters, the evolution in the three countries between the two wars, from mid-1997 to mid-1998 will be analysed.

# 5

# Congo: Waiting for Another War

Contrary to what many in the region and in the wider international community had hoped and believed, Kabila's accession to power heralded neither the reconstruction of the Congolese state nor the end of regional instability. On the contrary, all the ingredients for the resumption of war came to the fore during the first half year of Kabila's presidency. This chapter analyses the interbellum and why it inexorably led to renewed conflict.

## 5.1 THE 'LIBERATED TERRITORIES' IN THE EAST

### Two Problems Worse Than Before

While the populations living in the 'liberated territories' initially welcomed the AFDL rebellion, mainly because it ended the abuse of the FAZ, they rapidly grew disenchanted with the 'new masters'.[1] As mentioned earlier, the problems which were at the origin of Kabila's 'rebellion' had not disappeared: the security of neighbouring countries and the status of the Banyarwanda.

Several security agreements were signed between the DRC on the one hand, and Rwanda, Burundi and Uganda on the other. For instance, it

---

[1] The following assessment of the first year of the 'liberation' is mainly based on contemporary visit reports: De Charybde en Scylla? Rapport de mission Kivu, Zaïre, January 1997; Tumepata morale. Report of a fieldtrip to South Kivu 1–8.5.1997, 17 May 1997; Report of a fieldtrip to South Kivu 15–22.10.1997: 'One Year After ...', 4 November 1997; Consultancy visit to North and South Kivu, 5–21 January 1998, March 1998. See also, J.-C. Willame, *L'odyssée Kabila...*, op. cit., pp. 125–159.

was agreed in early September 1997 that the new Forces armées congolaises (FAC) and the RPA were to carry out a joint campaign against the mai-mai and the *Interahamwe*, particularly in the Masisi region. At the end of April 1998, Congolese interior minister Kakudji announced that accords on security were agreed with Uganda and Burundi, while another agreement provided for the training by Uganda of the officer corps of the Congolese police. However, these official signs of goodwill only moderately convinced the eastern neighbours. Ugandan and Rwandan officials said in private that their countries had asked President Kabila to commit more military resources to the east or to allow them 'to do the job'.[2] Former U.S. Assistant Secretary of State for African Affairs Herman Cohen was very clear and indeed prophetic: 'Rwanda is saying eastern Kivu must be in friendly hands, and the only friendly hands are Tutsis (...). The others won't stand for Tutsi hegemony in their area, so they will therefore give safe haven to (...) those who will help their case, including defeated Rwandan Hutu and Zairean soldiers'.[3] While the presence of the Rwandan army in the Kivus officially ended at the end of September 1997,[4] in reality, the RPA remained very present on the ground and ignored the borders between the DRC and Rwanda.[5] From mid-December 1997, the RPA was again massively deployed in North Kivu, and in early 1998, Rwandan and Burundian troops patrolled the zones of Uvira and Fizi, and the RPA was openly circulating in Bukavu. Besides the RPA, most Congolese troops present in the east were initially composed of several thousand Banyamulenge and Banyarwanda from Masisi and Rutshuru. The new recruits were commanded by officers of the RPA.

The strong and visible presence of Rwandan and Congolese Tutsi military and their practices (cf. later text) were heavily resented by the local population and were to contribute to the exacerbation of the anti-Tutsi sentiments addressed later. When the Congolese government attempted to dilute the Tutsi presence[6] somewhat, this immediately

---

[2] K. Davies, 'Workers Report Fighting in Congo', *The International Herald Tribune*, 14 October 1997.

[3] J.C. McKinley, 'Mobutu is Gone, but Fighting Goes on', AP, Nairobi, 10 September 1997.

[4] Rwandan presidential spokesman Claude Dusaidi announced that the RPA had returned to Rwanda: 'Their job was finished'. However, his statement was ambiguous: 'All have been called back, except if some of them are still there in virtue of an accord with Laurent-Désiré Kabila, something I am not informed about' (*Le Monde*, 27 September 1997).

[5] The nickname given to the RPA by the local population was 'Soldiers without borders'.

[6] It will be recalled that Kabila already tried this at the start of the rebellion in the fall of 1996 (cf. earlier text).

caused new tensions. Thus, the resumption of fighting in the Goma region in September 1997 coincided with the arrival of the 10th brigade of the FAC, in which 2000–3000 troops redeployed from the Kasaï.[7] Problems had arisen between Tutsi and non-Tutsi elements during the rebellion (cf. the case of Katangese gendarmes who refused to obey the orders of Rwandan commanders, earlier text), but by the autumn of 1997, these incidents became real warfare. An observer in the region noted that the growing insecurity in the east was 'due to Kinshasa's wish to put new military chiefs at the command of its battalions'.[8] In November, Tutsi and non-Tutsi briefly fought each other in Kalemie and Baraka. In a communiqué of 4 December 1997, the Association zaïroise des droits de l'homme (AZADHO) human rights organisation asked the Congolese government 'to lift the ambiguity surrounding the nationality of the soldiers operating in Kivu province and to ensure that soldiers of the Rwandan army under no pretext be allowed to conduct military operations there'; the organisation called the RPA's presence 'an obstacle to peace in the region'. In early March 1998, the FAC sent a new contingent of 2000–3000 men to the east in order to contain 'Tutsi elements' who refused to obey the orders of non-Tutsi officers, Katangese in particular.

At the same time non-Tutsi elements of the FAC were less than enthusiastic in combating the mai-mai, ex-FAR and *Interahamwe* insurgents. Not only did they resent the killings of civilians by the RPA they witnessed first hand, but they also felt that the war was not theirs. Their (at least passive) complicity with the insurgents was made abundantly clear when on 11 December 1997 hundreds of Hutu combatants passed through Bukavu on their way to Rwanda. Knowing about this move, the rebel 'Voix du Patriote' warned civilians to stay at home. This incident was presented as a mai-mai and ex-FAR attack successfully repelled by the FAC, but, in reality, the Congolese military let the Hutu rebels through, while firing into the air to convince their 'colleagues' of the RPA that they were putting up a staunch resistance. In a number of other cases, elements of the FAC escorted Rwandan rebels to the border. Early in 1998, Kabila asked the governor of South Kivu 'to feed these boys', a reference to the mai-mai. It is not surprising under these circumstances that, from the spring of 1998 onwards, the press increasingly reported military preparations by Uganda and Rwanda, as these countries were convinced that Kabila had neither the means nor the will to meet their security concerns.

---

[7] AP, Nairobi, 10 September 1997.
[8] AFP, Kigali, 13 September 1997.

The second unresolved problem was that of the status of the Banyarwanda, and of the Tutsi in particular. We have seen that the anti-Rwandan sentiment was considerable even before the 'rebellion of the Banyamulenge' started. It grew dramatically, however, as a consequence of the attitude of certain Congolese and Rwandan Tutsi civilians and military, who behaved as if they were an occupying force. The Rwandan and Banyamulenge military used the whip, spat in people's faces and expressed a disdain that was heavily resented (the Congolese were called '*ibicucu*', a kinyarwanda word for good-for-nothing). This feeling was further reinforced by the way in which the soldiers presented themselves as 'we, your liberators' towards 'you, the Zaireans'. I shall first mention some practices introduced by the 'liberators' and then address the reactions of certain local groups and the ensuing 'dualisation' of Kivu society.

The first practice that profoundly shocked the local populations concerned the treatment of traditional leaders. For instance, at the origin of violence in Masisi (cf. later text) lay in the governor of North Kivu's replacement of customary chiefs by Tutsi in the zones of Rutshuru, Nyiragongo, Masisi and Walikale. Events were triggered by Tutsi military forcing chief Chabango of Kalehe and some of his dignitaries to serve them as porters.[9] In early December 1997, soldiers arrested several traditional chiefs, suspected of sympathising with the mai-mai, in the zones of Masisi and Walikale. On 26 December, the *bami* (kings) Ndeze of Bwisha and Kabutiti of Bukumu were killed in Goma. At the end of January 1998, the *bami* Kabare of Kabare and Ndataraye of Ngweshe were arrested, and *mwami* Cimanye of Kaziba was actively sought and went into hiding. Special Rapporteur Garretón observed 'the displacement of Rwandan Tutsi to North Kivu with a view to populating that region, as well as the replacement, by the new Tutsi authorities, sometimes in humiliating circumstances, of the traditional chiefs of the ethnic groups considered indigenous' (para 75); by mid-July 1997, 'practically all the traditional chiefs had been replaced' (para 28).[10]

Another practice which reinforced the feeling of living under a regime of occupation was the triumphalism displayed by some Rwandan and

---

[9] *Rapport sur la situation qui prévaut actuellement dans les provinces du Nord et du Sud Kivu*, undated report (early September 1997) by a team sent to the two Kivus by President Kabila. Extracts can be found in *La Libre Belgique*, 6–7 September 1997.

[10] Nations Unies, Commission des Droits de l'Homme, Rapport sur la situation des droits de l'homme dans la République Démocratique du Congo (ex-Zaïre), présenté par M. Roberto Garretón, conformément à la résolution 1997/58 de la commission, 30 January 1998, E/CN.4/1998/65, hereafter cited as Garretón Report.

Congolese Tutsi, who seized houses in town and land in the countryside, 'requisitioned' vehicles and claimed the best positions in the new administration and army. As early as February 1997, civil society organisations complained about 'the almost mono-ethnic composition' of the AFDL and of the 'army of liberation', and expressed similar concerns about pivotal positions in the civil service and the public sector generally. The text explicitly condemned the process of 'Tutsisation'.[11] An anonymous document circulated in June 1997 complained about the 'economic pilfering': vehicles, furniture, equipment and industrial tools were taken to Rwanda and Burundi.[12] AZADHO reported the arrival and settlement, since February 1997, of dozens of Tutsi families from Rwanda and Uganda with the support of the RPA and 'certain elements of the AFDL': the 'indigenous' populations were reportedly dispossessed of their land in favour of these cattle-breeders.[13] In July 1997, former Minister Gérard Kamanda wa Kamanda denounced the 'transfer of large sums of money, coffee, gold and diamonds to Rwanda and Uganda'.[14] Local industries in Beni-Butembo were dismantled and taken to Uganda. According to *Le Soir* of 20–21 September 1997, Rwandan officers and soldiers took home sixty-eight kilograms of gold taken from the Kilo-Moto mine, papaine produced in a plantation belonging to Bemba Saolona,[15] coffee harvested in the Katale domain, fuel, large numbers of vehicles confiscated from 'Mobutists' and dollars extorted from the 'wealthy'.

It is not surprising under these circumstances that the anti-Tutsi feelings rapidly became widespread. An anonymous document presented a macabre inventory of abuse and concluded: 'Rather than being really liberated, the population is caught in a ferocious dictatorship and lives under a domination imposed by Rwanda'.[16] In November 1997, the report of a peace mission sent by President Kabila observed that the practices of the Tutsi military had spoiled the relations between Tutsi and other groups

---

[11] Société civile du Sud Kivu and Groupe Jérémie, *Pour une paix durable dans la région Est du Zaïre*, Bukavu, February 1997.
[12] La violation des droits de l'homme dans le territoire occupé par l'AFDL, June 1997.
[13] AZADHO, Droits de l'Homme au Nord-Kivu. Une année d'administration AFDL: plus ça change, plus c'est la même chose, Kinshasa, October 1997.
[14] AFP, Abidjan, 12 July 1997.
[15] J.-C. Willame (*Banyarwanda et Banyamulenge...*, *op. cit.*, p. 137) found out that 'the Rwandan embassy in Brussels is looking for a buyer for 32 tons of Papaine, a commodity Zaire is the only country to produce, that belongs to a company financed by the Belgolaise bank'. This information proves that the Rwandan authorities were involved in these activities of plunder.
[16] Les morts de la libération, June 1997.

'to the point that in certain places in Kivu province the presence of a Tutsi is not tolerated any longer'.[17] The AZADHO report quoted earlier mentioned 'the will of the indigenous populations to free themselves from Tutsi hegemony' and thought that at the heart of the instability lay 'the attempts by Tutsi officials and military to impose a new social and political order on these populations'.[18] The frustrations noted by these observers rapidly translated into a dangerous culture of bipolar confrontation.

Movements that came into being explicitly stated as their goal the fight against 'Tutsi hegemony', an objective couched in increasingly violent terms. Already at the end of December 1996, CRLK claimed that 'the killers-invaders are known. They are the Tutsi Banyarwanda refugees who massacre the Bantu'. Among the 'options, aims and objectives' of the CRLK were 'the total refusal to cohabit with the Tutsi refugee; the rejection (...) of any kind of negotiation with the enemy, the Tutsi; the expulsion of the Hima from the territories of the east of Zaire'. The document also announced the creation of a military wing, the Forces de résistance armée du Kivu (FRAK). Reports of CRLK meetings suggested that a sort of 'Bantu front' was being established. Thus, reference was made to 'the pursuit of contacts with movements for the liberation of the Bantu people, such as [the Burundian rebel movements] Palipehutu and Frolina. These contacts led to the signing on 8 January 1997 of a protocol of agreement on co-operation'.

In January 1997, certain Bembe formed an Alliance pour la Résistance Démocratique (ARD), led by former first deputy speaker of the HCR–PT Célestin Anzuluni Bembe. The ARD's military leader was said to be Charles Simba, a former Kabila ally, who, however, did not remain in the region but went into exile in Sweden. Like the CRLK to which it was probably close, the ARD established links with Palipehutu and Frolina. However, at the time the Bembe were not just fighting the Tutsi, but Kabila as well. In May 1997, a Bembe intellectual stated that 'Kabila is no liberator. He is a dictator worse than Mobutu', and he recalled the terror and the massacres perpetrated when Kabila maintained his *maquis* south of Uvira.[19] A press release of the Cercle des Ressortissants du Kivu on 8 February 1997 referred to a 'Tutsi invasion' and the establishment of 'their famous Tutsi empire, the Republic of Kilimanjaro'. In October 1997, a Mouvement national pour la sauvegarde de la démocratie

[17] The quote is from *La Libre Belgique*, 17 December 1997.
[18] AZADHO, *Droits de l'Homme au Nord-Kivu..., op. cit.*
[19] *The Washington Post*, 19 May 1997.

(MNSD), apparently close to the mai-mai, wrote that 'the abuse of the Tutsi military within the Alliance have caused antipathy and even visceral hatred on the part of the different ethnic groups of the region (Hunde, Nyanga, Tembo, Hutu, Nande, Vira, Fuliru ...) against the Tutsi populations'. It also denounced a project of 'the annexation pure and simple of eastern Zaire by Rwanda, even at the price of blood'.[20] In November 1997, a clandestine radio station, 'La Voix du Patriote', invited the (Tutsi) 'visitors' to go home. This station was apparently linked to the Front de Libération contre l'Occupation Tutsi (FLOT), founded in October, which also claimed to have a political wing, the Union des Forces Vives pour la Libération et la Démocratie (UFLD).

This fastidious list of radical positions could be continued. Whatever the real weight of all these movements and organisations (most were never heard of again), one thing was clear: in the context of the territorial extension of the Rwandan problem, the Kivu region entered a phase of profound social and political 'dualisation'.[21] As a result of near instant ethnogenesis, 'Bantu'[22] were opposed to 'Hima', 'Hamites' or 'Nilotics', just as 'Hutu' were opposed to 'Tutsi' in Rwanda and Burundi.[23] The semantic extension of the term 'mai-mai' showed this very convincingly: while it initially referred to a mainly Hunde ethnic militia, the expression came to include all forms of armed opposition to the new 'Tutsi' political–military order in the region. The extension of the term 'Banyamulenge' was as significant: the expression tended to refer to all the Tutsi from Kivu and even elsewhere in Congo.

The anti-Tutsism went hand in hand with the fear of an enlargement of the Rwandan zone over the whole Kivu region, a fear that for many *Kivutiens* became a reality. After the presentation of maps of 'Greater Rwanda' and the suggestion by the Rwandan political leadership at the beginning of the 1996 war that a 'Berlin-II' conference should be organised

---

[20] MNSD, Congo–RDC-Bilan: Gouvernement arrogant et irresponsable, enquête des Nations-Unies mort-née, démocratie confisquée, 15 October 1997.

[21] The term was coined by E. Lubala Mugisho, 'La situation politique au Kivu: vers une dualisation de la société', in: F. Reyntjens, S. Marysse (Eds.), *L'Afrique des grands lacs. Annuaire 1997–1998*, Paris, L'Harmattan, 1998, pp. 307–333.

[22] It should be recalled here that the term 'Bantu' refers to a linguistic classification ('Bantu languages') and that, scientifically speaking, a 'Bantu ethnic group' makes no sense. Moreover, certain so-called Bantu groups speak Nilotic languages, while some 'Nilotic' groups (e.g., the Tutsi) speak a Bantu language (e.g., Kinyarwanda or Kirundi).

[23] A good illustration of the bipolar drift is offered by the Cercle des ressortissants du Kivu, which claimed that 'the Tutsi clandestinely spread a theory (...) according to which the *Kasaïens* are Tutsi rather than Bantu' (press release, 4 February 1997).

(cf. earlier text), this prospect was made even more concrete by the way in which the RPA ignored borders (cf. 'soldiers without borders', earlier text) and by the promotion in certain circles reputedly close to Kigali of the concept of a 'transboundary citizenship' in the region. Thus, the NGO Synergie Africa co-organised a seminar around this theme in Cape Town in June 1997.[24] Kennes noted that 'this Tutsi "transbordership" has obviously fed a generalised fear, the more so since the Tutsi diaspora shows a great deal of coherence, an obvious economic power, and a strong mobilising capacity'.[25] The central government attempted belatedly and ambiguously to contain the anti-Tutsi feelings, in vain. In a speech to civilian, traditional and military leaders in Bukavu in January 1998, Kabila stated that the *Interahamwe* 'who as you know have committed atrocities at home (...) have started to contaminate you because they self-identify as "Bantu"'.[26]

The behaviour of many Tutsi reinforced the perception among non-Tutsi that their allegiance was ethnic rather than national. Two examples should suffice to illustrate this point. In February 1998, several hundred Banyamulenge soldiers deserted in Bukavu, taking with them large quantities of arms and ammunition. This incident, which followed a confrontation between Tutsi military and re-integrated elements of the FAZ, was a consequence of the Banyamulenge's refusal to be dispersed over other units and elsewhere in Congo. The mutiny ended in early March, when the Banyamulenge reintegrated Saio military barracks in Bukavu as a result of negotiations led by Chief of Staff James Kabarebe,[27] but this incident confirmed the already existing impression that the Banyamulenge elements of the FAC behaved like an ethnic militia rather than as part of the national army. Exactly the same phenomenon was to occur after the second war, with profoundly destabilising consequences (cf. later text). A second example occurred in Masisi in September 1997, when thousands of Tutsi left the area in the wake of the (temporary, cf. earlier text) withdrawal of the RPA. Lauras observed that this showed the obvious ambiguity between ethnic and national belonging of many Tutsi in the region.[28] This unease about populations without a clear national loyalty

---

[24] A report on this meeting can be found in *Dialogue*, 199, July–August 1997, pp. 3–30.

[25] E. Kennes, 'La guerre au Congo ...', *op. cit.*, p. 236.

[26] Excerpts of this address can be found in *L'Autre Afrique*, 27 May–9 June 1998. As we shall see in Chapter 7, less than a year later, former FAR and *Interahamwe* were combating 'Tutsi hegemony' on the side of Kabila.

[27] A detailed account of this episode can be found in *Le Phare*, 795, 13 March 1998.

[28] D. Lauras, 'Tensions récurrentes entre les Tutsi de RDC et la population congolaise', AFP, Goma, 23 September 1997.

transpired in November 1997, when interior minister Mwenze Kongolo announced 'measures against these individuals who, during the day, act as Congolese citizens, but at night transform themselves into soldiers to commit acts of vandalism on Congolese soil and then withdraw quietly into Rwandan territory'.[29] The same irritation was expressed vividly by what Bagalwa Mapatano said about his Munyamulenge interlocutor during a conference: 'Before 1990, Enoch was Burundian, although he also claimed Zairean citizenship; when the RPF took power in Rwanda, he became Rwandan and even worked in the Rwandan civil service; and he returned to the east of Zaire only in January 1997, when this part of the country was conquered by the Rwando-Ugandan (sic) and Burundian armies'.[30] Obviously, in the eyes of many 'indigenous' Congolese, their past claims about 'doubtful citizenship' were vindicated by these shifting loyalties.

## Massive Human Rights Violations

From early 1997 onwards, reports mentioned daily 'disappearances' in Bukavu and Goma.[31] On 26 May, demonstrators in Uvira protested against the 'kidnapping' and murder of a dozen civilians by the RPA. The Rwandan army fired into the crowd, leaving between thirty and 126 people killed (the number varied according to the source) and many more injured. Early in September 1997, the team sent by President Kabila (cf. earlier text) reported large-scale killings by the RPA in the zones of Kalehe and Masisi. Several thousand civilians were allegedly killed by 'Tutsi military' in revenge for Bembe attacks against 'Tutsi officers' in the zone of Fizi-Baraka. The report mentioned 'ethnic cleansing' carried out by 'heavily armed men of Tutsi ethnicity' allegedly from Rwanda. These night-time operations spared no one: men, women, the elderly and children were targeted, and entire villages were burned to the ground.[32] On 5 September 1997, AZADHO estimated the number of civilians killed in Kivu since July to be in excess of 2000 and confirmed that Rwandan troops, transported by helicopter, set several villages ablaze. It added that former FAR soldiers and *Interahamwe* organised raids into Rwanda, thus provoking more reprisals from the RPA.

[29] *La Référence Plus*, 1138, 21 November 1997.
[30] Graz–Congo, *Comment rétablir la paix...*, *op. cit.*, p. 10.
[31] This part does not address the plight of the Rwandan, Burundian and Congolese Hutu, a theme discussed earlier (cf. earlier text).
[32] Rapport sur la situation..., op. cit.

The town of Masisi was badly damaged by an attack of 'Congolese or Rwandan Tutsi troops' in mid-August. Hundreds of civilians were killed in what appeared to be a retaliation after an attack against Tutsi military by the mai-mai.[33] As stated earlier, 8000 Congolese Tutsi from Masisi fled to Goma as a consequence of the RPA leaving the area. Between 7 and 16 November, more than 2000 people were picked up in South Kivu and taken to Rwanda and Burundi by these countries' armies, which operated a selection process: while most of those 'repatriated' were women and children, most men were never heard of again. In February 1998, AZADHO reported that the area of Walikale had become the setting for a killing spree organised by the Congolese army under the command of an officer only known to the population by his nickname 'Commander Kagame – Strongman'. Feared for his cruelty, he reportedly announced on 3 December 1997 that his troops' mission was to 'exterminate' the population because it was considered complicit with the mai-mai.[34] Following a mai-mai attack against Butembo at the end of February 1998, FAC elements mainly composed of Katangese troops killed hundreds of people, most of them civilians. According to the Nande association Kyaghanda, massacres continued in Beni and Butembo throughout April.

In 1997–8, the human rights situation was disastrous in a region which had experienced grave insecurity since 1993. Fundamental rights other than the right to life too were seriously and consistently violated. Having endured pillaging by the fleeing FAZ at the beginning of the war, South and North Kivu were literally 'emptied' by the 'liberators': household appliances and audio-visual equipment, means of communication, vehicles, coffee and sugar stocks, food, ivory, and cattle were confiscated as 'contribution to the liberation' and taken to the other side of the border. Human rights abuses were even to intensify during the second war (cf. later text).

## Practices of Governance

As early as January 1997, the association of university staff of South Kivu addressed their complaints to Kabila. While recognising the achievements of the AFDL, they stressed that 'certain facts are in the process of tarnishing this laudable action'. The text denounced the anarchic occupation of private property and of positions in the civil service and the public

---

[33] AFP, Goma, 17 September 1997.
[34] AZADHO, Nord–Kivu: les massacres continuent au nom de la guerre contre les May–May, Kinshasa, 2 February 1998.

enterprises, 'the marginalisation of local competence', favouritism and nepotism, the violation of citizens' rights and 'the halting of the activities, for reasons unknown, of production units (...) and the setting up of a new chamber of commerce under obscure circumstances'.[35] Just as in Rwanda, a regime, which was strongly oriented towards security and intelligence, rapidly emerged. The use of communication equipment was closely monitored and radio, telephone and fax (if they had not simply been stolen or confiscated) were practically forbidden or used with extreme caution. The mail passing the Rwandan–Congolese border had to be kept in open envelopes and was read and controlled upon entry and exit. Likewise, the media were under close surveillance. From January 1997, RFI was no longer broadcast on FM by Radio Star in Goma; the only remaining radio station authorised was the rebel one, renamed 'La Voix du Peuple'. Although magazines and other publications were not formally prohibited, the requirements imposed[36] were such that not a single newspaper was published during the first six months of the 'liberation'. The monitoring of the territories under rebel control was organised through so-called chembe-chembe based on ten house cells that followed the Rwandan model of the *nyumbakumi*.[37] The Congolese authorities ordered the humanitarian agencies to leave the Goma area in early October 1997. This apparently occurred within the framework of the 'cleansing' of North Kivu; according to the logic of strong information management (cf. earlier text), clearly no witnesses were needed.

The preponderance of military structures over administrative authorities became clear from early on. When a new territorial administration was established, its autonomy proved very limited. Thus, for example, the newly appointed governor of South Kivu, Professor Magabe of the Institut supérieur pédagogique (ISP), was 'assisted' and in fact, controlled by a Munyamulenge vice-governor. After the 'General Commissioner of Information, Press and Communication' of the AFDL delivered a broadcasting permit to rural radio station Maendeleo on 19 April 1997, the station was closed down by military order on 3 May. Garretón observed that '[s]ince the capture of Bukavu, Ruhimbika Müller, chief of the Banyamulenge, has put in place a co-ordination of the NGOs to replace

---

[35] *Libération. Trois mois après*, Bukavu, 25 January 1997.

[36] Prohibition to discuss politics; a levy of a US$ 100 for each edition; submission of ten copies for the purpose of censorship.

[37] The system of the ten house cells was initially implemented in Tanzania and later in Uganda. Already during the Habyarimana years, it was introduced to monitor the population in Rwanda.

the Regional Council of the NGOs which they had elected. The activities of the NGOs are subject to the authorisation of Müller, which needs to be applied for one week in advance. Whatever their object, the meetings sometimes needed to take place in the presence of a Munyamulenge "facilitator" (...) In North Kivu, the Governor has announced (...) that the NGOs were to be placed under the control of the new authorities'.[38] Willame offers another illustration of military hegemony. The new authorities proposed only three alternatives to the students of the university and other institutions of higher education in Bukavu: enrolment in the municipal police, in the AFDL army or in the intelligence services.[39]

Just like during the war, information management remained an essential political tool. I have already mentioned the restrictions imposed on humanitarian organisation and the press, the control of communications by mail, fax, phone and radio and the ending of FM relay of international radio stations. A short unsigned article by an 'actor of international aid' in the region described the Kivu as 'a place of experiments by future rulers who were able to test modes of administration, human relations and political communication with humanitarian organisations and international media'.[40] The author warned that 'one can only be worried when a government rejects all dialogue, when its leaders retreat in an attitude of disdain for everything external and when its population is indoctrinated. This rupture of dialogue (...) can only lead to an attitude of defiance and fear (...) At the level of the country, it often results in hatred, and eventually in war'.[41] These were to prove prophetic words.

## 5.2 THE END OF AN ALLIANCE AND THE PRELUDE TO A NEW WAR

### The Regime Adrift

When looking at its historical emergence, the poor performance of the new Congolese regime was not surprising.[42] Indeed, de Villers and

---

[38] Garretón Report, para. 181.

[39] J.-C. Willame, 'Laurent-Désiré Kabila: les origines d'une anabase', *Politique Africaine*, 72, December 1998, p. 77.

[40] 'L'humanitaire et les pièges de la communication politique au Kivu (de mai 1997 à aujourd'hui)', *Politique Africaine*, 69, March 1998, p. 143.

[41] *Idem*, p. 147.

[42] A useful survey of the first year of the Kabila regime can be found in International Crisis Group, 'How Kabila lost his way: the performance of Laurent-Désiré Kabila's

Omasombo called Kabila's emergence an 'accident of history', rather than the outcome of a socio-political process of change.[43] We have indeed seen that Kabila's seizure of power was based on a number of internal and external factors he did not control: he happened to be at the right place, at the right time (admittedly, he helped put fate on his side). There was nothing in his past that suggested he had the capacity to build a viable polity: quite the contrary (cf. earlier text the 'management' of his *maquis* in Fizi–Baraka). De Villers and Omasombo rightly observed that '[a]lthough Laurent Désiré Kabila was a dubious revolutionary leader and *maquisard*, and rapidly became a political "has been", the way that he came to power was decisive for the political history of the country'.[44]

Space prohibits a detailed discussion of the performance of the Kabila regime between its seizing power in May 1997 and the outbreak of the second war in August 1998. I shall limit myself to a summary analysis of the political evolution in the DRC, in order to present the background to the destabilisation of the entire region. Statism, voluntarism, authoritarianism and incoherence appear to be the characteristics of the new regime since it came to power, and earlier during the rebellion. However, the statism was only apparent, as the regime did not really attempt to institutionalise itself; in addition, despite declarations of intent and even a short-lived attempt at implementation (e.g. the nationalisation of the railway company Sizarail), the economy was not placed under state control, but rather increasingly privatised and criminalised (cf. later text). This 'fake statism' expressed itself in a quasi-Jacobine urge to control and to have everything pass through the state, before its reconstruction had even started. Kennes observes that the regime seemed to adhere to the concept of the 'integral state', a term borrowed from Crawford Young, without bothering about the availability of the instrument.[45] In an address to the population of Bukavu on 14 June 1997, Kabila incited his audience to 'let the *Kinois* (population of Kinshasa) play, but the day will come that we shall have to put an end to the recreation (...). Discipline is the secret of

---

Government', 21 May 1999. For the same period, see G. De Villers, 'Identifications et mobilisations politiques au Congo-Kinshasa', *Politique Africaine*, 72, December 1998, pp. 81–97. A detailed account of the period between the beginning of the first and of the second wars (October 1996–July 1998) is offered in G. De Villers, J.-C. Willame, *République démocratique du Congo. Chronique politique...*, *op. cit.*

[43] G. De Villers, J. Omasombo Tshonda, 'An Intransitive Transition', *Review of African Political Economy*, 2002, p. 403.

[44] *Idem*, p. 404.

[45] E. Kennes, 'Du Zaïre à la République Démocratique du Congo ...', *op. cit.*, p. 198.

our victory and a disciplined youth is capable of everything'. Already during the rebellion, discipline and control were to be ensured by the 'chembe-chembe' (cf. earlier text) and the political training courses. Control mechanisms were to be consolidated by the creation of several intelligence and security services, such as the Détection militaire des actions anti-patrie (DEMIAP; 'military detection of anti-patriotic actions'); a law decree of 15 October 1997 created the National Service, a 'paramilitary organ of education, management and mobilisation of civic and patriotic actions' (Article 3).

The statist option was expressed particularly well in the attitudes of the regime toward civil society. As early as June 1997, National Reconstruction Minister Etienne Mbaya announced that the state assumed all responsibilities and that civil society was to function within the confines of actions and priorities defined by the government. At an inter-agency meeting in Uvira in December 1997, Mbaya stated that NGOs and churches played a positive role under the Mobutu regime, 'in the absence of a state'. But the new era was one of 'the Renaissance of state power' and all aid was henceforth to be direct and channelled through the state only.[46] Information Minister Raphaël Ghenda made a similar statement in October.[47] This position was formally adopted by the cabinet on 30 March 1998: 'The government of the Democratic Republic of Congo does not accept aid passing through non-governmental organisations or any other institution. All aid must be directly addressed to it'.[48] The government later even started creating its own 'NGOs', for example, 'Solidarité entre nous' (a development organisation) and the 'Union congolaise pour la défense des droits de l'homme' (a human rights organisation), but as with many of Kabila's initiatives, these were never heard of again; we will see many examples of stillborn initiatives in Chapter 8. Other non-state institutions were equally targeted: thus, on 30 April 1998, the government dissolved the board of the business federation Fédération des entreprises du Congo (FEC) and its provincial committees. Reflecting a similar logic, at the end of January 1998, the National Conference on Reconstruction (CNR) was annulled just two days before it was scheduled to start. The preparatory meetings in several provinces had been seized by participants

---

[46] IRIN, *Update on Uvira*, 18 December 1997.
[47] It is no coincidence that Ghenda and Mbaya belonged to the 'leftists' in the government. They were both sacked and arrested later (cf. later text).
[48] The report of this cabinet meeting can be found in *Le Soft International*, 736, 7–13 April 1998.

to 'talk politics', and the regime feared that the meeting might transform itself into a 'Sovereign National Conference'.[49]

The belief that things could be engineered was obvious from the first days of the new regime. In June 1997, Minister Mbaya published an extremely ambitious 'Programme on the feasibility of urgencies' that attempted to tackle everything at the same time: the economy, infrastructure, transport and communications, rehabilitation of the educational, cultural, medical and social sectors, the planning of humanitarian action, the financial sector, and so on. The inventory was impressive and translated the ambition to reconstruct a total state from scratch. Without false modesty, Mbaya wrote that his portfolio was, 'because of its mission, the hinge ministry between the President of the Republic and the other departments as well as the provinces'. However, this very interventionist programme did not contain the slightest indication on funding needs, nor on where the means were to be found. In a similar voluntarist vein, at the end of a 'course of ideological training' for former FAZ, Kabila announced his intention to create a 600,000 strong army.

Authoritarianism was the next characteristic. As stated earlier, during the rebellion, the AFDL had announced that it was to lead the transition alone and that the activities of other parties were to be 'provisionally suspended'. Less than a week after the change of regime, demonstrators marching in Kinshasa on 23 May 1997 chanted slogans hostile to Kabila: 'Kabila liberator' had already been replaced by 'Kabila dictator'. UDPS leader Tshisekedi declared that he did 'not recognise this government. To me it does not exist. I ask our people to do everything to resist this government (...) It should be obvious to everyone that the people are not at all ready to undergo a new dictatorship'.[50] The rally was dispersed by soldiers who fired into the air. On 26 May, the government prohibited party political activities and public demonstrations. The political parties were banned altogether in September.

The signs of an authoritarian exercise of power became rapidly visible. First, at the institutional level, a short (fifteen articles) constitutional law decree of 27 May 1997[51] attributed all powers to the president: he

---

[49] On the saga of the CNR, see J.-C. Willame, *L'odyssée Kabila...*, *op. cit.*, pp. 93–106.

[50] AFP, Kinshasa, 23 May 1997.

[51] Constitutional law-decree 003 of 27 May 1997 on the organisation and exercise of power in the Democratic Republic of the Congo (text in G. De Villers, J.-C. Willame, *République démocratique du Congo. Chronique politique...*, *op. cit.*, pp. 72–74). In a subsequent law-decree 074 of 25 May 1998, Kabila gave himself unlimited powers. These texts do not appear to have been officially published. According to one of his former aides,

exercised legislative power by law decree and executive power by decree; he appointed and dismissed the members of the cabinet, the ambassadors, provincial governors, the officers in the army, the civil servants and the judges.[52] The strong exercise of power was obvious as soon as the first government of the new regime had been formed. It immediately showed Kabila's unwillingness to open up the system: the team represented the AFDL, a few returnees from the diaspora and some converts from the opposition. This was a far cry indeed from the government of national unity many Congolese and international actors had hoped for. François Ryckmans rightly noted that here was a fundamental political misunderstanding. While the opposition founded its legitimacy on the Sovereign National Conference of 1991–2, the AFDL's foundation was its military victory. In other words, while the political class that remained in Kinshasa expected the rapid start of the 'second act' of the transition, Kabila closed that chapter and felt that the 'transition' had come to an end with the demise of Mobutu.[53] This message was very clear from the beginning. In his inauguration speech, Kabila stated that the new transition was possible 'only if the AFDL plays the role of a federating framework and of the conduit [*réceptacle*] of the national cohesion necessary at this stage'.[54] However, just as with the statist stance mentioned earlier, the notion of 'concentration of power' must be put into perspective: in a regime that rejected institutionalisation, this concentration did not, of course, take place in favour of a structure, but in the interest of individuals and factions engaged in processes of influence and accumulation.

The concentration in 'hands that can be trusted' was to become more visible still as later governments were formed and appointments made in the state apparatus. The more he felt isolated and threatened in a physical context he feared (he did not know nor understand Kinshasa, an environment which intimidated him), Kabila surrounded himself with those close to him, Katangans and Balubakat in particular. When a government

---

Kabila felt that publication in the *Journal officiel* was not necessary, 'because he himself announced the existence of these texts' (personal communication).

[52] For a useful analysis of this 'constitutional' system, see C. Lutundula, 'Analyse de la légitimation de la transition et de la nouvelle République Démocratique du Congo', *Afrika-Focus*, 1997, pp. 9–30.

[53] F. Ryckmans, 'Kinshasa: les malentendus de la "libération"', in: *Kabila prend le pouvoir*, *op. cit.*, p. 128.

[54] *Le Potentiel*, 1032, 30 May 1997. In this, Kabila was encouraged by one of his sponsors. President Museveni said that '[p]ersonally, I don't like political parties (...) I have limited their activities. I wouldn't be surprised if Mr. Kabila seeks inspiration in this kind of situation' (Reuters, Pretoria, 27 May 1997).

was formed in January 1998, *Le Soft International*'s front page title read
'*La montée au front du clan katangais*'.[55] In early 1998, Balubakat were
in charge of strategic positions such as home affairs (Kakudji), justice
(Mwenze Kongolo), the economy (Nyembo Kabemba), strategic development zones (Umba Kyamitala), the central bank (Masangu) and the security services (Kabwe).[56] Katangese former 'Mobutists' were more easily
'excused' for their past than others: thus, Lunda Bululu,[57] Umba Kyamitala
and Kyungu were soon rehabilitated. Finally, the members, all appointed by
Kabila, of the constitutional commission put in place on 22 October 1997
were veterans of pre-Mobutu Congolese politics, some people very close to
Kabila and members of his cabinet. The electoral timetable remained very
vague: as early as July 1997, Foreign Minister Bizima Karaha announced
during a visit to Washington that the promises made earlier were only 'an
objective'. He believed that elections could not take place 'before the country is reconstructed, the people fed, the voters educated and the provokers
in prison or exile. (…) As long as these conditions are not met, we shall not
organise elections for the sake of elections'.[58]

The concentration of power also showed in political practice. Already
in June 1997, the human rights organisation AZADHO published a
severe warning.[59] Indeed, as soon as the new regime assumed power,
journalists, leaders of civil society and opposition politicians were the
victims of arrests and other forms of harassment. It would be tedious
to mention practices of abuse and intimidation: suffice it to say that
dozens of leaders of parties and political movements, students, leaders
of NGOs, journalists, senior civil servants[60] and even members of the
cabinet[61] were arrested, sometimes ill-treated and often released later. In
early February 1998, Tshisekedi was arrested and deported to his home
village of Kabeya–Kamwanga in Eastern Kasai. With some dose of cyni-
cism, the minister of agriculture announced that Tshisekedi 'has returned
to his village to farm (…). We have given him seeds and a small tractor

---

[55] *Le Soft International*, 723, 9–15 January 1998.
[56] However, in Kabila's immediate environment not all were Balubakat: Victor Mpoyo was
from the Kasaï, Nyembwe Kazadi was of Burundian origin.
[57] By joining the anti-Kabila rebellion in August 1998, he did not show a great deal of
gratitude.
[58] UPI, Washington, 8 July 1997.
[59] AZADHO, Appel urgent 003/97. SOS au Congo-Zaïre: les espaces démocratiques menacés, Kinshasa, 10 June 1997.
[60] For example, the chief of the intelligence agency ANR Paul Kabongo and the chief
Inspector of the National Police Arsène Loange.
[61] For example, Mbaya, Ghenda and Sondji.

so as to allow him to engage in agriculture'.[62] The disastrous situation of human rights in the east was mentioned earlier. For the remainder, I refer to the highly critical reports published by international human rights organisations.[63]

Incoherence was the last characteristic of the new regime.[64] Although we have just seen that power was monopolised by the AFDL, or more accurately by Kabila and a few people close to him, this does not mean that the regime was monolithic or homogenous. While the regime was authoritarian, Willame rightly pointed out that it could not be dictatorial, simply because it lacked the internal coherence necessary to build and maintain a 'real dictatorship'.[65] I have already observed that the AFDL was an alliance of convenience, just like the regional coalition that supported the rebellion. The non-existence of the AFDL became increasingly obvious: after the elimination of Kisase during the war (cf. earlier text), Masasu was arrested on 25 November 1997 and condemned to twenty years in prison by a military court (Cour d'ordre militaire) in May 1998;[66] as a result of a reshuffle on 1 June 1998, Bugera lost his position as General Secretary of the AFDL and was given the portfolio without substance of minister of state in the president's office.[67] Thus, Kabila became the only 'survivor' of the four founders of the AFDL.[68] He later justified this evolution by saying that 'the AFDL was composed of allied political movements, three of which had no revolutionary experience nor ideological orientation. They relied on an external legitimacy. It was a conglomerate of opportunists and adventurers (...). You can see that the AFDL was a far cry from being at the forefront of the movement of liberation of our country'.[69]

The cohesion was not any greater inside the government, where 'progressives' and 'conservatives', 'technocrats' and 'politicians', 'old hand' and

---

[62] According to *Le Palmarès*, 14 February 1998.
[63] A few examples: Human Rights Watch, Transition and human rights violations in Congo, December 1997; Garretón Report; Amnesty International, Democratic Republic of Congo. Civil liberties denied, February 1998.
[64] Many anecdotal illustrations can be found in the story – not without bias, but often interesting – published by Justine Kasa-Vubu: *Douze mois chez Kabila (1997–1998)*, Brussels, Le Cri, 1998.
[65] J.-C. Willame, *L'odyssée Kabila...*, op. cit., p. 66.
[66] Masasu was eventually executed extrajudicially during the fall of 2000 (cf. later text).
[67] He was to join the anti-Kabila rebellion two months later.
[68] The AFDL was eventually dissolved and replaced by the CPP (*Comités du pouvoir populaire*) in April 1999 (cf. later text).
[69] L.D. Kabila, Discours-programme du Président de la République à l'ouverture du congrès des CPP, ACP, Kinshasa, 22 April 1999.

'new breed' were supposed to work together.[70] Kabila and his ministers constantly contradicted each other, stating one thing one day and the opposite the next.[71] During the year following the takeover, the cabinet was reshuffled three times in an atmosphere of intrigue, score-settling and clientelism. *Le Soir* of 22 October 1997 detected 'a whiff of the Roman Empire in Kinshasa': the rumour circulated that Bizima Karaha had been poisoned (in reality, he was simply overworked) and the chief of the security services Séverin Kabwe was severely wounded in an attempt on his life.

The army in particular remained a hazy affair. All officers were called 'commander' (just like the RPA's 'Afandi'), but no one exactly knew who commanded whom. Rather than being one single national army, the FAC continued to be made up of factions (Rwandan and Congolese 'Tutsi', Katangans, former FAZ, *kadogo* and others recruited during the advance of the rebellion). On 24 July 1997, Antoine Gizenga of the PALU party appealed to Kabila to end the existence of 'two armies, one possessing real command and comprising foreign contingents manipulated by the exterior, and the other consisting of Congolese nationals who are abused and oppressed'. Emile Ilunga, a political leader of the Tigres, recognised the tensions between Rwandans and Katangans in the army, which he said were the consequence of 'a lack of military and political leadership in the Kabila system. There is no Minister of Defence, no Chief of Staff, and therefore no one responsible for the settlement of conflicts (...). The confusion is total'.[72] The sacking and arrest on 25 November 1997 of Masasu Nindaga, widely considered until then to be the Chief of Staff, only confirmed this confusion. According to the president's office, Masasu was 'just a corporal in the Rwandan army'.[73] After his arrest, shooting in several places in Kinshasa led to a dozen deaths. On 1 December, the Rwandan Lt. Col. James Kabarebe (cf. earlier text) was appointed acting Chief of Staff; his replacement by Célestin Kifwa on 13 July 1998 was to be one of the accelerators of the second 'rebellion' (cf. later text). The cacophony was even greater inside the security services, where Katangans

---

[70] A survey of the very diverse nature of those who joined Kabila can be found in J.-C. Willame, *L'odyssée Kabila...*, *op. cit.*, pp. 67–72.

[71] In certain cases, deliberate attempts at sabotaging the government's work were probably made. The way in which Foreign Minister Bizima Karaha managed the DRC's external relations certainly contributed to the discredit of Kabila. Bizima Karaha joined the 'rebellion' in August 1998 (cf. later text).

[72] *La Libre Belgique*, 27–28 September 1997.

[73] AFP, Kinshasa, 29 November 1997. In his famous interview in *The Washington Post* of 9 July 1997, Kagame confirmed that 'General' Masasu was formerly in the RPA.

and Kasaiens were in constant competition,[74] mutually arresting each other without any one knowing who was really in charge.

Finally, the incoherence in the economic field was paralysing. Thus, in January 1998, the government unilaterally withdrew their rights of exclusive exploitation from a dozen mining companies; in March, it announced the revision of all contracts concluded by the previous regime.[75] Even contracts signed by the AFDL during the rebellion and by the government after taking power were not honoured, which led to important litigation and discouraged potential investors. Thus, for example, the Canadian 'junior' Banro started an arbitration procedure at the end of August 1998 with a view to obtaining the trifling sum of US$ 1 billion in compensation for the government's decision to dissolve Société aurifère du Kivu et du Maniéma (SAKIMA), in which Banro held a 93% stake, and to revoke its exploitation permit.[76] A similar dispute pitted the government against the Ghanaian company Ashanti Goldfields whose interest in Mindev (involved in the exploitation of the gold mines of Kilo-Moto) was suddenly 'transferred' to the Australian company Russell Resources.

Despite its many shortcomings, the new regime was also able to register a number of achievements during its first year in power. Except in the east (cf. earlier text), security improved considerably:[77] the army was paid, a rapid police intervention force (Police d'intervention rapide [PIR]) responded to the calls of citizens in major cities, soldiers committing abuse were punished (sometimes, it should be added, in a summary fashion). Efforts were made to reconstruct the state. This showed sometimes in punctual actions such as the refurbishing of public buildings, the creation of a certain degree of order at Ndjili airport (which used to be one of the most chaotic and hectic places in the world), the collection of waste and the cleaning of sewers, and even the purchase of a vehicle for the Kinshasa fire brigade, which had not experienced this luxury for years. Many of these actions resulted from initiatives taken at the intermediary level, where Congolese recovered their lost dignity and rolled up their sleeves.

---

[74] The attempt against Séverin Kabwe (cf. earlier text) must probably be seen in that context.

[75] For a survey of the legal insecurity resulting from these and other measures, see M.-F. Cros, 'Pour quelques pépites de plus: le centurion, la mine et les contrats', La Libre Belgique, 22 May 1998.

[76] Banro Resource Corporation, Press release, Toronto, 27 August 1997.

[77] A poll conducted in April 1998 by Bureau d'études, de recherche et de consulting international (BERCI) showed that 43% of respondents felt that the increased safety of persons and goods was the most important improvement since Kabila came to power.

The reconstruction was also visible at the level of a certain number of functions in the economic and financial sectors, which even a minimal state must perform in the exercise of its sovereignty. Thus, the monetary reform of June 1998, which introduced the new Congolese Franc (FC), made a promising start. The new currency was accepted everywhere[78] and the 'de-dollarisation' process started as planned. Inflation was brought under control at about 5% during the first half of 1998 and the value of the FC maintained itself against the dollar. However, this discipline had a price: the dearth of monetary flows in the form of private investments or foreign aid handicapped the economy, and the low availability of liquidity inspired a generalised complaint that 'there is no money'. Another economic sign of the restructuring of the state, fiscal income amounted to 9.1% of GDP during the second term of 1998, compared to a mere 3.4% a year earlier. Albeit at a very low level, the national budget was almost balanced, even if the practice of extra-budgetary 'gifts' had not disappeared. In addition, a master plan formulated by the National Bank aimed at correcting a number of macro-economic malfunctions. All these efforts were of course fragile, and the new war that erupted in mid-1998 was to undo them.

### The Art of Making Enemies

While, as we have seen, the regime isolated itself at home, where its base became increasingly narrow, at the same time it succeeded in rapidly losing the already reluctant international sympathy gained through the elimination of the previous regime. I shall refer here to the relations with the international community, and address the relations with the countries of the region in the next section. The psychology of the Kabila regime's international relations was aptly summarised by a Congolese priest who said 'ndokism' (ndoki means sorcerer) had returned: 'negative things happening to you are inevitably blamed on the malfeasance of a "sorcerer" who brings you bad luck – the World Bank, Belgium, France, the UN ...'.[79] With the advent of the AFDL in sight, French co-operation minister Jacques Godfrain warned early on: 'Let us be cautious and modest. Twenty years ago, the liberation of Phnom Penh by the *Khmers rouges*, whose humanity we have been able to appreciate since, was greeted in the

---

[78] This may seem obvious, but it is not in the Congo. When the new Zaïre replaced the old one in 1993, it was rejected in the two Kasaï provinces, which continued to use the old Zaïre, thus creating a separate monetary zone.

[79] Quoted in *La Libre Belgique*, 20 May 1998.

same words [as Kabila's coming to power]'.[80] While the French scepticism was certainly in part geopolitical (cf. her role, above), these doubts were soon shared by other bilateral actors, including the Americans, who attempted to maintain a modicum of control over Kabila, whom they felt had become an 'unguided missile'.[81]

On the one hand, the shadow of the frustrated United Nations inquiry into the massacres of Rwandan refugees (cf. earlier text) darkened the relations between Kabila's Congo and the international community.[82] On the other hand, and more damaging in the long run, the regime showed an extraordinary capacity to create animosity for no good reason. Just as with regard to the human rights situation discussed earlier, it would be tedious to mention all the incidents, big and small, that soured the relations between the Congolese regime and the outside world. I will limit myself here to a few examples. On 16 November 1997, the DRC left the 'Francophonie'. According to Congolese television, Kabila stated that 'the Francophonie is the continuation of neo-colonialism, where independent countries remain under France's umbrella'. Less than two weeks later, Kinshasa expelled the DCM of the French embassy; as a reprisal, France expelled the number two of the Congolese embassy in Paris. These incidents took place just before a crucial meeting of the 'friends of the Congo', due to take place in Brussels on 3 and 4 December. At the end of the meeting, which decided to create a financial support fund for the DRC – although no cheques were made out,[83] Minister Mawampanga seemed to announce a volte-face: 'France has always been a friend of the Congo. We are very satisfied with France, which has done nothing to put a spoke in our wheels'. Kabila's advisor Sakombi added that 'we are at a decisive turning point in the relations between France and the Congo.

---

[80] *Le Figaro*, 6 May 1997.
[81] This was the expression used by a high ranking State Department official during a conversation with the author.
[82] At the beginning, his African partners supported Kabila in his quarrel with the UN and the donor community. Dutch Minister Jan Pronk was the exception in the western camp. After meeting with Kabila on 21 October 1997, he said the Congolese regime had nothing to hide for the UN investigative team, adding that the UN was 'clumsy' and accusing the international community of 'arrogance' and 'a lack of understanding for the new regime, which has come from nowhere'. This was not the first time that Pronk, who – despite his interest for Rwanda since the genocide – did not know the region well, acted as an apprentice–sorcerer (cf. earlier text, his position on the Rwandan refugees and his unconditional support for the AFDL rebellion).
[83] However, in the margins of the meeting, the European Union decided to earmark Ecus 77 million for the DRC. On 5 August 1997, the EU troïka, during a visit to Kinshasa, recommended that structural co-operation be resumed.

We have turned over a new page and we start from a new base'. Hardly two months later, the 'new base' seemed compromised again, when on 28 January 1998 Kabila accused France, together with the UNHCR and the aid organisation Caritas, of aiding the mai-mai in their rebellion against the regime; on the same day, Minister Kakudji claimed that France and the Vatican supported the insurrection in the east.

The Americans' turn came in February. On 11 February, Kabila refused to meet with Clinton's special envoy, the Rev. Jesse Jackson, 'because he has not respected diplomatic usage'.[84] Madeleine Albright addressed a severe warning to Kabila on 19 March: she expected him to lift the ban on party political activities, to free political prisoners and respect human rights. Belgium, although it had kept a low profile and refrained from publicly criticising the new regime, was in turn challenged through an incident that was artificially engineered: in April, after the 'discovery' and seizure of two boxes of weapons coming from the Belgian consulate in Lubumbashi,[85] the chief of the office of the information minister called Belgium a 'terrorist state'. When Minister Ghenda decided to go to Belgium on a 'mission of clarification', he was refused an entry visa. Thus, in less than six months' time, the Congolese regime succeeded in antagonising the few partners of the old 'troïka' that still showed some interest in the DRC. More generally, the old *maquisard* Kabila was quite unaware of the functioning of international relations and of the basics of diplomatic etiquette. He said openly what crossed his mind, did not show up where he was expected, showed up where he was not expected and so on. While this undoubtedly had a negative impact, for example, on the level of development aid, which remained very limited, the souring of relations with some of the countries in the region was to have much more serious consequences.

## Towards a New War

We have seen that the embarrassing presence of the Rwandan army and the 'conqueror' attitude of some Tutsi were bitterly resented in the Kivu region. Likewise in Kinshasa, Laurent Kabila was soon confronted with

---

[84] The real reason was that Jackson met with opponents, including Tshisekedi, who was arrested a few days after the meeting and internally deported (cf. earlier text).

[85] In reality, these were light weapons used by elements of the Détachement d'assistance à la sécurité (DAS), a Belgian army unit charged with close protection and infiltration sent to Lubumbashi to protect and possibly evacuate Belgian nationals during the last stage of the 1996–7 rebellion. At the time, the AFDL was informed of this operation and the Congolese government was therefore fully aware of the existence of these weapons.

a similar problem that forced him into adopting a duty of ingratitude[86] towards his eastern sponsors. As soon as he assumed power, he was faced with a serious dilemma. Already during the rebellion, it was clear that his own military and political base was thin and that external forces – mainly Rwanda and Uganda during the first phase of the war, Angola (in part through the Katangese gendarmes) during the second phase – carried him to power. Although Kabila was initially well received, even if it was only because he had put an end to the abuse committed by the FAZ, this dependency soon became a mortgage in terms of internal legitimacy.[87] The continuing and highly visible presence of foreign troops and officers, particularly those of the RPA, raised accusations that Kabila was but a puppet of Rwanda and, to a lesser extent, Uganda. When Kagame recognised, or rather claimed, the decisive role played by Rwanda during the war, this was a considerable source of embarrassment for the new Congolese regime (cf. earlier text).

In addition, the opposition smelled blood. Hardly was Kabila inaugurated, when on 23 May 1997 Etienne Tshisekedi 'thanked' Rwanda and Uganda for their 'contribution to the liberation' and asked them 'to kindly recall their units put at the AFDL's disposal for this struggle'.[88] Faced with a strong nationalist sentiment, Kabila could not afford to remain aloof. Since the autumn of 1997, the regime, therefore, attempted to be seen as 'liberating' itself from what Congolese opinion increasingly perceived as Rwandan overrule. We have seen earlier that attempts to dilute the Rwandan military presence in the east by ferrying Congolese troops from other regions led to tensions and even violent confrontations between non-Tutsi elements of the FAC and the RPA. Well before the end of 1997, Kagame publicly stated he did not rule out a new operation in the Congo.[89]

In a communiqué of 4 December 1997, the human rights organisation AZADHO insisted that the government 'lift the ambiguity surrounding the nationality of the soldiers in the Kivu province and ensure that the soldiers of the Rwandan army are barred from operating there, under whatever pretext'. On 28 January 1998, Interior Minister Kakudji

---

[86] The expression comes from Colette Braeckman, 'La quadrature du cercle, ou l'ingratitude obligée', in: *Kabila prend le pouvoir, op. cit.*, pp. 175–180.

[87] A poll conducted in August 1997 by BERCI showed that 82% of the respondents were opposed to the presence of foreign troops. In an October 1997 poll, 71% of the respondents felt that 'Kabila is under foreign influence'; 62% expressed the feeling that Rwanda and Uganda 'are in the process of colonising the Congo'.

[88] AFP, Kinshasa, 23 May 1997.

[89] *Le Figaro*, 23 November 1997.

stated that Kabila was considering declaring a state of emergency in the
east, 'where a war is in the process of beginning'.[90] In the meantime, the
Kinshasa regime was increasingly embarrassed by the attempts by the UN
Secretary General's investigative team to carry out its mandate. While it
was the Congolese government that systematically obstructed the team's
work and thus paid the price in terms of international public relations, it
also realised it was doing Kigali's 'dirty job', as most of the massacres of
refugees were perpetrated by the RPA (cf. earlier text). Here was Kabila's
dilemma: either he pointed an accusing finger at his Rwandan allies (running the risk of antagonising them and, at the same time, admitting they
had fought his war), or he assumed full responsibility himself (conceding
his guilt of crimes against humanity and possibly genocide).

By the beginning of 1998, the signs of a grave deterioration in the
relations between the Kabila regime and his Rwandan and Ugandan god-
fathers had become very visible. In a declaration made on 6 April, the
South Kivu civil society denounced the 'threats of foreign aggression' and
observed 'a strong concentration of foreign troops on the other side of the
border in the [Burundian] province of Cibitoke, as well as the infiltration
of men in the direction of the Uvira highlands, fief of the Banyamulenge'.
It recalled that this scenario matched the one that preceded the 'rebellion' of 1996. During the same period, the MNC-Lumumba claimed that
'the regime of Kigali (...) is implementing a genuine expansionist plan'.
Rwanda and Uganda refused to participate in a conference on regional
security, which Kabila organised in Kinshasa on 17 May, to mark the first
anniversary of his coming to power. The only heads of state present were
those of Zimbabwe and the Central African Republic.

At a press conference held on 22 May, Minister Mpoyo – considered very close to Kabila – demanded that President Museveni 'takes
care of the affairs of his own country rather than denigrating President
Kabila (...). We know that Mobutu was a good friend of Museveni and
that the two got along very well (...). If this continues, we will have to
deal with him the way he treats us'. Mpoyo also accused a high Ugandan
official (whose name he did not reveal, but who was probably Museveni's
brother Salim Saleh) of fraudulent trade in Congolese timber, gold and
diamonds. In addition, he claimed that Ugandan officials had seized
mining concessions without the approval of the Congolese government.[91]
A western diplomat quoted by *The Washington Post* of 19 May 1998 felt

[90] AP, Bukavu, 29 January 1998.
[91] AFP, Kinshasa, 22 May 1998.

that the major cause of Ugandan irritation was the incoherent conduct of an inexperienced Congolese government, as well as its ambition to appear as a more important regional power than it really was. According to *The Monitor* (Kampala) of 20 May, another source of discontent, particularly on the part of Rwanda, was that the DRC, in its attempts to 'liberate' itself from Kigali, turned to Tanzania for military training. Rwanda suspected Tanzania of turning a blind eye on armed groups opposed to the RPF, and relations between the two countries were far from cordial. On 28 April, *The Monitor* asked a question, which at the same time contained the answer: 'Time for Museveni to drop Kabila?' Rwandan newspapers could have asked Kagame the same question.

The escalation continued on 4 July, when the UPDF installed an operational base against the ADF rebellion in Ntabi, 15 km inside Congolese territory; as this occurred without the authorisation of Kinshasa, this measure obviously violated the territorial integrity of the DRC. An atmosphere of an impending *coup d'état* was at the same time hanging over Kinshasa. The distrust between 'Tutsi' and 'Katangans' increased, and a persistent rumour had it that James Kabarebe was plotting against Kabila. Fearing a *putsch*, Kabila on 11 July appointed his brother-in-law Célestin Kifwa, a former officer of the Katangese gendarmes, as the new acting Chief of Staff; Kabarebe was sidelined to the position of 'special military advisor' to the army high command, a function without much substance. This change at the army top distanced the DRC even further from its eastern neighbours and brought it closer to Angola. However, it did not end the plot against Kabila. In the second half of July, several hundreds of Kinshasa Tutsi left the country, advancing all sorts of pretexts; this of course increased suspicion. The proverbial straw that broke the camel's back came on 26 July, when the *directeur de cabinet* of the Defence Ministry, a portfolio managed by Kabila himself, declared that 'the Rwandan and other foreign military' were to leave the Congolese territory. On 29 July, some 600 Rwandan soldiers left Ndjili airport to destination Kigali. In the making for several months, a new war had become inevitable.[92]

---

[92] But not unannounced. Among many of the 'chronicles of a catastrophe foretold', three titles can be quoted by way of example: C. Monsel, 'Le Kivu au bord d'une nouvelle explosion', *L'autre Afrique*, 27 May–9 June 1998; M.-F. Cros, 'La situation se détériore au Kivu: vers l'explosion?', *La Libre Belgique*, 29 June 1998; G. Prunier, 'Une poudrière au coeur du Congo-Kinshasa', *Le Monde diplomatique*, July 1998. I myself warned in the Belgian daily *De Morgen* on 30 July, three days before the second war started.

# 6

## Impasse in Rwanda and Burundi

Between the two wars, some phenomena were common to both countries: the continuation of the civil war in Burundi, its spread and intensification in Rwanda; widespread violations of civil rights, especially the right to life; the impasse in which the judicial systems found themselves; economic regression due to the enormous budgetary constraints imposed in part by defence efforts, insecurity and, for Burundi, sanctions; poor political governance; and finally, the prevailing atmosphere of fear and distrust. Other characteristics were peculiar to each country. Thus, in Burundi, and not in Rwanda, the paths for political dialogue remained open, even if they were full of pitfalls. The Rwandan government, for its part, opted for a military and police mode of management of political space, even beyond its borders. Another difference was to be found in the attitude of the international and regional communities: while Burundi was relatively isolated, the authorities in Kigali continued to benefit from the 'genocide credit', even if it was slowly eroding.[1] Finally, Rwanda, contrary to Burundi, claimed a role as a regional power, acquired as a result of its military successes in the Congo, but the country remained fragile and potentially destabilising for itself and its neighbours.

### 6.1 THE CIVIL WARS

As seen earlier, Burundi's civil war began as the *coup d'état* of October 1993 continued in a creeping manner, thereby bringing to a 'negotiated'

---

[1] On this, see S. Marysse, A. Ansoms, D. Cassimon, 'The aid "Darlings" and "Orphans" of the Great Lakes region in Africa', *European Journal of Development Research*, 2007, 433–458.

end the 1993 elections and the 1992 constitution. Faced with this evolution, whose first signs were already noticeable in early 1994, some leaders of the elected majority chose to go underground and created the National Council for the Defence of Democracy (CNDD) as well as its armed wing, the Forces for the Defence of Democracy (FDD). This rebel movement, joining those of Palipehutu and Frolina already endemically present in the field, really began in-depth military operations in the beginning of 1995. Destabilised for some time by the 'rebellion of the Banyamulenge', which destroyed its rear bases in South Kivu during the autumn of 1996, the CNDD–FDD nevertheless continued the insurrection.

Some of the rebel forces based between Uvira and Bukavu withdrew into the interior of Burundi, where they already had a strong presence, while others retreated to Tanzania, a country they were able to reach either by crossing Lake Tanganyika or passing through Burundi. This movement partly explains why the south of the country saw more intense fighting than before. Throughout 1997 and the beginning of 1998, the western provinces (Makamba, Bururi, rural Bujumbura, Bubanza and Cibitoke) were heavily affected by the war, whilst elsewhere security improved at the cost of a massive military presence, numerous civilian casualties and major human rights abuses (cf. the 'regroupment camps' in the following discussion). A source of some comfort for the Burundian army was the continued conflict between and even within the rebel movements.

The regime's response to the insurrections was twofold and somewhat contradictory, as it combined military action and dialogue. The military option, which implicitly believed that it was possible to put down the rebellion, was visible through several indicators. During the period 1996–7, the army probably doubled in size, thereby increasing to approximately 40,000 men[2], mainly by recruiting from secondary schools and institutes of higher education. Thus, at the beginning of February 1997, about 2250 students left for military service; after three months of training, they served for a period of nine months. On 10 November 1997, the minister of defence announced a new recruitment drive from among the final year students of secondary schools. At the end of 1997, the government, within the framework of 'civilian self-defence', had weapons distributed in the regions affected by the rebellion. All these efforts were reflected in the national budget, which, according to the UN Special Rapporteur

[2] However, official figures were unavailable.

Pinheiro,[3] allocated 38% of current expenditure to defence; according to other sources, defence claimed more than half of the budget. Moreover, in order to meet this overwhelming burden, the government translated its military option into fiscal terms by the introduction of a 'contribution to national solidarity', which was in fact a tax to support the war. Six percent of civil servants' salaries were deducted, while farmers were forced to contribute 1000 Burundi Francs per year per household (thus, the rural populations were to some extent requested to fund their own repression).

A final measure, severely criticised by the international community, was the 'regroupment' of populations in camps. This policy, launched in February 1996 in the province of Karuzi and extended elsewhere from October of the same year, officially aimed to protect the populations, but was in fact an anti-insurrection measure seeking to deprive the rebels from the active or passive support from which they benefited. Major Buyoya explicitly acknowledged this when he stated in an interview that 'these camps were needed to isolate the rebellion'.[4] In mid-1997, more than 600,000 people (about 10% of the population) were displaced, half of whom were in 'regroupment camps'. Amnesty International concluded that 'a pattern of mass human rights violations committed during or after the process of regroupment, undermines any argument that this regroupment provides protection'.[5] In June 1997, the government announced that the 'regroupment camps' were to be dismantled in September at the latest. Although this was far from being implemented at the beginning of 1998,[6] some camps were effectively closed in the provinces of Muramvya and Kayanza; however, in some areas, notably in Kayanza, they were replaced by a policy of 'villagisation' along major trunk roads, which in turn allowed close monitoring of the population. Besides the military option, the government also embarked on the path of dialogue, not only with the armed rebellion, but also with the civilian opposition (discussed below).

---

[3] United Nations, General Assembly, Interim Report on the Human Rights Situation in Burundi Submitted by the Special Rapporteur of the Commission on Human Rights, pursuant to Economic and Social Council Decision 1997/280, 7 October 1997 (A/52/505).

[4] *Libération*, 23 February 1998.

[5] Amnesty International, Burundi: Ethnic 'regroupement' takes place in the context of massacres, 15 July 1997. For a critical evaluation of this practice from a legal point of view, see: Humanitarian Law Consultancy, Burundi's regroupment policy: A pilot study on its legality, The Hague, June–July 1997.

[6] In this previously mentioned interview, Buyoya extended the timeframe by more than a year: 'Our aim is for all the peasants to return home by the end of the year (1998)', *Libération*, 23 February 1998.

Contrary to the Rwandan government's expectations, which hoped that the 'voluntary-forced' repatriation of hundreds of thousands of refugees in November 1996 was going to put an end to the insecurity and allow better control of these populations, it in fact re-imported the civil war. Indeed, from the beginning of 1997, barely two months after the massive return of the refugees, an increasingly important insurrection began in the northwest. As described by Marie-France Cros[7] and Olivier Rogeau,[8] for Kagame the dismantling operation was a double failure: there was even more insecurity in Rwanda and Kivu than before and, as seen earlier, anti-Tutsi hatred in Congo increased dramatically.

As 1997 unfolded, the rebel attacks became increasingly daring, organised and important. The UN 'Phases and Standard Security Procedures' for the month of July 1997 classified the entirety of Cyangugu, Gisenyi, Kibuye and Ruhengeri prefectures in 'phase 4', meaning that for security reasons, they were in principle out of bounds for UN personnel. According to the report of the Special Representative of the Human Rights Commission Michel Moussali, some months later, parts of Byumba, Gikongoro, Gitarama, Kibungo and rural Kigali were added to this list, thereby classifying more than half of the national territory under phase 4.[9] Even though the UN was undoubtedly excessively prudent, this was a good illustration of the spread of the guerrilla movement. According to Colonel Kayumba Nyamwasa, the commander of operations in Gisenyi, the rebellion counted over 15,000 fighters.[10]

At the end of 1997, an increasing number of rebel attacks took place outside the northwest, notably in the prefectures of Gitarama and rural Kigali, followed in March 1998 by Kibungo and Butare. The army suffered considerable losses, much more than was believed by the international community,[11] which undoubtedly explains the high degree of nervousness within the army, faced with the abandonment of positions, and even desertions. Moreover, the enemy was faceless, putting forward neither spokespeople nor claims.[12] What came to be known as the Armée

---

[7] *La Libre Belgique*, 17 September 1997.

[8] *Le Vif/L'Exprès*, 3 October 1997.

[9] United Nations, General Assembly, Report of the Special Representative of the Commission on Human Rights on the Situation of Human Rights in Rwanda, 22 October 1997 (A/52/522).

[10] AFP, Kigali, 19 November 1997.

[11] Several independent sources in Rwanda.

[12] This caused an important deficit of information. As the rebellion neither claimed nor denied the actions attributed to it, the only voice heard was that of the regime via

de libération du Rwanda (ALIR) was a number of relatively well-equipped and organised ex-FAR soldiers and former Interahamwe, operating under a single command and clearly better motivated than when they lost the war in 1994. They had the advantage the RPF possessed from 1990 to 1994, as they were fighting a guerrilla war against the RPA, which had become a conventional army operating in an unfavourable human environment. Although the rebel forces operated on a permanent basis inside the country, Kabila's conquest of Congo did not bring an end to the sanctuaries in that country, where the east, in particular, was barely under the control of the new regime in Kinshasa, and where, moreover, anti-Tutsi sentiment objectively favoured the Rwandan rebellion. The areas of Masisi and Rutshuru bordering Rwanda served as bases for attack and retreat, facilitated by an alliance with the Hunde mai-mai militia native to this region.[13]

The regime tried to manage this situation exclusively in a military fashion. In February 1997, Romania delivered arms via Yemen, through the mediation of the Israeli company LR Avionics Technologies. At the beginning of July, Rwanda acquired MI-24 fighter helicopters, flown by mercenaries from former Soviet Republics (Ukraine and Belarus). At the end of July, South Africa resumed its arms sales, suspended a year earlier.[14] In November, the RPA purchased about ten tanks; these were apparently old Soviet T-55 models, and experts doubted their usefulness for combat in the northwest. Obviously, the budget continued to reflect the military option: about 50% of current expenditure was allocated to defence, an obvious underestimate, since in a budget, which was hardly transparent, some revenue and expenses were not registered.

The military mode of management was also visible through the warnings given to the population; these became openly threatening at the end of 1997. On 21 December 1997, Prime Minister Rwigema declared that 'whoever acts in connivance with them (the rebels) will suffer a fate similar to theirs'. During a visit to Nkuli (Ruhengeri) at the beginning of 1998, Kagame firmly warned the population of the northwest. These declarations somehow 'justified' the massacres of civilians, about which something must now be said.

---

spokespeople from the Rwanda News Agency (RNA), presented as being a 'private' agency, but which in reality was controlled by the RPF.
[13] Several sources within the Rwandan and mai-mai diaspora.
[14] A decision subsequently criticised by Amnesty International: South Africa ignores grave human rights violations in Rwanda by resuming sales of military equipment, 25 July 1997.

In Rwanda as well as Burundi, most victims of these civil wars were unarmed outsiders to the conflict. In Burundi, the year started very badly when, on 10 January 1997, the army massacred 126 refugees on their return from Tanzania. Almost a year later, on New Year's Eve 1997, a confrontation near Bujumbura airport and the military camp of Gakumbu caused the death of several hundred civilians in Rukaramu. Between these two incidents, an unknown number of Burundians were killed. Adding up the figures from available data, which were, however, incomplete and often unconfirmed, a total of between 5000 and 10,000 civilians may well have been killed in 1997; this figure was obviously very high, but it was on the decline compared to previous years. The perpetrators of these massacres were not only the army but also the rebel movements; the army implicitly recognised its responsibility when the minister of defence, Colonel Firmin Sinziyoheba, asserted that 'all Hutu males of combat age are the enemy'.[15]

On the other hand, in Rwanda, the number of victims increased considerably as the year 1997 progressed. According to Amnesty International, at least 6000 people, mainly unarmed civilians, were killed between January and August, mainly by the RPA; according to the report, the real number was undoubtedly much higher, since numerous massacres were not reported.[16] These facts were implicitly acknowledged by the regime, when, refuting the observations made by the human rights observation mission (UN Human Rights Field Operation for Rwanda [UNHRFOR]), presidential advisor Claude Dusaidi claimed that 'if civilians had been killed, they were accomplices, people who sympathised with these armed men'.[17] Strangely enough, this language reminds one of that used by the former regime when it sought somehow to justify the persecution of the *ibyitso* (accomplices) of the RPF, a coded expression referring to the Tutsi. Just as in the past, U.S. Ambassador Gribbin carefully toed the regime's line. He claimed that 'on January 18 [1997], insurgents killed three Spanish aid workers in Ruhengeri town'[18] and he attributed the killing of the Canadian priest Guy Pinard and the Belgian school teacher Griet Bosmans to those same insurgents,[19] while the revelations of RPA defector Abdul Ruzibiza[20] and a Spanish judicial inquiry[21] uncovered

[15] Reuters, Bujumbura, 10 August 1997.
[16] Amnesty International, Rwanda. Ending the silence, 25 September 1997.
[17] AFP, Nairobi, 8 August 1997.
[18] R.E. Gribbin, *In the Aftermath of Genocide...*, *op. cit.*, p. 226.
[19] *Idem*, p. 227.
[20] A. Ruzibiza, *Rwanda. L'histoire secrète*, Paris, Editions du Panama, 2005.
[21] Juzgado central de instrución No. 4, Audiencia Nacional, Decision of 6 February 2008.

the RPA's responsibility for these (and many other) crimes attributed to the 'insurgents'. Against all evidence, Gribbin wrote that '[a]lthough the RDR and some critics abroad alleged that the attacks were perpetrated by the RPA in order to scare the international community out of zones where reprisals against Hutu were underway, I never doubted that insurgents orchestrated the attacks'.[22] On which basis – apart from his unwavering support for the regime – this lack of doubt was founded remains a mystery.[23]

Violence was clearly on the increase in the second half of 1997, especially from October onwards. In a new report, Amnesty observed that 'during the months of October, November and the beginning of December, AI received almost daily reports of slaughters of unarmed civilians in Rwanda, namely extra-judicial executions conducted by soldiers of the RPA and deliberate and arbitrary slaughters by armed opposition groups'.[24] Adding up available data that were often incomplete and imprecise, the death toll for the period October 1997 to January 1998 was close to 10,000 victims at the hands of the RPA, and several hundred (almost 2000 if one includes the massacre of Mudende, see the later text) at the hands of the rebels. Moreover, there was no news about large population groups, in particular in the sub-prefecture of Kabaya, the highly populated region of origin of former president Habyarimana, where, in January 1998, a team from Belgian public television was able to film the hills and town centres completely void of their populations. Were these people dead or detained? Were they hiding in the nearby forest of Gishwati? Another uncertainty: were all the incidents due to rebel activities or, were they, in some cases, staged by the RPA, with the aim of, as the human rights activist Joseph Matata wrote in a letter addressed to Mary Robinson on 4 December 1997, 'justifying retaliation operations against unarmed civilians'?[25] The latter, in reality, faced a murderous dilemma: if suspected of assisting the rebels, they were killed by the RPA; if they refused to collaborate with the rebellion, they became their target.

---

[22] R.E. Gribbin, *In the Aftermath of Genocide...*, *op. cit.*, p. 227.

[23] One learns without surprise that, when Gribbin's term came to an end, Kagame invited him to his ranch, and offered him a cow, 'a mark of esteem in Rwandan society' (R.E. Gribbin, *In the Aftermath of Genocide...*, *op. cit.*, p. 304). Gribbin probably did not realise that the gift of a cow also marks the link between a patron and a client.

[24] Amnesty International, Rwanda. Civilians trapped in armed conflict. 'The dead can no longer be counted', 19 December 1997.

[25] Furthermore, in several cases, the majority of those killed by 'assailants' were Hutu, fitting poorly into a campaign presented by the Government as 'the continuation of the genocide'.

Concluding this section on the civil wars, attention must be drawn to the shady side of a number of serious incidents. The feeling of manipulation was reinforced by the inaccessibility of the areas of conflict and by the absence in the field of impartial foreign observers. The targeted murders of, for example, ICRC workers in Burundi and members of Médecins du monde (MDM) in Rwanda prompted the departure of numerous foreigners from the affected areas, thereby allowing perpetrators of crimes against humanity to operate far from the eyes of the international community and to sow confusion. In order to illustrate this, I briefly present two atrocious episodes that took place barely three weeks apart.

On 11 December 1997, Mudende camp, a shelter for Congolese Tutsi refugees in northwestern Rwanda, was attacked. The Rwandan government claimed that the assailants were rebels. The RPA contingent of approximately 20 men who guarded the camp was overwhelmed and had to call back-up that managed to defeat the attackers. Depending on the source, the number of victims among the refugees varied between approximately 300 (Rwandan government) and more than 1500 (Congolese government). However, many disturbing facts surrounded this incident. How is it that the RPA reinforcements based in Gisenyi (a twenty-minute drive from Mudende) arrived so late that, according to survivors, the slaughter continued for several hours? How does one explain that, according to the UNHCR, the combats did not cause a single casualty among the RPA soldiers or the attackers?[26] Why did the accounts of survivors differ so much from those of the Rwandan government? At the very best, these contradictions suggest that the RPA allowed or, at worst, staged this incident, which took place very opportunely on the eve of Madeleine Albright's arrival in Kigali. Having been severely criticised by the UN High Commissioner for Human Rights less than a week before, it was in the government's interest to appear to be the victim. These doubts were apparently shared by the Americans. David Sheffer, the United States Ambassador for War Crimes, appointed by Secretary Albright to conduct an inquiry, stated that 'the RPA, in a pronounced manner, failed to adequately protect the refugees (of Mudende)'.[27] The State Department spokesman affirmed that 'the reasons for this failure of the RPA are uncertain but point in the direction of the actions of a local commander'.[28] A barely-known fact only reinforced the suspicion. On 16 December 1997, the Congolese ambassador to the United Nations, André

---

[26] UNHCR, Briefing Notes, Geneva, 12 December 1997.
[27] Reuters, London, 19 December 1997.
[28] AP, London, 18 December 1997.

Kapanga, addressed a formal submission to the Security Council, with the aim of setting up a commission of inquiry into the Mudende massacre. When its opinion was sought, Rwanda advised that the incident had already been the subject of two inquiries,[29] and that, as a consequence, another inquiry was unnecessary. On this note, Congo informally requested that this point be withdrawn from the agenda of the Security Council. Thus, the mist surrounding this serious incident remained.[30]

A second illustration is the attack on New Year's Eve near Bujumbura. Points of view converge on the following facts: during the night of 31 December 1997–1 January 1998, rebels attacked Bujumbura airport and the nearby military camp of Gakumbu; several hundred civilians were subsequently killed in the adjoining area of Rukaramu. From this point onwards, accounts differed. According to the Burundian authorities, some 200 civilians were killed by the rebels; furthermore, about 100 rebels and 4 soldiers were said to have been killed during the fighting. As for the CNDD, they claimed responsibility for the attack, but asserted that 500 civilians were killed by the army.[31] It is impossible to verify which of the two versions is correct since, apart from a team from the official television station, no journalist or foreign observer was allowed to visit the area. An 'inquiry'[32] conducted by the ITEKA human rights league, which had become close to the regime since the ethnic cleansing in Bujumbura, was unconvincing. The international inquiry requested by the CNDD never took place. As in Mudende, the mist continued to float over Rukaramu.

---

[29] These 'enquiries' conducted by the observation mission for human rights (UNHRFOR) and by Ambassador Sheffer were extremely summary and did not offer firm and definitive conclusions.

[30] The presence of the UN Human Rights Field Operation for Rwanda (UNHRFOR) became increasingly symbolic. A telling example of this was seen on the occasion of a particularly serious incident during which several thousand people died in caves in Nyakinama at the end of October 1997. While the RPA claimed that the victims were rebels, it is likely that they were civilians who had fled the fighting in the commune of Kanama. Even confronted with a well-localised situation (do the caves contain armed or unarmed people?) easy to investigate, the UNHRFOR was unable or unwilling to establish the facts. On this incident, see: Centre de lutte contre l'impunité et l'injustice au Rwanda, Communiqué no. 22/97. L'armée rwandaise a massacré, dans la grotte de Nyakinama, plus de 8000 habitants de quatre secteurs de la commune Kanama (Gisenyi) entre les 24 et 27 octobre 1997, 24 November 1997; Amnesty International, Rwanda. Civilians caught in armed conflict..., *op. cit.*, pp. 9–12.

[31] CNDD, Communiqué no. 4. L'attaque de l'aéroport par les FDD, 2 January 1998.

[32] Ligue ITEKA, Communiqué sur les massacres de Rukaramu, Bujumbura, 6 January 1998.

## 6.2 POLITICAL OR MILITARY OUTCOMES?

I have stated earlier that the option of the Burundian government was not exclusively military in nature. Since the international aspects of this process have been analysed elsewhere,[33] only a brief overview of the positions of internal actors will be presented here. At the time when there were discreet contacts in Rome with the CNDD, things began rather badly inside the country. The first 'Seminar of Reflection on the National Debate and the Peace Process' was boycotted by Frodebu and Parena. The Forces for Democratic Change (FCD: Frodebu, RPB and PL) demanded a ceasefire and a cessation of the massacres committed by the army as a pre-condition, while Uprona, RADDES and Inkinzo declared they did not wish to negotiate with 'génocidaires'. As for the CNDD, they called the proposed meeting a 'masquerade'.[34]

While there were still contacts throughout the year in Rome, Arusha and Paris, in Burundi the process was relaunched towards the end of 1997. In a speech to the National Assembly, the prime minister presented a plan to revitalise the peace process. This plan had three main components: national debate, peace conferences and political dialogue open to all parties. However, when Mr. Ndimira addressed the state of affairs, the slowness of this progress became apparent. The 'seminars of reflection' organised within the framework of the 'national debate' did not commit anyone and were far from bringing together the relevant actors; this called to mind the 'colloquia on national unity', organised in 1989, whose cosmetic character became very apparent later. Concerning the 'conferences for peace', the Prime Minister had only a meeting organised by UNESCO in Paris on 26–28 September to report. As for the 'political dialogue.' which should have begun on 25 August 1997 in Arusha, Ndimira attributed the government's absence to 'difficulties linked to collaboration with the mediator (Nyerere) and the country hosting the negotiations'. We shall see later that by being almost the only political actor absent from Arusha, the regime was thereby contributing to its own isolation, a situation which it later reversed. Nevertheless, the speech showed a certain willingness towards dialogue, which was shared by parliament. On 4 December 1997, the Speaker of the National Assembly stated that the House, in collaboration with the government, was ready to involve itself in the peace process, but not without warning that the

---

[33] P. Dupont, 'La crise politique au Burundi ...', *op. cit.*, pp. 39–61.
[34] AFP, Nairobi, 9 January 1997.

Assembly 'will never support the regime in power if it chooses to resolve internal problems by means of war'. The option of dialogue seemed to be reinforced by the creation, on 14 August 1997, of a ministry responsible for the peace process. The action plan for 1998, published at the end of 1997 by its incumbent Ambroise Niyonsaba, proposed a large number of different types of meetings. However, there was still no question of political negotiations, though it was obvious that these were necessary.

The fragile nature of the process was illustrated by the fact that, within the space of barely one week, two crucial actors (temporarily) closed the door during the second half of February 1998. In communiqué No. 17 of 17 February 1998, the CNDD announced the suspension *sine die* of the dialogue, after seven people were sentenced to death on suspicion of having planted mines in Bujumbura.[35] On the other hand, the Frodebu, through a press communiqué of 25 February 1998, rejected the conclusions published by the government after the round table meeting held in Gitega from 18 to 21 February. Claiming 'manipulation', the party felt that they did not reflect the content of the meeting and announced the suspension of its participation in subsequent meetings until the document was amended.

But the Burundians were speaking of dialogue and the various political and military forces maintained channels of communication. This was not the case in Rwanda: the RPF refused to speak to anyone, asserting that 'everything has been negotiated in Arusha', that 'those who would like to participate in the reconstruction of the country are welcome to do so', and that, at any rate, there were no valid interlocutors. However, this presupposed that the Arusha accords were applied (which they were not) and that those who wanted to effectively participate be allowed to do so (which they were not). On the other hand, the third argument was not unfounded. In fact, there were two types of potential negotiators, one legitimate and the other much less so. The former comprised a certain number of associations and movements in exile, such as 'Rwanda pour Tous' and the FRD[36], whose discourses were similar, putting the former genocidal regime and the RPF (which they claimed was hardly better) back to back. While these groups advocated a third path, the extent of their political base was unknown and probably limited. The second potential negotiator was this faceless

---

[35] However, this did not prevent the president of the CNDD Nyangoma from having discreet contacts with Major Buyoya during his visit to Europe in March.

[36] On this subject, see F. Reyntjens, 'Rwanda et Burundi: les acteurs politiques', *op. cit.*, pp. 120–121.

rebellion that included some of those bearing heavy responsibility for the genocide of 1994. This was clearly the perception of the Rwandan government, as was demonstrated in a revealing incident at the beginning of 1998. On the occasion of the signature of a grant agreement, the Japanese ambassador to Rwanda encouraged Kigali to 'forget hatred, distrust and pride', so that 'the fighting may cease and negotiations may begin'. The Rwandan reaction was like lightning. On 29 January, Minister of Foreign Affairs Anastase Gasana stated that he was 'surprised to hear the ambassador of a country friendly towards Rwanda (...) request negotiations with criminal groups, which should be brought before the courts', adding that 'given the historical heritage of Japan, it is regrettable that Mr. Shinsuke proposes negotiations with the forces of genocide'.[37] Four days after this diatribe, the Japanese government, by means of a communiqué announced that 'it did not speak out in favour of a negotiation between Rwanda and the rebels'; there had been a 'misunderstanding'.[38]

The marginalisation of the 'third way' by the RPF, supported by those – including some foreign observers – who made a mockery of it, closed the door to one of the rare opportunities for a negotiated solution. The decision to discredit all potential partners for dialogue was very clearly expressed by Tito Rutaremara, a very influential RPF MP, when he stated that 'the only organised anti-RPF movements are genocidal movements'.[39] with which, obviously, one does not negotiate. Even if the problem of a valid negotiating partner was indisputable, the excuses used by the FPR to reject any type of dialogue profoundly contributed to the impasse and caused deep frustration, thereby promoting increased radicalisation.

### 6.3 JUSTICE IN DEADLOCK

Justice in Rwanda was confronted with a mathematical impossibility. At the beginning of 1998, there were 135,000 people in detention, while slightly over 300 sentences were passed in 1997. At this rate, it would take over four centuries to judge all the prison population; this period even tended to increase, as the number of new arrests surpassed those of the sentences. Furthermore, between November 1997 and February 1998, the trials almost ceased, as they did again later in 1998. The impasse was acknowledged by the passing of the law of 26 December 1997, which

[37] AFP, Kigali, 29 January 1998.
[38] AFP, Kigali, 4 February 1998.
[39] AFP, Kigali, 16 March 1998.

purported to retroactively regularise detentions on remand until 31 December 1999 (previously, a law of 8 September 1996 extended detentions until 31 December 1997). This meant that people arrested in 1994 were to spend five years in prison without a judge ruling on their detention; moreover, this was a dangerous precedent, as nothing would prevent the regularisation being extended once again at the end of 1999,[40] which indeed it was. It goes without saying that even the most effective judicial system could not reasonably address such a backlog, which explains why the idea of non-judicial methods of processing these cases gained support, even among the higher realms of power. In an interview, General Kagame stated that it would be necessary 'to separate those cases of direct perpetrators of genocide from the others', asserting that 'we will have to find other solutions; we will explain this to the survivors'.[41]

The Rwandan justice system did not only face a mathematical problem. 'Justice must not only be done, but seen to be done'. The 'Tutsification' of the judicial apparatus[42] contributed to the perception of partiality, that is, of 'victors' justice', in which even the most objective judiciary would have difficulties convincing. The impression that Hutu defendants were prosecuted by mainly Tutsi prosecutors and sentenced by mainly Tutsi judges considerably limited the legitimacy of the judicial process and hampered the dual objective set for the rehabilitation of the system, namely national reconciliation and the fight against impunity. Two phenomena reinforced this feeling. On the one hand, associations close to the regime acted both as denunciation syndicates and as structures to intimidate defence witnesses. On the other hand, the regime refused to tackle the problem of crimes against humanity and war crimes committed by the RPA. Even though a few soldiers were tried and sentenced, these trials nearly always concerned members of the armed forces who committed military or common law offences; the convictions for civilian massacres were very few and the punishments symbolic.[43]

---

[40] Attorneys without Borders was concerned about the consequences of this law which they felt was 'extremely open to criticism': Avocats sans Frontières, Projet 'Justice pour tous au Rwanda'. Rapport annuel 1997, Brussels, 1998, p. 19.

[41] *Le Soir*, 20 January 1997. On non-judicial approaches see S. Vandeginste, 'L'approche "vérité et réconciliation" du génocide et des crimes contre l'humanité au Rwanda', in: F. Reyntjens, S. Marysse (Eds.), *L'Afrique des grands lacs. Annuaire 1997–1998*, Paris, L'Harmattan, 1998, pp. 97–140.

[42] On which, see F. Reyntjens, 'Rwanda. Evolution politique en 1996–1997' in: S. Marysse, F. Reyntjens (Eds.), *L'Afrique des grands lacs. Annuaire 1996–1997*, Paris L'Harmattan, 1997, pp. 46–47.

[43] A list of RPA military prosecuted for crimes committed in 1994 can be found in Annex 2 of Human Rights Watch, 'Law and Reality. Progress in Judicial Reform in Rwanda',

The third judicial impasse in relation to Rwanda was at the level of the International Criminal Tribunal for Rwanda (ICTR), which was confronted with three main problems. The first was its slow pace. Four years after its creation, only two sentences had been handed down. The second problem concerned the selection of suspects brought before the ICTR. In fact, the tribunal inherited a certain number of 'small fry', charged before the prosecutor's office was able to develop a coherent inquiry and prosecution policy. Even though important suspects were later charged and detained in Arusha, this situation considerably slowed down the processing of the cases of the 'masterminds' of the genocide. A third problem concerned the credibility of the ICTR, suspected – as were the Rwandan jurisdictions – of practising 'victors' justice'.[44] In fact, while it was admitted that elements of the RPA committed crimes within the temporal and material jurisdiction of the tribunal, no inquiry was conducted against it nor, *a fortiori*, was any prosecution launched. The prosecutor's office, set up in Kigali, was subject to barely veiled pressure from the Rwandan regime; according to several internal sources, they were well aware that they would be forced to end their activities in Rwanda if they were to conduct inquiries into the crimes committed by the RPF.

Burundi faced similar challenges, though of a lesser magnitude. Some of the presumed plotters of October 1993 were tried before the Supreme Court, while thousands of prisoners were waiting to be tried by the criminal chambers of the courts of appeal for their presumed responsibility in the massacres of Tutsi and Hutu from Union pour le progress national (UPRONA), in the days following the assassination of President Ndadaye. Dozens of death sentences were pronounced by predominantly Tutsi jurisdictions, a state of affairs that of course created a perception already mentioned in relation to Rwanda. Six of those condemned were executed on 31 July 1997, after trials considered 'grossly unfair' by Amnesty International.[45]

At the level of international justice, the Burundian government requested the setting up of an international criminal tribunal, but on 16 June 1997 Secretary General Kofi Annan announced that he could not support such a proposal. It could well be that his refusal was inspired

---

July 2008. Only 14 individuals were convicted; of these, one was given a six-year sentence, while the others received between two and four years.

[44] On this issue, see T. Cruvellier, *Le tribunal des vaincus. Un Nuremberg pour le Rwanda?*, Paris, Calmann-Lévy, 2006.

[45] Amnesty International, Burundi: Government carries out political executions after grossly unfair trials, 1 August 1997.

in part by the experience of the ICTR, but also by the fear of a political exploitation of the 'genocide' in Burundi. In fact, the UN itself contributed to this problem: the report published by the UN Commission of Inquiry on Burundi (UNICIB) in July 1996 concluded that 'acts of genocide' had been committed against the Tutsi at the end October 1993,[46] a finding immediately (and predictably) exploited by some political forces seeking to exclude 'the génocidaires' – in reality, their political opponents – from the negotiation process. The qualification of the crimes committed in 1993 as genocide was, however, not established and remained open to discussion. An international commission of NGOs which, barely two months after the events, conducted investigations in much more favourable conditions than the UN, did not believe that there were elements constituting a crime of genocide, although the report noted that some local officials incited or participated in these crimes. However, the proof of organisation was lacking (it was not demonstrated in the report of UNICIB either).[47]

## 6.4  INSTITUTIONAL DEVELOPMENTS AND PRACTICE OF GOVERNANCE

For Rwanda, 1997 was a year of commotion at several levels. Firstly, the government was reshuffled on three occasions. The first reshuffle took place on 28 March 1997 and deserves some attention. Several ministers left the government, some changed portfolios, others entered, state secretariats were created. The most noticeable departure was that of the Minister of the Interior, Alexis Kanyarengwe, also the chairman of the RPF at the time. He was not officially dismissed, but resigned because he wanted 'to devote himself to other duties'. However, besides the chair of the RPF – more of an honorary post than anything else – he has not performed any 'other duties' since. Moreover, Kanyarengwe was to lose the chair of the RPF a year later. In reality, his removal from office came after protests from Kanyarengwe and the prefect of Ruhengeri, Ignace Karuhije against the massacres committed by the RPA in that prefecture, which was also that of Kanyarengwe (several members of his family were

---

[46] UNICIB, Final Report, New York, 23 July 1996.
[47] I am well aware that this point of view is heavily resented by those who exploit the 'genocide credit'. At the end of February 1998, the Uprona and RADDES parties called for a demonstration against the Special Envoy of the European Union, Aldo Ajello, who was visiting Bujumbura, because he reportedly stated that the term 'genocide' was not appropriate in the case of Burundi.

among the victims). Furthermore, Karuhije was fired on the same day 'for incompetence and his inability to curb insecurity'; he was replaced by Boniface Rucagu (see the later text). Finance Minister Marc Rugenera was demoted to the ministry of handicraft, mines and tourism with little substance (and without avenues for accumulation). He was replaced by the Minister of Planning, Jean Birara, who, flanked by a Secretary of State (Donat Kaberuka), was entrusted with a 'super-ministry' of finance and planning.

While on the occasion of previous reshuffles, attempts had been made to be seen to apply the provisions of the Arusha protocol on power sharing, this was now no longer the case. Not only was the allocation of ministerial portfolios among the different political parties stipulated in the accord no longer respected,[48] but also, and above all, it was the president and not the Assembly who carried out the reorganisation, while the appointments were made without consulting the political parties. This episode only confirmed and reinforced the dominance of the executive branch, a feature that was in profound contradiction to the principles agreed in Arusha. On 7 October 1997, it was the turn of Jean Birara to be dismissed; he was replaced by his deputy Kaberuka. Birara was known for his firm stand on corruption,[49] and his departure came at a time when the Rwandan press carried reports on numerous embezzlements. The last reshuffle came on the occasion of changes in the military apparatus, which will be addressed later. On 10 January 1998, Major Emmanuel Habyarimana (ex-FAR), the former permanent secretary at the ministry of defence, was promoted as secretary of state for defence, a newly created post.

There were also several changes at the level of the préfectures. We have already seen that Ignace Karuhije was replaced by Boniface Rucagu as the prefect of Ruhengeri, after the murderous expeditions of the RPA; this episode also sealed the political fate of Alexis Kanyarengwe. Rucagu's appointment was surprising, as he was number 120 on the first list of genocide suspects as published by the public prosecutor of the Supreme Court in 1996[50]; moreover, his name had been cited as a member of the

---

[48] This infringement was rather understandable: strict adhesion to this division over a long period of time would cause unsustainable rigidity and would inhibit rational management.

[49] He had already resigned as the governor of the National Bank under the government of Habyarimana, deeming that he could no longer cover a certain number of fraudulent practices in the mid-1980s.

[50] *Official Gazette*, 30 November 1996.

'death squads' of the former regime since 1992.[51] At the beginning of June 1997, the National Assembly called for his suspension, in order to conduct an investigation, before demanding his arrest in July. At first sight, Rucagu's appointment and his survival in office was one of those Rwandan paradoxes, but on closer inspection, it was clearly a strategy to ensure relative peace in a préfecture where Hutu radicalism has ancient roots and was still very present.

Another reshuffle concerned the RPF itself. On 8 February 1998, the political bureau was dissolved; it was unclear who took the decision and on what statutory basis. According to an AFP interview with second vice-president and acting general secretary Denis Polisi, the RPF 'is pausing for reflection', i.a. regarding its leadership.[52] The 'reflection' was to be very brief, as one week later, on 15 February, it was announced that Paul Kagame was now the chairman of the party; the new vice chairman was the president of the Republic, Pasteur Bizimungu, while the rector of the National University, Charles Murigande, became the general secretary. Kanyarengwe was no longer in the picture. According to the press,[53] Kagame was elected 'by a narrow margin' after a meeting lasting two days; depending on the source, 'more than 150 members' (AFP) or '230 members' (Voice of America) reportedly took part in the decision. It is unclear which body took the decision: according to AFP, it was the political bureau, which, however, only comprises five members. According to a press communiqué from the RPF,[54] the decision was taken by the 'National Consultative Board (which includes) representatives of members from all regions, reference being made to the month of December 1993'. At least in part, the confusion stemmed from the fact that the RPF had no statutes, and there were no known regulations concerning the duration of mandates, the power to appoint and dismiss and the composition and competence of the various bodies. The new composition of the leading bodies slightly reduced the 'extraneous' character of the RPF as, henceforth, three of the eight commissioners were not from the former diaspora. However, the Tutsi character of the movement was even reinforced (among the three members of the executive committee and the eight commissioners, Pasteur Bizimungu was the only Hutu).

---

[51] Cf. F. Reyntjens, Données sur les 'escadrons de la mort au Rwanda', Antwerp, 9 October 1992.

[52] AFP, Kigali, 8 February 1998.

[53] AFP, Kigali, 16 February 1998; VOA, 16 February 1998.

[54] Dated 16 February 1998 and signed by Denis Polisi, 'Youth Commisssioner', for Charles Murigande.

The reshuffle at the top of the RPF confirmed the political elimination of Kanyarengwe and the central role of Kagame, but also illustrated the opaque functioning of the regime. This feeling was increasingly shared by many in the RPF membership.

Indeed more and more serious doubts were expressed on the RPF's mode of governance. Under the heading 'The RPF has renounced itself', the *Tribun du Peuple* – though considered a supporter of the RPF – in August 1997 stated that 'the revolution' had failed and that the new regime was plagiarising the methods of the former government. It denounced the misappropriation of funds, nepotism, clientship and corruption, and asserted that 'the liabilities of Habyarimana and company's management of the country at the end of the first fifteen years of his time in office, has been largely attained by the new leaders of the country over the last three years'. Referring to the abuses committed by the RPA, it observed that – contrary to Article 5 of the RPF's programme – the military 'are neither honest, competent nor patriotic'.[55] During this same period, members of the RPF published a memorandum denouncing the 'decadent nature' of the RPF and pointing to 'organisational shortcomings', 'moral decline', and 'intellectual bankruptcy', as 'elements of the crisis'. Joining the analysis of the *Tribun du Peuple*, the memo denounced 'the inexplicable accumulation of wealth, the lack of accountability, arrogance, clientship, political patronage'. The final verdict was severe: 'The RPF as an organisation has ceased to exist (...) From 1994, a group of individuals, members of the RPF, have monopolised the RPF by excluding the general membership'[56]. A document circulating in Kigali in June or July 1998 and largely discussed after it was posted on the Internet, claimed that a new *akazu*,[57] united by kinship and other bonds, was unduly accumulating material resources, jobs and privileges.[58]

In a generalised atmosphere of corruption, racketeering, trading of favours and nepotism, the elite – concerned about its future – took some precautions. Some ministers placed their assets in banks and purchased real estate in Europe; other politicians and officers of the RPA mainly

---

[55] *Le Tribun du Peuple*, No. 97, August 1997; for an overview of other criticisms in the national press, see *Dialogue*, No. 200, September–October 1997, pp. 75–86.

[56] Memo des membres de (sic) FPR (Rwanda, Afrique du Sud, Canada, Etats-Unis), Michigan, 31 August 1997.

[57] This term, literally meaning 'little house', was first used to refer to President Habyarimana's inner circle; see F. Reyntjens, *L'Afrique des grands lacs...*, *op. cit.*, pp. 189–190.

[58] Analyse politique du phénomène Akazu, document signed by 'a disappointed patriot [i.e. a member of the RPF]'.

invested in Uganda and South Africa. Those denouncing or fighting this downhill slide were sidelined or terrorised. Minister Birara, mentioned earlier, was a case in point. In the same vein, the French scholar Gérard Prunier was violently taken to task after the publication of a critical but on the whole appropriate analysis.[59] The director of the government information office ORINFOR reacted through a diatribe against 'Prunier who claims to be an academic', who makes a 'pseudo-analysis of Rwandan society' and who – no more, no less – 'is indirectly responsible for the 1994 genocide'.[60] In fact, many foreign critical voices simply became *persona non grata*. On 9 February 1997, Reuters correspondent Christian Jennings was expelled, probably for having written two days earlier that, during a press conference, General Kagame had asserted that 'Rwanda has the right to divert a part of international aid to contribute to the internal war against Hutu extremists'.[61] On 28 November 1997, Stephen Smith of the French daily *Libération* was refused a visa and became another *persona non grata*. The chargé d'affaires at the Embassy of Rwanda in Paris explained that 'Smith only has himself to blame, given the horrors he has written about the country'.[62] Some researchers specialised in the region were also declared undesirable.[63] The regime attempted by all possible means to silence Rwandans in exile, even – and perhaps, especially, because they were the most dangerous – those who had no blood on their hands. Thus, the former minister James Gasana, chairman of the association 'Rwanda pour tous' and promoter, along with Nkiko Nsengimana, of the New Hope for Rwanda (NOER) project, became the victim of an orchestrated campaign in his country of asylum, Switzerland, where his detractors tried to manipulate the press and the political world, in order to get the federal authorities to launch criminal proceedings against him and to deprive him of employment. Relayed by a certain press[64] of doubtful ethical standards, which had already been condemned for libel in a dispute involving the Fondation Hirondelle (also targeted by the regime

---

[59] G. Prunier, *Rwanda: the Social, Political and Economic Situation in June 1997*, Writenet (UK), July 1997.

[60] W. Rutayisire, Gérald (sic) Prunier: A Eulogy for Genocide, Kigali, 24 October 1997. A juicy detail: Prunier was also accused of 'anglophobia', while some French quarters reproached his 'anglophilia', as he had the audacity to publish in English and to criticise France for her 'Fashoda syndrome'.

[61] Reuters, Kigali, 7 February 1997.

[62] Communiqué of RFS/IFEX, Toronto, 2 December 1997.

[63] The author of this book being the first, in February 1995, to be hit by this measure. Several of his colleagues have since joined him.

[64] See *L'Objectif*, No. 147, 13–26 February 1998; No. 150, 27 March–8 April 1998.

in Kigali), this campaign was led by some 'associations' of Rwandans in Switzerland with close ties to the RPF.[65]

Even the criticisms formulated by UN bodies or international NGOs were systematically rejected or discredited, sometimes even stifled. In June 1997, the Rwandan government, through a large-scale diplomatic offensive, succeeded in having the mandate of UN Special Rapporteur René Degni-Segui abolished, as he had increasingly become a nuisance; he was replaced by a Special Representative whose ability to harm the regime's interests was much more limited. On 7 December 1997, the new UN High Commissioner for Human Rights Mary Robinson, considered a friend of the 'New Rwanda' (she visited the country on several occasions when she was president of Ireland), released a communiqué evoking the absence of a reconciliation policy and the practice of serious human rights violations. That same day, there was a vehement declaration by the spokesman of the Rwandan presidency, categorically denying Robinson's observations and accusing her of being influenced 'by informants whose aims are to mislead international public opinion on the situation in Rwanda'. Other critics suffered the same fate; hence, several reports published by Amnesty International in 1997 and 1998 were described by the regime as 'misinformation'.[66] In an interview published in the Ugandan newspaper *The Monitor* on 26 December 1997, General Kagame affirmed that 'we have international observers of human rights (...) they have to justify their existence; therefore, in order to be able to stay, they compile alarming reports which give them a purpose'. As a result of the government's refusal to allow it to continue its monitoring activities, the UN observer mission HRFOR left the country at the end of July 1998.

While there remained some degree of press freedom, the scope for dissidence was reduced through a number of measures. First, by intimidation pure and simple: at the end of 1997, an estimated hundred people 'disappeared' every month in the city of Kigali alone[67]; this of course encouraged those who would otherwise express critical sounds to be

---

[65] In a decision that was incoherent, to say the least, the Swiss government in June 1998 decided that Gasana was innocent of the accusations levelled against him, while at the same time ending his contract with the Intercoopération agency.

[66] After the publication of a communiqué (cf. footnote 67) by Amnesty International on 12 March 1998, the spokesman of the RPA Dr. Ndahiro accused the organisation of just being the 'relay of Hutu extremists' and of taking sides with the 'forces of genocide' (Xinhua, Nairobi, 14 March 1998).

[67] Amnesty International, confronted with the magnitude of this phenomenon, sounded the alarm in a communiqué published on 12 March 1998: Rwanda: selon des délégués d'Amnesty International, les 'disparitions' atteignent un taux alarmant; in their

extremely cautious. Second, some measures specifically targeted 'trouble-makers': in 1997, one journalist was killed, two others arrested, as were two leaders of human rights associations (ADL and ARDHO) and several judges, including a vice-president of the Supreme Court. Third, the regime neutralised civil society by infiltrating it or otherwise. The election of the vice-president of the Ibuka association, which at the time maintained close ties to the regime, at the head of the CLADHO (a human rights collective), and that of another influential member of Ibuka as chair of the CCOAIB (a collective of development NGOs) were part of this strategy,[68] which was quite openly acknowledged by the general secretary of the RPF, Denis Polisi: passing through Brussels on 15 June 1997, he denounced 'those business enterprises called NGOs' and lambasted 'the latest invention of the NGOs, namely civil society'.[69]

At the institutional level, Burundi was shaken up to a lesser extent than Rwanda during 1997. At the level of the government, there were two reshuffles, which only had a limited impact. Changes were more important within the two main political formations. While Uprona split into two wings, Frodebu, which started the year divided, seemed to reunite somewhat. The split in Uprona was mainly on the basis of the attitude to be adopted in negotiations, in particular with the CNDD, but was also influenced by the presence (or absence) of antagonists in the wheels of the state. One wing formed around the party chairman Charles Mukasi, who was opposed to any dialogue with the CNDD, labelled 'génocidiaire', and as a consequence also to Major Buyoya, supposedly open to negotiations. The other wing, close to Buyoya and including personalities such as Antoine Nduwayo, Jean-Baptiste Manwangari, Alphonse Kadege, Adrien Sibomana and Libère Bararunyeretse,[70] believed that UPRONA should be present in the search for peace. This tendency also rejected Mukasi's authoritarian style, committing the party as he did without consulting the competent bodies. The split was once again openly visible when, in a letter addressed to the minister of the interior and public security, dated 21 January 1998, some twenty members of Uprona's central committee demanded that no authorisation be given for a party congress which

---

      communiqué no. 006/98 of 23 February 1998, the Resistance Forces for Democracy (FRD) had already drawn attention to this phenomenon.

[68] The resolutions and recommendations of the extraordinary general assembly of CLADHO held on 28 February 1998 made no mention of the abuses committed by the army at that very moment.

[69] Transcribed on the basis of the reports of two persons present at the meeting.

[70] The latter was expelled from the party by Mukasi on 11 March 1998.

Mukasi had announced. A non-political reason could also explain this division: in fact, most politicians in the anti-Mukasi tendency held positions in the government, in the higher echelons of the civil service or at the head of public enterprises, which probably explains their loyalty to the government in place. These divisions showed that Burundian politics are less Manichaean than many outside observers believe: Hutu and Tutsi were found on both sides of the political divide.[71]

The CNDD–FDD fell prey to a major division at around the same time. In March 1998, the 'political-military General Staff' excluded or suspended a number of leaders and claimed to henceforth assume the movement's leadership. While he was initially maintained as the 'Commander of the CNDD–FDD', Léonard Nyangoma was in turn 'suspended' on 26 May and replaced by Col. Jean-Bosco Ndayikengurukiye. In the decision signed by the latter, who thus proclaimed himself leader of the movement, he announced he was to proceed rapidly 'to get the political and military activities back on track, and to reorganise and restructure the movement'.

Frodebu, for its part, achieved some reconciliation between its wings outside and inside the country, on the occasion of its congress held in Bujumbura on 6 December 1997. The decision was taken to renew the mandates of the national steering committee as well as those of Jean Minani as president, Augustin Nzojibwami as general secretary and Domitien Ndayizeye as permanent national executive secretary. Thus, members within and outside the country were found in the same bodies. This prompted the minister of the interior to seize the Supreme Court, where he argued that the holding of party political office by people not residing in Burundi was forbidden by the law on political parties.[72]

While the Mukasi wing of Uprona entered into open conflict with the government, there was some rapprochement between the latter and Frodebu. Although the general declaration of the congress on 6 December 1997 continued to reject power exercised as a result of a *coup d'état* and generally had a negative view of the government's activities,[73] the communication channels remained open. Some of this was visible in the speech of the (Frodebu) speaker of the National Assembly on 4 December

---

[71] The conflict was openly admitted in a text of Charles Mukasi: La nature de la crise entre le parti Uprona et le gouvernement, Bujumbura, 12 November 1997, 35 pp.

[72] On 8 December, the minister ordered Frodebu to suspend its activities for six months, a sanction repealed on the same day and followed by judicial proceedings.

[73] Frodebu, Déclaration générale du deuxième congrès ordinaire du parti Sahwanya-Frodebu, Bujumbura, 6 December 1997.

1997, in which some forms of collaboration with the government were not excluded.[74]

This did not prevent the government from being increasingly isolated. The most striking illustration was a meeting in Arusha on 25 August 1997, where – in the absence of the government and Uprona – nearly the entire political spectrum of Burundi gathered, including those considered extremists on both sides: Frodebu, PRP, CNDD, Parena, Frolina, RPB, PL, PP, Sojedem and Palipehutu. This rather surprising coalition, hardly conceivable six months earlier, declared that it supported the mediation efforts of Julius Nyerere and condemned Major Buyoya for his refusal to participate. The participants in what became an anti-Buyoya platform 'vehemently condemn the government of Major Buyoya, who has just proven his arrogance to the world, and forms the real obstacle to peace in Burundi'.

At the same time, Frodebu forcefully denounced the way in which it had been pushed away from power and the ethnic fundamentalism practised by the regime. A document, convincing in its accuracy and, based on some sample controls, apparently reliable, offered a survey of the political–ethnic composition of the public sector. The picture was disconcerting: at all levels Uprona and its allies, as well as Tutsi, claimed the lion's share. The general synthesis (ministries, local administrations and public enterprises) showed, in ethnic terms, 11% Hutu versus 89% Tutsi, and, in political terms, 7% Frodebu and allies (FCD) versus 93% Uprona and allies.[75] These figures were the clearest indication of the success of the *coup d'état*, both in its 'creeping' form since early 1994 and after it was made official in July 1996.

At the same time, the path of dialogue was pursued, through the combination of the search for an internal settlement and the Arusha process under Nyerere's leadership. Both tracks were indeed complementary. Internally, the Partenariat intérieur pour la Paix ('Internal Partnership for Peace') was an important step. On 6 June 1998, the National Assembly and the government signed an 'accord on the political platform for a transitional regime', which was translated into law the same day in the 'Constitutional Act for the Transition'. This new fundamental law

---

[74] According to some sources in Bujumbura, the reason for this relative flexibility on the part of Frodebu MPs could also be more mundane. Since their mandate (and, with it, their parliamentary earnings) was to come to an end in June 1998, by collaborating with the government, they reportedly hoped to have their terms in office extended beyond that foreseen under the constitution. This is eventually what happened.

[75] Frodebu, *Burundi. Un apartheid qui ne dit pas son nom*, Bujumbura, August 1997, 72 pp.

replaced the 1992 constitution and the law-decree of 13 September 1996 and was to remain in force 'until the date of the promulgation of the new constitution'. Not only did the Partnership confer some measure of legitimacy to Buyoya's regime, it also put in place a new government and kept parliament (the membership of which was broadened) alive beyond its constitutional term, and it gave a new impetus to Nyerere's mediation efforts. Indeed, the regime now joined the Arusha peace process, which was eventually to lead to the signing of an accord on 28 August 2000.

# 7

# 'The First African World War'

What has often been called the 'second war'[1] was in reality the continuation of the first one. As seen at the end of Chapter 5, for Rwanda and Uganda, a great deal of unfinished business was left, and the rationale behind the launch of a new 'rebellion' was in large part similar to the one prevailing in the fall of 1996. Admittedly, the outcome of the 'second war' was different from the first, but it was part of one and the same war, which is why I use the singular in the title of this book.

## 7.1 FROM GOMA TO KITONA, AND TO MILITARY STALEMATE

During the evening of 2 August 1998, Sylvain Mbuki, the commander of the FAC 10th brigade, read out a message over Goma radio, announcing that '[w]e the army of the DRC have taken the decision to remove President Laurent-Désiré Kabila from power'. The statement accused Kabila of 'misrule, nepotism and corruption', and urged the Congolese people to remain calm and carry out their normal activities. The next day, the Bukavu-based 12th brigade joined the uprising, and an unidentified person even announced on Bukavu radio that the Kivus were to become 'an autonomous zone, no longer part of the country'.[2] Supported by Rwandan troops, the rebels took over Goma, Bukavu and Uvira

---

[1] Many Congolese refer to the 1996–7 war as the 'war of liberation' and to the one that started in 1998 as the 'war of occupation'.
[2] 'Fighting in east as army vows to topple Kabila', Nairobi, IRIN, 3 August 1998.

without much of a fight,[3] while some combat was reported in the Fizi-Baraka area south of Uvira, as well as in Kindu, the capital of Maniema province. At the same time, there was heavy fighting at the Tshatshi and Kokolo military camps in Kinshasa, where FAC troops clashed with Banyamulenge soldiers who had remained in Kinshasa after the RPA pulled out a couple of days earlier.[4]

Just as in 1996, the rebellion received a name and showed visible leadership faces only after the outbreak of the war. Initial statements were made by military figures and by a Munyamulenge spokesman, identified only as André, who again placed the problem of the Banyamulenge on the agenda and claimed that his group was in control of most of the Kivu region.[5] According to a Munyamulenge NGO worker, the rebellion took place amid increased feelings of marginalisation among the Banyamulenge community, after several of their civilian officials were sacked and some of their soldiers killed.[6] Only on 5 August did a 'co-ordinator' for the rebellion come forward in the person of Arthur Z'Ahidi Ngoma. On 12 August, ten days into the war, it was supposed to have initiated, the 'rebellion' received a name, Rassemblement Congolais pour la Démocratie (RCD).[7]

However, it was clear from day one that it was masterminded in Kigali, and moreover that it was endorsed by the Americans: 'The United States accepted Rwanda's national security rationale as legitimate. We also recognised that the RCD was a proxy, directed in many respects from Kigali'.[8] During the early days of the war, the United States knew that the RPA had again invaded the DRC. A Rwandan source told Ambassador Gribbin that 'Rwanda would withdraw, once a responsible regime was installed (in Kinshasa)',[9] and Kagame himself told him that 'Rwanda felt honor bound to support (the Banyamulenge mutiny) on grounds of ethnic solidarity,[10] but also to rectify the error of putting Kabila in

---

[3] On 3 August, hundreds of FAC soldiers who had surrendered were massacred by the RPA at Kavumu airport near Bukavu. Most of them were Katangan, and this massacre further fuelled anti-Rwandan resentment.

[4] The Banyamulenge were thus abandoned in a hostile environment; we shall see that they were to try later to get even with the RPA.

[5] Kinshasa, AP, 3 August 1998.

[6] 'Fighting in east ...', op. cit.

[7] More information on the RCD's creation and subsequent evolution is offered later in this book.

[8] R.E. Gribbin, In the Aftermath of Genocide..., op. cit., p. 283.

[9] Idem, p. 279.

[10] A surprising statement, coming from the leader of a regime pretending to fight ethnic considerations.

power'.[11] The support of the United States was taken for granted to such an extent that Bizima Karaha, Kabila's former foreign minister who joined the new 'rebellion', told Gribbin: 'Ambassador, we are here again for another green light'.[12] In addition to the security rationale, Rwanda also justified its intervention on humanitarian grounds. This argument was well rendered at the end of August, when Rwandan minister Patrick Mazimhaka accused Kabila of launching a genocide against Congolese Tutsi and warned that Rwanda 'would be drawn into the war (…) if the killing of Tutsi is not stopped'.[13] Coming from the Rwandan regime, with its specific and tragic background, this kind of argument was difficult to challenge for the international community, which was constantly reminded of its failure to intervene in 1994 (cf. earlier text).

Just like Rwanda, Uganda justified its intervention on the ground that Kabila was not providing the hoped for security along its western border, but Clark arrives at the 'most plausible explanation (…) by putting the Rwanda–Uganda alliance at the center of the argument'. The insurrection in the northwest (cf. earlier text) put Kagame's regime at risk, and 'Museveni could not afford to see the Kagame regime fall from power at the time without suffering major security problems'.[14] In light of the Rwandan–Ugandan conflict that erupted less than a year later, this analysis is not convincing, and it underestimates Museveni's own agenda, which was to be part of the game and not to abandon the entire Congolese theatre to Kigali, a desire illustrated by the presence of the Uganda People's Defence Forces (UPDF) alongside the nascent Mouvement de Libération du Congo (MLC) as early as in November 1998 (cf. later text).

While the rebellion spread at a fast pace in the east, an RPA co-ordinated airborne operation was launched on 5 August against the Bas-Congo, west of Kinshasa. The RPA impounded cargo aircraft at Goma airport, and troops were airlifted to Kitona army base, where several thousand ex-FAZ were undergoing 're-education'. This very daring operation, 2000 km away from the RPA's bases, offered a huge potential dividend. It not only tied FAC reserves in the west, while they were needed in the east to

---

[11] R.E. Gribbin, In the Aftermath of Genocide…, op. cit., p. 280.

[12] *Idem*, p. 281.

[13] 'Foreign Troops in Congo Fighting, Rwanda Levels Genocide Charges', DPA, 28 August 1998, quoted by T. Longman, 'The Complex Reasons for Rwanda's Engagement in Congo', in: J.F. Clark (Ed.), *The African Stakes…, op. cit.*, p. 131. In this short sentence, Mazimhaka manages to lie twice: the Rwandan army was already in the DRC and the anti-Tutsi pogroms started *after* the beginning of the war, and indeed as a reaction to it.

[14] J.F. Clark, 'Museveni's Adventure in the Congo War. Uganda's Vietnam?', in: J.F. Clark (Ed.), *The African Stakes…, op. cit.*, p. 151.

counter the advancing rebellion, but it also threatened Kinshasa directly (the distance between the capital and Kitona is only 350 km) and indirectly (the port of Matadi and the Inga power plant are vital lifelines for the capital). The Rwandan, Ugandan and Banyamulenge troops, joined by ex-FAZ and ex-DSP, rapidly took control of Banana, Muanda and Boma. Matadi fell on 9 August, followed by Inga two days later. The power switch was turned off, and Kinshasa was left without electricity. Rebels also started infiltrating Kinshasa, where Kabila[15] organised 'popular self-defence', with the inevitable abuses I shall address later.

Although at first the rebel advance was much faster and penetrating than in 1996, this was not to be a remake of the first war. In the context of the shifting alliances that will be analysed later, Angola, Zimbabwe and Namibia intervened on the side of Kabila against their erstwhile Rwandan and Ugandan allies. On 20 August, a first battalion of Zimbabwean troops arrived in Kinshasa. On 22 August, the entry from Cabinda of several Angolan battalions, supported by the air force, heavy artillery and armoured vehicles, rapidly defeated the insurgent forces in the Bas-Congo.[16] Rwandan and Ugandan forces retreated, either by air or through UNITA-held territory in Angola. By the end of August, control over the region west of Kinshasa was re-established by the government coalition.

At the end of August, Kinshasa was infiltrated by heterogeneous rebel groups, comprising Rwandan and Congolese soldiers who had dispersed after their failed insurgency earlier in the month, elements of the expeditionary force defeated in the Bas Congo, and military of the former FAZ and the DSP who had fled or gone underground when Kabila took power in May 1997. The Zimbabwean contingent successfully defended the airport, while the civilian population – which had been less than enthusiastic about Kabila before – closed ranks to fight the invaders: 'Together with a certain patriotism mixed with anti-Tutsi racism and the fear of the restoration of Mobutism, the perspective of taking the losers' money has probably played a part in this bellicose mobilisation'.[17] Self-defence committees, in large part set up

---

[15] He himself and some of his ministers moved to Lubumbashi, only to return to Kinshasa on 9 September, when the situation was under control again.

[16] The operation encountered other snags as well. The Nigerian pilot of one of the hijacked planes, told to return to Kigali for another rotation, flew to Lagos instead, and from there returned to Kinshasa to tell his story. Other planes had accidents or broke down.

[17] G. de Villers, *République démocratique du Congo. Guerre et politique. Les trente derniers mois de L.D. Kabila (août 1998–janvier 2001)*, Tervuren-Paris, Institut Africain-L'Harmattan, Cahiers Africains, No. 47–48, 2001, pp. 28–29.

spontaneously by the *Kinois* (inhabitants of Kinshasa), organised patrols in the vast popular neighbourhoods. Youngsters armed with sticks, machetes and other traditional weapons, as well as tyres used for 'neck-lacing', took on the invaders in an atmosphere that was almost festive. The violence was massive and indiscriminate: being Tutsi or looking like one, being 'suspiciously dressed' or dirty, all this entailed a serious risk of being killed. The authorities contributed to this frenzy by insisting, from the very first days of the war, on the need to 'find out the traitors and the enemy', and by suggesting that these were Tutsi. Kabila's *directeur de cabinet* Yerodia Ndombasi is said to have appealed on radio to 'destroy the vermin of the aggressors, the garbage, the microbes that need to be eradicated methodologically and resolutely'[18]. De Villers and Omasombo have pointed to a remarkable side effect of the popular reaction against the aggression, in that it generated a spectacular (and short-lived) reconciliation between the regime and the capital, which up to then had been mutually suspicious.[19]

The entry of Angola and Zimbabwe made the difference compared to the first war, when the Mobutu regime was totally isolated against a unified regional coalition. It was a meeting of Southern African Development Community (SADC) held in Harare on 19 August that formally authorised the deployment of Angolan, Zimbabwean and Namibian troops, thus compensating for the weakness of the FAC, which were no more of an army than the FAZ had been in 1996–7. By the end of September, Chad, Libya and Sudan had entered the fray directly or indirectly. On 24 September, a number of francophone Central and West African countries, meeting at a summit in Libreville, Gabon, expressed political support for Kabila and condemned the aggression against the DRC. Given the number of countries involved on both sides, this was thus rapidly becoming, in the words of U.S. Assistant Secretary of State for African Affairs Susan Rice, the 'first African World War'.

---

[18] Quoted by *Idem*, p. 39. After a complaint lodged in Brussels under the Belgian law on universal jurisdiction, an investigating judge issued an arrest warrant against Yerodia in July 2000. However, in the meantime Yerodia had become foreign minister, and the DRC challenged the warrant before the International Court of Justice (ICJ). In *Democratic Republic of the Congo v. Belgium*, the ICJ ruled on 14 February 2002 that the warrant needed to be cancelled, because it failed to respect the immunity from criminal jurisdiction and the inviolability which an incumbent minister of foreign affairs enjoys under international law.

[19] G. de Villers, J. Omasombo, 'La bataille de Kinshasa', *Politique Africaine*, 84, December 2001, 21.

Despite the setback in the Bas-Congo and the support of the alliance for Kabila, the 'rebellion' continued to advance rapidly in the east. By early September, some nine Rwandan and five Ugandan battalions had taken Moba, Kisangani and Watsa. On 12 October, the important strategic town of Kindu fell after heavy fighting. This deprived the government side of an airport within striking distance of Rwanda, and it opened the road to the diamond-rich Kasai region. In mid-November, a new rebellion started in the northern Equateur province, which it largely occupied after defeating the FAC and their Chadian allies who suffered heavy losses. Jean-Pierre Bemba's MLC was supported by Uganda, which now had its own proxy and seized this opportunity to distance itself from the RCD, dominated by Rwanda.[20] Indeed, it was the Ugandan army that captured territory for Bemba, who initially had no troops of his own.

The fall of Kindu and the ensuing threat to the diamond mines in Eastern Kasai convinced Zimbabwe and Angola to dramatically extend their intervention. In addition to the fear that the rebellion and its allies would 'feed' on the proceeds of diamonds, for Angola, the perspective of the rebels making a junction with UNITA fighters was unacceptable. In support of several thousands of ground troops, Zimbabwe committed Sukoi fighter jets, while Angola sent in MI-24 and MI-25 combat helicopters. The rebel advance towards Mbuji-Mayi was halted.

The buildup of forces was considerable. By the Spring of 2000, the UN peacekeeping mission MONUC (Mission des Nations-Unies au Congo, known under its French acronym, see later text) estimated that troop strengths were as follows: Government/Zimbabwe/Angola around 85,000,[21] RCD-Goma/Rwanda around 35,000[22] and MLC/RCD-ML/Uganda around 19,000,[23] adding up to a total of around 140,000.[24] Fighting continued on several fronts, but the tendency was towards consolidation of positions. During 1999 and 2000, the RCD/RPA made some advances in the Kasai and North Katanga (even taking Kabila's town of origin Manono on 11 May 1999), but they were unable to capture Mbuji-Mayi and Kananga. In Equateur province, the MLC – with

[20] More information on the MLC's creation and subsequent evolution is offered later in this book.
[21] FAC 40,000; Zimbabwe 11,000; Namibia 1500–2000; Angola 1000+; Ex-FAR/*Interahamwe* 20,000; mai-mai 10,000.
[22] RCD-Goma 20,000; Rwanda 13,000–15,000.
[23] MLC 10,000; RCD-ML 3000; Uganda 6000.
[24] However, some of these figures may be inflated, and many of these troops were of poor quality and motivation.

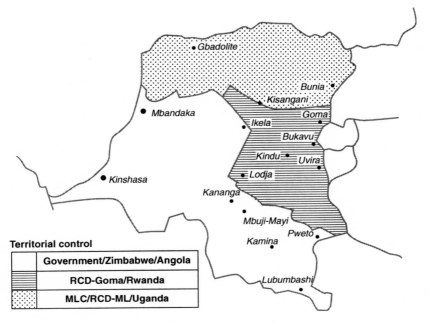

MAP 7. Military situation – early 2000.

the support of elements of UNITA and thousands of Ugandan troops –
extended its hold on the entire region, but was unable to take Mbandaka.
In Katanga, Pweto changed hands on several occasions, before being
captured by Rwandan troops in December 2000, but the rebel forces
were blocked west of the town, and failed in their attempts to push
towards Lubumbashi. Although occasional fighting continued, some
sort of a frontline stabilised, by and large along the line extending from
Mbandaka, via Kananga and Mbuji-Mayi, up to Pweto. In reality, the
term 'frontline' is inadequate to describe the situation: rather than a
contiguous war zone, there were pockets of enemy forces facing each
other, with large swathes in between without significant military presence. Together with political developments that will be discussed later,
this military stalemate contributed to the emergence of a negotiations
scenario. As stated earlier, here lies the main difference with the 1996–7
war: tens of thousands of troops from countries that were allies during
the previous war were committed on both sides, thus compensating for
the absent Congolese state and army, and for the ineptitude of the rebel
groups.

Space prohibits a detailed discussion of the war[25] and its humanitarian consequences. Amnesty International accused the RPA and the RCD of attacking and killing tens of thousands of Congolese civilians, pointing out that many massacres took place in areas rich in minerals.[26] A painstaking review covering the period from August 1998 to the end of 2000 conveys an image of large-scale systematic and deliberate atrocities in the Kivus, perpetrated mainly by the RCD/RPA.[27] Likewise, in the areas under its control and even in the Central African Republic,[28] the MLC committed grave human rights abuses, including – according to some sources – acts of cannibalism against Mbuti pygmies in the region of Mambasa.

## 7.2  SHIFTING ALLIANCES

Just as during the previous war, all players reasoned in the logic of 'the enemy of my enemy is my friend'. The fact that Mobutu mainly had enemies explains the emergence of the formidable regional alliance that eventually defeated him. But that such a circumstantial alliance is also very fragile was clear during the second war, when yesterday's friends became today's enemies almost overnight. Indeed, coalitions shifted dramatically.

We have seen that, right at the beginning of the war, Kabila was saved by Angola and Zimbabwe, who turned against their former allies Rwanda and Uganda. How can this choice be explained, since the relations of Angola and Zimbabwe with Kabila were far from perfect? Angola was

[25] For more information, see E. Havenne, 'La deuxième guerre d'Afrique centrale', in: S. Marysse, F. Reyntjens (Eds.), L'Afrique des grands lacs. Annuaire 2000–2001, Paris, L'Harmattan, 2001, pp. 143–174.

[26] Amnesty International, Democratic Republic of Congo. Rwandese-controlled East: Devastating human toll, 19 June 2001. I shall return later to the link between violence and exploitation of resources.

[27] J. Migabo Kalere, Génocide au Congo? Analyse des massacres de populations civiles, Brussels, Broederlijk Delen, 2002.

[28] A strong illustration of state weakness in the CAR, in May 2001 the Patassé regime was saved by an intervention of MLC troops, that is, non-state combatants from a neighbouring country (in addition to a Libyan contingent). On this episode, see O. Leaba, 'La crise centrafricaine de l'été 2001', Politique Africaine, 84, December 2001, 163–175. When Patassé was overthrown by Bozizé in March 2003, this deprived the MLC of its supply lines in the CAR, and it was further weakened when Kinshasa and Bangui resumed their defence co-operation in June 2003. On 24 May 2008, Bemba was arrested in Belgium at the request of the International Criminal Court (ICC), where he was indicted for crimes committed in the CAR.

concerned about two developments. Former Mobutu generals Nzimbi and Baramoto had been seen in Kigali before the new war broke out, and some politicians of the Mobutu era openly joined the rebellion, as did some former FAZ units. Because of their support for UNITA in the past, these elements were considered archenemies in Luanda. Moreover, Angolan intelligence was aware that there were contacts between UNITA and the rebel leadership and their Rwandan and Ugandan sponsors. Indeed, as seen earlier, elements of UNITA later fought alongside rebel forces, the MLC in particular. In the likely perspective of the resumption of the Angolan civil war (which indeed materialised a few months later), for Luanda the choice was clear: those supporting UNITA were the enemy, and their enemies merited support.

The motives behind the involvement of Zimbabwe were diverse. At the end of the previous war, the DRC had an important debt outstanding towards Zimbabwe, and the Zimbabweans were worried about repayment in the event of Kabila being overthrown.[29] A second motive was also economic: Zimbabwean business interests had made efforts during the past year to penetrate the Congolese market and to invest in the mining sector, partly at the expense of South African ventures; some of President Mugabe's business associates and high-ranking army officers stood to lose important assets if Kabila were defeated. Finally, the 'old revolutionary' Mugabe saw the Congolese crisis as an opportunity to reassert some of his leadership in the region,[30] lost to Mandela's South Africa, and to short-circuit the new leaders of the 'African Renaissance', such as Museveni and Kagame,[31] who were being promoted – notably by the Americans[32] – much to Mugabe's

---

[29] The exact amount, due mainly to the state-owned Zimbabwe Defence Industries (ZDI) is unknown, but estimates range from US$ 40 to 200 million.

[30] Zimbabwe happened to chair SADC's Organ on Politics, Defence and Security. As Kabila's Congo had become a member of SADC, it benefited from a defence agreement providing for member states' assistance in case of an attack. However, South Africa and Botswana disagreed with the intervention in the DRC. Although presented as such by the coalition of the willing, it is doubtful whether the operation of Angola, Namibia and Zimbabwe occurred under the SADC umbrella.

[31] Other members of the club included Eritrea's Afewerki and Ethiopia's Meles Zenawi. All four eventually turned out to be just banal African dictators.

[32] Addressing the Economic Commission for Africa in Addis Ababa on 9 December 1997, Secretary Madeleine Allbright stated, without mentioning their names, that 'Africa's best new leaders have brought a new spirit of hope and accomplishment to your countries – and that spirit is sweeping across the continent. (...) (Africa's new leaders) share a common vision of empowerment – for all their citizens, for their nations, and for their continent. (...) They are moving boldly to change the way their countries work – and the way we work with them'.

dismay. Rupiya nevertheless defends the intervention, along the lines of the Zimbabwean government's view, based on the legality and legitimacy of the SADC countries' response to the invasion by Rwanda and Uganda. He adds that, '[o]n balance, the country appears to have made a huge sacrifice for its involvement in the war, which has left it scarred, impoverished, and politically divided'.[33] However, that is certainly true for the people and the state, but not for some of Mugabe's cronies, who did use the war as a source of enrichment.

Other realignments soon occurred. Thus the mai-mai in the east, which had been fighting Kabila even before he came to power, now aligned with him in the context of an 'anti-Tutsi' coalition.[34] Within the same logic, an even more spectacular shift brought the ex-FAR and former *Interahamwe* militia into Kabila's camp, although less than a year earlier, the Rwandan Hutu had suffered massive loss of life during and after the previous rebellion at the hands of Kabila's AFDL and his erstwhile Rwandan allies (cf. earlier text). FAR were brought in from neighbouring countries, rearmed, retrained and deployed on the northern and eastern fronts.[35] A UN report noted that 'the changing alliances in and around the DRC have unexpectedly worked to the advantage of the former Rwandan government forces', because the ex-FAR and ex-*Interahamwe* 'have now become a significant component of the international alliance against the Congolese rebels and their presumed sponsors, Rwanda and Uganda'. The commission found it 'profoundly shocking that this new relationship has conferred a form of legitimacy on the *Interahamwe* and the ex-FAR'.[36] Likewise, the Burundian FDD's alliance with Kabila opened access to equipment, weapons, training and bases, and even to a degree

---

[33] M.R. Rupiya, 'A Political and Military Review of Zimbabwe's Involvement in the Second Congo War', in: J.F. Clark (Ed.), *The African Stakes...*, *op. cit.*, p. 103.

[34] Space prohibits a discussion of the mai-mai phenomenon. A useful treatment can be found in K. Vlassenroot, *The Making of a New Order...*, *op. cit.*, pp. 300–343. Vlassenroot insists on the fact that, while the mai-mai were also a resistance movement against foreign occupation, they can only be understood as an indigenous reaction to marginalisation and exclusion. The theme of the mai-mai militias as an experience of more egalitarian forms of solidarity based social organisation, with violence as its main discursive mode, is developed in F. Van Acker, K. Vlassenroot, 'Les "maï-maï" et les fonctions de la violence milicienne dans l'Est du Congo', *Politique Africaine*, 84, December 2001, 103–116.

[35] It is important to restate that, contrary to Rwandan claims (thus 'justifying' the invasion by the RPA), this occurred *after* the beginning of the war. In other words, the Rwandan invasion was not a consequence of the involvement of 'génocidaires', but rather its cause.

[36] United Nations, Security Council, Final Report of the International Commission of Inquiry (Rwanda), 18 November 1998, S/1998/1096, paras 86–87.

of respectability. They were headquartered in Lubumbashi, and troops recruited in Tanzanian refugee camps were transferred to the DRC.[37] At the end of 1999, the Zimbabwean press detailed the training of FDD fighters in Zimbabwe.[38] *The Zimbabwe Independent* of 24 December 1999 claimed that in June an agreement had been made between ZANU-PF and the FDD on training, equipment and funding. The training of hundreds of FDD fighters was later confirmed by several sources, but denied by the Zimbabwean army.[39] Another shift in the east concerned Sudan, which had supported the Mobutu regime against Kabila's rebellion, but now sided with Kabila against the new rebellion. The context here, of course, was the conflict between Khartoum and Kampala.

The frailty of the alliances again showed when conflict erupted between Rwanda and a major section of the Banyamulenge, who had earlier sought the protection of Kigali, while at the same time being used as a pretext for the Rwandan invasion in 1996 (cf. earlier text). Already by the autumn of 1996, Banyamulenge leaders had realised that they were being instrumentalised by Rwanda and that, rather than protecting their community, their close association with Kigali further marginalised and threatened them. This feeling of being used increased further when, in October and December of 1996, the RPA attempted to convince the Banyamulenge leaders to resettle their entire community in Rwanda, an idea most of them rejected.[40] Disagreements with RPA commanders of the FAC over command positions and deployment of troops further exacerbated the tensions in the early months of 1998. When the second 'rebellion' started in August 1998, the Banyamulenge were again faced with a crucial dilemma: on the one hand, they knew that they were going to be instrumentalised once again by Rwanda and that this would worsen their relations with other groups even further; but on the other, they needed the physical security provided by the RPA, including for their men in Kinshasa. When Banyamulenge leaders met in Bukavu just after the outbreak of the war, their reluctance to join the RCD was manifest. One of them wrote in a memo: 'Let us identify the real enemy, let us pursue

---

[37] International Crisis Group, Scramble for the Congo. Anatomy of an ugly war, 20 December 2000, p. 19.

[38] *The Zimbabwe Independent*, 21 November 1999; 10 December 1999.

[39] IRIN, Zimbabwe: IRIN focus on arms links to Burundi, Johannesburg, 3 February 2000; *Saturday Star*, 5 February 2000.

[40] On this strange episode, see M. Ruhimbika, *Les Banyamulenge...*, *op. cit.*, pp. 61–63, and K. Vlassenroot, 'Citizenship, Identity Formation & Conflict in South Kivu: The Case of the Banyamulenge', *Review of African Political Economy*, 2002, 510–511.

peaceful solutions to our problems in unity, without forgetting the other tribes in the Kivu, let us avoid petty interests, in brief: let us build together the future of our community', and he challenged 'those leaders of liberations who are more concerned with access to positions of responsibility and about the accumulation of personal material goods, at the expense of the Banyamulenge community',[41] a clear reference to the RCD.

As the second war progressed, it became increasingly clear that those Banyamulenge (like Ruberwa, Nyarugabo and Bizima Karaha) who had joined the RCD were a minority, and that most Banyamulenge opposed the RCD and Rwanda. This rejection received both a political and a military translation. On the one hand, leaders like Müller Ruhimbika and Joseph Mutambo created the Forces Républicaines et Fédéralistes (FRF) just after the beginning of the war. Operating from outside the territory occupied by the RCD/RPA, they vehemently opposed the RCD and the occupation by the Rwandan army.[42] On the other hand, the military response was the result of the growing distrust between Banyamulenge officers and the RPA. After repeated confrontations since early 1999, Munyamulenge commander Patrick Masunzu retreated to the Haut Plateau in early 2002, and in the following months several battles were fought between the RPA and Masunzu's men. Masunzu even joined forces with mai-mai, and he eventually joined the government army, becoming a commander of the Forces armées de la République démocratique du Congo (FARDC).[43]

The most dramatic shift occurred between the former core allies Rwanda and Uganda. In the words of Charles Onyango-Obbo, chief editor of the Ugandan daily *The Monitor*, in August 1999 'the impossible happened'[44]: the Rwandan and Ugandan armies fought a heavy battle in Kisangani, and more clashes followed later. In May–June 2000, the RPA and the UPDF again confronted each other in Kisangani; heavy weapons

[41] E. Ruberangabo, Mémorandum aux délégués de la communauté Banyamulenge réunis en session à Bukavu sur l'avenir de leur communauté, Bukavu, 13 August 1998.

[42] Ruhimbika explained that 'we have founded the FRF as a reaction to the invasion of our country by Rwanda and to express our refusal of the instrumentalisation of the Banyamulenge by Kigali' (*La Libre Belgique*, 1 September 2000).

[43] More details on the parting of ways between the RCD/RPA and most Banyamulenge can be found in M. Ruhimbika, *Les Banyamulenge...*, op. cit., pp. 80–109 and K. Vlassenroot, *The Making of a New Order...*, op. cit., pp. 235–250. Vlassenroot notes that, as a consequence of their instrumentalisation by Kigali, 'the future of the Banyamulenge community risks becoming very grim' (*Idem*, p. 248). As we shall see later, similar causes may have similar consequences for the Tutsi Banyarwanda in North Kivu.

[44] *The East African*, 30 August–5 September 1999.

were used and some 400 civilians and 120 soldiers were killed. The rift
had several causes. While Uganda wished to avoid repeating the mistake
made in 1996–7, when Kabila was parachuted into power without much
Congolese ownership, Rwanda preferred a quick military solution and the
installation of yet another figurehead in Kinshasa. Prunier has rightly noted
that Kampala had no problem with an independent and efficient government in the DRC, a vision dramatically opposed to the view of Kigali that
wanted to keep its Congolese proxies under control.[45] As we shall see later,
this divergence was also at the heart of the split of the RCD. In addition,
'entrepreneurs of insecurity' belonging to the elite networks in both countries were engaged in a competition to extract Congolese resources (see
later text).[46] Finally, Museveni resented the geopolitical ambitions of his
small Rwandan neighbour and the lack of gratitude displayed by Kagame,
who owed his accession to power to the support of Uganda.

Just like the Rwandan civil war, the conflict with Uganda was fought
out on the soil of a weak neighbour and, in part, by proxy. Both countries supported rebel movements and (ethnic) militias in the context of
an increasingly fragmented political–military landscape. They continu-
ously traded accusations of supporting each others' rebel groups, which
both sides indeed did, and in March 2001, Rwanda was declared a 'hostile nation' by the Ugandan government. Despite attempts at appease-
ment during the following months, on 28 August 2001, Museveni sent
a long and bitter letter to the UK Secretary of State for International
Development Clare Short 'about the deteriorating situation in the bilateral relations between Uganda and the government of Rwanda, led by
President Kagame'. He stressed that he had 'no doubt that Rwanda is
planning aggression against us either using proxies or, even, directly', and
he pointed to training facilities offered by Rwanda to Ugandan dissidents
around Kigali and in the DRC. He even referred to the 'ideological bankruptcy' of the Rwandan regime. As a consequence, Rwandan–Ugandan
relations further deteriorated, and troops were massed on both sides of
their common border. On 6 November 2001, Short summoned her two
*protégés* to London to put an end to a situation that risked becoming a
fiasco for the United Kingdom, just like the Ethiopian–Eritrean war of
1998–2000 had been one for the United States. While relations did not
become cordial, the threat of direct war subsided.

---

[45] G. Prunier, 'L'Ouganda et les guerres congolaises', *Politique Africaine*, 75, October 1999, 47.
[46] A Congolese friend of mine compared the fighting in Kisangani to two neighbours breaking
     into his house, and then fighting in his living room over who would steal his television set.

A dangerous escalation occurred again when, in early 2003, Rwanda started sending troops and supplies to the Ituri region in support of the Union des Patriotes Congolais (UPC), which had been supported by Uganda until then.[47] The attempt by the RCD-Goma and Rwanda to link up territory, and thus conflict, in North Kivu and Ituri was seen by Kampala as a lethal threat and again brought the two countries to the brink of direct war.[48] In the summer of 2003, both countries were forced out of Ituri as a result of a great deal of pressure by the international community, while at the same time the political evolution in the DRC, where an agreement on political transition was arrived at and the war came formally to an end (cf. later text), made it more difficult for them to be seen to overtly derail the process. As Kigali and Kampala were held on a leash by the United States and the United Kingdom, the Congo offered less food for conflict between them, though relations were never again friendly.[49]

## 7.3 WARS WITHIN THE WAR

### The Kivus

While the war formally ended in 2003, the wars within the war continued. The Kivus, where it all started back in 1996, showed all the ingredients of the great war on a smaller scale: implication of neighbouring countries, state weakness, economy of plunder, large number of armed entities and ethnic mobilisation. In addition, just as in 1996 and 1998, again in 2003, the Kinshasa political class felt that Kivu was not really its business: not only was the east far away, but it was also difficult to apprehend and tackle, and its destabilising potential was once more underestimated. Warnings that the Kivus were 'the forgotten crucible of the Congo conflict'[50] were insufficiently heeded. The human toll of this negligence

[47] Only in the summer of 2003 were the supplies from Rwanda to the UPC cut off through airspace surveillance by the Interim Emergency Multinational Force (IEMF) (AIP, APFO, CSVR, FEWER, Ituri. Stakes, actors, dynamics, September 2003, p. 5).

[48] The war in Ituri is discussed below. On Rwandan and Ugandan involvement in the Ituri conflict, see e.g. Human Rights Watch, Ituri: 'Covered in Blood'. Ethnically targeted violence in north-eastern DR Congo, New York, July 2003; B. Leloup, 'Le contentieux rwando-ougandais et l'Est du Congo', in: S. Marysse, F. Reyntjens (Eds.), L'Afrique des grands lacs. Annuaire 2002–2003, Paris, L'Harmattan, 2003, pp. 246–252.

[49] On Rwandan-Ugandan relations in the context of the Congo war, see B. Leloup, Le contentieux rwando-ougandais et l'ordre politique dans la region des grands lacs d'Afrique, University of Antwerp, Ph.D. thesis, 2008.

[50] International Crisis Group, The Kivus: The forgotten crucible of the Congo conflict, Nairobi-Brussels, 24 January 2003.

has been immense. At the end of 2004, a report found that, eighteen months after the formal end of the war, more than 31,000 people still died every month as a result of the ongoing conflict.[51]

The extraterritorial Rwandan civil war[52] did not end with the signing of the Pretoria agreement on 30 July 2002 (cf. later text). Although Rwanda had pulled out most of its 'visible' troops by September 2002, it maintained a clandestine residual presence, particularly in North Kivu, in order both to address the security threat posed by the Hutu rebels operating there and to continue the exploitation of Congolese resources it badly needed (cf. later text). On 28 July 2003, by Resolution 1493 (2003), the UN Security Council imposed an arms embargo, which applied to the provinces of North and South Kivu and to the Ituri district, and to groups not party to the DRC peace agreement. The resolution stated that 'all states and in particular those in the region, including the DRC, ensure that no direct or indirect assistance, especially military or financial assistance, is given to the movements and armed groups present in the DRC'. However, large quantities of arms and ammunition remained readily available, partly as a result of failing territorial control by the DRC government, and partly because of continued involvement of the Rwandan, Ugandan and Congolese governments with armed groups, in blatant violation of the embargo.[53] Although UN expert panels produced several reports on this issue, because of political differences the Security Council failed to act decisively, even though it extended the embargo on 18 April 2005 through resolution 1596 (2005).[54]

---

[51] Burnet Institute and International Rescue Committee, Mortality in the Democratic Republic of Congo: Results from a Nationwide Survey, 9 December 2004, 26 pp. The report concluded that approximately 3.8 million people died as a result of the conflict between the beginning of the (second) war in August 1998 and the end of April 2004, making this the deadliest war in the world since World War II and the deadliest in Africa ever recorded. An abridged and updated version of the report can be found in *The Lancet*, 7 January 2006, 44–51.

[52] This was also the case for Burundi up to the end of 2003, but this aspect has almost disappeared as a result of the Burundian peace and transition process, and it will therefore not be addressed here.

[53] The International Human Rights Law Group, a U.S. advocacy organisation, therefore called upon Washington to 'reinstate its own bilateral arms embargo on Rwanda (...), and it should condition its bilateral assistance to Rwanda and Uganda on their ceasing to support armed militias in the DRC' (J. Shattuck, P. Simo, W.J. Durch, *Ending Congo's Nightmare. What the US Can Do to Promote Peace in Central Africa*, Washington, International Human Rights Law Group, October 2003, p. 3).

[54] On this problem, see Amnesty International, Democratic Republic of Congo: arming the east, July 2005, 73 pp. The report detailed massive purchases of weapons by Rwanda in Eastern Europe and the way in which they were supplied by power brokers in Kigali to

After ALIR was defeated by the end of 1998 (cf. earlier text), the
Congolese peace talks led the remnants of the FAR, which had fought
alongside Kabila, to regroup and to move to the east, where they
started operating as the Forces démocratiques pour la libération du
Rwanda (FDLR) in 2000–1.[55] Although Rwanda succeeded in broker-
ing some desertions of FDLR commanders[56] who were incorporated
into the Rwanda Defence Forces (RDF; the new name of the RPA since
2002), and while there were several splits in the FDLR leadership, they
remained a factor of instability. Indeed, although they were no longer
a genuine military threat for Rwanda, they offered the regime in Kigali
the pretext to intervene in eastern DRC, which may well be the reason why – according to Human Rights Watch – Rwanda and the RCD-
Goma 'have for several years hindered efforts by MONUC to disarm
and repatriate Rwandan rebel combatants in Congo'[57]. Throughout
2003–6, Rwanda indeed regularly threatened to intervene, and it did so
on several occasions, sometimes directly, sometimes by proxy (cf. later
text). The Congolese government formally ended supporting the FDLR
in 2002, but the rebels frequently continued to co-operate with the mai-
mai, which allowed them access to weapons and ammunition. In addition, the defeat of the FARDC during the battle for Bukavu in May 2004
(cf. later text) worked to the advantage of the FDLR, allowing them to
strike new alliances with the Congolese government forces. A UN panel
noted that 'the Bukavu crisis enhanced the position of the FDLR (as)
forces of the tenth military region reinvested in the superior military
prowess of FDLR and new, circumstantial, alliances were formed'. It
found that the commander of a FARDC brigade had supplied weapons,
munitions and other equipment to both the FDLR and the Burundian

the RCD-Goma, to local defence militia and even to civilians in the Kivus, as well as to the
UPC in Ituri (cf. later text). It also showed how the Ugandan and Congolese governments
too were involved in supplying armed groups, albeit to a lesser extent, as well as the role
of Victor Bout (cf. later text) in arming all sides. For an interesting view from below on
arms dissemination in the region, see R. Kasereka Mwanawavane, N. Bauma Bahete, C.
Nasibu Bilali, *Trafics d'armes. Enquête de terrain au Kivu (RDC)*, Brussels, GRIP, 2006.
[55] On the FDLR, see M. Rafti, South Kivu: Sanctuary for the rebellion of the Democratic
Forces for the Liberation of Rwanda, Antwerp, University of Antwerp, Institute of
Development Policy and Management, Discussion Paper 2006–5, 32 pp.; African Rights,
A welcome expression of intent. The Nairobi Communiqué and the ex-FAR/*Interahamwe*,
Kigali, December 2007, 88 pp.
[56] The most important 'catch' occurred in November 2003, when General Paul Rwarakabije
deserted and joined the RDF, along with four other high-ranking officers.
[57] Human Rights Watch, D.R. Congo: Civilians at Risk During Disarmament, New York,
29 December 2004.

FNL. These realignments were mainly local initiatives of which Kinshasa was not necessarily aware. The report also quoted a number of instances where alliances were inspired by an economic and criminal, rather than a political agenda.[58] Although the FDLR and their ALIR predecessors, through intermarriage, farming and trade during their long stay in the DRC had become part of Congolese social reality, they also, like all other armed groups, committed atrocities against civilians.[59] They were therefore more of a threat for the Congolese population than for Rwanda, particularly since, by mid-2007, over 5000 combatants had been repatriated. According to the UN group of experts, only around 6000 FDLR fighters remained in the DRC.[60]

The resolve to eliminate the threat posed by the FDLR was therefore mainly inspired by the need to deprive Rwanda of a pretext to intervene in the DRC. Although everybody agreed in principle, remarkably little was done to act on this resolve. On 26 October 2004, the United States brokered a tripartite agreement between the DRC, Rwanda and Uganda, with the aim of putting an end to the threat posed by 'negative forces' in eastern DRC, including the FDLR. Despite the establishment of a mechanism for information exchange under U.S. auspices, not much happened on the ground. A few months later, an AU Peace and Security summit in Libreville, Gabon, announced its intent to support the DRC in disarming the FDLR, and the AU started consultations to send in a disarmament force. The FDLR reacted promptly, stating that they would 'forcefully resist plans to disarm (them)'.[61] Despite initial support from the EU for the idea, the initiative failed to materialise and quietly disappeared from the agenda.

For its part, MONUC announced on 31 March 2005 that those who refused to be disarmed by the next day 'would face the consequences', but again no attempts at forcible disarmament followed this robust statement.

---

[58] United Nations Security Council, Report of the Group of Experts on the Democratic Republic of the Congo, S/2005/30, 25 January 2005, paras 156–169.

[59] It is uncertain whether this widespread abuse was committed by the mainstream FDLR or by the so-called 'Rasta', a splinter group that was not under the control of the FDLR leadership and that was engaged in criminal rather than political violence. Although it was never proven, several sources even suggested that the Rasta were supported by the Rwandan regime. This caveat does not mean that the FDLR proper did not commit major human rights abuses.

[60] United Nations Security Council, Report of the Group of Experts on the Democratic Republic of the Congo, S/2007/423, 18 July 2007.

[61] 'Rwandan rebels warn of resistance to planned AU disarmament force', Nairobi, AFP, 2 February 2005.

In the same period, the community of Sant'Edigio in Rome brokered an agreement on voluntary repatriation. On 31 March, the FDLR chairman Ignace Murwanashyaka announced that his movement was to end the armed struggle and would engage in political combat instead. While he condemned the genocide for the first time, he added the condition that the FDLR should be allowed to freely exercise political activities in Rwanda, a demand considered unacceptable by the Rwandan government, which had not participated in the Rome talks anyway. In light of the fact that the Rwandan political landscape had been completely closed by the RPF in 2003–4, it is no surprise that the Rome agreement never even came close to implementation.

In June 2005, MONUC again announced the launching of a large-scale military operation, together with the FARDC, to root out the FDLR, and EU special envoy Aldo Ajello pledged logistical support. Operations 'Falcon Sweep' and 'Iron Fist' began in early July with Congolese troops and MONUC special forces from Guatemala, but they again failed to produce tangible results, despite a new split in the FDLR during the same period. Another ultimatum was addressed to the FDLR to disarm and return to Rwanda before 30 September, but operation 'Virunga Clearance' in late October to early November resulted in the capture of a mere seventeen FDLR fighters. New operations conducted in the spring of 2006 were no more successful, so that, by the time of the elections, the problem had not been resolved.

The other major threat to stability in the Kivus came from a number of Tutsi officers who, during the months following the signing of the Sun City accord in early 2003 (cf. later text), refused to accept their appointments in the new national army. Among them was General Laurent Nkunda, who stood accused of involvement in the massacre of civilians in Kisangani in May 2002. He claimed that he would not be safe in Kinshasa, but it appears that Rwanda persuaded the renegade officers to refuse integration,[62] and the link between Kigali and the insurgents was soon to become clear.[63] In part as a reaction to the way in which the presidential side was managing

[62] International Crisis Group, The Congo's transition is failing: Crisis in the Kivus, Nairobi-Brussels, 30 March 2005, p. 5.
[63] In early January 2004, meetings took place in Bukavu, where Nkunda and some other ex-RDC officers, together with politicians of the RCD-Goma (including the South Kivu governor Xavier Chiribanya), reportedly set up a new rebel movement, the Front de Libération de l'Est du Congo (FLEC). The presence of Rwandan officers at the meeting suggested support from Kigali for this new development. However, the FLEC did not get off the ground.

the transition, a first incident occurred in Bukavu in February 2004 and again, on a larger scale, in May–June, when Nkunda and Colonel Jules Mutebutsi briefly captured the town, thoroughly looting it and leaving several hundred combatants and civilians dead in the process. This was a major event that profoundly threatened the transition, as it was a show of force between the government and the RCD-Goma over the control of South Kivu.[64] As we shall see later, the outcome of the Bukavu events, occurring at about the same time as a split within the RCD-Goma and the massacre of Banyamulenge in Gatumba (Burundi), led RCD chairman and interim vice-president Ruberwa to (briefly) pull out of the transition. A UN panel found evidence of Rwanda 'aiding and abetting' the two officers' mutinous forces. The violations by Rwanda of the sanctions regime were both direct and indirect: it exercised a degree of command and control of Mutebutsi's troops, allowed the use of its territory as a rear base for military operations, participated in the – partly forcible – recruitment of troops, and supplied weapons and ammunition.[65] Kigali clearly misread the international mood and the reaction of its usual backers, chief among them the United States and the United Kingdom, who refused new attempts to derail the Congolese peace process, and they made this clearly known to the Rwandan regime. Under strong international pressure, Nkunda was forced to withdraw from Bukavu on 10 June.

This adverse military development also meant that the RCD-Goma lost most of its political and military hold on South Kivu, which made it all the more determined to retain control over North Kivu, its last bastion of power.[66] From then on, insurgent activity concentrated on North Kivu, and despite the Bukavu setback, Rwanda continued to support the insurgents in a covert, and sometimes overt fashion, for instance by openly approving Nkunda's argument that his military actions were necessary to protect the Tutsi. On 15 June 2004, Rwandan foreign minister Charles Murigande stated that 'if General Nkunda has intervened to attempt to halt (genocide), his intervention was probably justified'.[67] On 24 November 2004, Kigali warned that it was about to attack the FDLR on Congolese

---

[64] International Crisis Group, Pulling back from the brink in the Congo, Nairobi-Brussels, 7 July 2004.
[65] United Nations Security Council, Report of the Group of Experts on the Democratic Republic of the Congo, S/2004/551, 15 July 2004.
[66] Human Rights Watch, Democratic Republic of Congo: Civilians attacked in North Kivu, New York, July 2005, pp. 5–6.
[67] 'Intervention des dissidents en RDC: "probablement justifiée", selon Kigali', Kigali, AFP, 15 June 2004.

territory, but MONUC reacted vehemently: 'The United Nations cannot accept this kind of threat and the reaction from the international community will be very firm', and an additional MONUC brigade was deployed to North Kivu.[68] At the beginning of December, MONUC nevertheless found that Rwandan troops had crossed the border, barely ten days after Kigali committed itself in Dar-Es-Salaam to respect the territorial integrity of the DRC. Several other reports and satellite imagery obtained by the United Nations showed a considerable RDF presence in the Rutshuru, Walikale and Lubero areas. They attacked villages, burned down houses and killed civilians. A Rwandan–Congolese joint verification mission later confirmed that Rwandan troops had been present in the DRC, but said reports of burned villages had been exaggerated.[69] Despite all the evidence, the Rwandan government's reaction was blunt denial, as usual: Kagame's special envoy Sezibera stated that '[a]ll reported sightings of Rwandan troops in the DRC are false (…) Rwanda does not have any troops (in the DRC)'.[70] The United States, the United Kingdom and the EU again firmly warned Rwanda against any intervention in the DRC. On 7 December, the UN Security Council ordered it to withdraw the forces it might have in eastern Congo. UN sources also found that Nkunda's troops had received weapons and support from Rwanda,[71] which allowed them to stave off an offensive by the government army and to consolidate their hold on a widening part of North Kivu. As a result of the fighting, over 100,000 civilians were again displaced. With elections still scheduled for 2005 at the time, this was a major threat to the political transition. In addition, the violence exacerbated ethnic tensions: in December 2004, Tutsi demonstrators, including a number coming from Rwanda, marched in Goma to oppose the deployment of the FARDC, and this led to counter-demonstrations of pupils and students carrying pictures of President Kabila and protesting against the 'Rwandan aggression'.

Despite the signing of the 2004 tripartite agreement (cf. earlier text), and the establishment of the joint verification mechanism, the UN group

---

[68] 'UN sends Congo troops east as Rwanda threatens raid', *The Financial Times*, 25 November 2004.

[69] Human Rights Watch, Democratic Republic of Congo: Civilians attacked… *op. cit.*, p. 13.

[70] 'DR Congo Troops "to repel Rwanda"', BBC News, 3 December 2004, quoted by D. Barouski, Laurent Nkundabatware, his Rwandan Allies, and the ex-ANC Mutiny: Chronic Barriers to Lasting Peace in the Democratic Republic of the Congo, electronic document, 13 February 2007, p. 179 (www.zmag.org/racewatch/LKandexANC.pdf).

[71] 'UN evidence suggests Rwanda role in Congo', *The Financial Times*, 17 December 2004; 'Rwanda threatens to reignite Africa's bloodiest conflict', *The Independent*, 17 December 2004.

of experts stated in January 2005 that 'Rwanda continues to be used for recruitment, infiltration and destabilisation purposes', for example, with Nkunda openly enlisting youngsters in Kiziba refugee camp (Rwandan Kibuye province).[72] The group was 'cognizant of the presence of RDF soldiers in North Kivu (and) aware that Rwanda continues to retain a covert residual presence' in the DRC.[73] Although Kigali dismissed the charge in its usual style,[74] even the United States and the United Kingdom, countries who knew full well how the Rwandan regime functioned, had now become wary of their *protégé's* persistent threats and lies.[75]

On 25 August 2005, Nkunda again threatened to relaunch the war, barely a day before the UN group of experts issued a new report, which stated that the Congolese government 'should use all necessary measures to locate him and address the issue of his ongoing impunity'.[76] In September, the Congolese General Military Prosecutor issued international arrest warrants against Nkunda and Mutebutsi for 'the creation of an insurrectional movement, war crimes and crimes against humanity'. However, this did not deter Nkunda, who during the autumn of 2005 and in early 2006 benefited from many desertions of Kinyarwanda-speaking military who were previously integrated in the FARDC. With the elections nearing, he launched a new offensive in January 2006, gaining sizeable territory and uprooting tens of thousands of civilians. There were again strong suspicions that Rwanda delivered arms and equipment in preparation for the attack, and that RDF soldiers participated in the fighting.[77]

This was a crucial phase in the political transition, and Nkunda chose this moment to try and position himself as a political leader rather than as a mere renegade general. On 25 July 2006, just a few days before the first round of the presidential election and the parliamentary polls, he announced the creation of the Congrès national pour la défense du peuple

---

[72] United Nations Security Council, Report of the Group of Experts on the Democratic Republic of the Congo, S/2005/30, 25 January 2005, paras 185–192.

[73] *Idem*, paras 199–200.

[74] Army spokesman Colonel Patrick Karegeya said: 'We are not surprised because that is the usual UN trend. Where they have no facts, they have to falsely create their own' ('Rwanda dismisses UN reports on Congo arms violation', Nairobi, Reuters, 25 January 2005).

[75] An exhaustive demonstration of RDF military activities in the DRC during late 2004 and early 2005 is given in a section 'Rwandan Reinvasion' in D. Barouski, Laurent Nkundabatware…, *op. cit.*, pp. 168–202. While some of the information comes from less reliable sources, the overall image is convincing.

[76] United Nations Security Council, Report of the Group of Experts on the Democratic Republic of the Congo, S/2005/436, 26 July 2005, para. 44.

[77] D. Barouski, Laurent Nkundabatware…, *op. cit.*, pp. 220–222.

(CNDP), and presented himself as the political protector of minorities.[78] Nkunda refrained from disrupting the electoral process, but the CNDP's explicit and exclusive Tutsi agenda was very dangerous for the Tutsi themselves, as it reinforced their fears and enhanced the perception among other communities that they were 'different', dangerous, disloyal and even alien, a perception reinforced by their strong reliance on Rwandan support and protection.[79] Nkunda's claim that the Tutsi were victims who constantly faced the prospect of genocide – a claim supported by Kigali – thus became, in the words of the International Crisis Group, a dangerous self-fulfilling prophecy: 'While Nkunda has defended the Tutsi community in North Kivu, he has become a potential danger to the community's security as a whole'.[80] The transfer of Rwandan support from the RCD-Goma to the CNDP made sense in that the RCD-Goma ceased to be of use: it performed very poorly in the elections (cf. later text), while at the same time having integrated the national political process and having ceased to be a rebel force, with its fighters either enrolled in the FARDC or the CNDP, or demobilised.[81]

### Ituri

Despite the deep involvement of Uganda, and to a lesser extent of Rwanda, and unlike the one in the Kivus, the conflict in Ituri was not really part of the larger war, which is why it was only mentioned in passing earlier in this book. Although, as we shall see, the violence was

[78] International Crisis Group, Congo: Bringing peace to North Kivu, Nairobi-Brussels, 31 October 2007, p. 7.

[79] Longman notes that the RPA's actions in eastern DRC have increased the resentment and hatred of Tutsi, thus heightening their need for protection. 'The RPA, thus, is simultaneously a threat to the Tutsi and offers them protection' (T. Longman, 'The Complex Reasons ...', *op. cit.*, p. 133). In the long run, it will prove more a threat than a protection. Nzongola rightly stresses the fact that the assimilation of the interests of the Congolese Tutsi with those of the RPF regime is a danger, 'as they became victims of officially inspired hatred and violence, and some of the biggest losers of the second Congo war' (G. Nzongola-Ntalaja, *The Congo from Leopold to Kabila...*, *op. cit.*, pp. 229–230).

[80] International Crisis Group, Congo: Bringing peace to North Kivu, Nairobi-Brussels, 31 October 2007, p. 8.

[81] The most recent update on the Kivu crisis can be found in Human Rights Watch, Democratic Republic of Congo. Renewed crisis in North Kivu, New York, October 2007. For an excellent and full treatment of the Nkunda story, see J.K. Stearns, 'Laurent Nkunda and the National Congress for the Defence of the People (CNDP)', in S. Marysse, F. Reyntjens, S. Vandeginste (Eds.), *L'Afrique des grands lacs. Annuaire 2007–2008*, Paris, L'Harmattan, 2008, pp. 245–267.

fuelled by outside forces, it had rather ancient indigenous roots. Lendu and Hema, the district's most important ethnic groups, had already clashed in the early 20th century. More recently, in 1966, Lendu rebelled against Hema authorities, and there were new violent confrontations in the early 1990s. In an essentially bipolar setup, these appeared to be 'classical' ethnic confrontations over power and assets (land). The relations between both main groups were presented as akin to those between Hutu and Tutsi in Rwanda, Burundi and the Kivus, the Lendu (like the Hutu) being predominantly peasants and the Hema (like the Tutsi) being predominantly pastoralists. In addition to inequalities in access to land, the minority Hema, just like the Tutsi, were given a privileged position in education, the administration, politics and the economy during the colonial period. While considerations of economic gain and the actions of outside players played an important role in the violence, the agency of local actors should not be ignored. Vlassenroot and Raeymaekers insist on the need to place the conflict in its social setting and to recognise its own historicity. They invite us to take into account, on the one hand, the constant renegotiation by elites of the local political, social and economic space, and, on the other, the impact of these processes on local power structures.[82]

From late 1998 onwards, Ugandan involvement started to profoundly exacerbate an already fragile situation.[83] On 22 June 1999, Ugandan General James Kazini, commander of the UPDF occupying force, decided to merge the districts of Ituri and Haut-Uélé into the new 'province' of Kibali-Ituri, and he appointed Adèle Lotsove, at the time a member of the RCD-ML (which by then had settled in Bunia, cf. later text), as the 'Governor'. She was a Hema, and to Lendu political leaders, this confirmed their suspicions that the Ugandan army was siding with the Hema, which it had already done during a few earlier incidents. In early July, a UPDF unit killed dozens of Lendu and destroyed some of their villages. In clashes in the following weeks, scores of Lendu and Hema were killed and tens of thousands displaced. However, after the RCD-ML had set

---

[82] K. Vlassenroot, T. Raeymaekers, 'The Politics of Rebellion and Intervention in Ituri: The Emergence of a New Political Complex?', *African Affairs*, 2004, 385–412; K. Vlassenroot, T. Raeymaekers, 'Emerging Complexes in Ituri', in: K. Vlassenroot, T. Raeymaekers (Eds.), *Conflict and Social Transformation in Eastern DR Congo*, Ghent, Academia Press, 2004, pp. 177–196.

[83] A survey of the way in which Uganda intervened in the politics of Ituri with disastrous consequences can be found in Human Rights Watch, Uganda in Eastern DRC: Fuelling political and ethnic strife, New York, March 2001.

up a 'Pacification Committee', the violence subsided, but the displaced Hema did not return to areas where the Lendu were a majority.[84]

The lull in fighting was not to last. While it initially started in the territory of Djugu, the violence spread over most of Ituri in the following years. This dramatic extension was the consequence of external involvement, most prominently by Ugandan military–commercial figures, who cynically played one Congolese rebel or militia proxy against the others, thus creating the chaos necessary to remain present in Ituri and to unscrupulously exploit the region's riches. Later on, both Rwanda and the government in Kinshasa armed Hema and Lendu militias in a game of shifting alliances, resulting in massive human rights abuse.[85] Uganda had the closest interests and was the main culprit: 'For four years, every Congolese rebel in charge of Ituri was enthroned by Uganda, then replaced by another of its creatures. Wamba dia Wamba, Mbusa Nyamwisi, John Tibasima, Jean-Pierre Bemba, Thomas Lubanga, Chief Kahwa, and others all briefly ruled Ituri as protégés of one or another Ugandan general'.[86] Indeed, every one of these leaders came to power with the support of Uganda, and lost it as soon as that support was withdrawn.

The giving and removing of support was based on economic and geopolitical considerations. We shall see later that Ugandan officers and businessmen, among others, were involved in the illegal exploitation of resources. Geopolitically, the keywords were control and staving off both Rwanda and Kinshasa. As will be seen, Uganda attempted and failed to merge the RCD-ML and the MLC into the Front de libération du Congo (FLC). After Mbusa Nyamwisi ousted Wamba, in February 2002 he sacked his 'minister of defence' Thomas Lubanga, a Hema, who in June 2002 created his own UPC, which in August took Bunia with UPDF support. This was accompanied by the ethnic cleansing of Nande (Nyamwisi's group) and Lendu, and by the widespread looting of Nande businesses by elements of the UPC and the UPDF. In early September, Nyamwisi's Armée populaire congolaise (APC) and Lendu militias reacted by committing

---

[84] On this early phase of the conflict, see ASADHO, Rapport de l'Asadho sur le conflit inter-ethnique Hema-Lendu en territoire de Djugu dans la Province Orientale, Kinshasa, 7 December 1999.

[85] It is useful to add that Uganda, Rwanda and Kinshasa continued to do so after July 1, 2002, meaning that they fall under the mandate of the International Criminal Court (ICC), which has indicted Ituri militia leaders (cf. later text), but not (yet) those who used them as their proxies.

[86] International Crisis Group, Congo crisis: Military intervention in Ituri, Nairobi-New York-Brussels, 13 June 2003, p. 3.

atrocities against Hema in Nyakunde, where about 1000 men, women, children and elderly were massacred. By the end of 2002, Lubanga's reign of terror and the continuation of the war with the APC in the countryside had installed a culture of extermination. The ICG noted the 'progression from land-based communal violence, to land-related operations of ethnic cleansing, to repeated acts of genocide by both Hema and Lendu'[87]: a dramatic extension of violence in a period of just three years.[88] Events became more complex still when, linked with the evolution of the Inter-Congolese Dialogue (cf. later text), the UPC struck an alliance with the RCD-Goma, and thus with Rwanda, at the end of 2002. For Uganda, this meant having the enemy in its backyard, a major threat to its economic and geopolitical interests. This development also implied the risk of the Kivu and Ituri conflicts merging into one vaster and even more intractable war. Uganda accused Rwanda of backing the Ugandan rebel People's Redemption Army (PRA) and supported the creation of militia hostile to the UPC: Hema chief Kahwa's Parti de l'unité et de la sauvegarde de l'intégrité du Congo (PUSIC) and Tutsi commander Jérôme Kakwavu's Forces armées du people congolais (FAPC).

In the meantime, the increasing fragmentation of Ituri made matters worse. By February 2003, no less than a dozen militias were active, some supported by Uganda, others by Rwanda, and others still going it alone and not representing much in military terms, but all were involved in violence against civilians, pillaging and extortion.[89] The UPC received support from Rwanda under the form of military advisors, weapons and ammunition, in addition to elements of the PRA, trained and equipped by Rwanda. Taking pretext in an incident where the UPDF detachment at Bunia airport came under attack from the UPC, the UPDF took Bunia on 6 March with the support of an anti-UPC alliance. According to some sources, Lubanga was wounded during the fighting and evacuated to Kigali by the RDF.

Ugandan control brought a short spell of calm, which allowed the holding of a meeting of the often delayed Ituri Pacification Commission (IPC) in early April. It agreed to set up an interim administration, with a five-member executive and a 32-member assembly. MONUC promised that it would actively engage in the pacification of the region, but failed

---

[87] *Idem*, p. 6.

[88] A survey of massacres and other massive human rights abuses can be found in Human Rights Watch, *Ituri:* 'Covered in blood'... , *op. cit.*, pp. 19–47.

[89] This fragmentation is detailed in International Crisis Group, Congo crisis: Military Intervention in Ituri, *op. cit.*, pp. 9–10 and Human Rights Watch, Ituri: 'Covered in blood'... , *op. cit.*, pp. 15–16.

to deliver, for two reasons. First, both Kampala and Kinshasa tried to pre-empt the deployment of MONUC, the former by attempting to have a coalition of militias take control of Bunia, the latter by despatching a battalion of the Police d'intervention rapide (PIR); both initiatives resulted in more violence and widespread looting. Second, MONUC was unable to deploy the numbers and quality of troops needed under the circumstances. The ICG severely reprimanded MONUC on its failure: 'The UN appears to have intentionally misled the IPC on its capacity to deliver a security mechanism in order to demonstrate its ability to manage a political negotiation and clinch a political deal, however unimplementable. The Ituri interim administration and the civilians face the consequences'.[90]

Although Uganda offered to postpone the UPDF's withdrawal from Bunia 'in order to support the pacification process', an extraordinary claim in view of its responsibility for the chaos,[91] it was forced to leave and cede control over Bunia to MONUC. By 6 May, the UPDF withdrawal was complete, with thousands of frightened Hema following them into Uganda. An extremely violent week followed: Lendu militias entered the town, killing and looting, with MONUC unable to offer minimal protection to civilians under threat[92]; indeed it was barely able to protect its own staff. The UPC retook Bunia on 12 May, and it started committing the same abuse as the Lendu a week earlier, with MONUC again standing by. A new attempt to again launch the pacification process, this time facilitated by Tanzania, failed to produce any result, and militias continued fighting each other and killing civilians in town.

Faced with increasing media coverage of the unfolding disaster and with the obvious ineptitude of MONUC, on 30 May 2003, the UN Security Council authorised the deployment of an Interim Emergency Multinational Force (IEMF), which, though French-led, was the first ever European Union peacekeeping mission. Its mandate, as formulated by Resolution 1484 (2003) under Chapter VII of the UN Charter, included the stabilisation of the security conditions and the improvement of the humanitarian situation in Bunia, the protection of the airport and the IDPs in the Bunia camps, and the security of the civilian

---

[90] International Crisis Group, Congo crisis: Military intervention in Ituri, *op. cit.*, p. 11.

[91] Human Rights Watch observed that 'the UPDF claimed to be a "peacemaker" in a region torn by ethnic strife. In reality the Ugandan army provided political confusion and created insecurity in areas under its control. (It) more often aggravated than calmed ethnic and political hostilities' (Human Rights Watch, Ituri: 'Covered in blood'... , *op. cit.*, p. 6).

[92] MONUC's mandate included the power to 'protect civilians under imminent threat of physical violence'. People were killed just metres away from the MONUC compound.

population, the UN staff and the humanitarian presence in town. The mission was to be strictly limited in time and location, and to be replaced by 1 September at the latest by an expanded and reinforced MONUC detachment. Rwanda withdrew its initial rejection of the IEMF under strong pressure from the United States and the United Kingdom, and so did Lubanga. Of course, Uganda was in favour, as the operation would weaken the UPC and hinder Rwandan involvement in Ituri, and Kampala allowed the use of Entebbe airport as the main logistical platform. The IEMF showed that the deployment of 1400 troops can make a difference, provided the intervention is credible and robust. Although it only operated within Bunia, on one occasion, it successfully dislodged the UPC and seized weapons in a camp 20 km out of town, without sustaining casualties among its own troops. French Mirage patrols of airspace deterred supplies to the UPC and probably to other militias as well. This reduced the influence of Rwanda and weakened the UPC.[93] However, elsewhere in Ituri, villages continued to be attacked and people to be displaced in large numbers.

MONUC's Ituri brigade was in place in early September, with a broad mandate. UN Security Council Resolution 1493 (2003) increased MONUC's overall authorised troop strength to almost 11,000. Under chapter VII, it was allowed to use all necessary means to carry out its mandate in Ituri and the Kivus, and it was instructed to create improved security conditions in Ituri and to protect UN personnel and facilities. The resolution also imposed an arms embargo on all armed groups operating in Ituri and the Kivus. Contrary to the expectations of many, the Ituri brigade soon started operating outside of Bunia. Bunia itself was declared a weapon-free zone, and MONUC conducted searches and seized weapons. Just before the Ituri brigade deployed, a number of Ituri militia leaders moved to Kinshasa in the hope of being included in the transition process, although they had not been involved in the Sun City talks (cf. later text).[94] Only much later, at the beginning of 2005, were five of them, including Thomas Lubanga, appointed as generals in the FARDC. Human Rights groups protested vehemently, arguing that this decision amounted to offering a reward to militia leaders who had

---

[93] FEWER, AIP, APFO, CSVR, Ituri…, *op. cit.*, p. 18.

[94] Mbusa Nyamwisi's RCD-ML was the only Ituri-based organisation to participate in the Inter-Congolese Dialogue (cf. later text), but it did not in any way 'represent' the district and its local political dynamics. Indeed, Mbusa Nyamwisi is a Nande from Beni (North Kivu) and most of his troops were from that region.

committed grave human rights abuses.[95] However, the fact that these men were now far away from Ituri was helpful in pacification attempts and, eventually, in their elimination as a threat.

In the meantime, despite MONUC's enhanced presence, peace was far from re-established, as fighting between militias resumed in October 2003 and continued throughout 2004. On 24 February 2005, the killing in an ambush of nine Bangladeshi peacekeepers finally convinced MONUC to change tactics. Having always advocated voluntary disarmament, it now engaged in a more robust policy, and issued an ultimatum that was to expire on 1. April From then on, MONUC embarked on a campaign of forced disarmament and the dismantling of militia camps. The killing of the peacekeepers had another important effect. After calls from the UN Security Council and the Comité international d'accompagnement de la transition (CIAT, see later text) for the arrest of those responsible, the interim government did indeed arrest five militia leaders, including Lubanga. The loss of their leadership weakened the militias, and – more tellingly – the arrests did not provoke violent reactions. Thus, after the arrest of Lubanga, the UPC merely issued a statement demanding his release; this was considered a strong sign of stabilisation, as an event like this would previously have generated violent demonstrations in Ituri. It was also an indication that the grip of the militia groups on their own communities had weakened in such a way that they no longer had the capacity to manipulate their people at will as they did in the past.[96] In the months that followed, more than 15,000 of an estimated 20,000 militiamen were disarmed and, despite some continued violence, ever larger areas of Ituri returned to relative calm. However, while militia activity subsided significantly, the FARDC became a new factor of insecurity up to the present day.

## 7.4 PRIVATISATION AND CRIMINALISATION

### State Collapse and the Privatisation of Public Space

We have seen earlier that, as a result of decades of Mobutist misrule, empirically speaking the Congolese state had virtually disappeared, and

---

[95] This was undoubtedly the case, but it held also true for many people who occupied senior posts in the transition government and the FARDC, as well as for the militias' sponsors in Kampala and Kigali.

[96] Africa Initiative Programme, Ituri Watch, Kinshasa, April 2005, p. 6.

this hardly changed after Kabila came to power.[97] The void left by the state was filled by other, non-state actors. Some of these – like NGOs, churches, local civil society or traditional structures – assumed some functions abandoned by the state, but other less benign players also seized the public space left by the retreating state: warlords, (ethnic) militias and 'entrepreneurs of insecurity', both domestic and from neighbouring countries.[98]

This not only explains the extreme weakness in battle of the FAZ/FAC, which were the mirror of the collapsed state, but also why a small country like Rwanda was able, without much of a fight, to establish extraordinary territorial, political and economic control over its vast neighbour (cf. my reference to Nzongola in the introduction). What Achille Mbembe has called the 'satellisation' of entire provinces by (much) smaller but stronger states was accompanied by the emergence of new forms of privatised governance. It is worth quoting Mbembe at length, because he perfectly captures the situation in the Great Lakes region:

'A new form of organizing power resting on control of the principal means of coercion (armed force, means of intimidation, imprisonment, expropriation, killing) is emerging in the framework of territories that are no longer fully states. For, in these states, borders are poorly defined or, at any event, change in accordance with the vicissitudes of military activity, yet the exercise of the right to raise taxes, seize provisions, tributes, tolls, rents, *tailles*, tithes, and exactions make it possible to finance bands of fighters, a semblance of a civil apparatus, and an apparatus of coercion while participating in the formal and informal international networks of inter-state movements of currencies and wealth (such as ivory, diamonds, timber, ores). This is the situation in those countries where the process of privatizing sovereignty has been combined with war and has rested on a novel interlocking between the interests of international middlemen, businessmen, and dealers, and those of local plutocrats'.[99]

In eastern DRC, all functions of sovereignty were thus privatised, as some examples show. In 1996 and 1998, the Zairean/Congolese government forces hardly engaged in combat; during the war that started

[97] I describe recent developments here. For a longer historical look, see D. Renton, D. Seddon, L. Zeilig, *The Congo. Plunder and Resistance*, London-New York, Zed Books, 2007.

[98] The expression is from S. Perrot, 'Entrepreneurs de l'insécurité: la face cachée de l'armée ougandaise', *Politique Africaine*, 1999, 75, 60–71. It refers to rational makers of cost–benefit analyses, who realise that war, instability and absence of the state are more profitable than peace, stability and state reconstruction.

[99] A. Mbembe, *On the Postcolony*. Princeton, NJ, Princeton University Press, 2001, pp. 92–93.

in 1998, foreign and non-state forces faced each other – the Angolan and Zimbabwean (and, at one point, Chadian and Namibian) armies, and Rwandan and Burundian rebel groups on Kabila's side, and on the other the Rwandan and Ugandan armies with their RCD and MLC proxies. Territorial control, the provision of (in)security and the management of populations were taken over by militia, rebel groups – both domestic and from neighbours Rwanda, Uganda and Burundi – and the armies of neighbouring countries (and even the former Rwandan government army).

A UN panel monitoring an arms embargo reported compelling data on the total absence of the state in controlling cross-border traffic, including at ports and airports; indeed 'irregular aircraft practices are the norm'.[100] An extreme illustration occurred in January 2004, when access to Gbadolite airport was denied to the official aviation authorities while aircraft ferrying weapons and ammunition on behalf of Vice-President Bemba were unloaded.[101] In the summer of 2004, Bemba seized the opportunity of renewed fighting in the east to expand his private war business. Formally integrated into the FARDC, MLC troops were airlifted to North Kivu between June and October 2004 by aircraft owned by the vice-president. Not only did the MLC troops remain separate from other FARDC soldiers based in Beni, thus suggesting that Bemba continued to consider them his private militia, but in addition he charged the government twice the market price for the use of his planes, whereas other air operators were forced to transport FARDC troops and provisions without payment.[102]

The fiscal function too, which was limited anyway, was lost by the state.[103] Import and export levies collected by militias, rebel groups and Rwandan and Ugandan 'elite networks' (see later text for this notion) funded the wars and lined the pockets of individuals. Toll barriers (*péages*) were put up to extract resources from peasants taking their meagre surplus products to markets; so the possession of a gun was a sufficient means to impose internal taxation. In North Kivu, travellers passing between the zones controlled by the RCD-Goma and the RCD-ML were required to declare goods and pay duties at the 'border'. There were fixed tariffs for

[100] United Nations Security Council, Report of the group of experts on the Democratic Republic of the Congo, S/2004/551, 15 July 2004, para. 56.
[101] *Idem*, paras 64–69.
[102] United Nations Security Council, Report of the group of experts on the Democratic Republic of the Congo, S/2005/30, 25 January 2005, paras 149–151.
[103] The use of the past tense in the following paragraphs does not suggest that these realities have disappeared.

pedestrians and vehicles, and traders were required to hand over some of their merchandise. In areas controlled by the RCD-Goma, there were annual taxes on vehicles and a panoply of charges for individual journeys, road 'tolls' and 'insurance'.[104] The RCD-Goma taxed the coltan trade, sold mining rights, and demanded licence fees, non-refundable deposits, various export taxes and a 'war effort tax'.[105]

A UN report offers a good illustration, not just of the privatisation of the fiscal function, but even of 'fiscal competition' between private political/military entrepreneurs:

'[Chief] Kahwa had been able to establish a financial and logistical network spanning both (DRC and Uganda) sides of the lake (Albert) to support his political and military agendas. Using his political and business muscle, Kahwa has tried to compel merchants to use Kasenyi port as an entry point into the DRC rather than Tchomio, because if Tchomio was used he would lose out on taxes on imports collected there by Chief Kisembo. In addition to normal import taxes, a special "Kahwa tax" was levied on merchants trading in Kasenyi'.[106]

The panel documented a number of other examples showing that borders and their control became prized assets for armed groups and their sponsors in Rwanda and Uganda, allowing them the necessary revenue to maintain and resupply troops.[107] It concluded that 'as an institutionally weak state, the DRC significantly lacks control over both customs and immigration'.[108]

## Criminalisation of States and Economies

There is of course a strong link between the privatisation of public space and the criminalisation of states and economies in the region. A UN panel[109] set up in 2001 published a number of increasingly detailed reports

---

[104] Amnesty International, *Democratic Republic of Congo: Rwandese-controlled East...*, *op. cit.*, pp. 16–18.

[105] *Idem*, p. 33.

[106] United Nations Security Council, Report of the Group of Experts on the Democratic Republic of the Congo, S/2004/551, 15 July 2004, para. 41.

[107] *Idem*, para. 44.

[108] *Idem*, para. 31.

[109] The Panel's early work was criticised on account of both its focus on the activities of the rebel groups and their sponsors, and its definition of 'illegality'. While these criticisms were not unfounded, the value of the Panel's work was considerable: it has unearthed a large amount of empirical data and, in the later phase of its work, redressed the balance by inquiring into the predatory practices of the Kabila regime and its allies, Zimbabwe in particular.

on the criminal practices of 'elite networks', both Congolese and from neighbouring countries, and identified elements common to all these networks. They consisted of a small core of political and military elites and business people and, in the case of the occupied territories, rebel leaders and administrators. Members of these networks co-operated to generate revenue and, in the case of Rwanda, institutional financial gain. They derived this financial benefit from a variety of criminal activities, including theft, embezzlement and diversion of 'public' funds, under-evaluation of goods, smuggling, false invoicing, non-payment of taxes, kickbacks to officials and bribery. International players were closely involved in this criminal economy, as the local and regional actors drew support from the networks and 'services' (such as air transport, illegal arms dealing and international transactions of pillaged resources) of organised international criminal groups.[110] Thus, two different UN panels pointed out that Viktor Bout,[111] a notorious and internationally sought arms dealer and transporter featuring prominently in illegal activities in the region, operated from Kigali, among other places.[112]

The linkage between military engagement and illegal economic activities was a particularly worrying trend. Indeed pillaging was no longer an unfortunate side effect of war, but economic interests rather became its prime driving force. Dietrich has drawn attention to the dangers inherent in what he calls 'military commercialism', whereby a stronger state deploys the national military in a weaker neighbouring country, supporting either the sovereign power (as did Zimbabwe) or insurgents (in the cases of Rwanda and Uganda), in exchange for

[110] United Nations Security Council, Final Report of the Panel of Experts on the Illegal Exploitation of Natural Resources and Other Forms of Wealth of the Democratic Republic of the Congo, S/2002/1146, 16 October 2002. The Panel produced another 'Final Report' in October 2003 (see below).

[111] After Bout's companies started providing logistical support to U.S. forces in Iraq, he disappeared from the radar screen. Under U.S. pressure, his name was taken off a draft UN list of mercenaries and arms dealers (J. Godoy, Special Report: Wanted in Africa, Needed in Iraq, Paris, IPS, 20 May 2004). Cynically enough, Bout was arrested in Thailand in March 2008, on the basis of a U.S. warrant issued for weapons deals with the Colombian FARC rebels.

[112] United Nations Security Council, Report of the Panel of Experts on Violations of Security Council Sanctions against UNITA, S/2000/203, 10 March 2000, para. 26; United Nations Security Council, Final Report of the Panel of Experts on the Illegal Exploitation of Natural Resources and Other Forms of Wealth of the Democratic Republic of the Congo, S/2002/1146, 16 October 2002, paras 72–73. Aircraft owned by Bout and his frontmen continued to operate in the region during 2004 (United Nations Security Council, Report of the Group of Experts on the Democratic Republic of the Congo, S/2005/30, 25 January 2005, paras 67, 69, 73, 151).

access to profits.[113] Under these circumstances, economic criteria invade military decision-making, for example with regard to troop deployment and areas of operation.[114] In addition, if domestic resources are scarce or cannot be illicitly mobilised as a result of the scrutiny of the international community, cross-border predatory behaviour, out-of-sight and/or hidden-behind political and military concerns provides an alternative resource. Finally, when control over resources has become a military objective in itself, this is a strong disincentive for troop withdrawal, simply because the 'expeditionary corps' and those they support, whether rebels or governments, need each other. Put simply by Samset, 'war facilitates excessive resource exploitation, and excessive exploitation spurs continued fighting'.[115] As late as in mid-2007, a panel monitoring the UN arms embargo confirmed that 'the most profitable financing source for armed groups remains the exploitation, trade and transportation of natural resources. (...) All supply chains from areas controlled by armed groups are compromised'.[116] Crawford Young notes that this 'ability to sustain themselves through traffic in high value resources under their control' distinguishes contemporary insurgents from their predecessors.[117]

Nowhere is this as clear as in the case of Rwanda, a small and very poor country devoid of natural resources, but with an elite needing to maintain

[113] C. Dietrich, The Commercialisation of Military Deployment in Africa, Pretoria, ISS, 2001; C. Dietrich, Hard Currency. The Criminalized Diamond Economy of the Democratic Republic of the Congo and its Neighbours, Ottawa, Partnership Africa Canada, Occasional Paper #4, June 2002.

[114] Several reports point to the direct link between the exploitation of resources and the continuation of the conflict. The UN Panel notes that the control of mineral-rich areas 'could be seen primarily as an economic and financial objective rather than a security objective for Rwanda' (United Nations Security Council, Report of the Panel of Experts on the Illegal Exploitation of Natural Resources and Other Forms of Wealth of the Democratic Republic of the Congo, S/2001/357, 12 April 2001, para. 175); 'Most of the fights between Rwandan soldiers and mai-mai have occurred in the so-called "coltan belt"' (*idem*, para. 176). Under the title 'Rwanda's unusual tactics', the Panel found that 'attacks (by the RPA) seem to coincide with the period when coltan has been extracted and put in bags for evacuation by the mai-mai. Attacked, the mai-mai abandon their coltan, which is then taken away by small aircraft' (*idem*, para. 177).

[115] I. Samset, 'Conflict of Interests or Interests of Conflict? Diamonds & War in the DRC', *Review of African Political Economy*, 2002, 477.

[116] United Nations, Security Council, Final Report of the Group of Experts on the Democratic Republic of Congo, pursuant to Security Council Resolution 1698 (2006), S/2007/423, 18 July 2007, para. 37.

[117] C. Young, 'Contextualizing Congo Conflicts. Order and Disorder in Postcolonial Africa', in: J.F. Clark, *The African Stakes...*, *op. cit.*, p. 25.

a lavish lifestyle and possessing a large and efficient army.[118] In 2000, the revenue collected by the RPA in the DRC from coltan alone was believed to be US$ 80–100 million, roughly the equivalent of official Rwandan defence expenditure (which stood at US$ 86 million).[119] In a similar vein, a UN panel report found that in 1999–2000, 'the RPA must have made at least US$ 250 million over a period of 18 months'.[120] Marysse calculated that in 1999, the total value added of diamond, gold and coltan plundered in the DRC amounted to 6.1% of Rwanda's GDP,[121] and to 146% of its official military expenditure.[122] The Kigali economy, which is virtually disconnected from the Rwandan economy as a whole, was largely dependent on mineral and other extraction in the DRC (as well as on international aid). Pillaging the Congo not only allowed the Rwandan government to beef up the military budget in a way that was invisible to the donor community,[123] but also bought much needed domestic elite loyalty. This is what Jackson calls the 'economisation of conflict': a process whereby conflicts progressively reorient from their original goals (in the case of Rwanda: securing its borders) towards profit, and through which conflict actors capitalise increasingly on the economic opportunities that war opens up.[124]

The Rwandan military and civilian elites thus benefited directly from the conflict.[125] Indeed a UN panel noted a great deal of interaction

[118] Indeed, I have already indicated that post-1994 Rwanda has been called 'an army with a state', rather than a state with an army. In the Kivus, the Rwandan army was nicknamed 'Soldiers without borders', a wink to the international NGO 'Médecins sans frontières'.

[119] Sénat de Belgique, Rapport fait au nom de la commission d'enquête Grands Lacs par MM. Colla et Dallemagne, session 2002–3, 20 February 2003, No. 2 – 942/1, p. 72.

[120] United Nations Security Council, Report of the Panel of Experts on the Illegal Exploitation of Natural Resources and Other Forms of Wealth of the Democratic Republic of the Congo, S/2001/357, 12 April 2001, para. 130.

[121] This may seem a modest figure, but in light of the structure of the Rwandan economy, it is gigantic. Indeed in that same year, the production of export crops (mainly coffee and tea) only accounted for 0.4% of GDP (International Monetary Fund, Rwanda: selected issues and statistical appendix, IMF Country Report No. 04/383, 2004, p. 80).

[122] S. Marysse, 'Regress and war: the case of the DR Congo', European Journal of Development Research, 2003, 88.

[123] Of course, it was not really invisible, but the international community preferred to turn a blind eye to these practices. U.S. Ambassador Gribbin, for one, candidly acknowledged this reality: 'Rwanda had discovered during the first war that war in Congo was relatively cheap -even profitable (...) [W]ell connected Rwandans (...) could seize opportunities (...) to accumulate wealth' (R.E. Gribbin, In the Aftermath of Genocide..., op. cit., pp. 282–283).

[124] S. Jackson, 'Making a Killing: Criminality & Coping in the Kivu War Economy', Review of African Political Economy, 2002, 528.

[125] Marysse ('Regress and war ...', op.cit., p. 89) added that 'as military spending (...) was limited as a condition for access to financial flows provided by the Bretton Woods

between the military apparatus, the state (civil) bureaucracy and the business community. It found that the RPA financed its war in the DRC in five ways: (i) direct commercial activities; (ii) benefits from shares it held in companies; (iii) direct payments from the RCD-Goma; (iv) taxes collected by the 'Congo desk' of the external military intelligence office External Security Organisation (ESO)[126] and other payments made by individuals for the protection the RPA provided for their businesses; and (v) direct uptake by soldiers from the land.[127] In sum, the Congolese funded their own occupation by neighbouring countries' armies. Local coltan diggers were even forced out of the market in 2001–2, when Rwanda used its own forced labour, that is, under the form of prisoners 'imported' from Rwandan jails. After officially withdrawing its troops from the DRC in September 2002 as a result of discreet but intense international pressure, Rwanda therefore changed tactics by seeking alternative allies on the ground and sponsoring autonomist movements, in order to consolidate its long-term influence in eastern Congo and make the most out of the Kivu region.[128] In addition, even after its official withdrawal, Rwanda maintained a clandestine military presence in the DRC.[129]

The unpublished part of the UN panel's final report of October 2003[130] is particularly revealing in this respect. At the request of the panel, this section was to remain confidential and not to be circulated beyond the members of the Security Council, as it 'contains highly sensitive information on actors involved in exploiting the natural resources of the DRC, their role in perpetuating the conflict as well as details on

---

institutions, (...) wartime plunder has helped finance the conflict'. He denounced the 'ostrich policy' of a number of bilateral donors and the International Financial Institutions which, by continuing to fund the invading countries (Rwanda and Uganda) in the knowledge that their aid is fungible, indirectly supported the continuation of the war.

[126] The 'Congo Desk' had an office called 'Production', which oversaw the economic aspects of Rwandan operations in the DRC.

[127] United Nations Security Council, Report of the Panel of Experts on the Illegal Exploitation of Natural Resources and Other Forms of Wealth of the Democratic Republic of the Congo, S/2001/357, 12 April 2001, para. 126.

[128] International Crisis Group, The Kivus: the forgotten crucible..., *op. cit.*

[129] Many civil society sources in North and South Kivu reported Rwandan troop movements, and MONUC openly suspected the presence of the Rwandan army on Congolese soil (see, for instance, 'DRC: MONUC denounces obstruction of verification missions in east', Nairobi, IRIN, 29 October 2003).

[130] United Nations Security Council, Final Report of the Panel of Experts on the Illegal Exploitation of Natural Resources and Other Forms of Wealth of the Democratic Republic of the Congo, S/2003/1027, 23 October 2003.

the connection between illegal exploitation and illicit trade of small arms and light weapons'.[131] The findings showed an ongoing presence of the Rwandan army in the DRC. It had, the panel found, continued shipping arms and ammunition to the Kivus and Ituri, provided training, exercised command, supported North Kivu Governor Serufuli's militia and manipulated ex-FAR/*Interahamwe* by infiltrating RDF officers into them. The 'Rwanda Network' was considered by the panel 'to be the most serious threat to the Congolese Government of National Unity. The main actor in this network is the Rwandan security apparatus, whose objective is to maintain Rwandan presence in, and control of, the Kivus and possibly Ituri'.[132] Rwandan support for dissident forces went on throughout 2004, while the DRC was engaged in its delicate and fragile political transition. A later UN panel was concerned that 'the territory of Rwanda continues to be used for recruitment, infiltration and destabilisation purposes',[133] and it observed a 'residual presence' of the RDF in North Kivu.[134]

Uganda too greatly benefited from its military/commercial presence in the DRC. Although, unlike Rwanda, it did not set up an extra-budgetary system to finance its activities there, the UN panel found that the 're-exportation economy' had a significant impact on the financing of the war in three ways: by increasing the incomes of key businessmen, traders and other dealers; by improving Uganda's balance of payments; and by bringing more money to the treasury through various taxes on goods, services and international trade.[135] By way of example, Ugandan gold exports totalled US$90 million in 2000, while the country produced practically no gold.[136]

The logic of military commercialism could also be seen in the strategies developed by domestic armed groups. Thus the Walikale region west of Goma became a battleground between RCD-Goma rebels and mai-mai, both supposedly integrated into the FARDC, but who ceased to obey the FARDC eighth military region commander, an RCD General

---

[131] Letter dated 20 October 2003 from Mahmoud Kassem, chairman of the Panel, to UN Secretary General Kofi Annan.

[132] Para. 2 of the unpublished Section V.

[133] United Nations Security Council, Report of the Group of Experts on the Democratic Republic of the Congo, S/2005/30, 25 January 2005, para. 185.

[134] *Idem*, paras 199–200.

[135] United Nations Security Council, Report of the Panel of Experts on the Illegal Exploitation of Natural Resources and Other Forms of Wealth of the Democratic Republic of the Congo, S/2001/357, 12 April 2001, paras 135–142.

[136] Sénat de Belgique, *op. cit.*, p. 119.

who himself refused to obey orders from Kinshasa. In their fight for control over Walikale's cassiterite mines, these ex-mai-mai units co-operated with FDLR troops. Small aircraft based in Goma collected the cassiterite 'caught' by the RCD for purchasing agents; once it arrived in Goma, shares were distributed to local military and political authorities before being transported across the border to Gisenyi (Rwanda), where a smelting plant is located, or exported to South Africa.[137]

Clearly, criminal or informal regional integration was very real, and it was certainly more effective than the often called for formal integration. Cuvelier[138] has shown how the support of Rwanda for the RCD-Goma heralded a growing co-operation between businesspeople, politicians and high-ranking military on both sides of the border. The establishment of Société minière des grands lacs (SOMIGL) and of the Congo Holding Company (CHC) were instruments set up by the rebel group and Rwanda to get as much financial benefit as possible out of the international interest in Kivu's natural resources. Two Rwandan companies with close links to the RPF and the army, Rwanda Metals and Grands Lacs Metals were key in the organisation of the Congolese commercial ventures of the Kigali regime. What is novel about what Taylor suggests are 'neo-imperialist' regional networks of violence and accumulation is that they are managing to develop their own links and ties to the international arena, often on their own terms.[139] The type of alliances and transboundary networks currently reconfiguring Central Africa may well, in his view, offer a prophetic vision of what may be in store for vulnerable and peripheral areas of the world.[140]

That said, while this section has focused on local and regional players, international actors have played their part. The 1996–7 war was launched with the approval and support of the United States, and France intervened briefly (and inefficiently) on the side of Kinshasa (cf. earlier text). Acting as a patron for Rwanda and the AFDL, and later the RCD, the United States replaced the former neo-colonial powers France and Belgium,[141] subcontracting a number of clientship functions to South

---

[137] United Nations Security Council, Report of the Group of Experts on the Democratic Republic of the Congo, S/2005/30, 25 January 2005, paras 140–146.

[138] J. Cuvelier, 'Réseaux de l'ombre et configurations régionales: le cas du commerce du coltan en République Démocratique du Congo', *Politique Africaine*, 2004, 93, 82–92.

[139] I. Taylor, 'Conflict in Central Africa …', *op. cit.*, p. 48.

[140] *Idem*, p. 52.

[141] For instance, from 2002 onwards, the United States made clear to Kigali that Rwanda was to refrain from derailing the transition process in the DRC. The United States was instrumental in the official withdrawal of the Rwandan army in September 2002, and on several occasions called a halt to RDF/RCD-Goma military offensives (e.g. when they

Africa, which has emerged as a regional sub-hegemonic power showing increasing political, military and economic muscle. We have seen that speculative international 'juniors' attempted to seize the opportunities offered by Laurent Kabila's 'rebellion', but established Western business interests played little or no role.[142] For reasons that were both financial (the diminished availability of risk capital) and political (the chaos in Congo deterred even the most daring speculators), this outside influence decreased considerably as the second war unravelled.[143]

took Lubero in June 2003). It appears that, in exchange, Rwanda was allowed to do as it pleased inside its own borders.

[142] According to Grignon, '[a]fter the end of the Cold War, not only did Congolese resources lose their strategic political value, but the costs associated with their exploitation (deteriorated extractive capacity, corruption, political risks) also reduced their basic economic value' (F. Grigon, 'International response to the illegal exploitation of resources in the DRC', in: M. Malan, J. Gomes Porto (Eds.), *Challenges of Peace Implementation. The UN Mission in the Democratic Republic of the Congo*, Pretoria, Institute for Security Studies, 2004, p. 43).

[143] An excellent analysis of the recent political economy of the mining sector in the DRC can be found in E. Kennes, 'Le secteur minier au Congo: "déconnexion" et descente aux enfers', in: F. Reyntjens, S. Marysse (eds.), *L'Afrique des grands lacs: Annuaire 1999–2000*, Paris, L'Harmattan, 2000, pp. 299–342. Also see Global Witness, Same Old Story. A background study on natural resources in the Democratic Republic of Congo, Washington, June 2004; Global Witness, Under-Mining Peace. Tin: The Explosive Trade in Cassiterite in Eastern DRC, Washington, June 2005.

# Negotiating the Transition

## 8.1 THE POLITICAL LANDSCAPE

### The Regime in Kinshasa

In Chapter 5, I discussed the nature of the Congolese regime, between Laurent Kabila's coming to power and the outbreak of the second war. Despite the new conflict and the occupation of more than half the national territory by rebel and foreign forces, the regime continued to attempt to institutionalise (in the sense indicated in the text later) its authoritarian rule. As will be seen, at the same time Kabila was blocking attempts to find a negotiated settlement to the military conflict. This dual attitude was inspired by one and the same consideration: giving in to demands for power-sharing by either or both the opposition forces and the rebel groups would have been a major threat to his position. Although there was no state worth mentioning and while half the national territory was outside government control, Kabila represented a sovereign legal entity recognised by the international community. This recognition of juridical, rather than empirical statehood,[1] gave him an edge over his challengers, at least in the short run, and it allowed him to get away with an erratic mode of governance, which external partners, both African and more broadly international, disliked but were unable or unwilling to counter. It also allowed Kabila to 'play state' and to try to create the impression of institutional/legal normality.

---

[1] On this, see R.H. Jackson, C.G. Rosberg, 'Why Africa's Weak States Persist: The Empirical and the Juridical in Statehood', *World Politics*, 1982, 1–24.

A constitutional commission established in October 1997 thus adopted a draft constitution in March 1998, and a law-decree of 25 May 1998 provided for the creation of a Constituent and Legislative Assembly. The constitutional process was to be firmly controlled by the president, and the war only reinforced this tendency. Indeed, a law-decree of 21 September 1998 created a 'Commission for institutional reform attached to the Presidency', which would 'depend on the authority of the President'; as far as constitutional matters were concerned, it replaced the Constituent and Legislative Assembly, which anyway was never convened. After being submitted to 'opinion groups', the selection of which was widely criticised,[2] a draft constitution was adopted by the commission on 10 February 1999. For obvious reasons this text was never implemented, and there is no need to discuss it here,[3] except to point out that the political regime proposed was semi-presidential, along the lines of the French constitution, with an elected president and a prime minister appointed by the president; the government needed to command a majority in parliament and retain its confidence. Other pieces of legislation confirmed that the regime was not intent on liberalisation. While political parties remained suspended (though not banned), a law-decree of 29 January 1999, though recognising and even 'guaranteeing' political pluralism, imposed stringent conditions for their recognition. On the same day, another law-decree subjected demonstrations and meetings to the requirement for prior notice to be given to the 'competent political-administrative authority'; if they were organised in a public place, prior authorisation was required. Again on 29 January, a law-decree on civil society organisations allowed the government to control their creation and functioning, and to ban them.

Another attempt at strengthening control was made through the replacement of the moribund AFDL by the Comités du pouvoir populaire (CPP). We have seen earlier that the AFDL was a loose coalition which essentially served to provide the 1996–7 'rebellion' with a Congolese face. As a matter of fact, the AFDL had never been a coalition of parties

---

[2] Let us recall that the political parties had been suspended, which excluded the political opposition from the 'consultation'. When Health Minister Dr. Sondji criticised the selection of the 'opinion groups', he was promptly sacked (G. de Villers, *République démocratique du Congo. Guerre et politique….*, op. cit., p. 167). In any case, the impact of the 'opinion groups' must have been minimal, as the final text was almost identical to the October 1998 draft.

[3] For an analysis, see G. de Villers, *République démocratique du Congo. Guerre et politique...*, op. cit., pp. 167–172.

or movements, but rather a platform of four men 'who, with support
from Rwanda and Uganda, each relied on informal networks of friends,
allies, clients and armed factions.'[4] By August 1998, Kabila was the only
of the four initial leaders remaining: Kisase Ngandu was assassinated in
January 1997 (cf. earlier text); Masasu was jailed since November 1997[5];
and Bugera joined the new rebellion. Given that it coincided with the
executive branch and that there was no political competition, the AFDL
effectively ceased to exist as a political party. Although he had already
earlier referred to 'direct democracy', Kabila for the first time addressed
his 'friends of the committees of popular power' during a speech on 21
January 1999.[6] The CPP were finally launched on 20 April 1999, when
Kabila announced the disappearance of the AFDL, which as a party was
a 'centre of mediocrity and opportunism': the three other constituent
movements (not his own PRP of course) 'had no revolutionary experience or ideological orientation' and were manipulated by outside forces.
The relationship between the CPP and the state, as Kabila outlined it,
was ambiguous: on the one hand, 'the CPP are the organs of popular
state power, they assume political power'; but on the other hand, 'they
must apply the decisions of the government, the laws, the law-decrees, the
regulations of Ministers and Governors'.[7]

No one, presumably not even Kabila himself, really understood the
formula he proposed to summarise what the CPP were to be: 'the organ
of expression of state power assumed by the people'. The confusion did
not disappear when Kabila issued his law-decree of 6 July 1999 on 'the
institution, organisation and functioning of the Committees of Popular
Power'. Article 1 stated: 'Popular power is instituted in the DRC. It is
non-partisan and implies the exercise of direct democracy'. Article 3 continued as follows: 'Popular power aims at determining the policies to be
followed by the public services, at ensuring their implementation and, if
need be, at controlling this implementation'. From the very local level
(village or street) via the neighbourhood, the chiefdom, the district or the
town, up to the provincial and national levels, popular assemblies were
to be put in place, with committees of popular power acting as executive
bodies. However, rather than direct democracy, what the law-decree put

---

[4] G. De Villers, J. Omasombo, 'An Intransitive Transition', *op. cit.*, p. 406.
[5] He was released in March 2000, rearrested twice during 2000, and eventually killed in
November 2000, along with other officers from the Kivus.
[6] This speech is analysed and large extracts are offered in G. de Villers, *République démocratique du Congo. Guerre et politique...*, *op. cit.*, pp. 180–184.
[7] Extracts of the speech can be found in *Idem*, pp. 185–187.

in place was a system of 'democratic centralism', well known in communist days and in African single party systems, where decision-making went from top to bottom and not the other way round. At the top, where the reality of power was to be exercised, decisions were to be taken by a 'National Directorate' whose members were to be appointed by the president.[8] So much for 'popular power'... De Villers reminds us that, when Kabila opened the CPP congress, he had just returned from Libya, where he had signed the Syrte accord (cf. later text), and that the AFDL secretary general had recently paid visits to Libya and Cuba. The source of inspiration is clear indeed, although it must be said that during the early 1970s, in his *maquis* in Fizi-Bara, Kabila had advocated similar ideas – in a confused fashion, one should add. What all this boiled down to was a form of radical and indeed despotic populism,[9] and a very inconsistent one at that.

As they amounted to nothing, it is not useful to discuss the establishment of the CPP in any detail.[10] The National Directorate was set up in February 1999, before the actual creation of the CPP. At the municipal level, CPP were put in place in Kinshasa and Lubumbashi, after 'elections' that looked more like appointments. Popular interest in popular power was very limited, and most of those attending meetings were present in the hope of receiving gifts. By October 1999, the CPP were already in need of 'reorganisation' and fresh 'elections' were organised in Kinshasa in January 2000, when many people were forced to vote and conditions were chaotic. The CPP received a subsidy from the state, but the management of these moneys was far from collegial and even less 'popular': many CPP chairmen used them as their private coffers, a practice that led to a great deal of discontent and contestation. In the course of 2000, the CPP withered away and, by Kabila's death in January 2001, they had effectively ceased to exist.[11]

Well before the Inter-Congolese Dialogue started, a number of civil society organisations insisted on the need for political dialogue. This demand became even stronger after the beginning of the second war, which many organisations saw as a war of aggression, but also as a consequence

[8] An analysis of the law-decree is offered in *Idem*, pp. 188–189.
[9] *Idem*, pp. 190–192.
[10] See *Idem*, pp. 192–202.
[11] Interestingly, the CPP were only formally abolished by law-decree on 28 March 2003, when Joseph Kabila repealed the law-decree of 6 July 1999. Although everyone had forgotten about the CPP, this piece of legislation was seen as necessary, as Joseph Kabila was then creating his own party (cf. later text).

of the lack of democracy after Kabila's accession to power. During the months following the outbreak of the war, meetings organised on the initiative of civil society organisations were held in Kinshasa, Antwerp, Montreal and Durban, and they all called for some sort of round table. The regime was firmly opposed to these initiatives, which it attempted to boycott, for example, by preventing the internal opposition from participating or by arresting participants on their return. However, faced with increasing pressure, it decided to take pre-emptive action and so keep the initiative. On 27 March 1999, Kabila signed three law-decrees on the 'National Debate', which was to be firmly controlled by the regime: all the members of the organising committee, headed by Foreign Minister Yerodia Ndombasi, were close associates of Kabila, and both the agenda and the selection of the participants were to be decided by the president himself. Although opposition parties and civil society organisations were highly critical of the initiative, some also indicated that the holding of a national debate was necessary, but they of course proposed terms and conditions very different from the ones decreed by the regime. However, Kabila made it very clear that the national debate was not about discussing the legitimacy of his government; on the contrary, it was to approve the system of the CPP.[12]

At the end of April, the organising committee published its list of participants, among them a number of people whose advice had not been sought, such as rebel leaders like Wamba dia Wamba, Bemba and Thambwe. Many refused to join the debate, and its start kept being postponed, until on 10 July the Lusaka Accord was signed (cf. later text). As we shall see, it provided for the organisation of a 'national dialogue', and it was unclear what its relation with Kabila's national debate was to be. The two initiatives started from very different premises, and many Congolese players felt that the national debate had now been replaced by the national dialogue, all the more so since Kabila had signed the Lusaka Accord, and therefore seemed to have endorsed the national dialogue. Although it was never formally abandoned by the regime, the national debate never started, nor did the national dialogue, at least as long as Laurent Kabila and his inner circle were there to prevent it from happening.

This did not deter Kabila from further attempting to institutionalise and legitimise his regime. In February 2000, he resurrected the idea of

---

[12] For declarations made to that effect by Kabila on 20 March and 17 May 1999, see G. de Villers, *République démocratique du Congo. Guerre et politique...*, op. cit., pp. 213–214.

a Constituent and Legislative Assembly abandoned in September 1998 (cf. earlier text), despite the fact that more territory was now under rebel control than in the fall of 1998. It took some time, but the assembly, now called the Assemblée constituante et législative – Parlement de transition (ACL-PT), was finally put in place in early July 2000, at a moment when Kabila was on a collision course with Facilitator Masire (cf. later text). Among (officially) over 10,000 candidates, 240 were 'co-opted' by an obscure commission of close Kabila associates, while another sixty were appointed by Kabila himself, who also designated the members of the ACL-PT Bureau. The total lack of separation of powers was also illustrated by a provision in the decree of 10 July 2000 on the control powers of the ACL-PT to the effect that 'the procedure concerning commissions of inquiry and interpellation is put in motion upon the advice of the President of the Republic'. Although it met on a few occasions in Lubumbashi[13], the ACL-PT was to be another of Kabila's stillborn initiatives. By the end of 2000, it had quietly passed away.

It should be clear that the attempts at 'institutionalisation' outlined above were a far cry from genuine institutionalisation. On the contrary, throughout Kabila's almost four years in office, it was quite impossible to map out the exercise of power, which was in the hands of obscure and changing circles of individuals and factions, without clear links or, *a fortiori*, a coherent political vision or project. Just like Mobutu before him, Kabila co-opted, arrested, liberated, dropped or re-appointed members of government and holders of high civil, judicial or military office, thus compounding their feeling of insecurity and their dependence on the good disposition of their boss.[14]

As will be seen, only after Laurent Kabila's death did the long search for a negotiated transition start. For two years after he came to power, his successor Joseph Kabila and his mentors did not feel the need for a party political structure, and only in early 2003, during the final stage of the Sun City talks (cf. later text), did Kabila set up the Parti populaire pour la reconstruction et le développement (PPRD). Among the 200 founding members were former and current ministers, as well as close associates of Kabila, thus making the PPRD a party closely intertwined

[13] A decree of 20 July 2000 decided that the seat of parliament was in Lubumbashi. Kinshasa remained the seat of the government, while Kisangani (which was occupied by rebel forces) was to be the seat of the Supreme Court.
[14] For an attempt to identify trends in 'Who Governs', see G. de Villers, *République démocratique du Congo. Guerre et politique…, op. cit.*, pp. 238–266.

with state power and having limited autonomy. It was effectively run by its secretary general Vital Kamerhe, who had previously been minister of information and a key negotiator in Sun City. It is the start of the transition and the perspective of elections that generated the need for a party, which has been aptly described as 'essentially a shell organisation which exists to dole out favours to old friends and to provide Kabila with a political vehicle in the run-up to elections'.[15] As will be seen later, that is exactly what it did, not without success. But the circumstantial, almost 'non-political' nature of the PPRD might also prove to be its main weakness in the future.

### The Rebel Movements

We have seen that the RCD received a name and a visible leadership only after the 'rebellion' had started on 2 August 1998. On 5 August, the name of Arthur Z'Ahidi Ngoma[16] was mentioned as the co-ordinator, but when the RCD published a 'political declaration' on 12 August, Ernest Wamba dia Wamba[17] appeared as chairman, with Z'Ahidi Ngoma as first deputy chairman. The other deputy chairman was Moïse Nyarugabo, a munyamulenge lawyer. Clearly, on 2 August the RCD's sponsors were ready to start the war, but they were still looking for rebel leaders. While it was created on the initiative of Kigali, the RCD attracted all sorts of opponents from different political and regional origins, and it soon was as heterogeneous as the AFDL before it. Its history was to be marked by changes in leadership and divisions, as a result both of disagreements and incoherence, and of constant interference by Rwanda. As the RCD's disastrous performance during the 2006 elections was to confirm later, its association with Rwanda destroyed the legitimacy it might otherwise have had from day one. Indeed Dorsey has rightly noted that '[f]or the Congolese policy-makers, the alliance with the RPA has accumulated immediate inconveniences for uncertain perspectives (...) A dignitary, a traditional chief or a politician who allies himself with the RPA runs the

---

[15] S. Wolters, *Update on the DRC: Is the Transition in Trouble?*, Pretoria, ISS, 20 July 2004, p. 8.
[16] High UNESCO official in Paris, who returned to the DRC after Kabila took power. He founded a political party, *Forces du Futur*, but soon got into trouble with the new regime. He was imprisoned and again went into exile.
[17] Professor of History at the University of Dar-Es-Salaam, he was an academic rather than a politician, although he did participate in the sovereign national conference in 1992. He probably joined the RCD at the behest of President Nyerere, who knew Wamba well.

risk of total isolation'.[18] That is exactly what happened, and this gross misreading of Congolese national sentiment was a fundamental mistake of both Rwanda and its proxies: 'The Rwandan regime was faced with the negative effects of its own methods based on total control, violence, victimisation of its own position and a complete negligence of the existing internal dynamics of the local society (in the Kivus)'.[19]

At the end of January 1999, Z'Ahidi Ngoma left in protest over the refusal of the RCD to reach out to other forces that had fought Mobutu first, and Kabila later. It is very likely that he hoped that the broadening of the RCD's base would allow the dilution of Rwanda's influence, an issue that has been at the origin of bickering throughout the movement's existence. Wamba dia Wamba was the next leader to distance himself. At the end of 1998, he denounced the lack of internal democracy and accountability within the RCD, and, in March 1999, he set up headquarters in Kisangani, while the governing bodies remained in Goma. The main reason for this strange move – coming from the organisation's chairman – was a security concern. Goma was controlled by Rwanda, and Wamba felt more comfortable under Ugandan protection in Kisangani. But he again also expressed concern over political practices within the RCD, particularly the growing influence of former Mobutists and dissidents of the AFDL who wanted to 'install Kabilism without Kabila'.[20] Not much more was needed to provoke a split in the RCD, and this process happened in parallel with the emerging rift between its sponsors Rwanda and Uganda (cf. earlier text). We have indeed seen that, by November 1998, Uganda was supporting the new rebel group MLC and that it abandoned the mainstream RCD to the Rwandans.

On 16 May 1999, a group around Lunda Bululu, the co-ordinator of the RCD executive committee, decided to dissolve all the movement's bodies and replaced Wamba as chairman with Dr. Emile Ilunga.[21] Wamba denounced the move as a putsch and returned to Kisangani, taking with him a fraction of the RCD. The divorce was consummated, as Wamba set up the RCD-Mouvement de Libération (RCD-ML), for the time being – but not for long – based in Kisangani. The broader context must be considered. Indeed, a month earlier, the Syrte accord had been signed by Kabila

[18] M. Dorsey, 'Violence and Power-Building ...', *op. cit.*, p. 346.
[19] K. Vlassenroot, *The Making of a New Order...*, *op. cit.*, p. 273.
[20] G. de Villers, *République démocratique du Congo. Guerre et politique...*, *op. cit.*, p. 56.
[21] A medical doctor from North Katanga, Ilunga used to claim that he represented the former Katangan Gendarmes or 'Tigres'. Before becoming chairman, he headed the RCD health department.

and Museveni, in the absence of Rwanda (cf. later text). This led to the withdrawal of the Chadian troops on Kabila's side and allowed the UPDF to considerably extend the territory under the MLC's (nominal) control. While the Rwandan and Ugandan armies had maintained a common command until then, upon the creation of the RCD-ML, the UPDF withdrew their troops from areas where the Rwandan army was present, and all co-ordination between the two countries ceased. Except in Kisangani, they occupied separate territories and they supported competing rebel groups.

Upon returning to Kisangani, Wamba traded his usual RCD-RPA escort for UPDF protection. This occurred in an environment that had become quite complex after the split in the RCD, as the forces present included elements from both RCD wings, the RPA and the UPDF, and in the context of rapidly deteriorating relations between Rwanda and Uganda. The events leading to the escalation cannot be discussed here.[22] Suffice it to recall that fighting broke out between the UPDF and the RPA in Kisangani in May–June, and again, even more seriously, in August 1999.[23] Depending on the sources, the death toll was between 50 and over 500. Wamba and his supporters were forced to flee the city, which was probably one of the main objectives of the Rwandans.

Let us first look at the evolution of the RCD-Goma before returning to Wamba dia Wamba's RCD-ML. As seen earlier, Ilunga became chairman in May 1999, seconded by Commander Jean-Pierre Ondekane[24] and Moïse Nyarugabo as first and second deputy chairmen, respectively. However, this reshuffle did not put an end to the internal squabbles. Ilunga was accused of financial abuse and resented for his dictatorial style of management. Purges and defections followed in quick succession, and political disagreements set factions against each other.[25] At the end of October 2000, Ilunga, Ondekane and Nyarugabo resigned and were replaced on 3 November by Dr. Adolphe Onusumba[26] as chairman and

---

[22] See B. Leloup, 'Rwanda-Ouganda: chronique d'une guerre annoncée?', in: F. Reyntjens, S. Marysse (Eds.), *L'Afrique des grands lacs. Annuaire 1999–2000*, Paris, L'Harmattan, 2000, pp. 138–141; G. de Villers, *République démocratique du Congo. Guerre et politique...*, *op. cit.*, pp. 60–64.

[23] On this second occasion, the RPA was assisted by Burundian troops.

[24] A former FAZ officer who joined the AFDL rebellion in 1996. Previously, he held the post of chief of the general staff and commander in chief of the RCD army.

[25] These came to a head when, on 11 August 2000, Ilunga decreed the instauration of a federal system in the territory under the RCD's control. This move was hotly contested by others, including Ondekane, and it was not implemented.

[26] A medical doctor from East Kasai, he was previously in charge of the RCD department of external relations.

by Azarias Ruberwa[27] as general secretary and co-ordinator of the executive committee. However, it was very clear in Goma that Onusumba was a mere figurehead and that Ruberwa, seen as a 'man of Kigali', was the real leader. On 16 July 2003, on the eve of the setting up of the transitional institutions, Ruberwa formally became the chairman of the RCD-Goma, and he remained so throughout the transition, during which he was one of the vice-presidents (cf. later text).

We have seen that Ernest Wamba dia Wamba and his RCD-ML were forced to leave Kisangani as a result of the fighting between the RPA and the UPDF. In September 1999, they settled in Bunia, the capital of the Ituri region. This choice was not accidental, as the district borders Uganda, Wamba's protector, and as the UPDF were already present there (see earlier text). A 'government' was formed, with Wamba serving as President and Commissioner for Defence. Mbusa Nyamwisi[28] was appointed General Commissioner and thus became second in command, while John Tibasima[29] became Deputy General Commissioner. The RCD-ML was under the effective control of the UPDF, and Mbusa Nyamwisi and Tibasima were fully engaged in the exploitation of Ituri's resources, in partnership with Ugandan 'elite networks' (cf. earlier text), Generals Salim Saleh and Kazini in particular. As the RCD-ML only 'controlled' the newly constituted provinces of Kibali-Ituri and Beni-Lubero, its territory was small compared to the other rebel groups, and the RCD-ML inevitably practised a local form of governance, involved as it was in regional dynamics of political and economic power. This was much to the disadvantage of Wamba, whose region of origin was the far away Bas-Congo, while Nyamwisi and Tibasima hailed from neighbouring North Kivu and Ituri proper, respectively. So they had local networks and interests. Therefore, while Wamba pursued a national political project (admittedly in a fashion that was at the same time too intellectual and clumsy[30]), his two associates were involved in short-term projects that

[27] A munyamulenge lawyer who was *directeur de cabinet* of Foreign Affairs Minister Bizima Karaha after the AFDL's victory. He was previously the deputy of Onusumba in the RDC department of external relations.

[28] A Nande businessman from North Kivu, he previously held the post of president of the RCD General Assembly.

[29] A Hema businessman from Ituri, he was previously in charge of the RCD finance department.

[30] Space forbids a description of the astonishing accord that was signed on 15 June 1999 between Wamba ('in the name of the Democratic Republic of Congo') and Grenada-based Van A. Brink ('in the name of the African Union Reserve System'), involving the issuing of a currency based on the collateral offered by the Congolese gold and diamond

were essentially local and economic. This happened against the background of violent conflict between the Hema and the Lendu, of the fragmentation of militia, and of the manipulation of these local forces by
UPDF officers (see earlier text). Museveni attempted to reconcile Wamba
with Mbusa Nyamwisi and Tibasima, but in vain, summoning the opponents to Kampala on several occasions. When Nyamwisi and Tibasima
attempted to unseat Wamba in November 2000, the UPDF sided with the
latter, but Nyamwisi and Tibasima raised the support of militias, some of
them trained and equipped by the same UPDF. Space prohibits a detailed
discussion of the ensuing events,[31] but a summary follows.

In January 2001, Uganda attempted to regain control by merging the
MLC and the RCD-ML in a new Front de libération du Congo (FLC).
Wamba opposed the move, but Mbusa Nyamwisi and Tibasima agreed,
and Bemba transferred his headquarters to Beni, though not for long. In
June, fighting broke out between Nyamwisi's militia and the FLC, and
in August, both Nyamwisi and Tibasima parted ways with Bemba over
representation at the Inter-Congolese Dialogue, but also because Bemba
had taken control of the border crossings at Kasindi and Mahagi, thus
depriving them of an important source of revenue. After new fighting in
November, Bemba was finally chased out of Ituri, and Nyamwisi sacked
Wamba, becoming chairman of the RCD-ML himself, while Tibasima
remained deputy chairman. This was to be just the next step in the dis-
integration of the movement. On the one hand, fighting between the
RCD-ML and the MLC continued, and a new movement created with
the support of UPDF general Kazini, the RCD-National headed by Roger
Lumbala, joined the fray, making the picture even more complex and
fragmented. These movements fought each other, although they were
all supposedly allies and indeed proxies of Uganda, or more accurately
of Ugandan factions. On the other hand, after the signing of the Gobal
and Inclusive Agreement (AGI) in Sun City (cf. later text), to which the
RCD-ML was a party, Nyamwisi involved himself in the new political dispensation in Kinshasa. Lubanga vehemently disagreed: he formed a new
movement, the Union des Patriotes Congolais (UPC), which attacked the

---

reserves. The whole affair was of course a sham. For details, see G. de Villers, *République
démocratique du Congo. Guerre et politique...*, op. cit., pp. 79–82; J. Cuvelier, 'Linking
the Local to the Global: Legal Pluralism in the DRC Conflict', in: K. Vlassenroot,
T. Raeymaekers (Eds.), *Conflict and Social Transformation...*, op. cit., pp. 202–207.

[31] For more details see K. Vlassenroot, T. Raeymaekers, 'Le conflit en Ituri', in: S. Marysse,
F. Reyntjens (Eds.), *L'Afrique des grands lacs. Annuaire 2002–2003*, Paris, L'Harmattan,
2003, pp. 216–220.

positions of the RCD-ML and, with the support of the UPDF, took Bunia in August 2002 (see the earlier discussion for more details). In June 2003, Nyamwisi became Minister of Regional Co-operation in the central government, and the RCD-ML disappeared from the scene in Ituri, but now participated in the exercise of power at the national level.

The last rebel movement to be examined is the MLC. According to several sources, Jean-Pierre Bemba[32] initially wanted to join the RCD at the beginning of the rebellion, but he was not offered the position he sought.[33] He had previously been involved in business deals with Salim Saleh, and was therefore known in Ugandan circles of power. As the Ugandans were worried about the way in which the RCD was dominated by Rwanda, Bemba's ambitions offered opportunities to create a Ugandan proxy and to develop a Congo policy distinct from that of Rwanda. In November 1998, Ugandan troops occupied some territory in the Equateur province and in the north of the Oriental province, to the benefit of the MLC which, though officially founded in September, had not carried out any military action.

Contrary to the RCD, which was run in a collegial fashion (a feature that goes some way towards explaining the highly volatile nature of its leadership), the management of the MLC was distinctly presidential, run by Bemba as if he was its CEO. He appointed and presided over the Political-Military Council, the office of the President, and the General Secretariat; he was also the 'commander in chief' of the Liberation Army of Congo (Armée de liberation du Congo [ALC]), the MLC's military wing. Although the leading bodies were manned by a plethora of staff from all over the country, the only leader who visibly appeared next to Bemba was General Secretary Olivier Kamitatu.[34] The personalised nature of the exercise of power was underscored by the fact that the MLC only adopted bye-laws in June 1999; they confirmed the concentration of power in the hands of the chairman, but – interestingly – said nothing about how he was designated, again an indication that the MLC was Bemba's private property.

After the withdrawal of the Chadian expeditionary force as a result of the April 1999 Syrte accord (cf. later text), the MLC conquered the largest part of the Equateur province with Ugandan support, and Bemba

---

[32] Son of businessman Jean ('Jeannot') Bemba Saolona, he is from the Equateur province, and like his father, he was a businessman close to Mobutu.

[33] G. de Villers, *République démocratique du Congo. Guerre et politique...*, op. cit., pp. 90–91.

[34] Born in Belgium, where he received his complete education, he got to know Bemba during his studies in a Brussels business school.

installed his headquarters in Gbadolite on 3 June 1999. Unlike the RCD, the MLC appeared quite popular in the area under its control: indeed, Bemba was a 'son of the country' and he was seen as 'anti-Tutsi', a strong rallying factor among Congolese whose national(ist) feelings were hurt by Rwandan aggression and domination (cf. earlier text). Ugandan military presence was massive and very visible,[35] but it did not arouse the resentment the Rwandan presence did in the east. That said, the behaviour of the MLC too was reprehensible. Just like the other rebel groups and their foreign sponsors, it was involved in large-scale pilfering and exploitation of natural resources and it committed grave violations of human rights (cf. earlier text).

### 8.2  THE FALSE START OF NEGOTIATIONS: FROM VICTORIA FALLS TO THE DEATH OF LAURENT KABILA

### Many Cooks In The Same Kitchen[36]

The military stalemate discussed earlier prompted the parties to consider a negotiated outcome to the conflict, but it was clear from the beginning that the Congolese players were quite unable to embark on such a process by themselves. Not only was there no forum to do so, but their autonomy was limited and the weight of external actors was considerable. However, the number of outside facilitators trying to be helpful was even larger than during the first war: SADC, the UN, the OAU, South Africa, Libya, Belgium, the United States, the *Francophonie* and NGOs – whether out of self-interest or motivated by a genuine concern to engineer peace – all intervened at one point or another. If only because the war was so complex and protracted and the interests involved were so contradictory, this inevitably became a long diplomatic saga.

As shown earlier, SADC, which took the first initiatives, found itself in an awkward position, as three of its members sided with Kabila and

---

[35] Most of the 10,000 UPDF troops were stationed in MLC territory and their headquarters were in Gbadolite (G. de Villers, *République démocratique du Congo. Guerre et politique...*, *op. cit.*, p. 104).

[36] In his 1999 report on conflict resolution, Kofi Annan insisted on the need to 'avoid the temptation to undertake rival or competing efforts'. Lack of co-ordination 'should not (...) provide opportunities for the protagonists to divide the international community, or to play one effort off against another' (United Nations, Security Council, The Causes of Conflict and the Promotion of Durable Peace and Sustainable Development in Africa, Report of the Secretary General, S/1998/318, April 1998, para. 22).

were actively engaged in the war, making it difficult for the organisation to act as an honest broker. Contrary to what the Zimbabwean defence minister stated at the time, the decision to intervene on Kabila's side was far from unanimous. Nevertheless, it was during a SADC summit held at Victoria Falls on 8 September 1998 that the logic of a negotiated settlement was first subscribed to. A joint communiqué signed by the heads of state and government of all the countries directly concerned (Angola, DRC, Namibia, Rwanda, Uganda and Zimbabwe), joined by Zambia and the Secretary General of the OAU, reaffirmed their support for 'the unity, stability and territorial integrity of the DRC' and called for 'the immediate cessation of hostilities' and for an 'internal political dialogue'.[37] It is quite ironic that Rwanda and Uganda, which had invaded the DRC, would insist on its territorial integrity, but at that stage they denied having troops there, despite all the evidence to the contrary.

The Victoria Falls meeting also agreed that two days later, on 10 September, the defence ministers were to meet at the OAU headquarters in Addis-Ababa 'to establish the modalities for effecting an immediate ceasefire and a mechanism for monitoring compliance with the ceasefire provisions, especially those relating to the withdrawal of foreign forces from the DRC'. This rare involvement of the OAU in the conflict was not successful, as the Rwandan and Ugandan delegations walked out of the meeting in protest over the fact that the RCD had not been invited; this was, in fact, an acknowledgment that it was their proxy. That the OAU subsequently remained quite aloof throughout the peace process was to be one of its striking features.

The next player attempting to put his foot in the negotiation door was Libyan president Qadhafi, who had been trying for some time to be accepted as an African, rather than as an Arab leader. Libya was involved in the war through the funding of the Chadian expeditionary force, which made it less than an ideal honest broker. A first inconclusive meeting, during which Qadhafi appointed himself as the 'co-ordinator of the peace process in the Great Lakes', was organised in Syrte on 30 September 1998. Continued contacts led to a second Syrte summit on 18 April 1999. A Peace Accord, signed by the presidents of Uganda, the DRC, Chad, Eritrea and by Qadhafi, provided for a ceasefire, the withdrawal of all foreign troops and the deployment of an international neutral force. Although

---

[37] The text of the communiqué can be found in J.-C. Willame, *L'Accord de Lusaka. Chronique d'une négociation internationale*, Paris, L'Harmattan, Cahiers Africains, No. 51–52, 2002, pp. 26–27.

it did outline the contours of the eventual solution, the Syrte accord was unrealistic, if only because neither Rwanda nor the rebel movements were involved. Even Uganda reneged on the deal two days after signing it, as Foreign Minister Amama Mbabazi stated that the accord was merely an expression of his country's wishes concerning the Congo.[38]

The 20th Franco-African summit, held in Paris at the end of November 1998, could of course not ignore what was happening in the largest 'francophone' country. As a number of non-francophone countries involved in the war were also present (Uganda, Zimbabwe, Angola), the summit allowed for face-to-face meetings between the warring parties, as well as for President Chirac to advocate the idea of a regional conference on peace and security in the Great Lakes region, a proposal which France had already made in 1996, but which was resisted by the United States. What was called the 'Louvre Accord' did not contain more than a declaration of intent to cease hostilities. Again, crucial players such as the rebel groups and Rwanda were absent.

Also there to offer their good offices were NGOs, among which the Rome-based Catholic Community of Sant'Egidio, which had built up considerable mediation expertise in countries affected by civil strife, such as Mozambique and Burundi. While Sant'Egidio had contacts with the rebel movements, the internal opposition and civil society during the first semester of 1999, the regime was unwilling to engage into any kind of dialogue that might legitimise other parties. The initiative led to nothing for the same reason that was to block attempts at the Inter-Congolese Dialogue until Laurent Kabila's death: the regime would not engage with an agenda other than its own, and would certainly not embark on a course that might, somewhere down the road, challenge its position in power. However, the regime's attitude was not the only cause for the collapse of the Sant'Egidio initiative, as neither the eastern neighbours nor the rebel movements wanted to go to Rome. In addition, competition in the diplomatic market played a role: on the one hand, the United States and the United Kingdom distrusted an initiative that was supported by the 'Francophonie', while, on the other, there was even a 'Protestant counteroffensive' against what was seen as an action emanating from the Vatican.[39]

Despite the direct involvement of some of its members, SADC soon became the principal vehicle in the search for a negotiated settlement, and

[38] Kampala, AFP, 20 April 1999.
[39] For more details on the Sant'Egidio initiative, see J.-C. Willame, *L'accord de Lusaka...*, *op. cit.*, pp. 30–34.

South Africa assumed a clear leadership role. The day after Zimbabwe, Namibia and Angola decided to intervene on Kabila's side under the guise of SADC (cf. earlier text), Nelson Mandela stated that '[w]e would not worsen the situation by sending in a military force. We are committed to peace'.[40] A first SADC summit on the DRC was held in Pretoria on 23 August 1998, with the heads of state of Kenya, Rwanda and Uganda present, alongside the presidents of SADC member-states with the exception of Angola. The summit asked for an 'immediate ceasefire' and for the 'initiation of a peaceful process of political dialogue'. While it expressed support for Kabila, it also 'noted with appreciation the commitment of the Government of the DRC to the holding of democratic elections (which) should take place within a reasonable period of time',[41] an indication that there was some doubt about the democratic credentials of the regime in Kinshasa.

The situation was again debated at the SADC summit held in Mauritius on 13 and 14 September. President Kabila reiterated his refusal to admit the rebels to the negotiations, arguing that they were mere proxies for Rwanda and Uganda.[42] The final communiqué was a boost for Kabila, as it legitimised the intervention of Angola, Zimbabwe and Namibia: the summit 'commended the Governments (of the three countries) for timeously providing troops to assist the Government and people of the DRC defeat the illegal attempts by rebels and their allies to capture the capital city, Kinshasa, and other strategic areas'.[43] As he was seen as a neutral regional leader,[44] the summit entrusted Zambian president Frederick Chiluba with a mediation mission, assisted by the presidents of Tanzania and Mozambique.

## The Lusaka Process

It would be tedious to describe in detail the process which eventually led to the Lusaka Accord of July 1999. Therefore, a summary outline will be offered here.[45] By embarking on his mission with visits to Kigali

[40] 'DRC: Zimbabwe says SADC to back Kabila', Nairobi, IRIN, 13 August 1998.
[41] SADC Summit on the Democratic Republic of Congo, Communiqué, Pretoria, 23 August 1998.
[42] 'Focus: Congo at SADC insists no talks with rebels', Grande Baie, Mauritius, 13 September 1998.
[43] Final communiqué of the 18th SADC Summit – Mauritius, 13 and 14 September 1998, Grande Baie, Mauritius, 15 September 1998.
[44] As seen earlier, having on several occasions supplied weapons and ammunition to Rwanda, South Africa was considered biased by the members of the Kabila coalition.
[45] For detailed analyses, see J.-C. Willame, *L'accord de Lusaka…, op. cit.*; V. Parqué, 'Le rôle de la communauté internationale dans la gestion du conflit en République démocra-

and Kampala in order to discuss a ceasefire, Chiluba showed that he
understood very well where the real roots of the 'rebellion' lay. Several
regional meetings were subsequently held, but they all stumbled on the
issue of whether the rebel groups should be included in the negotiations. Supported in this stance by Zimbabwe in particular, Kabila refused
to meet them, arguing throughout that the DRC had been invaded by
Rwanda and Uganda, and that the rebel movements were mere proxies. On the other side, Rwanda and Uganda, supported in this by South
Africa, insisted on their inclusion, attempting to present the rebellion as
a strictly Congolese affair. However, Uganda (on 26 October 1998) and
Rwanda (on 6 November 1998) finally admitted to the presence of their
troops in the DRC. In a first stage, the rebels were brought in indirectly,
by having them discuss with SADC members in Gaborone (Botswana)
on 20 November 1998; Kabila refused to attend that meeting. After the
failure of a new SADC summit in Lusaka in mid-January 1999, Chiluba
convinced Kabila that he should talk directly with the rebels. However,
Kabila insisted that the meeting should take place in Kinshasa, a condition rejected by the rebel leaders for security reasons. Chiluba shuttled
between capitals, and attempted to convince the Angolans to put pressure
on Kabila, who was very dependent on them. At the end of February,
Chiluba proposed a new peace plan, including a ceasefire, the withdrawal
of foreign troops, the deployment of an international force, and security
guarantees for Rwanda and Uganda.[46] The first three points were the
same as the ones agreed in Syrte two months later (cf. earlier text).

Several factors allowed the Lusaka process to get out of hiberna-
tion: the failure of the April Syrte accord, the increased pressure of both
Chiluba and Thabo Mbeki (who had just been elected president and
who needed a South African diplomatic success), the division of the
RCD into two wings (cf. earlier text), the increased isolation of Rwanda,
and the mounting uncertainty on all sides on the prospects of a military
victory (cf. the stalemate mentioned earlier in this book). On 10 July
1999, a 'ceasefire agreement' was finally signed in Lusaka by the countries involved in the war (Angola, DRC, Namibia, Rwanda, Uganda and
Zimbabwe). The MLC signed on August 1st, while the RCD, undermined
by internal divisions (cf. earlier text), did not sign up until 31 August.

---

tique du Congo', in: F. Reyntjens, S. Marysse (Eds.), *L'Afrique des grands lacs. Annuaire
1999–2000*, Paris, L'Harmattan, 2000, pp. 343–376.
[46] 'Analysis: Zambia's Congo peace plan needs UN', Johannesburg, Reuters, 22 February
1999.

The accord was witnessed by Zambia, the OAU, the UN and SADC. After Kabila had resisted this development for a long time, all parties were thus put on the same footing: the internationally recognised government in Kinshasa, the 'invited' countries, the 'aggressor' countries, and the rebel movements.

Although modestly called a ceasefire agreement, the Lusaka Accord was much more than that. It combined external and internal approaches to the conflict in an often confusing fashion, and in ways sometimes difficult to accommodate under international and domestic law. Smis and Oyatambwe have pointed to the paradox of 'the war being somewhat legitimised as an attempt to push the Congolese to a dialogue that must lead to a new political dispensation; a dialogue in which the foreign countries dictate the agenda, and when Congolese agree on a new political dispensation, the same foreign countries will act as the guarantors of this new order'.[47] The ceasefire proper was to apply to all the parties' forces in the DRC, and it committed them to 'immediately address the security concerns of the DRC and her neighbouring countries'. The UN Security Council was to be requested to deploy a peacekeeping force, and the parties were to constitute a Joint Military Commission (JMC) which, together with a UN/OAU Observer group, was to be responsible, immediately after the agreement came into force, for starting peacekeeping operations until the deployment of the UN force. But the agreement went well beyond the concerns of a mere ceasefire, as it addressed a number of broader issues, both regional and domestic, that were seen as among the causes of the conflict. Regional issues concerned the taking of measures aimed at securing the normalisation of the situation along the DRC's borders, including the control of illicit trafficking of arms and the infiltration of armed groups. More broadly, the parties affirmed the need to address the security concerns of neighbouring countries, a code for Rwanda and Uganda. This was a diplomatic victory for these neighbours, as it legitimised their military presence, while confirming the *de facto* partition of the DRC into three spheres of influence (including economic exploitation), that is, Government-Angola-Zimbabwe, RCD-Rwanda, MLC-Uganda, each administered by a belligerent party. 'Such leeway gave Rwanda and Uganda full leverage to exploit and extract Congolese resources without restriction'.[48]

---

[47] S. Smis, W. Oyatambwe, 'Complex Political Emergencies, the International Community & the Congo Conflict', *Review of African Political Economy*, 2002, 419.

[48] F. Grignon, 'International response to the illegal exploitation of resources in the DRC', in: M. Malan, J. Gomez Porto (Eds.), *Challenges of Peace Implementation…, op. cit.*, p. 45.

Domestically, it was agreed that 'all ethnic groups and nationalities whose people and territory constituted what became Congo (now DRC) at independence must enjoy equal rights and protection under the law as citizens', an obvious reference to the Kinyarwanda speakers in the east. As the central government controlled just half of the country,[49] 'state administration shall be re-established throughout the national territory'. Other elements supposed to contribute to state reconstruction were 'the formation of a national, restructured and integrated army, including the forces of the Congolese parties who are signatories to this Agreement' and the establishment of a 'mechanism for disarming militias and armed groups, including the genocidal forces', an intention which also purported to address neighbours' concerns, in particular those of Rwanda. Finally, the agreement also opened up the perspective of a fundamental reshuffling of political cards within the DRC. It was indeed agreed that the government, the RCD, the MLC, the unarmed opposition, as well as civil society were to enter into an 'open national dialogue': 'These inter-Congolese political negotiations (...) shall lead to a new political dispensation and national reconciliation (and they) shall be under the aegis of a neutral facilitator to be agreed upon by the Congolese parties'.

Clearly, the domestic part of the accord held a serious political threat for Kabila, as his government was to be a party like others in the dialogue, while the reference to a new political dispensation suggested the need for a transition with an uncertain outcome for the incumbent. On paper, the Lusaka Accord covered the issues at the core of the conflict and offered an outline for their resolution. It was also the first attempted settlement to have all the relevant parties at the time on board, both from within the DRC and among the countries engaged in the war. However, as is often the case with agreements in Africa (and elsewhere), the signing of the accord was not the end of negotiations and the beginning of implementation, but merely a step in a long process. Indeed the timetable annexed to the agreement proved highly unrealistic, and its implementation turned out to be a hazardous obstacle race.

### From Lusaka to the Assassination of Laurent Kabila

I shall now look at this obstacle race by checking the main subjects agreed in Lusaka and the timetable for their implementation. First, the 'cessation

---

[49] Of course, in the absence of a functioning state, even there this control was essentially nominal.

of hostilities between all the belligerent forces' was to take place within 24 hours after the signing of the accord. As the RCD was the last party to sign on 31 August 1999, the ceasefire should have been effective on 1 September. However, ceasefire violations were rampant; the parties continued to take and lose territory, and troops were redeployed and reinforced. During a regional meeting in Lusaka on 22 February 2000, March 1st was agreed as the new implementation date, but to no avail. As they continued fighting, the parties traded accusations for these breaches.

The next chronological step was to be the constitution of the JMC, to be put in place at the latest seven days after the signing of the agreement and to be composed of two representatives from each party under a neutral chairman appointed by the OAU in consultation with the parties. It was to be answerable to a political committee composed of the ministers of foreign affairs and defence or other representatives appointed by the parties. After the appointment of Algerian[50] General Rashid Lalali, the JMC met for the first time on 11–12 October 1999. Subsequent meetings mostly dealt with procedural issues, in addition to the deployment of thirty observers. With limited financial means, only a handful of observers and liaison officers on the ground, and lacking a permanent structure, the impact of the JMC could only be minimal.

A neutral facilitator for the inter-Congolese political negotiations was to be appointed on 15 September 1999 at the latest. After quite some insisting by both the OAU and the UN, former Botswana president Sir Ketumile (Quett) Masire accepted the mission in mid-December. While Masire immediately started his consultations, he was faced with considerable difficulties: frequent ceasefire violations, the reluctance of Kabila to negotiate under any terms other than his own and insufficient funding. Although the dialogue was to start 45 days after the signing of the Lusaka Accord, it only began on 25 February 2002, almost two and a half years after the projected date. These negotiations will be analysed later.

The UN peacekeeping force was to be deployed within 120 days. Its mandate included peacekeeping and peace enforcement operations. Even before the RCD signed the Lusaka Accord, the UN Security Council authorised, on 6 August 1999, the deployment of 90 liaison staff, of which a first group of 21 started a reconnaissance mission in September. Five of them were to set up the headquarters of MONUC. A technical mission that arrived in October met with many obstacles, most of them created by the Congolese government, which limited its movements in the

[50] This choice can be explained by the fact that Algeria was chairing the OAU at the time.

territory it controlled, while similar problems handicapped the deployment of the liaison officers. Only on 24 February 2000 did the Security Council authorise the deployment of an additional 500 military observers, supported by some 5500 troops. Analysts considered the force too small, given the size of the country, the need to disarm several militias, and the diversity of areas of operation. However, although they would not have troops on the ground, the United States favoured a minimalist approach, essentially on account of the cost of the operation.[51]

Faced with the constant threat of stalemate, mostly as a result of sabotage by Kabila, in early June 2000, Masire attempted to unblock the situation by organising a 'preparatory meeting to the national dialogue' in Cotonou, Benin. However, not only did the government refuse to participate, but it prevented delegates of political parties and civil society from attending. On 19 June, the office of the facilitator in Kinshasa was sealed, and on 19 October the DRC Minister of Information announced that Masire was no longer acceptable: 'From now on, every act implying the recognition of President Masire as facilitator of the inter-Congolese dialogue will be considered an attempt against the DRC's sovereignty'.[52] We have seen that, in strictly domestic politics too, Kabila refused any opening. His constant sabotaging of developments he considered threatening to his position led to total deadlock by the end of 2000.[53]

## 8.3 TOWARDS AN IMPOSED SETTLEMENT: FROM THE ACCESSION OF JOSEPH KABILA TO SUN CITY

### A Dynastic Succession

In the early afternoon of 16 January 2001, Kabila was killed by one of his bodyguards. Space forbids an extensive treatment of this major event.[54] Suffice it to say that Braeckman identifies five conspiracies

---

[51] S. Field, E. Ebrahim, 'Peace and Security in the DRC', in: D. Kadima, C. Kabemba (Eds.), *Whither Regional Peace and Security? The Democratic Republic of Congo after the War*, Pretoria, Africa Institute of South Africa, 2000, p. 9.

[52] On this saga, see P. Bouvier, *Le dialogue intercongolais. Anatomie d'une négociation à la lisière du chaos*, Brussels-Paris, Institut Africain-L'Harmattan, 2004, Cahiers Africains No. 63–64, pp. 36–37.

[53] A survey of this new obstacle course can be found in International Crisis Group, Scramble for the Congo..., *op. cit.*

[54] For a survey of theses on this assassination, see O. Lanotte, *République démocratique du Congo. Guerres sans frontières*, Brussels, GRIP-Editions Complexe, 2003, pp. 137–151; C. Braeckman, *Les nouveaux prédateurs. Politique des puissances en Afrique centrale*, Paris, Fayard, 2003, pp. 97–125. A trial held before the Cour d'ordre militaire from March 2002 to January 2003 against 135 defendants was grossly flawed and failed

aimed concurrently at the elimination of the president: she suspects former Mobutists settled in Brazzaville; military from Kivu[55], disgruntled after the execution of their leader Anselme Masasu Nindaga (cf. earlier text); a Katangan Lunda network around Kabila's *aide de camp* Colonel Eddy Kapend, linked to Angola[56]; Lebanese diamond traders upset by the granting of a purchasing monopoly to IDI Diamonds of Israeli Dan Gertler; and inevitably the U.S. Defence Intelligence Agency (DIA). Braeckman concludes that 'the assassination was obviously the fruit of a plot, and perhaps of a series of several conspiracies',[57] but the problem with these theories is that it is impossible to find proof of links between these different plots.[58] The most likely scenario, proposed by de Villers,[59] is that of a process in two times: the assassination itself, committed by Rachidi in connivance with other *kadogo* and *Kivutiens*, followed by an attempt to recuperate the situation in their favour by Kapend and his Lunda and Angolan backers.[60] It was indeed Kapend who seemed to take control after the assassination: he read a statement on national television, announcing a curfew, the closure of airports and borders, and the confinement to barracks of all troops. The government claimed that Kabila was wounded, and went as far as transporting his body to Harare 'for treatment'. In the absence of constitutional rules on succession, the inner circle needed to buy time to agree on a successor.[61] In a dynastic fashion, Kabila's son Joseph was declared the new president, and he took the oath of office on 26 January.

to uncover the truth. Thirty suspects (including Kapend) were sentenced to death, 59 received prison sentences and 46 were acquitted.

[55] Kabila's alleged assassin, Rachidi Kasereka, was a *kadogo* from Kivu loyal to Masasu.

[56] Kapend allegedly killed Rachidi right after the latter shot Kabila.

[57] C. Braeckman, *Les nouveaux prédateurs...*, op. cit., p. 105.

[58] This book was in print when an additional scenario emerged. A witness told the Spanish National Court (*Audiencia Nacional*) that Kabila was assassinated at the order of the Kigali regime ('Un ex agente de Ruanda implica a su Gobierno en el asesinato de Kabila', *El País*, 21 December 2008).

[59] G. de Villers, *République Démocratique du Congo. Le temps de Joseph Kabila*, forthcoming in Cahiers Africains.

[60] Luanda wanted an end to the war, and felt that Laurent Kabila stood in the way of a negotiated settlement. Turner adds another motive, namely that, as the Pweto battle in December 2000 had shown, Kabila 'was quite capable of losing the war to a pro-UNITA coalition' (T. Turner, 'Angola's Role ...', op. cit., p. 75). He concludes that '[t]here is a fairly strong circumstantial case that Angola had Laurent Kabila killed, or at least allowed it to happen' (*Idem*, p. 87).

[61] Next to nothing is known about how this decision was reached. Apart from Laurent Kabila's immediate political entourage, it is very likely that foreign allies Angola and Zimbabwe had their say.

Although the young president inherited a situation worse than the one prevailing when his father took office, and while there was nothing in his history that predestined him to be a statesman, Joseph Kabila's coming to power soon unblocked a situation of profound political stalemate. His address to the nation on the day of his inauguration contained obvious, though on occasion hidden openings. He referred to the need to 'restore peace and consolidate national communion', the re-launching of the Lusaka Accord, the return to democratic life and the opening up of the political system, the organisation of the inter-Congolese dialogue and the liberalisation of the economy. He also made explicit overtures to the international community, a clear break with his father's discourse and practice. A window of opportunity had clearly opened to end the deadlock created, in large part, by Laurent Kabila and his inner circle. At a summit on the DRC held in Lusaka on 15 February, Joseph Kabila announced his intention to co-operate with Masire in order to get the inter-Congolese dialogue off the ground. Agreement was also reached on the deployment of the UN observer force, sub-plans for the disengagement of rebel forces were outlined and Kabila referred to his 'brothers in the rebellion' as partners in the peace process.

With the new president seemingly more forthcoming, the other side became more intransigent. Kigali raised new objections, both by formulating additional conditions for the withdrawal of its troops and by suddenly refusing to accept Zambia as an honest broker, accusing it of siding with the Hutu rebels. The conspicuous absence of Rwanda at the Lusaka meeting raised doubts about its commitment to the process, so much so that delegates and international observers openly expressed disappointment and worried that Rwanda 'is standing in the way of peace in the DRC'.[62]

Now that Kinshasa showed willingness to co-operate with him, Masire was in a position to move ahead. After intense diplomatic work, a 'declaration on the fundamental principles of the inter-Congolese political negotiations' was signed on 4 May 2001 in Lusaka by the Congolese government, the MLC, the RCD-Goma and the RCD-ML.[63] While this document did not add much to the Lusaka Accord, it did two things: on the one hand, the process was 'domesticated', as all the signatories were Congolese; on the other, the unarmed opposition and civil society were

---

[62] 'Rwanda criticised as Congo summit ends in a mood of optimism', Lusaka, DPA, 16 February 2001.
[63] As seen earlier, the RCD had split into two wings in 1999.

formally brought in, as the document invited them to select their representatives in the negotiations. It was agreed in addition that decisions
were to be taken by consensus.

After more consultations and the selection of delegates, a preparatory
meeting of the Dialogue, also referred to as the 'Pre-Dialogue', took place
on 20–24 August 2001 in Gaborone, with 74 representatives of all the parties involved. Several documents were approved: an 'Act of Commitment'
or 'Republican Pact'. which included basic principles on reconciliation,
human rights, political liberalisation, refugees etc.; draft internal regulations for the Dialogue; and a draft agenda. The momentum that emerged
in Gaborone was more important than the approval of texts: a follow-up
committee, with representatives of all the delegations, was set up, and it was
agreed that the Dialogue would start on 15 October. Optimism prevailed.

However, problems soon arose with regard to funding, but also, more
importantly, on the issues of which groups should be included and the
size of the delegations. The day before the Dialogue was due to begin,
Kabila referred to the principle of 'all inclusiveness' agreed in Gaborone
and protested that certain 'political and social components' were not
involved. This issue was to prove a major stumbling block throughout
the whole process. The inaugural session took place in Addis-Ababa
on 15 October as planned, and a number of African political leaders
expressed optimism and exhorted the Congolese participants to seize this
historic moment. However, the 'spirit of Gaborone', Masire referred to in
his speech, was nowhere to be found.[64] Several Congolese leaders, including Kabila and Bemba, were absent. As the number of delegates present
was well under the 330 agreed in Gaborone, the government and some
members of the opposition and civil society argued that the Dialogue
could not start. For their part, the RCD-Goma and the MLC accused the
government of seeking a pretext to stall the process. In turn, the government claimed the rebels were aiming to create stalemate, and so to find
a pretext to resume the war. On 19 October, the government decided to
stop participating, but it accepted that the official starting date of the
Dialogue was 15 October, and that it would continue in South Africa.
Diverse meetings, organised by all sorts of facilitators, were subsequently
held in Abuja (7–8 December 2001), Brussels (14–17 January 2002),[65]

---

[64] A summary of events in Addis Ababa is offered here, based on P. Bouvier, *Le dialogue intercongolais...*, *op. cit.*, pp. 40–46, where more details can be found.

[65] The Brussels meeting was organised by the Belgian government, which invited only members of the unarmed opposition and of civil society, fearing that these components faced

Blantyre (14 January 2002) and Geneva (4–8 February 2002). On 25 February 2002, the Dialogue was finally resumed in the South African resort of Sun City.

### From Sun City to Pretoria, and Back to Sun City[66]

It is not surprising that South Africa, which was about to play the lead role from now on, came in rather late in the process. Indeed, we have seen that Pretoria was seen as biased in favour of the invading countries. It neither condemned the rebellion nor Rwandan and Ugandan aggression, and it continued to sell arms to these two countries while refusing to sell weapons to Kinshasa.[67] However, this perception gradually changed after Thabo Mbeki took over from Nelson Mandela in mid-1999: his approach was seen as more evenhanded, as he pushed for a peace plan and urged all foreign forces to withdraw from the DRC.[68]

The opening session of the Inter-Congolese Dialogue immediately announced the difficulties that were to mark the process. At the start of the ceremony, which was delayed for four hours due to last-minute off-stage negotiations, the MLC and the unarmed opposition remained absent in protest over the non-inclusion of a number of opposition parties. A compromise solution was found, and Canada saved the day by sending a plane to transport leaders of the opposition from Kinshasa to Johannesburg. With everyone present, work could start in earnest on 6 March, but hassle over delegations immediately resumed; the issue was finally settled, with the total number of delegates set at 367. Other disagreements concerned the agenda, and more particularly the points on the 'new political order'[69] and the army.[70] These issues were settled, and both the agenda and the standing orders were approved on 11 March. The presentation by the delegations of their general declarations showed

---

marginalisation and needed to be strengthened against the government and the rebel movements.

[66] For a detailed treatment, see P. Bouvier, *Le dialogue intercongolais...*, *op. cit.*, pp. 129–186; pp. 235–301.

[67] C. Landsberg, 'The Impossible Neutrality? ...', *op. cit.*, p. 174.

[68] *Idem*, p. 178.

[69] How 'new' is 'new'? Predictably, the government thought in minimal terms, that is, the organisation and management of the transition, while the other parties insisted on a profound transformation of the institutions *ab nihilo*.

[70] The same type of disagreement arose as on the 'new political order': for the government, the 'rebel forces' were to be integrated into the existing national army, while the opposition wanted the creation of a new 'Republican' army.

that, while there was agreement, at least in principle, on items such as the need for peace, territorial integrity, and elections, the main points of divergence were on the withdrawal of foreign armies, the structure of the state, the type of political regime, and transitional justice.[71]

As a consequence of an attack launched on 14 March by Rwanda and the RCD on Muliro, a strategic town on the shores of Lake Tanganyika, the government decided to suspend its participation until the attackers withdrew to their original positions. It seemed initially quite isolated over this issue, but was unexpectedly saved by the UN Security Council which, on 19 March, adopted Resolution 1399 (2002), condemning the taking of Muliro by the RCD-Goma. It requested its withdrawal from Muliro, as well as from Pweto, and it recalled that rebel held Kisangani needed to be demilitarised. In addition, the Security Council exhorted Rwanda to use its influence on the RCD-Goma to make it respect the resolution. The government felt vindicated and decided to return to the negotiating table, but the incident was a new reminder of the frailty of the process.

Work in the commissions resumed on 22 March. Some made steady progress, such as the commissions on economic and financial matters, on peace and reconciliation, and on humanitarian, social and cultural matters; however, those on defence and security, and on political and legal matters failed to reach a consensus on crucial issues. Thabo Mbeki wanted the negotiations to be successful, but he also wished to avoid them dragging on for too long. On 11 April, the day initially set for the end of the dialogue, he announced that he would allow the talks to continue until 18 April, but no longer, thus increasing pressure on the participants. He was also successful in bringing positions closer together on the issue of the transitional institutions. Finally, the commission on defence and security, the last one still meeting, reached a consensus. Despite all this progress, tensions remained high, both in Sun City and on the ground in the DRC, and failure remained a possibility throughout.

On 17 April, there was a *coup de théâtre*: at a joint press conference the government and the MLC announced that they had reached an agreement, which they called the 'accord for the consensual management of the transition'. While some parties decided to join the deal, it was rejected by others, unsurprisingly including the RCD-Goma. The accord contained a broad outline of the institutional set-up for the transition and the distribution of power between the president, Joseph Kabila, and Jean-Pierre

---

[71] A useful synopsis of delegations' positions on the main issues can be found in P. Bouvier, *Le dialogue intercongolais…, op. cit.*, pp. 138–142.

Bemba who was to become prime minister. It was further provided that the National Assembly was to have 423 members designated by the parties present at the dialogue, and that it was to be chaired by the RCD. The Senate chair would come from the unarmed opposition. Although it was struck by two parties, the deal pretended to get everyone on board, but the accord of course remained partial, much to the dismay of Thabo Mbeki.

As some major players, the RCD-Goma in particular, were left out, this accord was never implemented, but it did paradoxically create a new momentum. The landscape was now bipolar, with the government, the MLC and those that joined them calling themselves the 'Camp of the Fatherland', which those outside 'for the time being' were free to join. On the other side, those 'outside' rejected the accord as contrary to the principles of inclusiveness and consensus agreed in Lusaka. For those adhering to the accord, the Dialogue had ended; for those opposed to it, the Dialogue had simply been suspended. A couple of days after the end of the Sun City meeting, the latter created the 'Alliance for the Safeguarding of the Inter-Congolese Dialogue' (*Alliance pour la sauvegarde du Dialogue inter-congolais* [ASD]). Both Mbeki and Masire rejected the government–MLC accord, as it was agreed outside of the Dialogue facilitated by them, and because it was not supported by a number of delegations. Unsurprisingly, Rwanda also rejected the deal, but even Uganda opposed it, although it supported the MLC. By and large, the wider international community welcomed the accord, but only saw it as a step and invited the parties to continue negotiating, in order to make it all-inclusive.

The logic of inclusiveness was to re-emerge soon, as it became clear that the government and the MLC were unable to implement their deal. Although some MLC leaders, chief among them General Secretary Olivier Kamitatu, settled in Kinshasa in order to set up the new institutions, Jean-Pierre Bemba, voicing concerns about his personal safety, remained holed up in Gbadolite. At the end of June 2002, Kabila declared that the accord was dead, and that he would again embark on the search for an 'inclusive' dialogue. This was to happen in adverse circumstances: in May, new fighting had broken out in Kisangani, where RCD-Goma troops committed atrocities; in June, South Kivu was the scene of renewed combat between the RPA and Patrick Masunzu's Banyamulenge (cf. earlier text); and in mid-August, violent confrontations took place in Ituri between different militias.[72]

---

[72] As in the past, the government, the MLC, the RCD-Goma, as well as Rwanda and Uganda stoked the fires in their constant game of making and unmaking alliances.

There was also better news. On 14 June 2002, the UN Security Council extended the mandate of MONUC until 30 June 2003. On 30 July, the DRC and Rwanda signed an accord in Pretoria which provided, on the one hand, for the withdrawal of Rwandan troops from the DRC, and, on the other, for the disarmament of Rwandan Hutu rebels operating in the DRC. Although this agreement did not add anything to what was already contained in the 1999 Lusaka accord, it was eventually to pave the way for the withdrawal of occupying forces, particularly after a similar accord was signed on 6 September in Luanda between the DRC and Uganda. All this reinforced President Kabila's position, as he signed these agreements as head of state and without the rebel movements being involved, thus suggesting that his status was no longer challenged. Quite surprisingly, Rwanda pulled out its forces without seeming to bother whether Kabila would fulfil his part of the deal. This was an indication that Kigali was being seen as a spoiler, and was therefore increasingly isolated. Kagame's intransigence and suspected duplicity started to raise criticism and attract international (including United States) pressure,[73] a trend that was to continue later. There was probably no better way for Kigali to defend itself against the accusations of obstructing peace efforts, plundering Congo's resources, and abusing human rights, than by withdrawing its troops.[74]

The designation by Kofi Annan of Moustapha Niasse as his special envoy allowed the dialogue to get back on track. As he had already occupied this position in 1999, Niasse knew the Congolese political class and the nature of the problem. In addition, he was energetic and had the advantage of being a French speaker. On 15 November 2002, negotiations resumed in Pretoria. Although he had effectively sidelined Masire, Niasse presented the meeting as taking place in the framework of his mission on behalf of the UN, rather than as a continuation of the inter-Congolese Dialogue, which was – formally speaking – run by the facilitator, that is, Masire. But no one was really fooled, and this was in effect the resumption of the Dialogue. The process was now firmly guided by Niasse and Mbeki, who exerted intense pressure on the Congolese players, who were able to capitalise on what had been achieved in Sun City, and who were backed by all relevant external powers. Nevertheless, the negotiations were again very difficult, and crept from one suspension to the next informal behind-the-stage contact. As the end of the session was set for 11 December and

[73] E. Rogier, 'The Inter-Congolese Dialogue: A Critical Overview', in: M. Malan, J. Gomez (Eds.), *Challenges of Peace Implementation...*, *op. cit.*, p. 34.
[74] *Idem*, p. 35.

failure was looming, Niasse postponed the closing to 12 December, when he presented a draft Global and Inclusive Accord (*Accord global et inclusif* [AGI]) to the participants. Again, 'final' sessions were scheduled on 13 and 15 December, to no avail. Finally, during the night of 16–17 December, Niasse handed out a new draft AGI, which delegates were given thirty minutes to study. He then invited the civil society representative to sign, which he did, followed by the other delegations, some of them under protest and expressing reservations. But the Accord was signed by all, it was 'global and inclusive', and the parties realised that they would be considered spoilers if they openly reneged on it. Just like when they signed earlier and later deals, this did not mean that the parties really adhered to them. Rather, '(their) motives for signing were to avoid being marginalised and to have their share of power preserved, confirmed or recognised, but probably not to offer the DRC an opportunity to rise from its ashes'.[75] Their subsequent behaviour was to confirm this assessment.

Between the signing of the AGI and the effective start of the transition, some important issues still needed to be settled, particularly on constitutional and security matters. This again required tedious negotiations in Pretoria, made more difficult by new flare-ups of violence in Ituri and by accusations of atrocities and even cannibalism levelled against the MLC. Faced with the problems created by the continuous bickering among the Congolese players, Mbeki and Niasse again decided to confront them with a *fait accompli*. On 6 March 2003, they presented drafts of a transitional constitution, of mechanisms aimed at establishing a new national army, and of security arrangements for those to take part in the transitional institutions. The documents were put forward in a 'take it or leave it' fashion and they were adopted without much debate. Thus, for the second time in a matter of months, the mediators imposed their view on the Congolese parties. This procedure caused surprisingly little protest, and it was actually approved of by a number of Congolese newspapers which felt that, otherwise, the debate could have lasted for another couple of years. Although all the substance had now been settled, the Pretoria meeting was not to be the end of the Dialogue. Indeed, technically speaking, this was not even part of the Dialogue, of which Masire, rather than Mbeki and Niasse, was in charge. He needed to be recognised, and it was up to him to formally conclude the process. On 1 April, 362 delegates who had participated in the Dialogue met in Sun City, the place where it had all started. Everyone endorsed the AGI and the day was rounded

---

[75] *Idem*, p. 36. Rogier aptly summarises each party's likely motives.

off with a concert given by the Congolese artist Niama Werra Son. An atmosphere of unity and reconciliation prevailed.

Let us conclude the narrative of this long and tortuous saga by briefly analysing the agreement arrived at after two and a half years of 'dialogue'. Three fundamental texts were to manage the transition: the AGI, the transitional constitution, and the 'memorandum on the army and on security'. The way in which they effectively functioned will be discussed later. According to the AGI, the transition was to last for two years, a period that could be extended twice by six months. The executive branch was to be made up of a president, four vice-presidents and a government. The former government side was to hold the offices of the president and of the vice-president in charge of the commission of reconstruction and development; the offices of vice-president in charge of the political commission, the economic and financial commission, and the social and cultural commission were attributed to the RCD-Goma, the MLC and the unarmed opposition, respectively. Ministerial portfolios were given to the entities involved in the Dialogue. Parliament was to be bicameral: a National Assembly with 500 members and a 120-seat Senate. MPs and senators were to be appointed by the same entities as those represented in the government. The positions these entities would have in government and parliament was spelt out in detail in the AGI. Provision was also made for two follow-up mechanisms: at the domestic level, this was to be the Commission de suivi de l'Accord, while a Comité international was to 'support the programme of transition'. The transitional constitution merely translated the principles agreed in the AGI. Indeed, the constitution was 'elaborated on the basis of the AGI. The AGI and the constitution constitute the only source of power during the transition (...)' (art. 1, transitional constitution). Article 197 provided that the president, the vice-presidents and the chairs of the National Assembly and the Senate would remain in place throughout the whole period of the transition. Finally, the 'memorandum on the army and on security' provided for the unification of the armed forces under the supervision of a 'meeting of the high commands' and for the security of the rebel leaders when they settled in Kinshasa.

## 8.4 POLITICAL TRANSITION IN CONFLICT

### The Bumpy Road Towards Elections

The institutions agreed in Sun City were soon created. At the summit of the executive branch, the so-called '1+4' formula brought together

President Kabila and four vice-presidents, representing the president's camp (Abdoulaye Yerodia), the unarmed opposition (Arthur Z'Ahidi Ngoma)[76], the RCD-Goma (Azarias Ruberwa) and the MLC (Jean-Pierre Bemba). On 30 June 2003, a 62-member government was formed, followed in July by a 500-member National Assembly and a Senate composed of 120 members. In a country where no competitive elections had been held since 1965, this plethora of political figures was of course totally unrepresentative, and the 2006 elections would later show that many organisations and parties, which had forced their way into the transitional institutions, had no constituency worth mentioning.

Despite this institutional progress, the transition moved forward painfully. Although a new integrated general army staff was theoretically in place in September 2003, command structures remained divided and the merging of the former government forces and the rebel groups into a national army proved difficult on the ground. The appointment of provincial governors and vice-governors, as well as of the CEOs of public and mixed (private and public) companies dragged on and was only completed in 2004 and 2005, respectively. In the meantime, little progress was made in areas such as the restoration by the state of full territorial control, human rights and the management of the economy and of the public finances.

Just as the process, from Lusaka to Sun City, towards the AGI had shown, the implementation of the transition which followed it confirmed again the incapacity of the Congolese players to make progress on their own.[77] The DRC was put under a *de facto* international trusteeship, which on several occasions prevented the process from collapsing. On the one hand, the Pretoria accord provided for the creation of an international

---

[76] The historical leader of the opposition, UDPS chair Etienne Tshisekedi, would have been the obvious candidate for this position. He signed the AGI in Sun City and could have been part of the transition. However, during the ICD, he flirted with the RCD-Goma and, worse still, with Rwanda: he met with Kagame in Kigali, and he was present in Kisangani when occupying forces marched there. All this had a considerable political cost for the UDPS (see C. Braeckman, 'Tshisekedi ou le front du refus', *Le Soir*, 18 May 2005). We shall see later that Tshisekedi disqualified himself for the remainder of the transition.

[77] Obotela observes that this was not new in Congo's history: 'The crises which the country has faced have always necessitated the intervention of third parties to be resolved. Antananarivo, Coquilhatville, The Lovanium Conclave... have seen an always present international community, under diverse forms. The Sovereign National Conference, the Lusaka Accord, the Inter-Congolese Dialogue have shown the limits of the Congolese actors' (N. Obotela Rashidi, 'L'an I de l'Accord global et inclusif en République démocratique du Congo', in: F. Reyntjens, S. Marysse (Eds.), *L'Afrique des grands lacs. Annuaire 2003–2004*, Paris, L'Harmattan, 2004, p. 123).

committee to accompany the transition. CIAT, which operated at ambassadorial level in Kinshasa, was instrumental in avoiding breakdown through flexible interventions, whenever the transition was in jeopardy. On the other hand, after a hesitant start, MONUC became the largest and most expensive mission run at the time by the UN Department of Peace Keeping Operations, with 17,000 troops and an annual cost of $1 billion at its height. Its mandate under Chapter VII of the UN Charter involved implementing and monitoring the ceasefire agreement, DDRRR (disarmament, demobilisation, repatriation, resettlement and reintegration), and the facilitation of the process leading to the elections. While MONUC has been rightly criticised for its lack of robustness, its sheer presence – in a sense acting as the military arm of CIAT – has been crucial in preserving the transition. During the electoral period, it was shouldered by a 2500-strong European Force (EUFOR) deployed in Kinshasa (cf. later text).

International persuasion did not prevent the transition from being marred by many grave incidents that constantly threatened it. For instance, at the end of March 2004, several military barracks in Kinshasa were attacked by assailants, which the government claimed were elements of Mobutu's old DSP who had fled to Congo-Brazzaville after the AFDL captured Kinshasa in May 1997. On 11 June, a bizarre *coup* attempt was staged by a few dozen elements of Kabila's own presidential guard under the command of Major Eric Lenge. The insurgents briefly took control of the national radio station and read out a message stating that the transitional government had been dissolved. They were routed by loyalist forces and withdrew to the Bas-Congo, where they 'vanished'. No attempts were made to trace them and no inquiry was conducted on what had happened, and it was suggested – but never proved – that this had been an attempt by hard-line elements belonging to Kabila's inner circle to derail the transition. During the same month of June, students rioted in Kinshasa, chanting the slogan 'one plus four equals zero', thus indicating that the presidential '1+4' formula had failed to deliver after one year of existence. In an angry reaction to the capture of Bukavu (cf. earlier text), street violence came close to the widespread pillaging which, in 1991 and 1993, had nearly destroyed the economy. In the meantime, the government and its army were unable to establish a modicum of territorial control in Ituri, the Kivus and North Katanga.

During the entire transitional period, plutocratic and indeed Mobutist political culture continued to prevail. Not only did Vice-Presidents Bemba and Ruberwa maintain command structures outside the FARDC, but President Kabila likewise behaved like a warlord, both by creating his

*Maison militaire* (a parallel army command) and by building a 12,000-
to 15,000-strong presidential guard (Groupe spécial de sécurité présidentielle [GSSP]), much better equipped and paid than the ordinary FARDC,
and dominated by officers from Katanga. In the economic sector too, it
was business as usual. A report produced in June 2005 by a parliamentary commission, which probed mining, financial and other contracts concluded between 1996 and 2003,[78] was not followed up; indeed it was not
even officially discussed in the Transitional Assembly. The report of the
Lutundula Commission, named after its chairman, was a thorough investigation, which uncovered and discussed dozens of deals that were either
illegal or grossly biased against the public interest. It recommended their
termination or renegotiation, and advocated judicial action against politicians and businesspeople involved in these transactions. While the report
was kept under wraps, the 'animators of the transition' continued to conclude new deals that were no more transparent than the previous ones.

The dangers facing the transition were compounded by splits in the
component parts of the transition government, the RCD-Goma and the
MLC in particular. In the RCD-Goma, a Kinshasa wing and a Goma wing
emerged increasingly clearly, divided along two lines: one separated those
who held functions in the transitional structures from those who did not,
the other pitted a number of Tutsi against the non-Tutsi, with chairman
Ruberwa uncomfortably caught in the middle. On 9 July 2004, eight
prominent MPs (seven Banyarwanda and one Munyamulenge) wrote a
long letter from Goma to Ruberwa, announcing that they were suspending
their participation in the transition parliament and demanding the summoning 'without delay' to Goma of the party's competent bodies 'to assess
the situation', which was presented as a total failure: '[A]n enormous deficit of confidence characterises the relations between the political parties in
the transition government. (...) The peace process in our country is seriously threatened and it would be a mistake to take this warning lightly'.
The MPs also mentioned the growing 'demonisation, racism, xenophobia
and unreasonable fear aimed at a particular community', an obvious reference to the Tutsi in the wake of the Bukavu events (cf. earlier text).[79]
The problem this caused to Ruberwa, a Munyamulenge himself, was made
worse by a dramatic coincidence, when almost 200 Banyamulenge were

---

[78] République démocratique du Congo, Assemblée Nationale, Commission spéciale chargée
de l'examen de la validité des conventions à caractère économique et financier conclues
pendant les guerres de 1996–1997 et de 1998, *Rapport des travaux*, 26 June 2005, 271 pp.
[79] This letter was published on *Lesoftonline.net* on 12 July 2004.

killed in the refugee camp of Gatumba (Burundi) on 13 August. Present at the victims' burial on 16 August, Ruberwa was no longer able to resist the pressure, and he demanded 'a halt to the transition': 'The fracture (in the peace process) is so serious that it is necessary to stop on the road of the transition, in order to take stock'.[80] As a consequence, a process that had been simmering for some time now openly manifested itself, when eleven other leading members of the party stated on 23 August that they would remain in Kinshasa and continue their participation in the transitional institutions. The split became even more apparent when, on 31 August, Ruberwa had the seat of the RCD-Goma in Kinshasa sealed by his guards. However Thabo Mbeki, who was in Kinshasa on that very day on a scheduled visit, was able to iron things out by offering Ruberwa a face-saving exit from a situation which dangerously isolated him. After meeting with Mbeki, Ruberwa announced that 'the college of founding members [of the RCD], under international guarantee and confident in the respect for commitments made by all partners in the transition, and especially by the President of the Republic, decides to lift the suspension measure'. The split, which threatened the entire process, was thus mended for the time being, but it was to have lasting effects for the RCD-Goma. At the end of December 2004, the party sacked a minister and both its general secretary and deputy general secretary, all suspected of having set up an 'RCD-Kinshasa', but these decisions were immediately challenged by other leading party members, who called them 'unfair and likely to threaten (the party's) cohesion'.[81] The 'Group of Reformers' (Goma)[82] and the 'Group of Kinshasa' were to confront each other right up to the 2006 elections, with Ruberwa trying to avoid the groups becoming separate parties.

During the Autumn of 2005, it was the MLC's turn to experience a first split. After disputes over appointments in public enterprises, in early September a number of members joined former MLC Minister José Endundo[83] in his breakaway party, the Union nationale des démocrates chrétiens (UNADEC). In early December, the MLC (or more accurately Bemba) decided to exclude its general secretary, Olivier Kamitatu, officially because he did not respect the party's discipline, but more probably because he had complained about the authoritarian tendencies

[80] 'Le vice-président congolais Ruberwa demande "un arrêt de la transition"', Gatumba, AFP, 16 August 2004.

[81] 'RCD: les suites d'une houleuse réunion', *Lesoftonline.net*, 30 December 2004.

[82] In a sense, General Nkunda acted as the military wing of this group (cf. earlier text).

[83] Endundo was among six ministers who were suspended in November 2004 and eventually sacked in January 2005 for corruption.

prevailing in the MLC. Kamitatu, who realised that Bemba did not stand much of a chance and who wanted to be on the winning side, immediately launched his own party, the Alliance pour le renouveau du Congo (ARC), which was later to join the presidential platform AMP (see later text). The MLC tried in vain to have Kamitatu sacked as speaker of the Transitional National Assembly, an attempt – though supported by a judgment of the Supreme Court – which led even more parliamentarians to leave the MLC. Occurring just months before the elections, these defections certainly weakened Bemba.

The failure to make steady progress on security sector reform remained another threat to the transition. Bizima Karaha, one of the 'renegade' RCD-Goma MPs, declared on 21 August 2004 that the integrated Congolese army 'existed only on paper'.[84] The vast majority of the FARDC indeed continued to obey the orders of their previous entities, that is, the pre-transition government or the former rebel forces. How could the transition be conducted and elections organised in the presence of armed factions rather than a national army? And why is it that, between mid-2003 and early 2005, the transitional government paid hardly any attention to this issue, while at the same time there was a general consensus that it was crucial? The former combatants were uncomfortably 'co-operating' in the same national government, but each continued controlling its troops and the territory where they were deployed. In other words, President Kabila and Vice-Presidents Bemba and Ruberwa continued behaving like militia leaders.[85] The saga of General Nkunda, discussed earlier, was just one example of the threat this phenomenon posed to the transition process, but it was and remains the most serious one to this day. Foreign military observers concluded that Kabila and the former rebel leaders kept their best soldiers and weapons in reserve.[86] Potential spoilers dissatisfied with the election results thus maintained the option of returning to war, a possibility reminiscent of the Angolan scenario. In addition, as a MONUC official remarked: 'Army integration is an industry and the

---

[84] 'L'armée congolaise intégrée "n'existe que sur le papier"', Goma, AFP, 21 August 2004.

[85] This was not just the case in the areas controlled by the MLC and the RCD-Goma, but in Kinshasa too: the troops protecting Bemba and Ruberwa 'arrested' people on several occasions and they maintained detention facilities ('cachots') in town. An example of these practices by Ruberwa is offered in a press release of the NGO La Voix des Sans Voix (VSV) ( 'M. Issa Tutu recherché par des officiers proches de M. Azarias Ruberwa, Vice-Président de la République', Kinshasa, 30 March 2006). For examples concerning Bemba acting as a warlord, see earlier text.

[86] Human Rights Watch, Democratic Republic of Congo. Elections in sight: 'Don't rock the boat'?, New York, 15 December 2005, p. 9.

Congolese have become very good at making money from it'.[87] Only in May 2005 was a military integration plan devised, which provided for the creation of eighteen infantry brigades, to be put in place before the elections. Troops were to be transported to six integration centres, where they would be disarmed, trained and integrated (a process referred to as 'brassage'). However, by mid-2006, only three brigades had effectively been formed and deployed.[88] The operational capacity of the FARDC remained very low: undertrained, underequipped, underorganised and underpaid, not only was the army unable to carry out its prime mission of exercising territorial control and ensuring the national territory's integrity, but it also continued to prey on the population and remained a major factor of insecurity.[89] A mirror of the state, the army remained an illustration of the 'informalisation' at the heart of national sovereignty.[90]

In the meantime, the legislative work needed to achieve the transition moved forward only slowly, and parliamentarians seemed more interested in their income than in making laws. One of the first things the senators did was to increase their salaries from the US$600 per month initially provided to US$1500, above the increase to US$1200, which the MPs had offered themselves; this difference was of course normal, as the Senate was a more 'august' house. The constitution drafting process dragged on because, among other reasons, the senators wished to organise costly 'popular consultations', as well as several meetings and seminars which allowed them to cash in *per diems*. In September 2005, each member of both houses took possession of a Nissan jeep worth US$22,000 a piece, which 'they paid for themselves' – in part by receiving their 'end of mandate indemnity' in advance. In the 2005 budget, parliament allotted itself six times the amount reserved for the entire justice sector. It should be added in fairness that President Kabila's 'civil list' represented eight times the state's health budget.[91]

---

[87] *Idem, Ibid.*

[88] S. Wolters, H. Boshoff, The Impact of Slow Military Reform on the Transition Process in the DRC, Pretoria, ISS, 10 July 2006, p. 8.

[89] A survey of army and police reforms can be found in International Crisis Group, Security Sector Reform in the Congo, Nairobi-Brussels, 13 February 2006.

[90] T. Vircoulon, 'République démocratique du Congo: la démocratie sans démocrates', *Politique étrangère*, 2006, 3, 572. On the informalisation of African politics more generally, see P. Chabal, J.-P. Dalloz, *Africa Works. Disorder as Political Instrument*, Oxford-Bloomington, James Currey-Indiana University Press, 1999.

[91] At the beginning of November 2005, a Ministry of Finance audit found that, between January and September, the President had overspent by 91% and that the Vice-Presidents had overspent by between 36% (Yerodia) and 242% (Bemba).

Only in June 2004 was the Independent Electoral Commission (Commission électorale indépendante [CEI]) created by law. Headed by the cleric Apollinaire Malu-Malu, the CEI became fully operational in November 2004, when its provincial offices were created. The CEI was to become a formidable operation, with 42,000 electoral agents, a number that rose to 250,000 at the time of the elections. However, the progress in legislative work remained slow. After long and, on occasion, bitter debate, the parliament passed the Nationality Act on 26 October 2004. In order to reassure those whose citizenship had been contested in the past, Article 6 stated: 'Is Congolese by origin, every person belonging to the ethnic groups and nationalities whose ascendants and territories were part of what became the Congo (...) at independence'. This was the formulation of the Lusaka Accord, including the strange reference to 'nationalities', which makes no sense in the Congolese context. Despite the poor drafting, this provision intended to put an end to the challenging of the citizenship of Banyarwanda and Banyamulenge in the Kivus.

As there was neither a constitution nor an electoral law in early 2005, the chairman of the CEI suggested that the polls might have to be postponed. This led to widespread unrest in Kinshasa, where a few people were killed and considerable damage occurred on 11 January. In protest over a possible postponement, but also over the sacking of two MLC Ministers and over delays in appointments to institutions and public companies, Vice-President Bemba left Kinshasa for his fief Gemena on 18 January, announcing that the MLC would withdraw from the transition if these appointments were not made by 31 January. However, a couple of days later, he returned to the capital, and just three hours of conversation with Kabila allowed them to 'harmonise' their positions. This made it possible to officially announce the postponement, by six months, of the elections. Strangely enough, the announcement was first made on 15 February by the EU special envoy Aldo Ajello, and only officially requested by the CEI on 28 April, before being approved by parliament on 17 June. In early April, UDPS leader Etienne Tshisekedi announced that the end of the transition being fixed for 30 June, 'the parenthesis of the AFDL' would draw to a close on that date. Indeed, for Tshisekedi things were quite simple: the institutional order of the Sovereign National Conference (which had appointed him as prime minister in 1992) would resume, and 'the people' would close the offices of the 'gravediggers of the transition'.[92] Some Kinshasa newspapers saw a

---

[92] 'Tshisekedi: "la paranthèse AFDL se referme le 30 juin 2005 à minuit"', Lesoftonline.net, 4 April 2005.

Ukrainian scenario unfolding, but the demonstration called by the UDPS on July 1 was blocked by the police. Although a few people were killed in Kinshasa and Tshikapa (Kasai), the violence did not approach what had been feared, and the rest of the country remained calm.

In the meantime, discussions on the constitution had started in earnest in February 2005, a mere five months before the initially fixed end of the transition. The debate in parliament centred on the structure of the state (unitary or federal), the type of political regime (presidential, parliamentary or mixed) and the minimum age for presidential candidates (Kabila was only 33 years old). The draft was finally adopted by the National Assembly on 16 May, in the presence of Kabila and Thabo Mbeki. The text introduced a unitary state that is, however, strongly decentralised: provision is made for 25 provinces plus the city of Kinshasa, and public revenue is to be shared (50% for the national level, 40% for the provinces and 10% for an 'Equalisation Fund'). The regime is semi-presidential, with a president elected by universal suffrage and a prime minister appointed by the president, but needing to command a majority in parliament. The minimum age for presidential candidates is 30 years, and a president can serve a maximum of two five-year terms. The judiciary is independent, and the Superior Council of the Judiciary is composed exclusively of judges. The Constitutional Court has considerable powers: it judges the constitutionality of statutes, treaties and executive instruments, interprets the constitution, adjudicates litigation on the distribution of competences between different levels of power and judges disputes arising from elections and referendums.[93] While the text was far from perfect, there was a widespread feeling that this was the best that could be achieved under the circumstances, a feeling well translated by de Saint Moulin: 'Our conclusion is therefore that it would be difficult today to reach a better result, and that it is preferable that the proposed text receives the legitimacy of its adoption by the referendum that is currently being proposed. Its rejection would merely prolong the transition that has already lasted for too long, without ensuring the drafting of a more democratic alternative text'.[94]

Although the adoption of the constitution was a major step forward, much more was needed before elections could be organised. On 14 June

[93] For more detailed analysis, see the special issues of *Congo-Afrique*, September 2005, No. 397 and of *Fédéralisme-Régionalisme*, 2004–5.

[94] L. de Saint Moulin, 'Projet de constitution de la RDC. Dimension sociale', *Congo-Afrique*, September 2005, 397, 94.

2005, the parliament adopted the Referendum Act, but the drafting of the crucial Elections Bill incurred such a delay that, on 17 October, the CIAT expressed deep concern over the 'accumulation of delays' and 'exhorted the government to proceed, without delay, to examine, adopt and table this essential bill before Parliament'. On 7 November, the UN Security Council likewise demanded 'that the process be accelerated, so that elections can be held on 30 June 2006 at the latest'.[95]

Nevertheless, voter registration had started on 15 June, and the process went much more smoothly than had been expected in a country as vast and derelict as the DRC. With the vital support of the international community and despite the UDPS's call for a boycott, the CEI successfully conducted this complex operation: over 25 million voters were registered between June and December 2005. This was a major feat in a country without population registers and where most people did not even carry an identity card. The close of the operation arrived just in time for the 18–19 December constitutional referendum. While CIAT called for a yes vote, a coalition of 44 parties was opposed to the draft constitution, and Tshisekedi again called for a boycott. The polling went surprisingly smoothly, with only a few irregularities. During what was the first free electoral exercise in the country since 1965, about 62% of the registered voters cast their ballot, of which about 84% were in favour of the draft. Both participation and approval rates were the highest in the east, which had borne the brunt of the successive wars: more than 90% of the vote was favourable in the two Kivus and in Maniema, and about 90% in Katanga. An even more pronounced east–west divide was observed during the 2006 elections (cf. later text).

Faced with its failure to convince people to boycott voter registration first and the referendum later, on 5 January 2006 the UDPS asked the CEI to re-open the registration process. Indeed, the party was now in deep trouble: many of its potential voters were not registered, candidates needed to be registered in order to run, and – after the referendum – it seemed that the transition was to go ahead without the UDPS. CEI chairman Malumalu refused the request, arguing that this would cause a new delay in the electoral process, but he left some openings, *inter alia* by allowing candidates to register when introducing their candidature. The UDPS was to continue its own marginalisation up to the end: in early April Tshisekedi announced that he would not run for the presidency and that his party would not field candidates for the parliamentary election. It

---

[95] While this had not yet been decided, the Security Council thus (rightly) anticipated that a second six-month extension of the transition would be necessary.

may well be that the UDPS, which had never prepared for polls, was simply not ready for an electoral exercise and feared defeat, despite being 'the historical opposition'. Tshisekedi's stubbornness eliminated the UDPS as a relevant political force, thus destroying over 25 years of courageous and risky battle in a difficult authoritarian environment.[96]

The adoption of the last piece of needed legislation, the electoral law, dragged on as MPs and senators fought pitched battles in pursuit of what they saw as their best interests. After lengthy debates, the text was finally approved on 21 February 2006. It provided for a majority system in the 59 single-seat constituencies and for a proportional system in the 441 others. As Kabila had promulgated the constitution a few days earlier, all the instruments were now in place for the electoral marathon. However, it was clear by then that the entire process could not be finished by 30 June. The day after the adoption of the electoral law, Malumalu stated that, provided the law was promulgated before the end of February, the first round of the presidential elections and the parliamentary polls could take place on 18 June, thus implying that the second round of the presidential elections and the polls for the provincial assemblies could not be organised before 30 June.[97] An institutional void, which some spoilers would certainly have seized to stall the process once again, was avoided thanks to article 222 of the constitution.[98]

## The 2006 Elections

In the absence of genuine political programmes proposed by the parties, other discourses were proposed during the campaign. Kabila, in particular, was the subject of vicious campaigning to the effect that he was not Congolese but Rwandan, a particularly virulent claim in light of the profound disgust of most Congolese for Rwanda. False genealogies, testimonies and documents were circulated,[99] while other candidates such as

---

[96] The philosophy underlying the self-destruction of the UDPS can be gleaned from UDPS-Belux, *L'UDPS face à la crise congolaise*, Paris, L'Harmattan, 1999.
[97] 'La date butoir du 30 juin ne sera pas respectée', *La Libre Belgique*, 23 February 2006.
[98] 'The political institutions of the transition remain in place until the effective installation of the corresponding institutions provided for by the present constitution; they exercise their functions in accordance with the transitional constitution' (author's translation).
[99] One example among many: in June 2005, a picture was circulated where Kagame is seen with some of his troops; an officer walking behind him was claimed to be Joseph Kabila and the photo was said to have been taken in May 1995. However, the uniforms worn by the Rwandan military dated from after mid-2004, and 'Joseph Kabila' was actually a Rwandan lieutenant.

Bemba exhibited their 'Congolité'. Kabila was also presented as the 'candidate of the white men', supported by the international community, a
claim that was not entirely false. On 23 May, 32 foreigners (3 Americans,
19 South Africans and 10 Nigerians) were arrested. The minister of the
interior claimed that they were mercenaries who aimed to 'overthrow
the institutions and disturbing the ongoing electoral process'. No one
really believed it, and CIAT denounced 'the political exploitation of this
so-called coup attempt'.[100] Other events increased the climate of fear preceding the elections. In early June, Human Rights Watch documented
increasing attacks, threats and detentions of journalists, human rights
defenders and members of the opposition during April and May, raising
concerns about free speech in the run-up to the polls.[101]

While it remained 'globally satisfied' by the campaign period, MONUC
expressed concern over incidents and irregularities, and denounced the
violent repression of a demonstration in Kinshasa on 11 July.[102] On 20
July, the National (Catholic) Episcopal Conference issued a declaration
which stated that 'all conditions for the organisation of genuinely transparent, free and democratic elections are not present. Quite to the contrary, the available information confirms the fears of manipulation and
fraud'. The bishops warned that they would not recognise the validity of
the polls if these irregularities were not corrected.[103]

Before turning to the elections themselves, two developments must
be mentioned. First, the fear that this was a very fragile situation that
might go disastrously wrong convinced the international community
that MONUC might not provide enough weight in terms of security.
That is why UN Security Council Resolution 1671 (2006) of 25 April
2006 authorised the deployment of a European military force, called
EUFOR, to support MONUC during the electoral period. The operation
was to be limited in time (four months starting from the first round of the
presidential elections) and space (an advance force stationed in Kinshasa
and a reserve on standby in Gabon). After Operation Artémis (cf. earlier
text), this was only the second EU peacekeeping mission. Second, the
first attempts at some consolidation of the fragmented political landscape

[100] 'RDC: Expulsion de 32 mercenaires présumés', Kinshasa, AFP, 28 May 2006.
[101] Human Rights Watch, Journalists and human rights defenders under fire, New York,
9 June 2006, 11 pp.
[102] MONUC, 'RDC: La MONUC dénonce incidents et irrégularités dans la campagne électorale', New York, 12 July 2006.
[103] Déclaration spéciale de la Conférence épiscopale nationale du Congo, Kinshasa, 20 July
2006.

were made before the elections. On 25 June, the Alliance de la majorité présidentielle (AMP) was formed, grouping the PPRD with thirty other, generally small parties and a few dozen 'personalities', with the aim of supporting Kabila's candidacy. On 24 July, the RCD-ML's candidate Mbusa Nyamwisi, withdrew from the race and rallied behind Kabila.

The first round of the presidential vote and the parliamentary polls took place on 30 July. During the campaign, the presidential side enjoyed obvious advantages, for instance in the media. Despite the fact that prior to the vote, a limited number of violent incidents took place, claiming the lives of a dozen people, and the fact that there was some intimidation by both the security forces and some candidates' militias, the polls themselves took place in relative calm, with a turnout of about 70%. Although some irregularities were noted during the voting and counting processes, national and international[104] observers concluded that the polls were generally free and fair.[105] Joseph Kabila, who ran as an independent candidate, came first with 44.81% of the vote, followed by Jean-Pierre Bemba (MLC) with 20.03% and Antoine Gizenga (PALU) with 13.06%. The other contenders obtained less than 5%.[106] The result meant that a second round was necessary, as no candidate had managed to obtain more than 50%.

As is shown in Map 8, the outcome revealed a marked east–west divide, with Kabila winning over 70% in Province Orientale, in North Kivu and in Katanga, over 80% in Maniema and over 90% in South Kivu. Conversely, Bemba's score was very poor in the east (0.3% in South Kivu being the extreme), but he obtained 64% in Equateur, almost 50% in Kinshasa, and around one-third of the vote in Bas-Congo and Western Kasaï. This split between the mainly Swahili-speaking east and the mainly Lingala-speaking west was a sizeable challenge for Kabila, who would have to gain legitimacy in the western part of the country, including Kinshasa.

When the final results were announced on 20 August, an incident broke out between Kabila's presidential guard, which behaved like a militia, and Bemba's men around the latter's residence. Kinshasa was the scene of three days of fighting with heavy weapons, leaving at least 23 people

---

[104] Among others the European Union, the Carter Center, a consortium of European and Congolese NGOs, and the Electoral Institute of Southern Africa.

[105] An interesting and nuanced survey of citizens' perceptions of the polls can be found in Konrad Adenauer Stiftung, *Le processus électoral 2006 en République démocratique du Congo. Perception de la population*, Kinshasa, s.d. (2007).

[106] The RCD-Goma candidate, Azarias Ruberwa, obtained a pitiful 1.69%, a very poor result for a party that once controlled about one third of the Congolese territory and a glaring testimony to its lack of popularity.

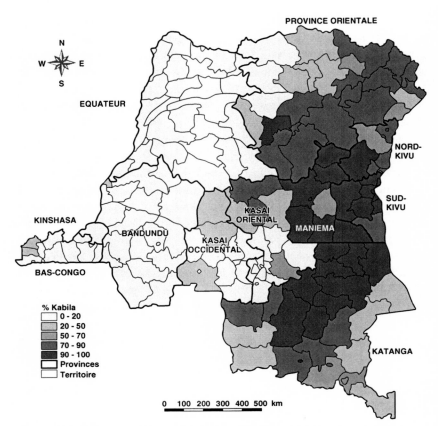

MAP 8. The east–west divide. (a) Results obtained by J. Kabila during the first
round. (b) Results obtained by J.P. Bemba during the first round.

*Source*: L. De Saint Moulin, E. Wolff, Cartes des résultats du premier tour de
l'élection présidentielle en RDC' (www.srbg.be).

dead, before it was quelled by MONUC and EUFOR peacekeepers.[107]
After fire gutted a television station owned by Bemba on 19 September,
tensions again flared up, and EUFOR warned that there were 'too many
men in arms and too many weapons circulating in Kinshasa'.[108] In mid-
October, with the second round approaching, MONUC noted a 'worrying

[107] On these events, see International Crisis Group, Securing Congo's Elections: Lessons
from the Kinshasa Showdown, Nairobi-Brussels, 2 October 2006.
[108] 'EUFOR: "trop d'armes à Kinshasa, où la situation peut vite s'embraser"', Kinshasa,
AFP, 21 September 2006.

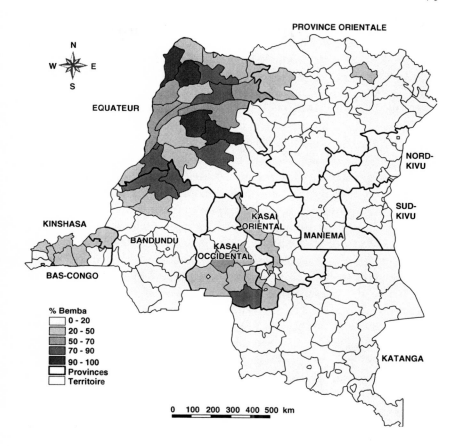

increase in violent incidents and political intolerance'.[109] These and other incidents showed both the frailty of the situation and the crucial nature of the international military presence.

The parliamentary polls confirmed the fragmented nature of the political landscape. Out of a total of 500 seats, five parties obtained 20 seats or more, but together these represented only slightly over half of the total. Sixty-three independent candidates were elected and 31 parties obtained only one seat; together these 94 single member 'groups' accounted for almost 20% of the Assembly. Not unexpectedly, the results matched those of the presidential vote, with Kabila's PPRD obtaining 111 seats, followed

---

[109] 'Elections en RDC: Les incidents violents sont en hausse, selon l'ONU', Kinshasa, AFP, 18 October 2006; also see Human Rights Watch, D.R. Congo: Halt Growing Violence Ahead of Elections, Brussels, 26 October 2006.

by Bemba's MLC with 64 and Gizenga's PALU with 34. Mirroring its poor result in the presidential poll, the RCD-Goma captured a mere 15 seats. No party thus came near to a majority needed to form a government.

However, platforms put together in advance of the second round of the presidential poll were a preview of a parliamentary majority. On the one hand, the AMP created before the first round was joined by PALU and by Nzanga Mobutu's Union des Démocrates Mobutistes (UDEMO).[110] On the other side, the Union pour la Nation (UN) rallied the MLC and a number of smaller parties behind Bemba's candidacy. Mathematically speaking, if all those who voted for Gizenga and Mobutu during the first round transferred their vote to Kabila, he would easily pass the 50%+ threshold.

While this transfer of votes was far from complete, Kabila quite comfortably won the second round, which – despite pre-electoral violence – took place on 29 October 2006 without significant incidents. He obtained 58.05% of the vote against 41.95% for Bemba. In addition to attaining an overall majority, through his alliances with Gizenga and Mobutu (two 'westerners'), Kabila also gained some foothold in the west. Nevertheless, the divide remained real: Bemba obtained over 60% in Bandundu and Kinshasa, over 70% in Bas-Congo and Kasaï Oriental, over 80% in Kasaï Occidental and almost 100% in Equateur; conversely Kabila secured over 80% in Province Orientale and over 90% in Katanga, the two Kivus and Maniema.

Even before the final results were made public, they were challenged. The archbishop of Kinshasa, Cardinal Frédéric Etsou, who hails from the same region as Bemba, increased the tension considerably by making an irresponsible statement to the French radio station RFI on 13 November. He claimed that 'there is already manoeuvring. In many places, the outgoing President does not have the results that are given, just like during the first round. (…) We must not allow the results of the ballot to be falsified'. The use of deliberately false rumours on preliminary results by the Bemba camp was another means of exacerbating a situation that became so dangerous that EU 'foreign minister' Javier Solana, EU Commissioner Louis Michel, World Bank boss Paul Wolfowitz and UN Undersecretary General Jean-Marie Guéhenno issued a joint statement on 15 November, insisting on restraint by the two candidates and inviting them to 'abstain from any

---

[110] The agreements signed in October 2006 between the AMP on the one hand and PALU and UDEMO on the other, in addition to setting up a majority behind Kabila's bid for the presidency, also announced that they would join forces to form a government based on a majority in the Assembly. The agreement with PALU contained a clause that the Prime Minister would be from PALU.

provocation so as to avoid challenges to the vote in which the Congolese people has placed such high hopes'. Claiming that the poll had been marred by many irregularities, Bemba rejected the outcome and took the matter to the Supreme Court, which, however, upheld the result on 27 November, thus making the outcome final. Although some of his supporters violently protested in Kinshasa, even setting fire to the Supreme Court building, Bemba eventually accepted the verdict and promised to engage in a 'strong and republican opposition'.[111] Kabila was sworn in on 6 December.

The institutional set-up could now be fully completed. On the same day as the second round of the presidential election, provincial assemblies were elected, mostly[112] by direct suffrage. In addition to their importance at the provincial level,[113] they were also in charge of electing the members of the Senate, which they did on 19 January 2007. Among those elected were two of the former vice-presidents, Bemba and Yerodia. Out of a total of 108 Senators, Kabila's AMP obtained 55 seats against 20 for Bemba's UN.[114] On 27 January, the provincial assemblies elected the governors and vice-governors.[115] The presidential coalition captured eight provinces, while the MLC managed only to gain the governorship of Equateur province. During both these indirect elections (senators and governors), widespread corruption explains why Kabila's camp was victorious even in provinces where it scored poorly during the presidential and parliamentary polls. Indeed votes were bought by money, presents and promises,[116] a very bad omen for the future of democracy in the DRC and a potential source of violence.

[111] It seems that quite some pressure was brought to bear on Bemba by the CIAT, which reportedly threatened him with prosecutions before the International Criminal Court for alleged war crimes, should he derail the process. He was eventually arrested on 24 May 2008 in Belgium following a warrant issued under seal by the ICC, where he will be prosecuted on four counts of war crimes and two counts of crimes against humanity committed in the Central African Republic from 25 October 2002 to 15 March 2003.

[112] Among the 690 provincial assembly members, 632 were directly elected and 58 were co-opted in early January 2007 from among the customary chiefs.

[113] As the constitution provides for a strongly decentralised state, this importance is set to increase in the future.

[114] Nevertheless, on 11 May 2007, the UN candidate for the chair of the Senate beat the AMP candidate by six votes, showing that the majorities are shaky. Léon Kengo wa Dondo, who supported Bemba's bid for the presidency, is a former minister and prime minister under Mobutu.

[115] Due to a dispute over the nationality of some candidates, the gubernatorial elections were postponed in the two Kasai provinces.

[116] This fraud was made possible by the fact that the provincial assemblies only count a few dozen members, who can be individually approached and 'bought', unlike the many millions of voters during the direct elections.

In the meantime, a parliamentary majority was sought for the formation of the national government. As agreed when PALU decided to back Kabila during the second round, it was to obtain the post of prime minister. The veteran politician Antoine Gizenga[117] was offered the position. He sought to build a coalition along the lines that emerged toward the second round of the presidential poll, but the combination of the AMP (197 seats), PALU (34) and UDEMO (9) gave only 240 seats, eleven short of a majority in the Assembly. Other smaller parties and a number of independent MPs joined in, in exchange for all sorts of perks, and Gizenga claimed to have rallied a coalition of 322 seats, well above the majority of 251 needed.[118] In early February 2007, he announced a vast government of 60 ministers and vice-ministers. A total of fifteen parties were represented, with all of them, except the PPRD (23 portfolios), PALU (7) and Forces du Renouveau (5), having just one or two (vice-) ministers. The parties represented a total of 252 seats in the Assembly, a majority of just two. Questions immediately arose as to how stable this opportunistic, heterogeneous and fragmented power base would prove.

As stated earlier, this process was to a large extent externally induced and imposed on a number of crucial and reluctant domestic stakeholders. Indeed, donors seemed to want the elections to succeed more than many Congolese political leaders. As one Kinshasa based diplomat told Human Rights Watch in September 2005: 'We are pushing and shoving to get elections done, but we are behind on everything. Most members of this government are just not interested in elections'.[119] The international community funded the process to the tune of over €400 million, an amount which does not include the deployment of MONUC and EUFOR and their contributions in kind. It had to keep the main Congolese players constantly on a leash, exercising considerable pressure to prevent potential spoilers prevailing. This was a major performance few observers would have believed could happen just two years earlier, but it does raise the issue of the solidity of externally induced political transitions, a point to which I will return in the conclusion.

[117] 81 years old, he was deputy Prime Minister in Lumumba's ill-fated cabinet in 1960.
[118] There was a clear indication that the presidential coalition was heading towards a majority when Vital Kamerhe, a close associate of Kabila (cf. earlier text) was elected Speaker of the Assembly with an overwhelming majority of 388 out of 465 votes cast.
[119] Human Rights Watch, Elections in sight..., *op. cit.*, p. 17.

# Conclusion

According to Lemarchand, political, economic and social exclusion are the principal dimensions necessary for understanding the dynamics of domestic and interstate violence in the region. '[T]he central pattern that recurs time and again is one in which ethnic polarization paves the way for political exclusion, exclusion eventually leading to insurrection, insurrection to repression, and repression to massive flows of refugees and internally displaced persons, which in turn become the vectors of further instability'.[1] He adds that '[w]here ethnic fault lines cut across national boundaries, conflict tends to spill over from one national arena to the next'.[2] This bottomline analysis perfectly captures the dynamics at play in the Great Lakes region in the 1990s. The exclusion of the Rwandan Tutsi after 1959 led to invasion by the RPF, which in turn led to anti-Tutsi violence and eventually genocide. After the RPF's victory, scores of Hutu left for Zaire, from where they attempted to recapture power. Transboundary ethnic alliances exacerbated the conflict, which escalated to become a regional war that ignored national borders. The current exclusion of Hutu (and indeed many Tutsi) in Rwanda may well cause a similar scenario in the years to come. The relative regional peace is probably a lull in the Rwandan civil war, but not its end.

In fact, Lemarchand explains one of the paradoxes appearing in this book, namely that the smallest country in the region has played such a decisive role. Without the lead taken by Rwanda, the 'AFDL rebellion'

---

[1] R. Lemarchand, *The Dynamics of Violence in Central Africa*, Philadelphia, University of Pennsylvania Press, 2009, p. 31.
[2] *Idem*, p. 41.

would not have taken place, and Kabila would not have replaced Mobutu. True, Uganda and Burundi were faced with similar security concerns, but they were less vital, and these countries would in all likelihood have limited their military action against the threats coming from Zaire to cross-border strikes. Only a few months into the conflict, Angola joined the fray, to carry the war to its ultimate conclusion – regime change in Kinshasa. Again in 1998, while Uganda was also unhappy with developments in the DRC, it was Rwanda that took the initiative to launch a new 'rebellion', with Uganda following suit. There are two main reasons for this Rwandan prominence. First, for Kigali, the stakes were very high. In 1996, the security threat emanating from the refugee camps across the border was acute, and there were solid indications that it would only increase. While there was no immediate threat in 1998, relations with the Kabila regime had become overtly hostile, and the risk of further deterioration and the subsequent destabilisation of Rwanda was real. In addition, Rwanda learned in 1996–7 that waging war in Congo was cheap, and even profitable. For a poor country with an elite that needed to maintain a lavish lifestyle, the exploitation of Congolese resources became an increasingly essential motivation. Second, its entire background and experience made the Rwandan regime rely on a military mode of managing political situations and spaces. The RPF leadership had gone from war to war and from one military victory to the next, ever since two of them joined Museveni's 'originals' in 1981. Similarly, its way of managing the Rwandan domestic scene was, and still is, based on physical control. Rwanda thus developed a formidable intelligence, security and military apparatus, which became the most effective in the region, and which went far beyond its defence needs. Its status as a regional superpower was attained on the basis of military might.[3]

This development was, at least in part, made possible by the tolerance shown by the international community. Indeed, the Rwandan regime constantly tested the limits of that tolerance, and realised there were none. So, it crossed one Rubicon after the other. A few examples may serve to illustrate this. Just six months after the RPF took power, at a moment when worrying signs were visible that the regime was sliding into authoritarianism and that its human rights record was dismal, a donor roundtable was held in Geneva in January 1995, during which almost US$600

---

[3] This is a major break with the past. Before 1990, the Rwandan army was only 6000–7000 strong, and it never operated outside of its borders. Today, it is seen as a threat by all its neighbours.

million were pledged. The failure to tie the pledges to improvements in a rapidly deteriorating situation convinced the regime that it could act without restraint, and that impunity was assured. The RPF was squarely supported by the 'friends of the New Rwanda', in particular the United States, the United Kingdom and the Netherlands. These countries were not burdened by much knowledge of Rwanda and the region, and, driven by an acute guilt syndrome after the genocide, they reasoned in terms of 'good guys' and 'bad guys', the RPF naturally being the 'good guys'. When the International Criminal Tribunal for Rwanda started operating, it soon became clear that the losers were being prosecuted, but that the victorious RPF/RPA was left alone, while it too had committed crimes against humanity and war crimes that fell squarely within the Tribunal's mandate. This reinforced the sense of impunity: had the threat of prosecution existed, the RPA would probably have acted with more restraint in the DRC. During the Congo wars, international criticism of Rwanda was muted, to say the least, and most international players adhered to the Rwandan discourse. Even after the war, when the DRC engaged in a tortuous and fragile transition, Rwandan attempts to derail the process only met with discreet representations. I have discussed the role the 'genocide credit' and its astute exploitation by the Rwandan regime played in this international tolerance. Van Leeuwen has observed that the RPF was successful in having its 'narrative of difference' accepted, although this discourse was based on ambiguous and doubtful assumptions.[4] Storey noted 'a strong sense of history repeating itself here: the (World) Bank is once again displaying a willingness to lend strong support to Rwandan state power, and the consequences for ordinary people – in Rwanda itself and in the DRC – may once more be bleak'.[5]

Further aggravating the destabilising impact of the Rwanda conflict, a combination of factors came into play, some intrinsic to the Congo, others emanating from Uganda, Burundi and Angola. As with all historical episodes, this combination of factors occurred in a unique and contingent environment, and explains the events, their sequence and their outcome. On the Zairean/Congolese domestic side, apart from the collapse of the state I have discussed extensively, the following elements have played their

---

[4] M. Van Leeuwen, 'Rwanda's *Imidugudu* programme and earlier experiences with villagisation and resettlement in East Africa', *Journal of Modern African Studies*, 2001, 623–624.

[5] A. Storey, 'Structural adjustment, state power and the genocide: the World Bank and Rwanda', *Review of African Political Economy*, 2001, 381.

role. The profound stalemate the 'democratisation' process had been in since 1990 led to increasing political apathy and eventually to a total lack of governance. Besides the impact this had on Zaire as a whole, it also caused the political class in Kinshasa to ignore the dangerous situation, which was developing in the east. Not only was that situation not anticipated, but when it exploded, the regime was unable to manage it. At least in part as a result of the imposition on Zaire of the neo-liberal paradigm, the Mobutu system had imploded: the pyramidal clientship structure on which it rested became fundamentally eroded and the little that remained of the army and security apparatus disappeared. The informalisation of the state, the armed forces and public service delivery was near complete. Political, administrative and economic links between the centre and the peripheries, and between the peripheries themselves, had become fictitious. In one of these peripheries, the Kivu provinces, the status of the 'populations of doubtful nationality', a code for the Banyarwanda, resurfaced acutely.

These problems combined with a regional factor, namely the territorial extension of neighbours' civil wars. There were spillovers from Angola, Uganda and Burundi, but the decisive factor occurred in mid-1994, when over a million Rwandan refugees settled in Zaire. They created an 'insurgent Rwanda' just across the border, and thus not only threatened the security of the new regime in power in Kigali, but also disturbed an already fragile ethnic situation in the Kivus. This, again combined with the reality of a virtual state in Zaire, both allowed and forced Rwanda to intervene. The attack by Rwanda, Uganda and Burundi was further reinforced by larger geopolitical interests and the ambitions of regional powers. Angola, in particular, would probably not have taken the initiative itself, but saw the war in the east as an opportunity to deal once and for all with Mobutu and his cronies who supported UNITA. While classical realism allows us to understand the relation between domestic situations and the foreign policy decisions of neighbouring states, Clark notes that the structural variety of realism shows that post-cold war changes in the international system considerably impacted on these policies. Indeed, 'the withdrawal of the Soviet Union and the reduction of American commitments in the region seems to have stimulated interstate confrontations and intervention'.[6]

After the Cold War, a number of international actors, the United States in particular, were happy to see Mobutu, whom they had supported in

---

[6] J.F. Clark, 'Introduction ...', *op. cit.*, p. 6.

the past, leave the scene, particularly as his removal was brought about through an operation mounted by their friends in the region, Rwanda and Uganda. They did not know Kabila, they ignored or underestimated subsequent regional dynamics, and they did not realise that they had opened a can of worms. The price has been immense, as it was the beginning of a decade of violent destabilisation and immense human suffering. Faced with the successive wars, the international community was unable to weigh effectively on events. Local and regional actors had the advantage of being on the ground, without being hindered by considerations of international (humanitarian) law, ethics or respect for human rights. As African forces set the agenda, the way in which the Central African wars unfolded was a new illustration of the end of the neo-colonial system. Besides governments and national armies, these players were nonstate entities of a very diverse nature. Among them were entrepreneurs of insecurity who engaged in rational cost-benefit analyses, and who realised that war, instability and the absence of state offer more opportunities than state reconstruction, stability and peace. Nevertheless, the relative absence and the impotence of the international community remain striking, hardly ten years after the hopes raised by the ambition to promote a 'new international order', and to engage in policies of conditionality, preventive diplomacy, and conflict prevention and management.

Of course, these internal and external factors were not all intrinsically linked, but they merged in a particular historical conjuncture, thus creating the conditions for war and determining its outcome. Contrary to conspiracy theories nurtured by many Congolese, there was no master plan, devised in Washington or elsewhere. Rather, opportunities presented themselves and were seized by the actors. This happened in an incremental fashion: thus, for instance, the RPA did not know in 1990 or even in 1994 that it would attack Zaire in 1996, nor did it know in 1996 that it would attack again in 1998, and start exploiting Congolese resources. It is even very likely that, in the autumn of 1996, Rwanda did not intend to overthrow the Mobutu regime and put Kabila in power; this resolve only came progressively, after Angola joined the war. Furthermore, to take the example of a 'great conspirator', the United States did not anticipate nor did they intend that their support for the 'AFDL rebellion' was to result in the profound destabilisation of the whole region, and to war between their allies.

In a context of informal/criminal regional integration, exchanges across largely theoretical borders facilitated links with the global economy and meant that states could be largely ignored. In reality, the phenomena

I have discussed – 'destatisation', 'deterritorialisation', criminalisation – have also been the translation of the disappearance of the post- or neo-colonial order, which provided state structures and spaces inherited from the colonial period, the protection offered by former colonial powers in exchange for a 'benevolent' trusteeship, the principle (though not always the practice) of the predominance of the public over the private, a structured economic exploitation by large established businesses. In the DRC, like elsewhere in Africa, these characteristics tend to disappear under the combined effect of globalisation and the activities of local, regional and international nonstate actors for whom quick benefits made in enclaves are more relevant than questions of formal sovereignty.

The political transition in the DRC was to a large extent externally induced. Indeed, we have seen that many Congolese players were not interested in democracy, which they actually feared, as they stood to lose the position they had gained through the use of arms. What was achieved was intrinsically difficult, as it involved a transition coupled with a war and combined domestic and regional conflicts of interest. In a way, it is a miracle that it happened at all. Without the strong pressure of South Africa, which at one point took control of the process and effectively imposed a settlement, the Inter-Congolese Dialogue might well have failed to produce an outcome. Similarly, the path towards elections was laid out by the international community and again imposed on very reluctant domestic players: without the presence of CIAT and MONUC, and the promotion of the elections with massive funding and logistical support, as well as with promises of aid, the Congolese might not have made it to the polling stations in 2006. The DRC was put under effective international trusteeship. This is also the weakness of the process. Poorly owned by the Congolese political class, the new political dispensation remains artificial, and the first year after the transition did not give grounds for exaggerated optimism.[7]

And yet, reconstructing a polity, which can perform minimal state functions is an essential condition for both national development and regional stability. In light of the extent of state decay, the sheer size of the country, the degree of fragmentation, and indeed the nature of the political leadership and of the political culture more generally, this is a colossal task. Obviously, a collapsed state cannot be entirely reconstructed

---

[7] In a report published a year after the first round of the presidential elections, the ICG listed a daunting number of challenges facing the new regime: International Crisis Group, *Congo: Consolidating the Peace*, Kinshasa/Brussels, 5 July 2007.

overnight. The cost will be immense and the effort will take many years. Therefore, putting Humpty Dumpty together again will have to happen sequentially, starting with the main functions of sovereignty. First, the state must regain control over its territory and re-establish links with its population. Territorial control means physical control, together with the presence of an effective administration. Physical control requires the rebuilding of a truly national army and police force. We have seen that the Congolese military mirrored the failed state, and it continues to do so. The FARDC often behave like a militia and perpetuate the practices of their predecessors: desertion, violence against civilians, racketeering and plunder. They are a source of insecurity rather than of security. Realising that security sector reform was failing, Amnesty International warned that it is a precondition for peace and stability.[8] Physical control also requires overseeing borders, including effective customs and immigration services both at land/river crossings and at airports and airstrips. Beyond physical security, territorial control means creating an effective administration – a way of establishing a link between the state and its citizens, a link that is now virtually nonexistent, even in the capital city Kinshasa.

Second, the state must simultaneously recover its funding capacity. The DRC is often depicted as a 'geological scandal' and as a potentially rich country that has the means of funding its own development. This is true, but one does not buy much with 'potential'. Therefore, the fiscal capacity of the state must be rebuilt, with revenues collected and spent in a transparent, efficient and honest fashion, and resources (mines, forests, hydropower and agriculture) harnessed as public goods. This presupposes that the criminalisation and privatisation of the state and the economy come to an end, again a matter of state capacity. A vicious circle needs to be broken: while the 'de-privatisation' of natural resources will prove an essential element of state reconstruction, only a reconstructed state can garner these assets as public goods.

A third priority is legal security and the rule of law, essential not only for the protection of the Congolese people's fundamental rights and for the fight against impunity, but also because considerable domestic and international investments will be needed for Congo's reconstruction. However, venture capital will be attracted only if, for instance, contracts are honoured, and, when they are not, if contract parties can rely on a well-functioning, predictable and honest judicial system to offer relief. In

---

[8] Amnesty International, DRC: Stability threatened as country fails to reform army, London, 25 January 2007.

a similar vein, entrepreneurs will need a reliable judiciary in their dealings with the state, for example, in the areas of tenders, taxation and investment incentives.

While state capacity or lack thereof has been a recurrent theme in this book, a number of other lessons can be learned. One is that impunity and international tolerance of aggressive and criminal behaviour can only encourage the perpetrators, even if, as in the case of Rwanda, they are small, poor and extremely aid-dependent. They test the limits of that tolerance, and – when realising there are none – they cross one Rubicon after the other, eventually reaching a point of no-return. They must be reined in at an early stage. Second, local and regional engineers of violence are constantly engaged in a rational calculation of costs and benefits, knowing that war, instability and state decay are more profitable than peace, stability and state reconstruction. In these conditions, the only way to come to terms with the spoilers is to make war more expensive and peace more attractive. Third, lessons one and two can only be applied if the so-called international community is minimally united and coherent. The contrary has happened, and the consequences of division have been disastrous for millions of people in the Great Lakes region. And yet, international involvement can make a difference: the combination of MONUC, the largest peace-keeping operation anywhere in the world, irrespective of its shortcomings, and the imposition of a *de facto* trusteeship, in the form of CIAT, has allowed the political transition in the DRC to take place, even if the process was painful and the outcome remains uncertain. Fourth, the fact that this process was, to a large extent, externally induced and imposed on a reluctant domestic political class, raises the question of how far the residual legacy of the Mobutist state will continue to stand in the way of political stability. A fifth and final lesson concerns the regional linkages. We have seen how easily conflicts cut across borders and by the same token have profoundly perverse effects on neighbouring communities. Despite the rhetoric on 'integrated regional approaches', this fact has been insufficiently taken into account in international diplomacy: this is nowhere more dramatically illustrated than in the assumption that governed the thinking of the international community in trying to promote a peaceful transition in the DRC; by turning a blind eye to Rwanda's hegemonic claims in eastern Congo, the future stability of the region remains in doubt. Rwanda may once again, in the not too distant future, become the focal point of regional violence.

# Appendix 1

## Sources on the Killings of Rwandan Refugees in Early 1997

### 1. UN DOCUMENTS

- United Nations, Commission on Human Rights, Report on the Situation of Human Rights in Zaire, prepared by the Special Rapporteur, Mr. Roberto Garretón, 1996/77, 28 January 1997 (E/CN.4/1997/6).
- United Nations, Commission on Human Rights, Report on the mission carried out at the request of the High Commissioner for Human Rights between 25 and 29 March 1997 to the area occupied by rebels in eastern Zaire, 2 April 1997 (E/CN.4/1997/6/Add.2).
- United Nations, Economic and Social Council, Report of the joint mission charged with investigating allegations of massacres and other human rights violations occurring in eastern Zaire (now Democratic Republic of the Congo) since September 1996, 2 July 1997 (A/51/942).
- United Nations, Security Council, Report of the Investigative Team Charged with Investigating Serious Violations of Human Rights and International Humanitarian Law in the Democratic Republic of Congo, 29 June 1998 (S/1998/581).

### 2. DOCUMENTS BY INTERNATIONAL NGOS

- Amnesty International, Great Lakes: Amnesty International condemns massacre of around 500 refugees in Eastern Zaire, 26 November 1996.
- Amnesty International, Zaïre: Hidden from scrutiny: human rights abuses in eastern Zaire, 19 December 1996.
- Amnesty International, Great Lakes region: Refugee crisis far from over, 24 January 1997.

- Human Rights Watch, Attacked by all sides. Civilians and the war in eastern Zaire, 20 March 1997.
- Human Rights Watch, Zaire. Transition, war and human rights, April 1997.
- Amnesty International, Amnesty International condemns abuses against Rwandese refugees, 30 April 1997.
- Human Rights Watch, Save Rwandan refugees, 30 April 1997.
- Médecins sans frontières, Refugee numbers analysis, 9 May 1997.
- Médecins sans frontières, Forced flight: A brutal strategy of elimination in eastern Zaire, 16 May 1997.
- US Committee for Refugees, Site visit to Eastern Congo/Zaire: Analysis of humanitarian and political issues, 10 June 1997.
- Physicians for Human Rights, Investigations in Eastern Congo and Western Rwanda, 16 July 1997.
- Human Rights Watch, Democratic Republic of The Congo. What Kabila is hiding. Civilian killing and impunity in Congo, October 1997.
- Amnesty International, Democratic Republic of Congo. Deadly alliances in Congolese forests, 3 December 1997.
- International Non-Governmental Commission of Inquiry into the Massive Violation of Human Rights Committed in the Democratic Republic of Congo (former Zaire) 1996–1997, Report Prepared by the International Center for Human Rights and Democratic Development and the Association africaine pour la défense des droits de l'homme en République démocratique du Congo, June 1998.

### 3. BOOKS

- C. Braeckman, *L'enjeu congolais. L'Afrique centrale après Mobutu*, Paris, Fayard, 1999.
- N. Eltringham, *Accounting for Horror: Post-Genocide Debates in Rwanda*, London, Pluto Press, 2004.
- H. French, *A Continent for the Taking. The Tragedy and Hope of Africa*, New York, Alfred A. Knopf, 2004.
- P. Mpayimana, *Réfugiés rwandais entre marteau et enclume*, Paris, L'Harmattan, 2004.
- G. Musabyimana, *L'APR et les réfugiés rwandais au Zaïre 1996–1997*, Paris, L'Harmattan, 2004.
- M. Niwese, *Le peuple rwandais un pied dans la tombe. Récit d'un réfugié étudiant*, Paris, L'Harmattan, 2001.

- L. Ntisoni, *J'ai traversé des fleuves de sang*, Paris, L'Harmattan, 2008.
- B. Rugumaho, *L'hécatombe des réfugiés rwandais dans l'ex-Zaïre*, Paris, L'Harmattan, 2004.
- B. Umutesi, *Surviving the Slaughter. The Ordeal of a Rwandan Refugee in Zaire*, Madison, WI, University of Wisconsin Press, 2004.

## 4. DOCUMENTS BY LOCAL NGOS

- Centre de lutte contre l'impunité et l'injustice au Rwanda, Communiqué n° 7/96. Massacres de réfugiés rwandais et burundais dans les camps du Sud-Kivu au Zaïre, 8 November 1996.
- AZADHO, Nord-Kivu: Existence de charniers et de fosses communes, 1 March 1997.
- Un animateur d'une association des droits de l'homme au Kivu, La violation des droits de l'homme dans le territoire contrôlé par l'AFDL, May 1997.

## 5. TESTIMONIES BY LOCAL PEOPLE OR CONCERNED GROUPS

- Génocide dans le territoire conquis par Monsieur Laurent-Désiré Kabila, Nairobi, 21 February 1997.
- Prêtres rwandais en diaspora, Cri d'alarme, Nairobi, 28 February 1997.
- Prêtres rwandais en diaspora, Second cri d'alarme, Nairobi, 6 March 1997.
- Témoignage sur le calvaire des réfugiés rwandais à l'Est du Zaïre, Kinshasa, 26 April 1997.
- Massacres perpétrés par Monsieur Laurent Désiré Kabila et ses rebelles de l'AFDL au Nord-Kivu, Nairobi, 6 May 1997.
- Témoignage des femmes rescapées de Tingi-Tingi, Nairobi, 8 May 1997.
- Assumani Muhima, Chronique: traces d'un génocide au Zaïre-Est, Bukavu, 10 May 1997.
- Vue rétrospective sur l'attaque contre les réfugiés rwandais à l'Est du Zaïre: Qui sont réellement ces assaillants?, s.l., 20 May 1997.
- Témoignage sur le calvaire des réfugiés rwandais, Bangui, 9 October 1997.
- Abbé Jean, Neuf mois de tragédie à l'Est du Zaïre. Mon journal, Nairobi, 14 October 1997.

## 6. OTHER TESTIMONIES

- Goma-Bukavu: Témoignage direct, January 1997, 10 February 1997, reprinted in CMI Informissi, February 1997, n° 3.
- Fax sur Kazindu, Bukavu, April 1997 (*Rwandanet*, 13 May 1997).
- H. Van Dyck, Rapport sur les violations des droits de l'homme dans le Sud-Equateur, 29 September 1997.

## 7. INVESTIGATIVE JOURNALISM

- B. Mseteka, 'Rwandan refugees massacred by Zairean rebels', Reuters, Nairobi, 23 April 1997.
- N.D. Kristof, 'Along a Jungle Road in Zaire, Three Wars Mesh', *New York Times*, 26 April 1997.
- 'La mort et la desolation planent sur Biaro', AFP, Biaro, 28 April 1997.
- 'Zaïre-réfugiés: Les rebelles tentent de repousser les réfugiés hutu rwandais', AFP, Biaro, 29 April 1997.
- D. Orr, 'Aid workers catalogue Zaire rebel "barbarities"', *The Times* (London), 30 April 1997.
- 'Zaïre: les agences humanitaires appellent le conseil de sécurité à l'aide', AFP, Geneva, 6 May 1997.
- J. Moore, 'Kabila's Soldier Shows Mass Graves', AP, Kisangani, 22 May 1997.
- D.G. McNeil, 'Reports Point to Mass Killings of Refugees in Congo', *The New York Times*, 28 May 1997.
- J. Pomfret, 'Killing Spree Blamed on Troops of New Congo Leaders', *The Washington Post*, 8 June 1997.
- J. Pomfret, 'Massacres Became a Weapon in Congo's Civil War', *The Washington Post*, 11 June 1997.
- J. Pomfret, 'Congo Leader Bars Helping U.N. Probers', *The Washington Post*, 19 June 1997.
- D. Cahn, 'Witnesses Detail Congo Killings', AP, Shabunda, 28 June 1997.
- 'What happened to Hutu refugees in Congo?', AP, Kisangani, 2 July 1997.
- C. McGreal, 'Truth Buried in Congo's Killing Fields', *Mail and Guardian* (Johannesburg), 21 July 1997.

# Appendix 2

## Chronology

### 1993

- 21 October. *Coup d'état* in Burundi: President Ndadaye killed, beginning of civil war.

### 1994

- April–July. Resumption of the civil war in Rwanda; genocide against the Tutsi by extremist Hutu, crimes against humanity and war crimes by RPF; RPF seizes power; 2 million Hutu, including defeated army and militia, flee to neighbouring countries, Zaire in particular.
- Fall. First signs of authoritarian rule, human rights abuse and 'Tutsification' in Rwanda.

### 1995

- Fall. Large-scale violence in North Kivu: Hutu vs. Hunde and Tutsi; Hunde vs. Tutsi and Hutu.
- Hit-and-run operations by Rwandan Hutu refugees, operating from Zaire, against targets in Rwanda.

### 1996

- June–July. Banyamulenge in South Kivu increasingly victimised and their organisation, Milima, banned.
- 25 July. *Coup d'état* returns Major Buyoya to power in Burundi.

- September. Start of the 'Banyamulenge rebellion' supported by Rwanda.
- October. Creation in Kigali of the AFDL, with Laurent-Désiré Kabila as its spokesman; U.S. support for the 'rebellion'; France sides with Kinshasa.
- October. Rwandan refugee camps attacked in North and South Kivu. Uganda joins the invasion of Zaire.
- 18 October. Fall of Uvira.
- 28 October. Fall of Bukavu.
- 31 October. Fall of Goma.
- 4–5 November. Nairobi-I regional summit on the Zairean crisis.
- November. Buffer zone established along Rwandan and Burundian borders. Hundreds of thousands of Rwandan refugees 'repatriated', while hundreds of thousands of others flee westwards.
- November–December. Aborted attempts at launching an international 'military-humanitarian' intervention to protect the Rwandan refugees.
- 16–17 December. Nairobi-II regional summit.
- 17 December. Mobutu returns to Kinshasa from France, where he was undergoing medical treatment.
- 18 December. General Mahele appointed chief of staff of the FAZ.
- 25 December. Fall of Bunia.

## 1997

- 8 January. Mobutu returns to France for medical checks.
- 22 January. Sahnoun appointed Special Representative of Kofi Annan.
- February. Angola joins the anti-Mobutu coalition.
- 18 February. UNSC adopts Resolution 1079, outlining a five-point peace plan.
- 28 February. Fall of Kindu.
- 15 March. Fall of Kisangani.
- 19 March. Nairobi-III regional summit.
- 21 March. Mobutu returns to Kinshasa
- Spring. Massive slaughter by the RPA of Rwandan refugees in Zaire. Later stated by a UN inquiry to have involved war crimes and crimes against humanity, and possibly genocide.
- 2 April. Tshisekedi appointed prime minister.
- 4 April. Fall of Mbuji-Mayi.

- 9 April. Fall of Lubumbashi. Tshisekedi sacked as prime minister and replaced by General Likulia.
- 29 April. Fall of Kikwit.
- 4 May. Meeting Mobutu-Kabila on board SAS Outeniqua in the port of Pointe-Noire.
- 17 May. Fall of Kinshasa.
- 27 May. Constitutional law-decree gives all powers to the President.
- 29 May. Kabila sworn in as president.
- Fall. Increased fighting in northwestern Rwanda. Thousands of civilians killed by the RPA.
- 1 December. Rwandan Lt. Col. James Kabarebe appointed interim chief of staff of the FAC.
- 11 December. Hundreds of Congolese Tutsi refugees killed in Mudende camp (Rwanda), probably by the RPA.
- 31 December. Hundreds of civilians killed during fighting near Bujumbura airport.

## 1998

- 15 February. Kagame replaces Kanyarengwe as chairman of RPF.
- February. Mutiny of Banyamulenge soldiers in Bukavu.
- 17 May. Rwanda and Uganda refuse to attend a conference on regional security, organised in Kinshasa to mark the first anniversary of the AFDL's victory.
- 26 July. 'Rwandan and other foreign military' ordered to leave the DRC.
- 2 August. Beginning of a new Congolese 'rebellion' masterminded by Rwanda. Goma, Bukavu and Uvira taken.
- 5 August. RPA raid on Kitona, defeated by Angolan intervention.
- 12 August. Creation of the RCD, with Ernest Wamba dia Wamba as chairman.
- 19 August. Deployment of Angolan, Zimbabwean and Namibian troops in support of Kinshasa regime authorised at SADC meeting in Harare.
- 23 August. Fall of Kisangani. SADC summit in Pretoria.
- 8 September. SADC summit in Victoria Falls.
- 13–14 September. SADC summit in Mauritius.
- 30 September. First Syrte summit under Libyan auspices.
- 12 October. Fall of Kindu.
- 26 October. Uganda admits having troops in the DRC.
- 6 November. Rwanda admits having troops in the DRC.
- November. Creation of MLC with Ugandan support.

## 1999

- 18 April. Second Syrte summit.
- 20 April. Launch of the CPP.
- May–June. Fighting between RPA and UPDF in Kisangani.
- 16 May. The RCD splits, as Wamba retreats to Kisangani and sets up the RCD-ML. Emile Ilunga becomes chairman of the RCD-Goma.
- 22 June. Ugandan General James Kazini creates the 'province' of Kibali-Ituri and appoints Adèle Lotsove as governor.
- 3 July. MLC headquarters installed in Gbadolite.
- 10 July. Signing of the Lusaka Accord.
- July. Beginning of mass violence in Ituri.
- August. Ten days of heavy fighting between the Rwandan and Ugandan armies in Kisangani. Wamba, forced to flee the city, settles in Bunia.
- October. Start of deployment of MONUC.
- Mid-December. Masire appointed as facilitator of the Inter-Congolese Dialogue.

## 2000

- Spring. In Rwanda, the Speaker of parliament, the prime minister and the president resign. Vice-President Kagame becomes president.
- 19 June. Offices of facilitator Masire in Kinshasa sealed.
- 28 August. Arusha Accord on Burundi signed.
- 3 November. Adolphe Onusumba replaces Ilunga as chairman of RDC-Goma.
- 19 October. Masire declared 'unacceptable' by DRC government.

## 2001

- 16 January. Assassination of Laurent-Désiré Kabila.
- 26 January. Joseph Kabila assumes office.
- January. Uganda forces the merger of the MLC and the RCD-ML to form the FLC.
- 6 March. Rwanda declared a 'hostile nation' by the Ugandan government.
- June–August. End of the FLC.
- 20–24 August. 'Pre-Dialogue' in Gaborone.
- November. Wamba removed and replaced by Mbusa Nyamwisi as chairman of RCD-ML.

### 2002

- 25 February. Launch of the Inter-Congolese Dialogue in Sun City.
- 17 April. 'Accord for the consensual management of the transition' signed between Kabila and Bemba.
- 30 July. Accord between the DRC and Rwanda signed in Pretoria.
- August. UPC takes Bunia with Ugandan support.
- 6 September. Accord between the DRC and Uganda signed in Luanda.
- September. Rwanda officially pulls out forces from the DRC.
- 17 December. Global and Inclusive Accord (AGI) signed in Pretoria.

### 2003

- 1 April. AGI formally endorsed in Sun City, during a ceremony presided by Masire.
- 6 May. UPDF complete withdrawal from Ituri.
- 26 May. Constitutional referendum in Rwanda.
- 16 July. Azarias Ruberwa becomes chairman of RCD-Goma.
- June. IEMF force deployed in Ituri, replaced by MONUC Ituri brigade in September.
- June–July. 1+4 presidency, transitional government and transitional parliament in place.
- August–September. Seriously flawed presidential and parliamentary elections in Rwanda. Kagame elected by 95% of the votes. RPF becomes *de facto* single party.

### 2004

- May. Renegade Tutsi officers Nkunda and Mutebutsi capture Bukavu.
- June. Independent Electoral Commission (CEI) put in place.
- 13 August. Almost 200 Banyamulenge killed by FNL rebels in Gatumba refugee camp (Burundi).
- 26 October. United States-brokered 'tripartite agreement' (DRC, Rwanda, Uganda) to deal with the threat of 'negative forces'. Parliament passes Nationality Act.

### 2005

- 28 February. Constitutional referendum in Burundi.
- 31 March. Rome agreement under the auspices of Sant'Egidio on voluntary repatriation of FDLR.

- 16 May. Constitution adopted by parliament.
- 14 June. Adoption of Referendum Act.
- June–August. Presidential, parliamentary and local elections in Burundi. The overall free and fair polls offer a decisive victory to the CNDD-FDD. Pierre Nkurunziza becomes President.
- 18–19 December. Referendum on the Constitution: 62% turnout, 84% yes votes.

## 2006

- 21 February. Adoption of Elections Act.
- 25 April. UN Security Council authorises the deployment of EUFOR, in order to secure the elections, together with MONUC.
- 30 July. First round of presidential elections: Kabila 44.81%, Bemba 20.03%, Gizenga 13.06%. Parliamentary elections: National Assembly: PPRD 111 seats, MLC 64, PALU 34, RCD-Goma 15.
- 20–22 August. After the official announcement of the results, three days of heavy fighting oppose Kabila and Bemba troops in Kinshasa.
- 29 October. Second round of the presidential elections. Kabila 58.05%, Bemba 41.95%. Elections for provincial assemblies.
- 27 November. Supreme Court rules on challenge of the results by Bemba. Kabila declared the winner. After violence by Bemba supporters, Bemba accepts the outcome.
- 6 December. Kabila sworn in as president.

## 2007

- 19 January. Indirect election of Senate.
- 27 January. Election of provincial governors and vice-governors.
- 5 February. Formation of government by Prime Minister Antoine Gizenga.

# Appendix 3

## List of Abbreviations

| | |
|---|---|
| ACL-PT | Assemblée constituante et législative-Parlement de transition (DRC) |
| ACODRI | Action communautaire pour le développement rural intégré (DRC) |
| ADF | Allied Democratic Forces (Uganda) |
| ADL | Association rwandaise pour la défense des droits de la personne et des libertés publiques |
| ADP | Alliance démocratique des peuples (DRC) |
| AFDL | Alliance des forces pour la libération du Congo–Zaïre (DRC) |
| AFP | Agence France-Presse |
| AGI | Accord global et inclusif (DRC) |
| ALC | Armée de libération du Congo |
| ALIR | Armée pour la libération du Rwanda |
| AMP | Alliance de la majorité présidentielle (DRC) |
| ANACOZA | All-North America Conference on Zaïre |
| ANC | Armée nationale congolaise |
| AP | Associated Press |
| APC | Armoured personnel carrier |
| APC | Armée populaire congolaise |
| ARD | Alliance pour la résistance démocratique (DRC) |
| ASADHO | Association africaine de défense des droits de l'homme (DRC) |
| ASD | Alliance pour la sauvegarde du dialogue intercongolais (DRC) |
| AU | African Union |

| | |
|---|---|
| AZADHO | Association zaïroise des droits de l'homme |
| AZAP | Agence zaïroise de presse |
| BBC | British Broadcasting Corporation |
| BERCI | Bureau d'études, de recherche et de consulting international (DRC) |
| CAR | Central African Republic |
| CCOAIB | Comité de concertation des organisations d'appui aux initiatives de base (Rwanda) |
| CEI | Commission électorale indépendante (DRC) |
| CEINUB | Commission d'enquête des Nations unies pour le Burundi |
| CIA | Central Intelligence Agency (United States) |
| CIAT | Comité international d'accompagnement de la transition (DRC) |
| CLADHO | Coordination des ligues et associations de défense des droits de l'homme (Rwanda) |
| CRLK | Conseil de résistance et de libération du Kivu (DRC) |
| CNDD | Conseil national pour la défense de la démocratie (Burundi) |
| CNDD-FDD | Conseil national pour la défense de la démocratie-Forces pour la défense de la démocratie (Burundi) |
| CNDP | Congrès national pour la défense du people (DRC) |
| CNE | Commission nationale des élections (DRC) |
| CNL | Conseil national de libération (DRC) |
| CNN | Cable News Network |
| CNRD | Conseil national de résistance pour la démocratie (DRC) |
| CNS | Conférence nationale souveraine (RDC) |
| CPP | Comités du pouvoir populaire (RDC) |
| CRAP | Commandos de recherche et d'action en profondeur (France) |
| CRONGD | Conseil régional des organisations non-gouvernementales de développement (DRC) |
| CSR | Conseil suprême de la révolution (DRC) |
| DAS | Détachement d'assistance à la sécurité (Belgium) |
| DDRRR | Disarmament, Demobilisation, Repatriation, Resettlement and Reintegration |
| DEMIAP | Détection militaire des actions anti-patrie (DRC) |
| DIA | Defence Intelligence Agency (United States) |
| DIC | Dialogue inter-congolais |

| | |
|---|---|
| DMI | Department of Military Intelligence (Rwanda) |
| DPA | Deutsche Presse-Agentur |
| DRC | Democratic Republic of Congo |
| DSP | Division spéciale présidentielle (DRC) |
| DST | Direction de la surveillance du territoire (France) |
| EO | Executive Outcomes (South Africa) |
| ESO | External Security Organization (Rwanda) |
| EU | European Union |
| EUFOR | European Union Force |
| FAA | Forças Armadas Angolanas |
| FAC | Forces armées congolaises |
| FAP | Forces armées populaires (DRC) |
| FAPC | Forces armées du peuple congolais |
| FAR | Forces armées rwandaises |
| FARDC | Forces armées de la République démocratique du Congo |
| FAZ | Forces armées zaïroises |
| FCD | Forces de changement démocratique (Burundi) |
| FDD | Forces pour la défense de la démocratie (Burundi) |
| FDLR | Forces démocratiques pour la liberation du Rwanda |
| FEC | Fédération des entreprises du Congo |
| FLC | Front de libération du Congo |
| FLEC | Front de libération de l'est du Congo |
| FLNC | Front pour la libération nationale du Congo |
| FLOT | Front de libération contre l'occupation tutsi (RDC) |
| FNL | Forces nationales de libération (Burundi) |
| FONUS | Forces novatrices pour l'union et la solidarité (RDC) |
| FP | Front patriotique (RDC) |
| FPC | Forces politiques du conclave (RDC) |
| FRAK | Forces de résistance armée du Kivu (RDC) |
| FRD | Forces de résistance pour la démocratie (Rwanda) |
| FRF | Forces républicaines et fédéralistes (RDC) |
| FRODEBU | Front pour la démocratie au Burundi |
| FROLINA | Front pour la libération nationale (Burundi) |
| GSPR | Groupe de sécurité de la présidence de la République (France) |
| GSSP | Groupe spécial de sécurité présidentielle (DRC) |
| HCR | High Commission for Refugees (UN) |
| HCR-PT | Haut conseil de la République-Parlement de transition (DRC) |

| | |
|---|---|
| HRFOR | Human Rights Field Operation for Rwanda (UN) |
| ICC | International Criminal Court |
| ICD | Inter-Congolese Dialogue |
| ICJ | International Court of Justice |
| ICRC | International Committee of the Red Cross |
| ICTR | International Criminal Tribunal for Rwanda |
| IEMF | Interim Emergency Multinational Force (DRC) |
| IMET | International Military Education and Training (United States) |
| IPC | Ituri Pacification Commission (DRC) |
| IRC | International Rescue Committee (United States) |
| ISP | Institut supérieur pédagogique (DRC) |
| JMC | Joint Military Commission (DRC) |
| MDM | Médecins du monde |
| MDR | Mouvement démocratique républicain (Rwanda) |
| MIBA | Minière de Bakwanga (DRC) |
| MLC | Mouvement de libération du Congo |
| MNC | Mouvement national congolais |
| MNF | Multinational Force (DRC) |
| MNSD | Mouvement national pour la sauvegarde de la démocratie (DRC) |
| MONUC | Mission de l'Organisation des Nations-Unies au Congo |
| MPR | Mouvement populaire de la révolution (DRC) |
| MPRI | Military Professional Resources Inc. (United States) |
| MRLZ | Mouvement révolutionnaire pour la libération du Zaïre |
| MSF | Médecins sans frontières |
| NCN | New Congo Network |
| NGO | Non Governmental Organisation |
| NOER | Nouvelle espérance pour le Rwanda |
| NRA | National Resistance Army (Uganda) |
| NRM | National Resistance Movement (Uganda) |
| OAU | Organisation of African Unity |
| ORINFOR | Office rwandais d'information |
| PALIPEHUTU | Parti pour la libération du peuple hutu (Burundi) |
| PALU | Parti lumumbiste unifié (DRC) |
| PARENA | Parti pour le redressement national (Burundi) |
| PDSC | Parti démocrate et social-chrétien (DRC) |
| PIR | Police d'intervention rapide (DRC) |
| PL | Parti libéral (Burundi) |
| PLC | Parti de la libération congolais |

| | |
|---|---|
| PP | Parti du peuple (Burundi) |
| PPRD | Parti populaire pour la reconstruction et le développement (DRC) |
| PRA | People's Redemption Army (Uganda) |
| PRP | Parti pour la réconciliation du peuple (Burundi) |
| PRP | Parti de la révolution populaire (RDC) |
| PUSIC | Parti de l'unité et de la sauvegarde de l'intégrité du Congo |
| RADDES | Ralliement pour la démocratie et le développement économique et social (Burundi) |
| RCD | Rassemblement congolais pour la démocratie |
| RCD-ML | Rassemblement congolais pour la démocratie-Mouvement de libération |
| RDF | Rwanda Defence Forces |
| RDP | Régiment de dragons parachutistes (France) |
| RDR | Rassemblement pour la démocratie et le retour des réfugiés (Rwanda) |
| RFI | Radio France internationale |
| RPA | Rwanda Patriotic Army |
| RPB | Rassemblement du peuple burundais |
| RPF | Rwanda Patriotic Front |
| RSF | Reporters sans frontières |
| RTBF | Radio-télévision belge francophone |
| RTLM | Radio-télévision des milles collines (Rwanda) |
| RTNC | Radio-télévision nationale congolaise |
| SADC | Southern African Development Community |
| SAKIMA | Société aurifère du Kivu et du Maniéma (DRC) |
| SARM | Service d'action et de renseignement militaire (DRC) |
| SOJEDEM | Solidarité jeunesse pour la défense des droits des minorités (Burundi) |
| SPLA | Sudan People's Liberation Army |
| UDEMO | Union des démocrates mobutistes (DRC) |
| UDI | Union des démocrates indépendants (DRC) |
| UDPS | Union pour la démocratie et le progrès social (DRC) |
| UFERI | Union des fédéralistes et des républicains indépendants (DRC) |
| UFLD | Union des forces vives pour la libération et la démocratie (DRC) |
| UN | United Nations |
| UN | Union pour la Nation (DRC) |

| UNADEC | Union nationale des démocrates chrétiens (DRC) |
|---|---|
| UNICOI | UN Commission of Inquiry (Rwanda) |
| UNITA | União Nacional para a Independência Total de Angola |
| UPC | Union des Patriotes Congolais |
| UPDF | Uganda People's Defence Forces |
| UPI | United Press International |
| UPRONA | Union pour le progrès national (Burundi) |
| URD | Union pour la République et la démocratie (RDC) |
| USAF | U.S. Air Force |
| USAID | U.S. Agency for International Development |
| USCR | U.S. Committee for Refugees |
| USOR(AL) | Union sacrée de l'opposition radicale (et alliés) (DRC) |
| VLD | Vlaamse Liberalen en Democraten (Belgium) |
| VOA | Voice of America |
| WFP | World Food Program |
| ZANU-PF | Zimbabwe African National Union-Patriotic Front |
| ZDI | Zimbabwe Defence Industries |

# References

Africa Initiative Programme, Ituri Watch, Kinshasa, April 2005.

African Rights, A Welcome Expression of Intent. The Nairobi Communiqué and the ex-FAR/Interahamwe, Kigali, December 2007.

AIP, APFO, CSVR, FEWER, Ituri. Stakes, actors, dynamics, September 2003.

Amnesty International, Zaïre: Amnesty International condemns human rights violations against Tutsi, 20 September 1996.

Amnesty International, Great Lakes: Amnesty International condemns massacre of around 500 refugees in Eastern Zaire, 26 November 1996.

Amnesty International, Zaire: Hidden from scrutiny: human rights abuses in eastern Zaire, 19 December 1996.

Amnesty International, Great Lakes Region: Refugee crisis far from over, 24 January 1997.

Amnesty International, Rwanda: Amnesty delegates back from Rwanda report new wave of human rights abuses, 19 February 1997.

Amnesty International, Amnesty International condemns abuses against Rwandese Refugees, 30 April 1997.

Amnesty International, Burundi: Ethnic 'regroupment' takes place in the context of massacres, 15 July 1997.

Amnesty International, South Africa ignores grave human rights violations in Rwanda by resuming sales of military equipment, 25 July 1997.

Amnesty International, Burundi: Government carries out political executions after grossly unfair trials, 1 August 1997.

Amnesty International, Rwanda. Ending the silence, 25 September 1997.

Amnesty International, Democratic Republic of Congo. Deadly alliances in Congolese forests, 3 December 1997.

Amnesty International, Rwanda. Civilians trapped in armed conflict. 'The dead can no longer be counted', 19 December 1997.

Amnesty International, DRC. Democratic liberties denied, February 1998.

Amnesty International, Rwanda: selon les délégués d'Amnesty International, les 'disparitions' atteignent un taux alarmant, 12 March 1998.

Amnesty International, Democratic Republic of Congo. Rwandese-controlled East: Devastating toll, 19 June 2001.

Amnesty International, Democratic Republic of Congo: Arming the east, July 2005.

Amnesty International, DRC: Stability threatened as country fails to reform army, 25 January 2007.

Asadho, Rapport de l'Asadho sur le conflit inter-ethnique Hema-Lendu en territoire de Djugu dans la Province Orientale, Kinshasa, 7 December 1999.

Autesserre, S., Local Violence, International Indifference? Post-conflict 'settlement' in the Eastern D.R. Congo (2003–2005), New York University, Ph.D. Thesis, September 2006.

Avocats sans frontières, Projet 'Justice pour tous au Rwanda'. Rapport annuel 1997, Brussels, 1998.

Azadho, Nord-Kivu: Etat d'urgence, Kinshasa, April 1996.

Nord-Kivu: Existence de charniers et de fosses communes, Kinshasa, 1 March 1997.

Appel urgent n° 003/97. SOS au Congo-Zaïre: les espaces démocratiques menacés, Kinshasa, 10 June 1997.

Droits de l'Homme au Nord-Kivu. Une année d'administration AFDL: plus ça change, plus c'est la même chose, Kinshasa, November 1997.

Nord-Kivu: les massacres continuent au nom de la guerre contre les May–May, Kinshasa, 2 February 1998.

Barnes, W., 'Kivu: l'enlisement dans la violence', *Politique Africaine*, 73, March 1999, 123–136.

Barnett, M.N., 'The UN Security Council, Indifference, and Genocide in Rwanda', *Cultural Anthropology*, 1997, 551–578.

Barouski, D., Laurent Nkundabatware, his Rwandan Allies, and the ex-ANC Mutiny: Chronic Barriers to Lasting Peace in the Democratic Republic of the Congo, electronic document, 13 February 2007 (www.Zmag.org/racewatch/LKandexANC.pdf).

Bayart, J.F., 'La guerre en Afrique: dépérissement ou formation de l'Etat?', *Esprit*, 1998, 55–73.

Berghezan, G., 'Une guerre cosmopolite', in: *Kabila prend le pouvoir*, Brussels, GRIP-Editions Complexe, 1998, pp. 94–97.

Bijard, L., 'Zaïre. La faim fera le travail ...', *Le Nouvel Observateur*, 14–20 November 1996.

Block, R., 'Lost in Africa: How U.S. Landed On Sidelines In Zaire', *The Wall Street Journal*, 21 April 1997.

Bouvier, P., *Le dialogue intercongolais. Anatomie d'une négociation à la lisière du chaos*, Brussels-Paris, Institut Africain-L'Harmattan, Cahiers Africains, No. 63–64, 2004.

Boyle, S., 'Rebels repel Zaire counter-offensive', *Jane's Intelligence Review*, 1 April 1997.

'The White Legion: Mercenaries in Zaire', *Jane's Intelligence Review*, 1 June 1997.

Bradol, J.-H., Guibert, A., 'Le temps des assassins et l'espace humanitaire, Rwanda, Kivu, 1994–1997', *Hérodote*, 86–87, 1997, 116–149.

Braeckman, C., 'Zaïre: la fin d'une prise d'otages', *Le Soir*, 16–17 November 1996.

'Zaïre: récit d'une prise de pouvoir annoncée', *Politique internationale*, No. 76, 1997.

'Christian Tavernier, du Zaïre au Congo', *Le Soir*, 3 October 1997.

'La campagne victorieuse de l'AFDL', in: *Kabila prend le pouvoir*, Brussels, GRIP-Editions Complexe, 1998, pp. 65–89.

'La quadrature du cercle, ou l'ingratitude obligée', in: *Kabila prend le pouvoir*, Brussels, GRIP-Editions Complexe, 1998, pp. 175–180.

*L'enjeu congolais. L'Afrique centrale après Mobutu*, Paris, Fayard, 1999.

*Les nouveaux prédateurs. Politique des puissances en Afrique centrale*, Paris, Fayard, 2003.

'Tshisekedi ou le front du refus', *Le Soir*, 18 May 2005.

Burnet Institute, International Rescue Committee, Mortality in the Democratic Republic of Congo: Results from a Nationwide Survey, 9 December 2004.

Centre de lutte contre l'impunité et l'injustice au Rwanda, Communiqué n° 7/96. Massacres de réfugiés rwandais et burundais dans les camps du Sud-Kivu au Zaïre, 8 November 1996.

Centre de lutte contre l'impunité et l'injustice au Rwanda, Communiqué n° 22/97. L'armée rwandaise a massacré, dans la grotte de Nyakinama, plus de 8.000 habitants de quatre secteurs de la commune Kanama (Gisenyi) entre les 24 et 27 octobre 1997, 24 November 1997.

Chabal, P., Daloz, J.-P., *Africa Works. Disorder as Political Instrument*, London, The International African Institute, 1999.

Chambon, F., 'La grande prudence de la diplomatie sud-africaine', *Le Monde*, 6 November 1996.

Charlier, T., 'Les mercenaires français au Zaïre', *Raids-Magazine*, No. 132, May 1997.

Chester, E.T., *Covert Network. Progressives, the International Rescue Committee, and the CIA*, Armonk-London, M.E. Sharpe, 1995.

Clark, J.F. (Ed.), *The African Stakes of the Congo War*, New York-Houndmills, Palgrave McMillan, 2002.

Clark, J.F. 'Introduction. Causes and Consequences of the Congo War', in: Clark, J.F. (Ed.), *The African Stakes of the Congo War*, New York-Houndmills, Palgrave MacMillan, 2002, pp. 1–10.

'Museveni's Adventure in the Congo War. Uganda's Vietnam?', in: Clark, J.F. (Ed.), *The African Stakes of the Congo War*, New York-Houndmills, Palgrave MacMillan, 2002, pp. 145–165.

*Conflits de l'Est du Zaïre. Repères et enjeux*, Kinshasa, Editions Secco, January 1997.

Consultancy visit to North and South Kivu, 5–21 January 1998, March 1998.

Coopération et Progrès, Zaïre. L'armée au service du développement, Brussels, March 1996.

Cosma, W.B., *Fizi 1967–1986. Le maquis Kabila*, Brussels-Paris, Institut Africain-L'Harmattan, Cahiers Africains, No. 26, 1997.

Cros, M.-F., 'Pour quelques pépites de plus: le centurion, la mine et les contrats', *La Libre Belgique*, 22 May 1998.

'La situation se déteriore au Kivu: vers l'explosion?', *La Libre Belgique*, 29 June 1998.

Cruvellier, T., *Le tribunal des vaincus. Un Nuremberg pour le Rwanda?*, Paris, Calmann-Lévy, 2006.

Cuvelier, J., 'Linking the Local to the Global: Legal Pluralism in the DRC Conflict', in: Vlassenroot, K., Raeymaekers, T. (Eds.), *Conflict and Social Transformation in Eastern DR Congo*, Ghent, Academia Press, 2004, pp. 197–215.

'Réseaux de l'ombre et configurations régionales: le cas du commerce du coltan en République Démocratique du Congo', *Politique Africaine*, 93, March 2004, 82–92.

Davies, K., 'Workers Report Fighting in Congo', Nairobi, AFP, 10 September 1997.

De Barba, P., 'L'engagement américain pendant la guerre au Zaïre', *Raids-Magazine*, 138, November 1997.

De Charybde en Scylla? Rapport de mission Kivu, Zaïre, January 1997.

Depelchin, J., From Pre-Capitalism to Imperialism. A History of Social and Economic Formations in Eastern Zaire (Uvira Zone, c. 1800–1965), Stanford University, Ph.D. Dissertation, 1974.

De Saint-Moulin, L., 'Projet de Constitution de la RDC. Dimension sociale', *Congo-Afrique*, 397, September 2005, 84–94.

De Schrijver, D., 'Les réfugiés rwandais dans la région des grands lacs en 1996', in: Marysse, S., Reyntjens, F. (Eds.), *L'Afrique des grands lacs. Annuaire 1996–1997*, Paris, L'Harmattan, 1997, pp. 221–253.

Des Forges, A., *Leave None to Tell the Story*, New York-Paris, Human Rights Watch-International Federation of Human Rights, 1999.

Desouter, S., Reyntjens, F., Rwanda. Les violations des droits de l'homme par le FPR/APR. Plaidoyer pour une enquête approfondie, Antwerp, University of Antwerp, Centre for the Study of the African Great Lakes Region, June 1995.

Destexhe, A., 'Contre une intervention au Kivu', *Le Monde*, 14 November 1996.

De Villers, G., 'Dernier acte au Zaïre de Mobutu: le Phénix et le Sphinx', in: *Kabila prend le pouvoir*, Brussels, GRIP-Editions Complexe, 1998, pp. 15–30.

'Identifications et mobilisations politiques au Congo-Kinshasa', *Politique Africaine*, 72, December 1998, 81–97.

*République démocratique du Congo. Guerre et politique. Les trente derniers mois de L.D. Kabila (août 1998-janvier 2001)*, Brussels-Paris, Institut Africain-L'Harmattan, Cahiers Africains, No. 47–48, 2001.

'La guerre dans les évolutions du Congo-Kinshasa', *Afrique Contemporaine*, 2005, 215, 47–70.

*République Démocratique du Congo. Le temps de Joseph Kabila*, forthcoming in Cahiers Africains.

De Villers, G., Omasombo Tshonda, J., Zaïre. *La transition manquée 1990–1997*, Bruxelles-Paris, Institut Africain-L'Harmattan, Cahiers Africains, No. 27–28–29, 1997.

'La bataille de Kinshasa', *Politique Africaine*, 84, December 2001, 17–32.

'An Intransitive Transition', *Review of African Political Economy*, 2002, 399–410.

De Villers, G., Willame, J.-C., *République démocratique du Congo. Chronique politique d'un entre-deux-guerres, octobre 1996-juillet 1998*, Brussels-Paris, Institut Africain-L'Harmattan, Cahiers Africains, No. 35–36, 1998.

DHA-IRIN, Update on South Kivu, 26 October 1996.

Update on Uvira, 18 December 1997.

Dietrich, C., *The Commercialisation of Military Deployment in Africa*, Pretoria, Institute for Security Studies, 2001.

Hard Currency. The Criminalized Diamond Economy of the Democratic Republic of the Congo and its Neighbours, Ottawa, Partnership Africa Canada, Occasional Paper #4, June 2002.

Dorsey, M., 'Violence and Power-Building in Post-Genocide Rwanda', in: Doom, R., Gorus, J. (Eds.), *Politics of Identity and Economies of Conflict in the Great Lakes Region*, Brussels, VUB Press, 2000, pp. 311–348.

Dumoulin, A., *La France militaire et l'Afrique*, Brussels, GRIP-Editions Complexe, 1997.

Dupaquier, J.-F., 'Rwanda: le révisionnisme, poursuite du génocide par d'autres moyens', in: Verdier, R., Decaux, E., Chretien, J.-P. (Eds.), *Rwanda. Un génocide du XXe. siècle*, Paris, L'Harmattan, 1995, pp. 127–136.

Dupont, P., 'La crise politique au Burundi et les efforts de médiation de la communauté internationale', in Reyntjens, F., Marysse, S. (Eds.), *L'Afrique des grands lacs. Annuaire 1997–1998*, Paris, L'Harmattan, 1998, pp. 39–61.

Eltringham, N., *Accounting for Horror: Post-Genocide Debates in Rwanda*, London, Pluto Press, 2004.

Emizet, K., 'The massacre of refugees in Congo: a case of UN peacekeeping failure and international law', *The Journal of Modern African Studies*, 2000, 163–202.

Field, S., Ebrahim, E., 'Peace and Security in the DRC', in: Kadima, D., Kabemba, C. (Eds.), *Whither Regional Peace and Security? The Democratic Republic of Congo after the War*, Pretoria, Africa Institute of South Africa, 2000, pp. 3–27.

Forum Baraza La Kivu, 'Banyamulenge', Roberto Garretón's report and Human Rights in Fizi, Uvira and Mwenga, Zaire: The anatomy of fraud and genesis of a conflict, Montréal, 10 May 1996.

'For US firms war becomes a business', *The Boston Globe*, 1 February 1997.

Francois, F., 'A la rencontre du Kivu libéré: carnet de route (janvier-février 1997)', in: *Kabila prend le pouvoir*, Brussels, GRIP-Editions Complexe, 1998, pp. 49–64.

French, H.W., 'Zaïre, in Arming the Hutu, is Making Human Shield of the Refugees', *The International Herald Tribune*, 20 February 1997.

'In Zaire, France Sees the Hand of Washington', *The International Herald Tribune*, 5 April 1997.

*A Continent for the Taking. The Tragedy and Hope of Africa*, New York, Alfred A. Knopf, 2004.

Frodebu, Burundi. Un apartheid qui ne dit pas son nom, Bujumbura, August 1997.

Frodebu, Déclaration générale du deuxième congrès ordinaire du parti Sahwanya-Frodebu, Bujumbura, 6 December 1997.

'Generals for Hire', *Time Magazine*, 15 January 1996.

Gerard-Libois, J., Van Lierde, J., *Congo 1965*, Brussels, CRISP, 1965.

Global Witness, Same Old Story. A Background Study on Natural Resources in the Democratic Republic of Congo, Washington, June 2004.

Global Witness, Under-Mining Peace. Tin: The Explosive Trade in Cassiterite in Eastern DRC, Washington, June 2005.

Godding, J.-P., *Réfugiés rwandais au Zaïre. Sommes-nous encore des hommes?*, Paris, L'Harmattan, 1997.

Godhoy, J., 'Special Report: Wanted in Africa, Needed in Iraq', Paris, IPS, 20 May 2004.

Gordon, N., 'Return to Hell', *Sunday Express*, 21 April 1996.

Gourevitch, P., *We Wish To Inform You That Tomorrow We Will Be Killed With Our Families. Stories from Rwanda*, New York, Farrar Strauss and Giroux, 1998.

Gowing, N., New challenges and problems for information management in complex emergencies. Ominous lessons from the Great Lakes and Eastern Zaire in late 1996 and early 1997, London, 27 May 1998.

GRAZ-Congo, Comment rétablir la paix à l'Est du Congo (ex-Zaïre)?, Geneva, November 1997.

Gribbin, R.E., *In the Aftermath of Genocide. The U.S. Role in Rwanda*, New York, iUniverse, 2005.

Grignon, F., International response to the illegal exploitation of resources in the DRC', in: Malan, M., Gomes Porto, J. (Eds.), *Challenges of Peace Implementation. The UN Mission in the Democratic Republic of the Congo*, Pretoria, Institute for Security Studies, 2004, pp. 43–52.

Guichaoua, A., *Le problème des réfugiés rwandais et des populations banyarwanda dans la région des grands lacs africains*, Geneva, UNHCR, 1992.

Haut Conseil de la République – Parlement de Transition, Rapport de la commission d'information du HCR-PT sur la situation des personnes déplacées dans les régions du Nord et du Sud-Kivu, Kinshasa, 30 November 1994.

Havenne, E., 'La deuxième guerre d'Afrique centrale', in: Marysse, S., Reyntjens, F. (Eds.), *L'Afrique des grands lacs. Annuaire 2000–2001*, Paris, L'Harmattan, 2001, pp. 143–174.

HRFOR, Preparation for a massive influx of Rwandan Refugees from Zaire, 6 November 1996.

Humanitarian Law Consultancy, Burundi's Regroupment Policy: a Pilot Study on Its Legitimacy, The Hague, June–July 1997.

Human Rights Watch, Rwanda. A New Catastrophe?, December 1994.

Human Rights Watch, Rwanda. The Crisis Continues, April 1995.

Human Rights Watch, Rearming with Impunity: International Support for the Perpatrators of the Rwandan Genocide, 29 May 1995.

Human Rights Watch, Local Rwandan Leaders Assassinated, August 1995.

Human Rights Watch, Attacked by All Sides. Civilians and the War in Eastern Zaire, 20 March 1997.

Human Rights Watch, Save Rwandan Refugees, 30 April 1997.

Human Rights Watch, Zaire. Transition, War and Human Rights, April 1997.

Human Rights Watch, Democratic Republic of The Congo. What Kabila is Hiding. Civilian Killings and Impunity in Congo, October 1997.

Human Rights Watch, Transition and Human Rights Violations in Congo, December 1997.

Human Rights Watch, Uganda in Eastern DRC: Fuelling Political and Ethnic Strife, March 2001.

Human Rights Watch, Ituri: 'Covered in Blood'. Ethnically Targeted Violence in North-Eastern DR Congo, July 2003.

Human Rights Watch, D.R. Congo: Civilians at Risk During Disarmament, 29 December 2004.

Human Rights Watch, Democratic Republic of Congo: Civilians Attacked in North Kivu, July 2005.

Human Rights Watch, Democratic Republic of Congo. Elections in Sight: 'Don't Rock the Boat'?, 15 December 2005.

Human Rights Watch, D.R. Congo. Journalists and Human Rights Defenders Under Fire, 9 June 2006.

Human Rights Watch, D.R. Congo: Halt Growing Violence Ahead of Elections, 26 October 2006.

Human Rights Watch, Democratic Republic of Congo. Renewed Crisis in North Kivu, October 2007.

Human Rights Watch, Law and Reality. Progress in Judicial Reform in Rwanda, July 2008.

International Crisis Group, How Kabila Lost His Way: the Performance of Laurent-Désiré Kabila's Government, Nairobi-Brussels, 21 May 1999.

International Crisis Group, Scramble for the Congo. Anatomy of an Ugly War, Nairobi-Brussels, 20 December 2000.

International Crisis Group, The Kivus: the Forgotten Crucible of the Congo Conflict, Nairobi-Brussels, 24 January 2003.

International Crisis Group, Congo Crisis: Military Intervention in Ituri, Nairobi-New York-Brussels, 13 June 2003.

International Crisis Group, Pulling Back from the Brink in the Congo, Nairobi-Brussels, 7 July 2004.

International Crisis Group, The Congo's Transition is Failing: Crisis in the Kivus, Nairobi-Brussels, 30 March 2005.

International Crisis Group, Security Sector Reform in the Congo, Nairobi-Brussels, 13 February 2006.

International Crisis Group, Securing Congo's Elections: Lessons from the Kinshasa Showdown, Nairobi-Brussels, 2 October 2006.

International Crisis Group, Congo: Consolidating the Peace, Kinshasa-Brussels, 5 July 2007.

International Crisis Group, Congo: Bringing Peace Back to North Kivu, Nairobi-Brussels, 31 October 2007.

International Monetary Fund, Rwanda: Selected Issues and Statistical Appendix, IMF Country Report No. 4/383, 2004.

International Non-Governmental Commission of Inquiry into the Massive Violation of Human Rights Committed in the Democratic Republic of Congo (former Zaire) 1996–1997, Report Prepared by the International

Center for Human Rights and Democratic Development and the Association africaine pour la défense des droits de l'homme en République démocratique du Congo, June 1998.

IRIN, Zimbabwe: IRIN focus on arms links to Burundi, Johannesburg, 3 February 2000.

Jackson, R.N., Rosberg, C.G., 'Why Africa's Weak States Persist: The Empirical and Juridical in Statehood', *World Politics*, 1982, 1–24.

Jackson, S., 'Making a Killing: Criminality & Coping in the Kivu War Economy', *Review of African Political Economy*, 2002, 517–536.

Jean, F., Rufin, J.-C. (Eds.), *Economie des guerres civiles*, Paris, Hachette, 1996.

Joint Evaluation of Emergency Assistance to Rwanda, The International Response to Conflict and Genocide: Lessons from the Rwanda Experience, 1996.

Kabila, L.D., Naufrage du processus de re-démocratisation, Hewa-Bora III, PRP, 6 December 1993.

Discours-programme du Président de la République à l'ouverture du congrès des CPP, Kinshasa, ACP, 22 April 1999.

Kajiga, G., 'Cette immigration séculaire des Rwandais au Congo', *Bulletin du CEPSI*, 1956, No. 32, pp. 5–64.

Kanyamachumbi, P., Les populations du Kivu et la loi sur la nationalité. Vraie ou fausse problématique, Kinshasa, Editions Select, s.d. (1993).

Kasereka Mwanawavane, R., Bauma Bahate, N., Nasibu Bilali, C., Trafics d'armes. Enquête de terrain au Kivu (RDC), Brussels, GRIP, 2006.

Kennes, E., 'La guerre au Congo', in: Reyntjens, F., Marysse, S. (Eds.), *L'Afrique des grands lacs. Annuaire 1997–1998*, Paris, L'Harmattan, 1998, pp. 231–272.

'Du Zaïre à la République Démocratique du Congo: une analyse de la guerre de l'Est', *L'Afrique politique 1998*, Paris, Karthala, 1998, pp. 175–204.

'Le secteur minier au Congo: "déconnection" et descente aux enfers', in: Reyntjens, F., Marysse, S. (Eds.), *L'Afrique des grands lacs. Annuaire 1999–2000*, Paris, L'Harmattan, 2000, pp. 299–342.

*Essai biographique sur Laurent-Désiré Kabila*, Brussels-Paris, Institut Africain-L'Harmattan, Cahiers Africains, No. 57–58–59, 2003.

Konrad Adenauer Stiftung, Le processus électoral 2006 en République Démocratique du Congo. Perception de la population, Kinshasa, s.d. (2007).

Kouchner, B., 'Monsieur Mandela, peut-on les laisser mourir?', *Le Monde*, 5 November 1996.

Krueger, R., Krueger, K.T., *From Bloodshed to Hope in Burundi. Our Embassy Years during Genocide*, Austin, University of Texas Press, 2007.

Landsberg, C., 'The Impossible Neutrality? South Africa's Policy in the Congo War', in: Clark, J.F. (Ed.), *The African Stakes of the Congo War*, New York-Houndmills, Palgrave McMillan, 2002, pp. 169–183.

Lanotte, O., *République démocratique du Congo. Guerres sans frontières*, Brussels, GRIP-Editions Complexe, 2003.

Leaba, O., 'La crise centrafricaine de l'été 2001', *Politique Africaine*, 84, December 2001, 163–175.

Leloup, B., 'Rwanda-Ouganda: chronique d'une guerre annoncée?', in: Marysse, S., Reyntjens, F. (Eds.), *L'Afrique des grands lacs. Annuaire 1999–2000*, Paris, L'Harmattan, 2000, pp. 127–145.

'Le contentieux rwando-ougandais et l'Est du Congo', in: Marysse, S., Reyntjens, F. (Eds.), *L'Afrique des grands lacs. Annuaire 2002–2003*, Paris, L'Harmattan, 2003, pp.235–255.

Le contentieux rwando-ougandais et l'ordre politique dans la région des grands lacs d'Afrique, University of Antwerp, Ph.D. Thesis, 2008.

Lemarchand, R., The Democratic Republic of Congo: From Collapse to Potential Reconstruction, Copenhagen, Centre of African Studies, Occasional Paper, September 2001.

*The Dynamics of Violence in Central Africa*, Philadelphia, University of Pennsylvania Press, 2009.

'L'Etat en voie de privatisation', *Politique Africaine*, 73, March 1999.

'L'humanitaire et les pièges de la communication politique au Kivu (de mai 1997 à aujourd'hui)', *Politique Africaine*, 69, March 1998, 143–147.

Ligue ITEKA, Communiqué sur les massacres de Rukaramu, Bujumbura, 6 January 1998.

Lizinde, T., Rwanda: la tragédie, Brussels, 1 May 1996.

Longman, T., 'The Complex Reasons for Rwanda's Engagement in Congo', in: Clark, J.F. (Ed.), *The African Stakes of the Congo War*, New York-Houndmills, Palgrave McMillan, 2002, pp.129–144.

Lubala Mugisho, E., 'La situation politique au Kivu: vers une dualisation de la société', in: Reyntjens, F., Marysse, S. (Eds.), *L'Afrique des grands lacs. Annuaire 1997–1998*, Paris, L'Harmattan, 1998, pp.307–333.

Lumuna Sando, C.K., *Zaïre: quel changement pour quelles structures?*, Brussels, Editions A.F.R.I.C.A., 1980.

Lutundula, C., 'Analyse de la légitimation de la transition et de la nouvelle République Démocratique du Congo', *Afrika-Focus*, 1997, 9–30.

McKinley, J., 'Serb Who Went to Defend Zaire Spread Death and Horror Instead', *The New York Times*, 19 March 1997.

'Mobutu is Gone, but Fighting Goes On', *The International Herald Tribune*, 14 October 1997.

Madsen, W., *Genocide and Covert Operations in Africa 1993–1999*, Lewiston, The Edwin Mellen Press, 1999.

Mamdani, M., 'Why Rwanda trumpeted its Zaire role', *Mail and Guardian*, 8 August 1997.

*When Victims Become Killers: Colonialism, Nativism, and the Genocide in Rwanda*, Princeton, Princeton University Press, 2001.

Marysse, S., 'Regress and war: the case of the DR Congo', *European Journal of Development Research*, 2003, 75–99.

Marysse, S., Ansoms, A., Cassimon, D., 'The aid "Darlings" and "Orphans" of the Great Lakes region in Africa', *European Journal of Development Research*, 2007, 433–458.

Mathieu, P., Willame, J.-C. (Eds.), *Conflits et guerre au Kivu et dans la région des grands lacs. Entre tensions locales et escalade régionale*, Brussels-Paris, Institut Africain-L'Harmattan, Cahiers Africains, No. 39–40, 1999.

Mbembe, A., *On the Postcolony*, Princeton, Princeton University Press, 2001.

MDR, Position du parti M.D.R. sur les grands problèmes actuels du Rwanda, Kigali, 6 November 1994.

Médecins sans Frontières, Report on Events in Kibeho Camp, April 1995, 25 May 1995.

Médecins sans Frontières, Refugee Numbers Analysis, 9 May 1997.

Médecins sans Frontières, Forced Flight: A Brutal Strategy of Elimination in Eastern Zaire, 16 May 1997.

Mémo des membres de (sic) FPR (Rwanda, Afrique du Sud, Canada, Etats-Unis), Michigan, 31 August 1997.

Mémorandum sur l'état de la situation engendrée par le coup de force de quelques militaires contre le pouvoir en date du 20 au 21 octobre 1993, Bujumbura, 27 October 1993.

Migabo Kalere, J., *Génocide au Congo? Analyse des massacres de populations civiles*, Brussels, Broederlijk Delen, 2002.

Misser, F., *Vers un nouveau Rwanda? Entretiens avec Paul Kagame*, Brussels-Paris, Luc Pire-Karthala, 1995.

Misser, F., Vallee, O., *Les gemmocraties. L'économie politique du diamant africain*, Paris, Desclée de Brouwer, 1997.

MNSD, Congo-RDC – Bilan: Gouvernement arrogant et irresponsable, enquête des Nations Unies morte-née, démocratie confisquée, 15 October 1997.

Moncel, C., 'Le Kivu au bord d'une nouvelle explosion', *L'Autre Afrique*, 27 May–9 June 1998.

Mpayimana, P., *Réfugiés rwandais entre marteau et enclume*, Paris, L'Harmattan, 2004.

M'Poyo Kasa-Vubu, J., *Douze mois chez Kabila (1997–1998)*, Brussels, Le Cri, 1998.

Mukasi, C., La nature de la crise entre le parti Uprona et le gouvernement, Bujumbura, 22 November 1997.

Mukendi, G., Kasonga, B., *Kabila. Le retour du Congo*, Ottignies, Quorum, 1997.

Musabyimana, G., *L'APR et les réfugiés rwandais au Zaïre 1996–1997*, Paris, L'Harmattan, 2004.

Musambuko Musemakweli, Toute la vérité sur l'assassinat du général-major André Kisase Ngandu, commandant en chef de l'Alliance (AFDL), Goma, 7 March 1997.

Musangamfura, S., J'accuse le FPR de crimes de génocide des populations d'ethnie hutu, de purification ethnique et appelle à une enquête internationale urgente, Nairobi, 8 December 1995.

'Museveni explains Great Lakes Crisis', *The Monitor*, 30 May, 1 and 2 June 1999.

Nations Unies, Commission des Droits de l'Homme, Rapport sur la situation des droits de l'homme au Zaïre, présenté par M. Roberto Garretón, rapporteur spécial, conformément à la résolution 1996/77 de la Commission, 28 January 1997 (E/CN.4/1997/6).

Nations Unies, Commission des Droits de l'Homme, Rapport sur la situation des droits de l'homme dans la République Démocratique du Congo (ex-Zaïre), présenté par M. Roberto Garretón, conformément à la résolution 1997/58 de la Commission, 30 January 1998 (E/CN.4/1998/65).

NCN Intelligence Reports, A US inspired covert coalition command and control center in Kigali?, Washington D.C., AfIS News Service, 15 July 1997.

Ndikumana, V., Afrika, J., Lettre ouverte au Conseil de sécurité de l'ONU sur la situation qui prévaut au Rwanda, Nairobi, 14 November 1994.

N'Gbanda Nzambo Ko Atumba, H., *Ainsi sonne le glas! Les derniers jours du Maréchal Mobutu*, Paris, Editions Gideppe, 1998.

Niwese, M., *Le peuple rwandais un pied dans la tombe. Récit d'un réfugié étudiant*, Paris, L'Harmattan, 2001.

Nkubito, A., Le harcèlement, les tracasseries, les menaces, bref la persécution du personnel judiciaire, Kigali, 10 May 1996.

Ntisoni, L., *J'ai traversé des fleuves de sang*, Paris, L'Harmattan, 2008.

Nzongola-Ntalaja, G., *The Congo from Leopold to Kabila. A People's History*, London-New York, Zed Books, 2002.

Obotela Rashidi, N., 'L'an I de l'Accord global et inclusif en République démocratique du Congo', in: Reyntjens, F., Marysse, S. (Eds.), *L'Afrique des grands lacs. Annuaire 2003–2004*, Paris, L'Harmattan, 2004, pp. 111–137.

Odom, T. P., *Journey into Darkness. Genocide in Rwanda*, College Station, Texas A&M University Press, 2005.

Overdulve, C. M., 'Fonction de la langue et de la communication au Rwanda', *Nouvelle Revue de science missionnaire*, 1997, 271–283.

Pabanel, J.-P., 'La question de la nationalité au Kivu', *Politique Africaine*, 41, March 1991, 32–40.

Parque, V., 'Le role de la communauté internationale dans la gestion du conflit en République démocratique du Congo', in: Reyntjens, F., Marysse, S. (Eds.), *L'Afrique des grands lacs. Annuaire 1999–2000*, Paris, L'Harmattan, 2000, pp. 343–376.

Parque, V., Reyntjens, F., 'Crimes contre l'humanité dans l'ex-Zaïre: une réalité?', in: Reyntjens, F., Marysse, S. (Eds.), *L'Afrique des grands lacs. Annuaire 1997–1998*, Paris, L'Harmattan, 1998, pp. 273–306.

Perrot, S., 'Entrepreneurs de l'insécurité: la face cache de l'armée ougandaise', *Politique Africaine*, 75, October 1999, 60–71.

Physicians for Human Rights, Investigations in Eastern Congo and Western Rwanda, Washington D.C., 16 July 1997.

Pomfret, J., 'In Congo, Revenge Became Rebellion', *The Washington Post*, 6 July 1997.

'Defense Minister Says Arms, Troops Supplied for Anti-Mobutu Drive', *The Washington Post*, 9 July 1997.

Pottier, J., *Re-Imagining Rwanda: Conflict, Survival and Disinformation in the Late Twentieth Century*, Cambridge, Cambridge University Press, 2002.

Pourtier, R., 'Congo-Zaïre-Congo: un itinéraire géopolitique au coeur de l'Afrique', *Hérodote*, 86–87, 1997, 6–41.

'Private US companies train armies around the world', *US News and World Report*, 8 February 1997.

Prunier, G., *The Rwanda Crisis. History of a Genocide*, New York, Columbia University Press, 1995.

Rwanda: the Social, Political and Economic Situation in June 1997, Writenet (UK), July 1997.

'La crise du Kivu et ses conséquences dans la région des Grands Lacs', *Hérodote*, 86–87, 1997, 42–56.

'Une poudrière au coeur du Congo-Kinshasa', *Le Monde diplomatique*, July 1998.

'L'Ouganda et les guerres congolaises', *Politique Africaine*, 75, October 1999, 43–59.

Rafti, M., South Kivu: Sanctuary for the Rebellion of the Democratic Forces for the Liberation of Rwanda, Antwerp, University of Antwerp, Institute of Development Policy and Management, Discussion Paper 2006–5.

Rapport sur la situation qui prévaut actuellement dans les provinces du Nord et du Sud Kivu, s.d. (early September 1997).

'RDC, la guerre vue d'en bas', *Politique Africaine*, No. 84, December 2001.

Reno, W., 'Shadow states and the political economy of civil wars', in: Berdal, M., Malone, M. (Eds.), *Greed and Grievance. Economic agendas in civil wars*, Boulder-London, Lynne Riener, 2000, pp.43–63.

Renton, D., Seddon, D., Zeilig, L., *The Congo. Plunder and Resistance*, London-New York, Zed Books, 2007.

Report of a fieldtrip to South Kivu 15–22.10.1997: 'One Year After ...', 4 November 1997.

République Démocratique du Congo, Assemblée Nationale, Commission spéciale chargée de l'examen de la validité des conventions à caractère économique et financier conclues pendant les guerres de 1996–1997 et de 1998, Rapport des travaux, Kinshasa, 26 June 2005.

Reyntjens, F., Données sur les 'escadrons de la mort' au Rwanda, Antwerp, 9 October 1992.

*L'Afrique des grands lacs en crise. Rwanda, Burundi: 1988–1994*, Paris, Karthala, 1994.

'Sujets d'inquiétude au Rwanda en octobre 1994', *Dialogue*, 179, November–December 1994, 3–14.

*Burundi: Breaking the Cycle of Violence*, London, Minority Rights Group, 1995.

'Un ordre constitutionnel dissimulé: la "loi fondamentale" du 26 mai 1995', *Dialogue*, 186, October–November 1995, 13–22.

'Rwanda. Evolution politique en 1996–1997', in: Marysse, S., Reyntjens, F. (Eds.), *L'Afrique des grands lacs. Annuaire 1996–1997*, Paris, L'Harmattan, 1997, pp.43–57.

'Estimation du nombre de personnes tuées au Rwanda en 1994', in: Marysse, S., Reyntjens, F. (Eds.), *L'Afrique des grands lacs. Annuaire 1996–1997*, Paris, L'Harmattan, 1997, pp.179–186.

'Rwanda et Burundi: les acteurs politiques', in: Verhasselt, Y. (Ed.), *Rwanda-Burundi*, Brussels, Royal Academy of Overseas Sciences, 1997, pp.111–126.

'Evolution politique au Rwanda et au Burundi, 1998–1999', in: Marysse, S., Reyntjens, F. (Eds.), *L'Afrique des grands lacs. Annuaire 1998–1999*, Paris, L'Harmattan, 1999, pp.124–157.

'Rwanda, Ten Years On: From Genocide to Dictatorship', *African Affairs*, 2004, 177–210.

Reyntjens, F., Marysse, S. (Eds.), Conflits au Kivu: antécédents et enjeux, Antwerp, University of Antwerp, Centre for the Study of the African Great Lakes Region, 1996.

Rogier, E., 'The Inter-Congolese Dialogue: A Critical Overview', in: Malan, M., Gomes Porto, J. (Eds.), *Challenges of Peace Implementation. The UN Mission in the Democratic Republic of the Congo*, Pretoria, Institute for Security Studies, 2004, pp.25–42.

Ruberangabo, E., Mémorandum aux délégués de la communauté Banyamulenge réunis en session à Bukavu sur l'avenir de leur communauté, Bukavu, 13 August 1998.

Ruberangeyo, E., Mes inquiétudes sur la gestion actuelle rwandaise des fonds publics, 31 May 1995.

Rugumaho, B., *L'hécatombe des réfugiés rwandais dans l'ex-Zaïre*, Paris, L'Harmattan, 2004.

Ruhimbika, M., *Les Banyamulenge (Congo-Zaïre) entre deux guerres*, Paris, L'Harmattan, 2001.

Rupert, J., 'Zaire Reportedly Selling Arms to Angolan Ex-Rebels', *The Washington Post*, 21 March 1997.

Rupiya, M. R., 'A Political and Military Review of Zimbabwe's Involvement in the Second Congo War', in: Clark, J.F. (Ed.), *The African Stakes of the Congo War*, New York-Houndmills, Palgrave McMillan, 2002, pp.93–105.

Rutayisire, W., Gérald (sic) Prunier: A Eulogy for Genocide, Kigali, 24 October 1997.

Rutazibwa, P., 'Cet ethnisme sans fin', *Informations Rwandaises et Internationales*, No. 5, November–December 1996.

Ruzibiza, A., *Rwanda. L'histoire secrète*, Paris, Editions du Panama, 2005.

Ryckmans, F., 'Kinshasa: les malentendus de la "libération"', in: *Kabila prend le pouvoir*, Brussels, GRIP-Editions Complexe, 1998, pp.119–133.

Samset, I., 'Conflict of Interests or Interests in Conflict? Diamonds and War in the DRC', *Review of African Political Economy*, 2002, 463–480.

Sanders, E. R., 'The Hamitic Hypothesis: Its Origin and Functions in Time Perspective', *Journal of African History*, 1969, 521–532.

Shattuck, J., Simo, P., Durch, W. J., *Ending Congo's Nightmare. What the US Can Do to Promote Peace in Central Africa*, Washington, International Human Rights Law Group, October 2003.

Scherrer, C. P., *Ethnisierung und Völkermord in Zentralafrica. Genozid in Rwanda, Bürgerkrieg in Burundi und die Rolle der Weltgemeinschaft*, Frankfurt, Campus, 1997.

Central Africa: Conflict Impact Assessment and Policy Options, Copenhagen Peace Research Institute, Working Paper 25/1997.

Sénat de Belgique, Rapport fait au nom de la commission d'enquête Grands Lacs par MM. Colla et Dallemagne, session 2002–3, No. 2–942/1, 20 February 2003.

Silverstein, K., 'Privatizing War. How Affairs of State are outsourced to corporations beyond public control', *The Nation*, 2 July–4 August 1997.

Smis, S., Oyatambwe, W., 'Complex Political Emergencies, the International Community & the Congo Conflict', *Review of African Political Economy*, 2002, 411–430.

Smith, S., 'Rwanda: enquête sur la terreur tutsie', *Libération*, 27 February 1996.

Société civile du Sud-Kivu, Groupe Jérémie, *Pour une paix durable dans la région Est du Zaïre*, Bukavu, February 1997.

Stearns, J.K., 'Laurent Nkunda and the National Congress for the Defence of the People (CNDP)', in: Marysse, S., Reyntjens, F., Vandeginste, S. (Eds.), *L'Afrique des grands lacs. Annuaire 2007–2008*, Paris, L'Harmattan, 2008, pp. 245–267.

Storey, A., 'Structural adjustment, state power and the genocide: the World Bank and Rwanda', *Review of African Political Economy*, 2001, 365–386.

Taylor, I., 'Conflict in Central Africa: Clandestine Networks & Regional/Global Configurations', *Review of African Political Economy*, 2003, 45–55.

Tull, D.M. 'A Reconfiguration of Political Order? The State of the State in North Kivu (DR Congo)', *African Affairs*, 2003, 429–446.

Tumepata morale. Report of a fieldtrip to South Kivu 1–8.5.1997, 17 May 1997.

Turner, T., 'Angola's Role in the Congo War', in: Clark, J.F. (Ed.), *The African Stakes of the Congo War*, New York-Houndmills, Palgrave McMillan, 2002, pp. 75–92.

*The Congo Wars*, London, Zed Books, 2007.

Twagiramungu, F., Sendashonga, S., F.R.D. Plate-forme politique, Brussels, March 1996.

UDPS-Belux, *L'UDPS face à la crise congolaise*, Paris, L'Harmattan, 1999.

Umutesi, B., *Surviving the Slaughter. The Ordeal of a Rwandan Refugee in Zaire*, Madison, University of Wisconsin Press, 2004.

United Nations, Commission of Inquiry on Burundi, Final Report, New York, 23 July 1996.

United Nations, Commission on Human Rights, Report on the situation of human rights in Zaire, prepared by the Special Rapporteur, Mr. Roberto Garretón, in accordance with Commission resolution 1995/69, 29 January 1996 (E/CN.4/1996/66).

United Nations, Commission on Human Rights, Report on the Situation of Human Rights in Zaire, prepared by the Special Rapporteur, Mr. Robert Garretón, in accordance with Commission Resolution 1996/77, 28 January 1997 (E/CN.4/1997/6).

United Nations, Commission on Human Rights, Report on the mission carried out at the request of the High Commissioner for Human Rights between 25 and 29 March 1997 to the area occupied by rebels in eastern Zaire, 2 April 1997 (E/CN.4/1997/6/Add.2).

United Nations, Economic and Social Council, Report of the joint mission charged with investigating allegations of massacres and other human rights violations occurring in eastern Zaire (now Democratic Republic of the Congo) since September 1996, 2 July 1997 (A/51/942).

United Nations, General Assembly, Interim Report on the human rights situation in Burundi submitted by the Special Rapporteur of the Commission on Human Rights, pursuant to Economic and Social Council decision 1997/280, 7 October 1997 (A/52/505).

United Nations, General Assembly, Report of the Special Representative of the Commission on Human Rights on the situation of human rights in Rwanda, 22 October 1997 (A/52/522).

United Nations, Security Council, The Causes of Conflict and the Promotion of Durable Peace and Sustainable Development in Africa. Report of the Secretary General, April 1998 (S/1998/318).

United Nations, Security Council, Report of the Investigative Team Charged with Investigating Serious Violations of Human Rights and International Humanitarian Law in the Democratic Republic of Congo, 29 June 1998 (S/1998/581).

United Nations, Security Council, Final Report of the International Commission of Inquiry (Rwanda), 18 November 1998 (S/1998/1096).

United Nations, Security Council, Report of the Panel of Experts on Violations of Security Council Sanctions against UNITA, 10 March 2000 (S/2000/203).

United Nations, Security Council, Report of the Panel of Experts on the Illegal Exploitation of Natural Resources and Other Forms of Wealth of the Democratic Republic of the Congo, 12 April 2001 (S/2001/357).

United Nations, Security Council, Final Report of the Panel of Experts on the Illegal Exploitation of Natural Resources and Other Forms of Wealth of the Democratic Republic of the Congo, 16 October 2002 (S/2002/1146).

United Nations, Security Council, Final Report of the Panel of Experts on the Illegal Exploitation of Natural Resources and Other Forms of Wealth of the Democratic Republic of the Congo, 23 October 2003 (S/2003/1027).

United Nations, Security Council, Report of the Group of Experts on the Democratic Republic of the Congo, 15 July 2004 (S/2004/551).

United Nations, Security Council, Report of the Group of Experts on the Democratic Republic of the Congo, 25 January 2005 (S/2005/30).

United Nations, Security Council, Report of the Group of Experts on the Democratic Republic of the Congo, 26 July 2005 (S/2005/436).

United Nations, Security Council, Final Report of the Group of Experts on the Democratic Republic of the Congo, 18 July 2007 (S/2007/423).

U.S. Committee for Refugees, Masisi. Down the Road from Goma: Ethnic Cleansing and Displacement in Eastern Zaire, Washington, June 1996.

U.S. Committee for Refugees, Military Deployment in Eastern Zaire Would Be Misguided; Talk of Deployment Threatens to Impede Humanitarian Relief, 28 November 1996.

U.S. Committee for Refugees, Site Visit to Eastern Congo/Zaire: Analysis of Humanitarian and Political Issues, 10 June 1997.

U.S. Institute of Peace, Special Report. Zaire's Crises of War and Governance, Washington D.C., April 1997.

U.S. Military Activities in Rwanda since 1994. Summary, 19 August 1997.

Van Acker, F., Vlassenroot, K., 'Les "maï-maï" et les fonctions de la violence milicienne dans l'Est du Congo', *Politique Africaine*, 84, December 2001, 103–116.

Vandeginste, S., 'L'approche "vérité et réconciliation" du génocide et des crimes contre l'humanité au Rwanda', in: Reyntjens, F., Marysse, S. (Eds.), *L'Afrique des grands lacs. Annuaire 1997–1998*, Paris, L'Harmattan, 1998, pp. 97–140.

Van Dyck, H., Rapport sur les violations des droits de l'homme dans le Sud-Equateur, 29 September 1997.

Van Leeuwen, M., 'Rwanda's Imidugudu programme and earlier experiences with villagisation and resettlement in East Africa', *Journal of Modern African Studies*, 2001, 623–644.

Verschave, F.-X., *La Françafrique. Le plus long scandale de la République*, Paris, Stock, 1998.

Vircoulon, T., 'République démocratique du Congo: la démocratie sans démocrates', *Politique étrangère*, 2006, No. 3, pp. 569–581.

Vlassenroot, K., The Making of a New Order. Dynamics of Conflict and Dialectics of War in South Kivu (DR Congo), University of Ghent, Ph.D. Thesis, 2002.

'Citizenship, Identity Formation & Conflict in South Kivu: The Case of the Banyamulenge', *Review of African Political Economy*, 2002, 499–515.

Vlassenroot, K., Raeymaekers, T., 'Le conflit en Ituri', in: Marysse, S., Reyntjens, F. (Eds.), *L'Afrique des grands lacs. Annuaire 2002–2003*, Paris, L'Harmattan, 2003, pp. 207–233.

'The Politics of Rebellion and Intervention in Ituri: The Emergence of a New Political Complex?', *African Affairs*, 2004, 385–412.

'Emerging Complexes in Ituri', in: Vlassenroot, K., Raeymaekers, T. (Eds.), *Conflict and Social Transformation in Eastern DR Congo*, Ghent, Academia Press, 2004, pp. 177–196.

Vlassenroot, K., Raeymaekers, T. (Eds.), *Conflict and Social Transformation in Eastern DR Congo*, Ghent, Academia Press, 2004.

Vunduawe Te Pemako, *A l'ombre du Léopard. Vérités sur le régime de Mobutu Sese Seko*, Brussels, Editions Zaire Libre, 2000.

Weiss, G., *Le pays d'Uvira*, Brussels, ARSC, 1959.

Willame, J.-C., *Banyarwanda et Banyamulenge. Violences ethniques et gestion de l'identitaire au Kivu*, Brussels-Paris, Institut Africain-L'Harmattan, Cahiers Africains, No. 25, 1997.

'Laurent-Désiré Kabila: les origines d'une anabase', *Politique Africaine*, 72, December 1998, 68–80.

*L'odyssée Kabila. Trajectoire pour un Congo nouveau?*, Paris, Karthala, 1999.

*L'Accord de Lusaka. Chronique d'une négociation internationale*, Brussels-Paris, Institut Africain-L'Harmattan, Cahiers Africains, No. 51–52, 2002.

Winter, R., "How Human Rights Groups Miss the Opportunity to Do Good", *The Washington Post*, 22 February 1998.

Wolters, S., Update on the DRC: Is the Transition in Trouble?, Pretoria, Institute for Security Studies, 20 July 2004.

Wolters, S., Boshoff, H., The Impact of Slow Military Reform on the Transition Process in the DRC, Pretoria, Institute for Security Studies, 10 July 2006.

Yoka Lye, *Lettres d'un Kinois à l'oncle du village*, Brussels-Paris, Institut Africain-L'Harmattan, Cahiers Africains, No. 15, 1995.

Young, C., 'Contextualizing Congo Conflicts. Order and Disorder in Postcolonial Africa', in: Clark, J.F. (Ed.), *The African Stakes of the Congo War*, New York-Houndmills, Palgrave McMillan, 2002, pp. 13–31.

Zolberg, A.R., Suhrke, A., Aguayo, S., *Escape from Violence: Conflict and Refugee Crisis in the Developing World*, New York, Oxford University Press, 1989.

# Index

ADF (Allied Democratic Forces), 58, 60, 141, 169

ADP (Alliance démocratique des peuples), 102, 105

AFDL (Alliance des forces pour la libération du Congo-Zaïre), 56, 62, 78, 87–99, 102–109, 114, 120, 137, 139–141, 233

Afewerki, Isaias, 118

AGI (Accord global et inclusif), 259–263

Ajello, Aldo, 118, 123, 135, 211, 268

Albright, Madeleine, 75, 166, 177

ALIR (Armée de libération du Rwanda), 174, 209

Alliances, 201–207

AMP (Alliance de la majorité présidentielle), 266, 273, 278

ANACOZA (All-North America Conference on Zaire), 106

Angola, 43, 169
  intervention in Congo (1998), 197–205
  intervention in Zaire (1996), 61–65

Annan, Kofi, 88, 91, 96, 114, 130, 183, 259

Anzaluni Bembe, Célestin, 149

Arusha (peace accord), 2, 185

Austin, Kathi, 76, 77

Autesserre, Séverine, 5

Axworthy, Lloyd, 86, 88

Bagalwa Mapatano, 152

Bagaza, Jean-Baptiste, 38

Balubakat, 159

Bangilima, 17

Bantu (ethnogenesis), 40, 141, 149–152

Banyamulenge, 21–23, 45–57, 61, 70, 72, 80, 98, 102, 105, 106, 109, 119, 145, 147, 150, 151, 154, 195, 204, 205, 268

Banyarwanda, 13–17, 22, 23, 50, 105, 119, 144, 147, 268

Banza Mukalay, 125

Baramoto, Kpama, 110, 111, 133, 136, 202

Bararunyeretse, Libère, 190

Baril, Maurice, 86

Barlow, Eben, 76

Barnes, William, 61

Bas Congo, 196–199

Bassole, Léandre, 40

Bayart, Jean-Francois, 3

Belgium
  AFDL 'rebellion', 55, 75, 81, 89, 124
  diplomacy, 118, 123, 135, 139, 166, 244
  international intervention, 85, 87, 127

Bemba Saolona, Jean (Jeannot), 243

Bemba, Jean-Pierre, 7, 217, 236,
    242–244, 258, 262, 263,
    265–267, 271–277
Bembe, 149, 152
Bimazubute, Gilles, 35
Birara, Jean, 185, 188
Bisengimana, Barthélémy, 14
Biya, Paul, 118
Bizima Karaha, 122, 125, 127, 129,
    160, 162, 196, 241, 266
Bizimungu, Augustin, 21
Bizimungu, Pasteur, 20, 50, 53, 81,
    118, 186
Boende, 93
Bogosian, Richard, 69, 119
Bolozi Gbudu Tanikpama, 134
Bonino, Emma, 72, 80, 82, 85,
    119, 142
Bosmans, Griet, 175
Bout, Viktor, 225
Boutros-Ghali, Boutros, 41, 96,
    118, 133
Bradol, Jean-Hervé, 84, 90
Braeckman, Colette, 84, 90, 135, 252
Bugera, Déo, 102, 105, 161, 234
Bukavu, 47–55, 62, 63, 68, 69, 84,
    96, 105, 109, 114, 115, 145, 146,
    151, 154, 156, 194, 204, 209,
    212, 264
Bunia. *See* Ituri
Burundi
    Banyamulenge, 48
    civil war, 40–41, 170–172, 178
    coup d'état 1993, 34–41
    coup d'état 1996, 41–42
    governance, 190–193
    human rights, 175–178
    intervention in Zaire (1996), 61
    justice, 183
    negotiations, 179, 180
Bush, George, 76
Buyoya, Pierre, 41, 42, 71, 172,
    190–193

CEI (Commission électorale
    indépendante), 268–271
Chabango (chief), 147

Chigovera, Andrew, 91
Child Soldiers, 105, 253
Chiluba, Frederick, 118, 247, 248
China, 111, 112
Chirac, Jacques, 81, 85, 88, 115,
    133, 246
Chrétien, Jean, 86
Chrétien, Raymond, 82, 86, 119, 133
Christopher, Warren, 74
CIA (Central Intelligence Agency), 67,
    70, 75
CIAT (Comité international
    d'accompagnement de la
    transition), 261, 263, 270,
    272, 277
Clark, John F., 196
Clinton, William, 69, 73
CNDD (Conseil national pour la
    défense de la démocratie), 39,
    178, 180,
    190, 192
CNDD-FDD, 61, 171, 191
CNDP (Congrès national pour la
    défense du peuple), 215
CNE (commission nationale des
    élections), 13
CNN (Cable News Network), 58,
    83, 87
CNRD (Conseil national de résistance
    pour la démocratie), 102, 104
Cohen, Herman, 76, 77, 145
Communication. *See* Information
Constitution, 134, 232–234, 260, 261,
    268–270
CPP (Comités du pouvoir populaire),
    233–236
CRAP (Commandos de recherche et
    d'action en profondeur), 116
Crimes against humanity, 87–99
Criminalisation, 224–231
Crocker, Chester, 78
Cros, Marie-France, 173
Cuba, 235
Cuvelier, Jeroen, 230

De Charette, Hervé, 88
De Saint Moulin, Léon, 269

De Villers, Gauthier, 10, 139, 155, 198, 235, 253
Degni-Segui, René, 189
Derycke, Eric, 87, 124, 135
Destexhe, Alain, 89
DIA (Defence Intelligence Agency), 69, 76, 253
Dietrich, Chris, 225
DMI (Department of Military Intelligence), 32, 33
Dorsey, Michael, 32, 238
Dos Santos, José Eduardo, 62
DSP (Division spéciale présidentielle), 18, 108, 112, 197
Dumoulin, André, 117
Dusaidi, Claude, 55, 175

El Turabi, Hassan, 112
Elections, 271–278
Elite networks (Rwanda, Uganda), 223, 241
Eluki, Monga Aundu, 17, 18, 110, 132
Elysée, 115
Emmanuelli, Xavier, 88
Endundo, José, 265
Eritrea, 43, 58, 62, 65
ESO (External Security Organisation), 33, 228
Ethiopia, 43, 62, 65
Ethnicity
ethnogenesis, 141, 149–152
mobility, 14
Etsou, Frédéric, 276
EUFOR, 272–275
Executive Outcomes, 76, 117, 143

FAA (Forças armadas angolanas), 63
FAC (Forces armées congolaises), 145, 146, 162, 198, 204
FAPC (Forces armées du peuple congolais), 218
FAR (Forces armées rwandaises), 7, 18, 21, 32, 113, 174, 203

FARDC (Forces armées de la RDC), 209, 211, 213–215, 221, 229, 266, 267
Farrakhan, Louis, 112
Fashoda syndrome, 78
FAZ (Forces armées zaïroises), 18, 21, 49, 54, 59, 108–117, 197
FDD (Forces de la défense de la démocratie) (also see CNDD-FDD), 39, 40, 203
FDLR (Forces démocratiques pour la libération du Rwanda), 6, 209–211
Foccart, Jacques, 115
Fondation Hirondelle, 188
FONUS (Forces démocratiques pour la libération du Rwanda), 136
Forces Politiques du Conclave (FPC), 13, 133
France, 44, 114–117, 130
FRD (Forces de resistance pour la démocratie), 180
Frodebu, 34–40, 179, 190–192
Frolina, 40, 149, 171

Gabiro, 27
Garang, John, 104
Garde Civile, 108
Garretón, Roberto, 22, 91, 97, 147, 154
Gasana, Anastase, 81, 118, 181
Gasana, James, 188
Gatumba (massacre), 212
Gbadolite, 104, 116, 132, 134, 139, 244
Genocide, 2, 19, 87, 88, 92, 184, 196
Gersony, Robert, 26, 27
Gertler, Dan, 253
Ghenda, Raphaël, 75, 138, 157, 160, 166
Gizenga, Antoine, 162, 273, 276, 278
Godfrain, Jacques, 164
Goma, 15, 16, 18, 47, 52–58, 62, 63, 67–71, 73, 74, 83, 84, 91, 96, 98, 103, 105, 115, 131, 135, 152, 154, 194, 196, 213, 229, 239, 240, 264

Governance, 153–164, 232–238
Gowing, Nik, 99
Gribbin, Robert, 68, 69, 77, 85, 89, 175, 176, 195, 196
GSPR (Groupe de sécurité de la présidence de la République), 117
Guéhenno, Jean-Marie, 276
Guibert, Anne, 84, 90

Habyarimana, Emmanuel, 185
Habyarimana, Juvénal, 36, 43, 187
HCR-PT (Haut Conseil de la République – Parlement de transition), 11, 22, 104, 121, 129, 131, 134, 136, 139
Hema, 215–219, 242
Human Rights
  investigations, 90–93
  violations, 93–99, 152–153, 175–178, 201
Humanitarian intervention, 80–88
Hunde, 14, 16–18, 99, 150, 174
Hutu (refugees), 16–21, 80–101

Ibuka, 31, 190
ICTR (International Criminal Tribunal for Rwanda), 21, 183
IEMF (International Emergency Multilateral Force), 219, 220
Ilunga, Emile, 162, 239, 240
Impunity, 32, 92
Information (manipulation), 57, 58, 83, 87, 90, 99–101, 154, 155
Inga (power plant), 197
Inter-Congolese Dialogue, 235, 246, 254–261
IRC (International Rescue Committee), 68, 76
Isnard, Jacques, 58
Israel, 112
Ituri
  intervention by Rwanda, 207, 220
  intervention by Uganda, 215–220
  RCD-ML, 243
  war, 221

Jackson, Jesse, 166
Jackson, Stephen, 227
Japan, 181
Jennings, Christian, 188
Justice, 181–184

Kabanda, Godfrey, 98
Kabare (mwami), 147
Kabarebe, James, 54, 98, 151, 162, 169
Kaberuka, Donat, 185
Kabila, Joseph, 8, 237, 257, 263, 266, 267, 271, 275
  _and the international community, 254
  dynastic succession, 253
  presidential election, 273, 276
Kabila, Laurent-Désiré, 8, 58, 60, 63, 75, 77, 83–85, 91, 102, 106, 107, 113, 123–130, 132, 135, 137, 140, 146, 151, 194, 246, 247, 253
  _and the international community, 92, 164–166
  contacts with the US, 67, 69
  governance, 153–164, 232–237
  inauguration, 66
  murder of, 252, 253
  smuggling, 104
Kabutiti (mwami), 147
Kabuya-Lumana, Sando, 141
Kabwe, Séverin, 160, 162
Kadege, Alphonse, 190
Kadogo. *See* Child Soldiers
Kafunda, 63
Kagame, Firmin, 54
Kagame, Paul, 19, 28, 45, 47, 53–57, 62, 64, 66, 71, 72, 76, 83, 85, 86, 100, 105, 107, 128, 140, 174, 186, 188, 189, 195, 206
Kahwa (chief), 217, 218, 224
Kakudji, Gaétan, 145, 160, 166, 167
Kakwavu, Jérôme, 218
Kamalata, Abilio, 113
Kamanda wa Kamanda, Gérard, 123, 125, 148

Kamerhe, Vital, 238
Kamitatu, Olivier, 243, 258, 265, 266
Kanyarengwe, Alexis, 187
Kanyenkiko, Anatole, 38, 39
Kapanga, André, 178
Kapend, Eddy, 253
Karibwami, Pontien, 35
Karuhije, Ignace, 184
Kasereka, Rachidi, 253
Katangese Gendarmes. *See* Tigres
Kayumba Nyamwasa, 173
Kazindu, Marc, 97
Kazini, James, 216, 241
Kengo Wa Dondo, Léon, 62, 111, 120,
    132–134, 136, 138
Kennes, Erik, 151, 156
Kibumba, 48, 49, 53
Kifwa, Célestin, 162, 169
Kindu, 199
Kinshasa
    fall of_, 139
    incidents, 273, 277
    threat, 197–198
Kisangani
    fall of_, 63, 123, 135, 136, 199
    fighting between RPA and UPDF,
        205, 240
    massacres, 94, 98
    seat of RCD-ML, 239
Kisase Ngandu, André, 99, 102, 104,
    106, 107, 161, 234
Kitona (army base), 196
Kivu, 13–22, 207–215
Kopelipa (Vieira Dias), 63
Kouchner, Bernard, 80
Krueger, Robert, 40
Kuwait, 112
Kyungu, Gabriël, 160

Lalali, Rachid, 251
Larkin, Barbara, 70
Le Carro, Alain, 116
Lemarchand, René, 11, 279
Lemera, 51, 102
Lendu, 216–219, 242
Lerge, Eric, 263
Libya, 104, 235, 245

Likulia Bolongo, Norbert, 138,
Lotsove, Adèle, 216
Lubanga, Thomas, 217, 220, 221, 242
Lubero, 17
Lubumbashi, 109, 126, 138, 200, 204
Lumbala, Roger, 242
Lunda Bululu, 160, 239
Lusaka (accord), 236, 247–250
Lutundula, Christophe, 264
Lwabandji, Lwasi, 50
Lye Yoka, 131

Magabe, Jean-Charles, 154
Mahele, Lieka Bokungu, 62, 110, 111,
    115, 132, 133, 136
Mai-mai, 14, 99, 145–147, 150, 153,
    166, 174, 203, 205, 229
Malumalu, Apollinaire, 268, 270, 271
Mandela, Nelson, 81, 122, 124, 127,
    130, 247, 256
Manipulation. *See* Information
Manwangari, Jean-Baptiste, 190
Marysse, Stefaan, 227
Masasu Nindaga, 102, 105, 161, 162,
    234, 253
Masire, Ketumile (Quett), 251–254,
    258, 260
Masisi, 14–18, 99, 105, 145, 147,
    152, 174
Masunzu, Patrick, 205, 258
Matata, Joseph, 176
Mazimhaka, Patrick, 57, 196
Mbabazi, Amama, 246
Mbandaka, 95, 98, 200,
Mbaya, Etienne, 157, 158, 160
Mbeki, Thabo, 64, 124, 126, 128,
    129, 133, 248, 256–261, 265,
    269
Mbembe, Achille, 222
Mbuji-Mayi, 126, 138, 199
Mbuki, Sylvain, 194
Mbusa Nyamwisi, Antipas, 217,
    241–243, 273
McCall, Richard, 53
MDR (Mouvement démocratique
    républicain), 31
Mercenaries, 114–117, 174

Michel, Louis, 276
Minani, Jean, 37, 39, 191
Misser, François, 47, 62
Mitterrand, François, 117
Mkapa, Benjamin, 118
MLC (Mouvement de libération du
    Congo), 199, 217, 223, 243, 244,
    265, 276
MNC (Mouvement national
    congolais) – Lumumba, 104, 168
Mobutu, Nzanga, 276
Mobutu, Sese Seko, 8, 43, 45, 57, 60,
    62, 81, 104, 107, 113, 115, 119,
    120, 127, 129, 131–138, 202
Moi arap, Daniel, 118, 124
Monsengwo, Laurent, 139
Montoya, Robert, 117
MONUC (Mission des Nations-
    Unies au Congo), 199, 209, 210,
    213, 218–221, 251, 259, 263,
    272–275
Moose, George, 75, 122
Moreels, Réginald, 89
Moussali, Michel, 173
MPRI (Military Professional
    Resources Inc.), 76, 143
MRLZ (Mouvement révolutionaire
    pour la libération du Zaïre), 102,
    105
MSF (Médecins sans frontières),
    19
Mudende, 176, 177
Mugabe, Robert, 202
Mugunga camp, 21, 53, 84
Mukasi, Charles, 38, 190, 191
Mulanda, 63
Munyangu, Gaston, 99
Munzihirwa, Christophe, 49
Mupenda, Christophe Moto, 18
Murigande, Charles, 186, 212
Murwanashyaka, Ignace, 211
Museveni, Yoweri, 43, 48, 59, 60, 64,
    105–108, 118, 119, 130, 168,
    196, 206, 242
Mutambo, Joseph, 205
Mutebutsi, Jules, 212, 214
Mwenze Kongolo, 125, 152, 160

N'Gbanda, Honoré, 19, 110,
    119–122, 133
Nagenda, John, 59
Nande, 14, 150, 153, 217
Natural resources, 224–231
Ndadaye, Melchior, 34, 35
Ndataraye (mwami), 147
Ndayikengurukiye, Jean-Bosco, 191
Ndayizeye, Domitien, 191
Ndeze (mwami), 147
Ndimira, Pascal-Firmin, 179
Nduwayo, Antoine, 38, 39, 41, 190
Netherlands (The), 47
Ngabu, Faustin, 89, 90
Ngendahayo, Jean-Marie, 40
Ngendakumana, Léonce, 38
Niasse, Moustapha, 259, 260
Nimpagaritse, Innocent, 40
Nkunda, Laurent, 6, 211–215,
    265, 266
Nkurunziza, Jackson. *See* Nziza, Jack
Nsengimana, Nkiko, 188
Ntaryamira, Cyprien, 35, 36
Ntibantunganya, Sylvestre, 37, 39, 41
Nyamwisi. *See* Mbusa Nyamwisi
Nyanga, 14, 16, 18, 99, 150
Nyangoma, Léonard, 39, 191
Nyarugabo, Moïse, 238, 240
Nyembo, Kabemba, 160
Nyerere, Julius, 42, 107, 118, 179,
    192, 193, 238
Nzimbi, Ngbale, 108, 111, 134, 136,
    202
Nziza, Jack, 98, 107
Nzojibwami, Augustin, 191
Nzongola, Georges, 3, 222

Oakley, Phyllis, 53
Ogata, Sadaka, 41, 53
Olenga Nkoy, Joseph, 136
Omasombo, Jean, 140, 156, 198
Ondekane, Jean-Pierre, 240
Onusumba, Adolphe, 240
Onyango-Obbo, Charles, 205
Orth, Richard, 69
Outeniqua, 127, 129
Oyatambwe, Wamu, 249

Palipehutu, 149, 171, 192
PALU (Parti lumumbiste unifié), 162, 276, 278
Parena, 41, 192
Pasqua, Charles, 115, 117
Physicians for Human Rights, 72
Pinard, Guy, 175
Pinheiro, Paulo Sergio, 41, 172
Plunder, 148, 153, 217, 221–231, 264
Polisi, Denis, 141, 186, 190
Pomfret, John, 61
Poncelet, Jean-Pol, 85
Pottier, Johan, 101
Pourtier, Roland, 50
PP (Parti du peuple), 40
PPRD (parti Populaire pour la reconstruction et le développement), 237, 238, 273, 275, 278
PRA (People's Redemption Army), 218
Pretoria, 256–261
Pronk, Jan, 88
PRP (Parti de la révolution populaire), 102, 104, 107, 234
Prunier, Gérard, 131, 188, 206
PUSIC (Parti pour l'unité et la sauvegarde de l'intégrité du Congo), 218
Pweto, 200, 257

Qadhafi, Moamer, 245
Quanyu, Fu, 112

Raeymaekers, Tim, 5, 216
RCD (Rassemblement congolais pour la démocratie), 199, 204, 206, 212
  creation, 195, 238
  RCD-Goma, 218, 223, 240, 276
  RCD-ML, 217, 223, 239–243
  splits, 239, 264, 265
RDF (Rwanda Defence Forces) (also see RPA), 209, 213, 214, 218
RDP (Régiment de dragons parachutistes), 116

RDR (Rassemblement pour la démocratie et le retour des réfugiés), 47, 49, 58, 176
Redmont, Ron, 51
Refugee camps, 52, 80, 93–96
Refugees. *See* Hutu (refugees)
Reno, William, 11
Rice, Susan, 122, 198
Richardson, William, 64, 75, 127–129
Rifkind, Malcolm, 85
Robinson, Mary, 176, 189
Rogeau, Olivier, 173
Ronco Consulting, 76, 143
Rosenblatt, Lionel, 86
RPA (Rwanda Patriotic Army) (also see RDF), 4, 7, 8, 19, 32, 48, 54, 61, 73, 74, 78, 89, 109, 113, 140, 145, 152, 153, 174, 177, 182, 194–201, 204, 205
RPF (Rwanda Patriotic Front), 2, 3, 8, 16, 100, 180, 186, 187
  domination, 23–34, 180
Ruberwa, Azarias, 241, 262–267
Rucagu, Boniface, 185, 186
Rugenera, Marc, 185
Ruhimbika, Müller, 21, 22, 105, 154, 205
Rukaramu, 175
Rupiya, Martin, 203
Rutaremara, Tito, 181
Rutazibwa, Privat, 29
Rutshuru, 15–17, 99, 145, 147, 174
Ruzibiza, Abdul, 175
Rwanda
  Banyamulenge, 204, 205
  civil war, 173–178
  communication strategy, 27
  conflict with Uganda, 205, 206, 218, 239, 240
  governance, 184–190
  human rights, 24–27, 33, 175–178, 189
  intervention in Ituri, 207, 220
  intervention in Zaïre/DRC, 45–58, 194–201, 222
  justice, 184
  plunder of DRC, 226–231

Rwanda (*cont.*)
    political evolution, 23–34,
       184–190
    regional power, 141
    support for Nkunda, 214
Rwarakabije, Paul, 209
Rwigema, Pierre-Célestin, 174
Ryckmans, François, 159

SADC (Southern African Development
    Community), 198, 203,
    244–249
Sahnoun, Mohamed, 64, 122–131
Sakombi, Dominique, 165
Salim Saleh, 168, 241, 243
Salim Salim, Ahmed, 118
Samset, Ingrid, 226
Sandline, 76
Sant'Egidio, 211, 246
Scherrer, Christian, 89
Serb mercenaries, 115
Serufuli, Eugène, 229
Sezibera, Richard, 213
Sheffer, David, 177
Shinsuke, Horiuchi, 181
Short, Clare, 206
Sibomana, Adrien, 190
Simba, Aloys, 15
Simba, Charles, 149
Simpson, Daniel, 74
Sinziyoheba, Firmin, 175
Slocombe, Walter, 72, 74
Smis, Stefaan, 249
Smith, Christopher, 70, 73, 85
Smith, Edwin, 69
Smith, Stephen, 132, 188
SOJEDEM (Solidarité jeunesse pour la
    défense des droits des minorités),
    38, 39, 192
Solana, Javier, 276
Sondji, Jean-Baptiste, 160
Songolo, Nira, 112
South Africa
    arms supplies, 174, 255
    diplomacy, 247, 248, 256–261
Soyster, Ed, 76
Soyster, Harry, 76

Spicer, Tim, 76
SPLA (Sudan People's Liberation Army),
    44
Stockton, Nick, 87
Sudan, 43, 111
Sun City, 256–261

Tavernier, Christian, 21, 112, 114, 116
Taylor, Ian, 5, 230
Thambwe, Alexis, 236
Tibasima, John, 217, 241, 242
Tigres, 62–65, 112, 162
Tindemans, Leo, 21
Tingi-Tingi, 69, 93, 94, 114
Tomlinson, Chris, 54
Transition (political_), 261–271
Tshisekedi, Etienne, 127, 132–139,
    158, 160, 167, 262, 268, 271
Tutsi, 17, 18
    anti-feelings, 18, 131, 145–152,
       173, 198, 264
    Tutsification, 29–30, 148, 182

UDPS (Union pour la démocratie et
    le progrès social), 134, 138, 158,
    262, 270, 271
Uganda, 43–44, 48, 55, 196
    conflict with Rwanda, 205, 206,
       218, 239, 240
    creation of the MLC, 242
    intervention in Ituri, 207, 215–220
    intervention in Zaïre (1996), 58–61
    plunder of DRC, 229
Umba Kyamitala, 160
UNITA (União Nacional para a
    Independência Total de Angola),
    43, 62, 63, 111–113, 197, 200,
    202
United States, 43, 47
    role in 1996–1997 war, 66–79,
       130
    role in 1998–2002 war, 195, 196
UPC (Union des patriotes congolais),
    207, 217, 221, 242
UPDF (Uganda People's Defence
    Forces), 55, 58, 73, 169,
    216–219, 240

Uprona, 35–39, 179, 190–192
USCR (US Committee for Refugees), 68
USOR (Union sacrée de l'opposition), 13, 134, 138

Verschave, François-Xavier, 115
Victoria Falls, 244
Vlassenroot, Koen, 5, 48, 216

Walikale, 17, 153, 229
Wamba dia Wamba, Ernest, 217, 236, 238–242
Whaley, Peter, 69
Wibaux, Fernand, 115
Willame, Jean-Claude, 155, 161
Winter, Roger, 68, 69
Wolfowitz, Paul, 276
Wolpe, Howard, 119, 122

Yerodia Ndombasi, 198, 236, 262, 277
Young, Crawford, 156, 226
Young, Doug, 85
Yugo, Dominic, 116

Z'Ahidi Ngoma, Arthur, 195, 238, 239, 262
Zambia, 65–66
ZANU-PF (Zimbabwe African National Union-Patriotic Front), 204
Zenawi, Meles, 118
Zimbabwe
    alliance with Burundian rebels, 203, 204
    role in 1996–1997 war, 65–66
    role in 1998–2002 war, 197–204